BETWEEN HEAVEN AND RUSSIA

Orthodox Christianity and Contemporary Thought
Aristotle Papanikolaou and Ashley M. Purpura, series editors

This series consists of books that seek to bring Orthodox Christianity into an engagement with contemporary forms of thought. Its goal is to promote (1) historical studies in Orthodox Christianity that are interdisciplinary, employ a variety of methods, and speak to contemporary issues; and (2) constructive theological arguments in conversation with patristic sources and that focus on contemporary questions ranging from the traditional theological and philosophical themes of God and human identity to cultural, political, economic, and ethical concerns. The books in the series explore both the relevancy of Orthodox Christianity to contemporary challenges and the impact of contemporary modes of thought on Orthodox self-understandings.

Between Heaven and Russia

RELIGIOUS CONVERSION AND POLITICAL
APOSTASY IN APPALACHIA

Sarah Riccardi-Swartz

FORDHAM UNIVERSITY PRESS   NEW YORK 2022

Visit us online at www.fordhampress.com.

Library of Congress Cataloging-in-Publication Data available online
at https://catalog.loc.gov.

Printed in the United States of America
24 23 22   5 4 3 2 1

First edition

for Clementine, who is proof of God's providence

Contents

Preface

Orthodox Christianity is thought to be both inside and outside of time, perhaps even beyond time or timeless. At the same time, it is a faith that is intimately tied to the mechanisms of dating and pacing that mark the chronological and theological passage of days, months, and years. This preoccupation with time is not only seen in the dedication of the Church to remembering and memorializing its historical people, events, and periods throughout world history, it is also central to the liturgical praxis and social ethos of the faith. Feast days, fast days, sunrise, sunset, Lent, Holy Week—each moment of time, each day is accounted for in the Orthodox calendar, a solar and lunar hybrid for religious timing and dating. In the case of Russian Orthodoxy, time takes on rhythm of difference, as I term it. Set apart by their adherence to a dating rubric known as the Julian Calendar, Russian Orthodox Christians are approximately, dependent upon the year, thirteen liturgical (solar) days behind many other Orthodox Christians around the world for most of their feast days. A difference in timing has social, cultural, theological, and ontological implications and effects; as the late Catherine Bell reminds us, calendars help form a "temporal series that molds time."[1]

The Appalachian community of converts to Russian Orthodoxy in this book adhered not only to the Julian Calendar, they also aligned themselves, in large part, with the daily services of the Church. Devoting themselves to the rhythmic liturgical cycles filled with kinetic worship—standing, crossing oneself, prostrating, bowing, kneeling—had an effect on both spirituality and temporality. As one monk noted, "Time moves differently here." While the daily implications of time were felt in repetitive cycles of prayers, services, and commitments of community members, the powerful social mechanisms of time in a globalized, digitized world also contoured their reality. Situated in the rural post-2016 United States, this ethnography provides a glimpse into a particularly transformative moment in both American religion and politics—the era of Vladimir Putin and Donald Trump.

While the Putin-Trump era is not limited by a set period of seconds, minutes, hours, days, or years, the election of Donald Trump in 2016 seems to have marked the beginning of a transformational social period in both Russian-American international relations and American conservative politics. An era, as a chronological denotation of time, has different meanings, but a decidedly important aspect is a particularly noteworthy event that seemingly marks a period of change. Vladimir Putin became the acting president of Russia in 1999 and was officially elected as president in the spring of 2000. Since then, Putin has been either the prime minster (2008–2011) or president. Putin's current term is set to end in 2024, but a referendum in 2020, formally signed into law in 2021, would allow Putin to run for two more presidential terms. Putin's seemingly illiberal tenure has been marked by two important social movements: the rise of the powerful and politically charged post-Soviet Russian Orthodox Church, and the engagement of western conservative actors with Russian politics, religion, and ideas. Putin's conservative social politics, his focus on keeping the Moscow Patriarchate as a close political ally, and his emphasis on marketing Russia as wholly outside of western secularism and liberalism set into motion a social transformation of Russia in the western conservative imagination, particularly during the 2010s. This shift had effects on the ground in Russia, at the United Nations, in transnational politics, and in international relations.

In many ways, Putin's strongman authoritarian leadership provided a model for Trump, and the Russian president may have realized he found a compatriot in the former reality television star. From the beginning, Donald Trump's ascendency to president of the United States in 2016 was marked by suspicions of Russian intervention. Trump, a longtime admirer of Putin, served in public office for a substantially shorter period of time than his Russian counterpart, but those four years of overlap are where we see the Putin-Trump era begin to unfold, and where we begin to see more substantial engagement between American and Russian far-right actors, both institutionally and individually. The 2018 Helsinki summit between Trump and Putin might have marked the apex of the era, but post-2020 America has been and continues to be shaped by the encounters between Trump and Putin that took place for their four years as political contemporaries. Both strongmen leaders, the two presidents focused on social initiatives for their respective countries that emphasized nationalism, conservatism, and the alterity of their political opposition. The end of Trump's tenure was marked by an insurrection at the Capitol on January 6, 2021, when members of his base, believing Trump to have fairly won the election, stormed the Capitol building. On the heels of this act of domestic terrorism, Trump was impeached and then acquitted on charges of inciting the insurrection. For Putin, 2021 marked the year that he signed into law a legal safety net to ensure access to continued power. In some respects, it might look like the Putin-Trump era has ended. Yet, those four years will have lasting social and political implications, not only for Russia, but also for Trump's successor—President Joseph Biden—and for American democracy.

From my vantage point, the Putin-Trump era is likely still unfolding. We are still witnessing its manifestation in the political ideologies that were unleashed from 2016 to 2020; the new global culture wars; right-wing, far-right, and alt-right groups that mobilized globally during this period; the continued political tensions between the U.S. and Russia; and the former Russia's potential political interventions in American democracy. Of course, Trump has not ruled out another presidential run. The year 2024 may see Trump return to power, just as Putin either leaves office or tightens his authoritarian grasp. The tightening grasp of other illiberal, arguably authoritarian politicians throughout Eurasia and Europe— Turkish president Recep Tayyip Erdogan, Hungarian prime minister Viktor Orbán, and Polish president Andrzej Duda—and the rise of the highly nationalistic, far-right America First movement in the United States signal that the first four years of the Putin-Trump era were an effective catalytic time period for social action among conservative actors globally. While the Putin-Trump era has contoured international relations and institutions that are found in this book, they were and are shaped by the history of American politics and religion, the framing of rural communities in the public consciousness, and myopic social understandings of Christianity outside of Protestantism and Catholicism. Set in the closing moments of the 2010s, this ethnography provides a window into a particular moment in the story of American religion—one of exceptionalism, panic parables, and nostalgic discontent.

Editorial note: Adapted and revised materials from this book appear in a variety of public scholarship pieces I have written over the years, all of which have been included at the end of the book for ease of reference.

Abbreviations and Terms

EP	Ecumenical Patriarchate
GOA	Greek Orthodox Archdiocese of America
MP	Moscow Patriarchate
OCA	Orthodox Church in America
ROC	Russian Orthodox Church
ROCOR	Russian Orthodox Church Outside of Russia

TERMS

Abbot	Ecclesiastical title for the head of a monastery
Altar	Sanctuary separated by an iconostasis from the nave
Antimins	A small piece of fabric containing holy relics that is consecrated and signed by a bishop before being placed on the altar of an Orthodox Church. The consecration of the Eucharist cannot take place without the antimins.
Aposticha	A set of hymns
Catechumen	Formal religious inquirer in the Orthodox Church
Chrismation	A sacrament of confirmation using anointing oil (chrism)
Church Slavonic (CS)	A Slavic liturgical language
Divine Liturgy	Eucharistic celebration
Eucharist	The sacramental body and blood of Christ
Hieromonk	A celibate monk who is also a priest
Icon	Painted or reproduced religious image

Iconostasis	Altar screen with icons that separates the altar from the nave
Matins	A daily morning prayer service in the liturgical cycle
Matushka	From Russian; an older, diminutive term for a priest's wife that is common in the Russian diaspora, meaning "mother"
Narthex (vestibule)	Similar to a lobby; opens into the nave
Nativity	Feast of the birth of Christ
Nave	Central part of the temple (church) where worshipers stand
New Calendar (NC)	The Revised Julian Calendar (approximately thirteen solar days ahead of the Old Calendar) is an Orthodox liturgical calendar that currently aligns with the Gregorian calendar. Both the NC and the OC are hybrid liturgical calendars, meaning they make use of solar and lunar timing. In writing, liturgical dating often includes both the NC and the OC (e.g., November 20/7, 1920).
Old Calendar (OC)	Julian Calendar (or Old Julian Calendar) (approximately thirteen solar days behind the New Calendar)
Pascha	Feast of the Resurrection of Christ
Temple	Church building
Theosis	Deification
Trapeza	Colloquial term meaning "common/shared meal"
Troparion	A type of hymn (also Tropar)
Vespers (Great)	A daily evening prayer service in the liturgical cycle

BETWEEN HEAVEN AND RUSSIA

Introduction: East of Appalachia

The New Russian Turn in American Christianity

The crash happened before I had time to react. I hit a pothole, blew a tire, and swerved into the concrete wall separating me from the side of the mountain and the wooded ravine below. Just a few weeks before I planned to return home from twelve months of living with a Russian Orthodox convert community in the mountains of West Virginia, I found myself on a back road, by an abandoned schoolhouse, in a totaled car with no cell phone reception. The roads in Woodford, where I lived in 2017–2018, were in terrible condition because of lack of funding and maintenance. Driving through the densely wooded mountains, I often encountered broken down vehicles; townsfolk changing blown-out tires; or drivers waiting while the fire department lifted fallen trees, dead deer, or boulders off the small, often, one-lane roads. As I shook off the shock of the event, chemicals from the airbags burned my face and eyes. Somehow, I managed to drive my mangled car the short distance to the home of Clotilde, a lay member at St. Basil's monastery, where I was headed that summer morning before the crumbling asphalt changed my plans. As I banged on her kitchen door, I realized Clotilde was already at the monastery. I checked my phone. Still no signal. Gathering my wits about me, I remembered that Clotilde spoke warmly of her neighbors just down the road. Leaving my car in her driveway, I walked until I spotted the house. I knocked on the door. An older woman answered. She was watching her grandchildren. I explained what happened, that I knew Clotilde, and that I needed to get to the monastery.

We piled into the family's dusty minivan and headed up the mountain to St. Basil's. As we drove, I managed to ask the woman and her husband if they had ever been to the monastery. They replied that they had not, but that they knew the monks to be good folks and that some of their kin had been hired by the abbot as part-time workers when they needed employment. I waved goodbye to them and headed to the monastery's chapel. Opening the door, I immediately saw Clotilde seated in the area assigned for women and I motioned for her to come outside. Over the course of the morning, Clotilde, the monks, and the abbot made sure I was physically safe before driving me back to my rented cabin. As I was about to return to my wasp- and bat-filled wooden abode, the abbot told the members gathered around that it was God's providence that spared me from flipping off the side of the mountain in my used silver Honda Civic that I had purchased at the only car lot in town.[1] The day the accident occurred also happened to be the festal holiday of St. Elias (Elijah) the Prophet, who is considered in Orthodox Christian hagiography to be the patron saint of bakers. Since I often baked cakes and other desserts for the monks, the abbot believed that God providentially spared me through the intercessions of St. Elias. Providence, for many of the people I worked with, directed them to Russian Orthodoxy; it was providence that guided them to West Virginia, and it was providence that governed their everyday lives through divine direction in social matters.

This book explores the sociopolitical practices and beliefs of this West Virginian community of converts to the Russian Orthodox Church Outside of Russia, a religious organization known most often simply by its abbreviation, ROCOR.[2] The late 2010s were a period of complex transnational politics and changing global religiosity, and the community I worked with was (and still is) part of that social transformation. Drawing together work on post-Soviet Russian politics and religion, the growing Russian Orthodox presence in the United States, conservative American Christianity, and digital information networks, this book asks what conversion to a foreign faith and its political trappings might mean for the future of Christianity and democracy in the United States. In doing so, I highlight various dimensions of a lively and vibrant community that I worked with for over a year.[3] From material piety, to social politics, to epistemological understandings of time and place, this book considers how worldbuilding (or worldmaking) is often religious and how spiritual conversion is political in nature.[4]

Worldbuilding is part design and part ideology. Creation, repair, conservation, and preservation are its cornerstones. To build a world requires time, patience, connectivity, and ideological confidence. It also requires, according to Jarrett Zigon, a politics of disappointment.[5] The disappointment, disenchantment, and disillusion that Appalachian converts to Russian Orthodoxy felt with the United States and with progressive politics in the late 2010s will unfold over the course of this book, expressed in their turn to Russia, to hierarchical authority, to boundary making, and to divine providence. While Zigon is writing a philosophical hermeneutics of liberative worldbuilding that emphasizes its plasticity and ability for infinite unfolding, despite its agonistic and durable nature, I engage worldbuilding as a reactionary development project that is attuned to temporalities, metaphysics, and cultural anxieties, one that is caught up with biopolitics, geopolitics, and constructions of religious soft power.[6] In Woodford, West Virginia, converts constructed an ideological world that was made possible by the social scaffolding of Russian Orthodoxy, with a firm foundation built on conversion comradery.

The history of religious conversion is one of ideological conviction. Persuader or persuaded, both parties typically have an affective desire to show the truthfulness of their position and why aligning with their group would be advantageous spiritually, socially, and, sometimes, politically. This book offers up such a story. Set against the backdrop of the New Cold War, in the year following the election and inauguration of Donald J. Trump as the forty-fifth president of the United States, this ethnography explores the political ideologies of Appalachian converts to Russian Orthodoxy, showing how their support of Vladimir Putin and his New Russia is both a symptom of increasing globalized networks of far-right conservatism and a continuing expression of the United States' fraught relationship with both Russia and secularism. Offering a contextualized and interdisciplinary account of the role this one community plays in the broader networks of religiopolitical fundamentalism, fascism, and extremism swiftly rising throughout the Western world, this ethnography engages with the philosophical and political history of Russian Orthodoxy and conservative Christianity, particularly Evangelicalism, in the United States to explore larger social movements that have shaped our current political moment.

For many ROCOR converts in Appalachia, and throughout the rural United States, Russia seemed to be their only hope for social salvation, for reclaiming America for God, and for preserving the status quo of Christian hegemony in an increasingly diversifying Western world. Anxious over America's path toward progressive secularism and its attached social moral politics, converts looked beyond the borders of United States and beyond the confines of democracy to a salvific home abroad. To align with post-Soviet Russia meant to align with God. This book asks and answers the question of why rural Americans adopted Russian Orthodox Christianity with all its political connotations in the twenty-first century. In doing so, it draws out how American Christians are carving out new political realities beyond U.S. democracy.

Community Context

The community I worked in was divided between two institutions: St. John's, a small ROCOR parish located in the heart of small-town Woodford, and St. Basil's, a ROCOR monastery situated several miles south of the town, but still within the city limits. While Appalachia has historically been home to ethnic Orthodox communities, particularly throughout much of New York State, Pennsylvania, and the coalfields of West Virginia, the migration of Orthodox converts to the region, along with the conversion of locals, is a far different social phenomenon for both Appalachia and ROCOR.[7] Historically, ROCOR had larger ethnic communities in urban areas, including San Francisco, Chicago, New York, and New Jersey. Since the early 2000s, however, it seems as if ROCOR has been on the rise in suburban and rural areas, predominantly among communities founded by and comprised of converts.[8] Woodford was the site of such ROCOR transformation. Located in the western region of Appalachia that has had stagnant population growth the last thirty-plus years, the small town of Woodford, which had approximately one thousand inhabitants, was home to St. John's parish and St. Basil's monastery. With about thirty-plus inhabitants, St. Basil's was, in the late 2010s, the largest English-speaking Russian Orthodox monastery in the United States. Attached to the monastery was a female monastic skete (a small, isolated dependency of the monastery) with one nun.[9] The town also had a family-owned Orthodox icon printing business with a few employees. Both St. Basil's and St. John's came to be in Woodford in the early 2000s when two converts—a local university professor, who donated land for the monastery, and a local politician, who built the parish building—began to missionize the region. Attendance at the parish of St. John's ebbed and flowed over the years. The amount of people on the roster was not always expressed in attendance on an average Sunday morning. To be sure, the parish was often filled to capacity, but there were Sundays with sparse turnout as well. Typical Sunday attendance at St. John's ranged from thirty to fifty people. While St. Basil's was located high in the mountains, remote with difficult access because of steep terrain, especially during the winter months, St. John's parish was located right off the main highway in a more commercial area of the town.

In most respects, Woodford was a typical small town in West Virginia during the late 2010s. Spread out among the rolling hills and mountains, pierced through by a state highway, the town had small-scale infrastructure that mostly consisted of a few fast-food shops and a Walmart. The post-coal decades had not been kind to Woodford, with its boarded up shops in the downtown area, and its scarcely populated strip mall fading in the shadow of the big-box store that shared its crumbling parking lot. Surrounded on all sides by the wild Appalachian Mountains, Woodford's deteriorating infrastructure was a symptom of the larger, historical, systemic extractive forces that have taken advantage of the region and its natural resources for over a century. By 2017, Woodford seemed to be a town people were leaving rather than moving to, seeking employment and opportunities in the larger cities throughout the state. Census data taken in 2010 and Census estimates gathered in 2019 provide a bit more insight into shifts in demographics for the county where Woodford was located. In 2010, the population was 42,481, and the Census Bureau estimated that by 2019 it had dropped to 39,402. In 2010, 97.7 percent of the population of the county identified as Caucasian, and that percentage dropped less than 1 percent by the 2020 Census. The 2010 Census recorded that almost 21 percent of the total county population lived below the poverty line, a figure that dipped less than 3 percent a decade later. Education rates stayed the same, with 15.1 percent of county residents holding a bachelor's degree or higher.[10] This quantitative data is helpful, since it both aligns with and diverges from the demographics of the Orthodox community in the area.

In a town where a large section of the population lived at or below the poverty line, and where jobs were virtually nonexistent, the ubiquitous Dollar General and Save-a-Lot were fixtures. What was not ubiquitous, however, was the three-bar Russian cross atop the onion-domed wooden church that shared a property line with the Save-a-Lot. As I explain throughout this book, ROCOR converts in Woodford were, in many ways, set apart from the town where they worshipped. This was most acutely expressed in educational and economic differences. On the whole, adherents at St. Basil's monastery and St. John's parish had at least college experience and most had undergraduate degrees. The parish had a wide range of professionals, including nurses, pharmacists, professors, teachers, social workers, IT workers, and lawyers. The majority of the parish could be considered middle class; most owned their homes and lived a bit removed geographically from Woodford. In addition to their educational opportunities, parishioners also had economic affordances, including owning a reliable vehicle that made finding work in larger towns and cities a reality.

These socioeconomic differences were not isolated to the parish. Many of the monks I spoke with at St. Basil's had undergraduate degrees and some had extended educational experience. Prior to renouncing their worldly lives, quite a few of the men had careers in a wide variety of fields, including broadcast television and education. While each monk was called to embrace poverty, the monastery as an institution was not. By no means wealthy, St. Basil's did have many generous benefactors who helped them fund building projects and obtain high-speed internet access for monastery residents, when the majority of Woodford had dial-up speeds. If we look at both the monastery and parish, it seems as if most of the Orthodox Christians in Woodford lived comfortably above the poverty line, and many had advanced and/or professional degrees. Their demographics suggest they were outliers when compared to the rest of the county, where approximately 21 percent of the population lived below the poverty level and roughly only 15 percent of the county had a bachelor's degree or higher. The stark differences in socioeconomic demographics and the fact that the majority of the Orthodox converts in this community moved to the region from elsewhere in the United States are key in understanding how this community saw themselves in relationship to locals.

St. Basil's monastery was first founded in eastern Missouri in 1986. Seeking more land on which to develop their community, the monks found financial hope from an older couple with property in West Virginia. They moved to Appalachia in the spring of 2000, setting up camp in a muddy valley with tents as shelter. St. Basil's monastery and St. John's parish were several miles apart but were part of the one overarching ROCOR community. St. John's was founded in 2002 by a group of converts, both local and those from other areas of the United States, who wanted a lay community to accompany the monastery that had moved to the area two years prior. From a handful of parishioners and a couple of monks, the community swelled to well over one hundred people, with believers spread geographically throughout West Virginia, southeastern Ohio, and Eastern Kentucky. Many parishioners drove well over two hours one way to reach the tiny town every Sunday in order to gather with the community, passing Greek and Antiochian Orthodox churches along the way, preferring to worship exclusively in a ROCOR setting. More than 90 percent of the Orthodox Christians in Woodford were converts. During my time with the community, the parish grew by 10 percent as converts from the surrounding area joined; additionally, the monastery welcomed four new novices hailing from around the United States. Alongside Orthodox locals, a steady influx of religious pilgrims meant that the town was often filled with Orthodox Christians from around the globe. A trip to the local Walmart typically included running into monks and Orthodox laypeople.[11]

ROCOR does not place a priority on gathering statistical data from parishes and monasteries, which means we know very little about the demographics of most communities. That being said, one way to glean some data about mission parishes is through cross-referencing the digital ROCOR directory with social media accounts and parish websites to learn more about why the parishes were created, who the priests are, and what communities they aim to serve. The Woodford group was and is typical of ROCOR communities springing up across the United States in rural and suburban areas, where upwardly mobile converts often come from fairly well-educated backgrounds.[12] Alabama, Georgia, Tennessee, and Virginia are among the states in which ROCOR mission parishes were and are growing. When I lived in Woodford, the parish had a convert priest; the congregation was predominantly composed of converts, with very few ethnic Russian members. Many of the converts came from the broader areas of Appalachia, the South, and Midwest, with less from Woodford proper. At the time, the monastery had one Russian lay member who attended sporadically, a married Canadian couple who attended regularly, a Romanian lay member with part-time employment at the monastery, and one monk from outside of the United States. The Orthodox presence in Woodford was roughly 10 percent of the town's population, although it ran higher during pilgrimage weekends that happen throughout the year.

Woodford's Orthodox community was originally pan-Orthodox; by 2018, however, it seemed more focused on serving converts than cradles.[13] Cradle is a colloquial term often used in Orthodox Christian communities to denote a person who was raised Orthodox or is ethnically Orthodox, meaning he or she comes from a country that has or used to have a dominant Orthodox presence, such Russia, Romania, or Greece. St. John's and St. Basil's were formed because of converts. This a distinct difference from historical ROCOR communities in major U.S. cities, such as San Francisco, Chicago, and New York, where the majority of founders and adherents were and are cradle Slavic Orthodox Christians.[14] This difference is crucial in understanding the social politics of the Woodford community and their implications for the future social trajectory of ROCOR. While neither cradle nor convert Orthodox Christians in the United States are the subject of much social science research, work on the latter is virtually nonexistent. In order to provide a thick, textured description and analysis of such a community, I faced considerable methodological complexities.[15]

Methodological Affordances and Considerations

As is always the case in anthropology, the identity of the researcher shapes how she is understood by interlocutors, since she brings certain preexisting knowledge and particular dynamics to the ethnographic encounter. Thus, I must note here that I am a member of the Orthodox Church in America Archdiocese (OCA).[16] I realize that this was crucial to my acceptance as a researcher in this community, as was made clear to me by many folks during my stay. Despite my own religious affiliation, however, I was not a community member. On any given day, in jest or not, I could be labeled a heretic, a schismatic, and a liberal from New York City. Part of this, it seemed, stemmed from the community's own understanding of the fraught historical relationship between ROCOR and the OCA, discussed in Chapter 1. During coffee hour after service on Sundays, the parish priest would often take playful jabs at my religious status. "You know you're in schism, right?" he laughed once while we were sipping coffee with a group of parishioners. This type of occurrence was not uncommon during my year in Woodford. Additionally, because I was a woman doing research without a husband present, despite the fact that my mother and daughter joined me for the entire stay while my husband held down his job in New York, I was considered to be a "liberal feminist." In fact, one of the stipulations given to me by the monastery's abbot in 2015 before he agreed to allow me to work with the community was that my husband would come visit me regularly. The first time I met with the abbot, my husband had to be present and give his blessing for my research to move forward. This is not surprising given the traditional gender dynamics found in many convert-heavy ROCOR communities, nor is it surprising given the hierarchical structure of Russian Orthodoxy, and Orthodox Christianity more generally, that places primacy on male leadership.[17]

While my religious affiliation, on some level, allowed me entry, it did not always provide me access. One thing it did do, however, was seem to make me a sort of neutral or seemingly sympathetic figure. Although I was labeled a liberal, none of the community members I worked with asked my political affiliation or social moral stances on issues they discussed. Perhaps they assumed that my silent listening was a symbol of solidarity. During Thanksgiving dinner with a prominent family in the community, the father joked about Hillary Clinton's failed 2016 presidential campaign and how a woman would never win the White House. I listened intently but said nothing. His teenage daughter said to him, "Papa, she might have voted for Hillary." To which the father replied, "Don't be ridiculous." He did not turn to me, nor did he ask me to confirm or deny who I voted for in that election. Instead, he went on to talk about Trump and what his election might mean for the United States. If he would have asked who I voted for, the evening might have gone differently. A few scholars who study what Agnieszka Pasieka calls the "unlikable others" focus on scholar-informant solidarity through a variety of creative means; this type of "immoral anthropology," as Benjamin Teitelbaum describes it, might be essential when dealing with radicalized groups, yet it gives me considerable methodological, not to mention ethical, anxiety.[18] This type of anthropological ethics is not part of my scholarly tool kit. Thus, rather than crafting fictive narratives of solidarity, I opted, like a number of other scholars who have worked with conservative communities, such as Faye Ginsburg, Susan Harding, and Omri Elisha, to simply to listen. This method proved to be effective, for many members told me that I was the first person outside of the community to care about their views or listen to their ideas. Of course, it was my job as an anthropologist to listen carefully and try to understand how they see the world and what motivates them.

Much in the vein of Faye Ginsburg's work in the 1980s on abortion proponents and opponents in Fargo, North Dakota, I carried out thirty-six life-story interviews, or what I have termed conversion narratives with Orthodox Christians. These conversion narratives were combined with formal interview questions about demographics and social issues; this hybrid interview methodology allowed me to glean a holistic understanding of each person. The conversion narratives helped explain why converts decided to be a part of this particular Orthodox community. In the following chapters, I use large sections of the narratives, focusing on the form and key elements of their stories, much in the tradition of life-story interviews.[19] Each interview followed a similar pattern; I would ask demographic questions at the outset, including age, race, gender preference, political affiliation, marital status, and family structure, in order to gather a data set on these Orthodox converts to ROCOR. I then asked each interviewee to tell me the story of his or her conversion to Orthodoxy. This life-story section of the interview became the basis through which I would ask questions once the personal narrative ended. After the reflexive question section, I returned to a standardized set of questions about global social politics, understandings of religious belief and practice, and views of Appalachia, the United States, and Russia. My goal was to understand why my interviewees converted to ROCOR and what social, political, and economic factors might have influenced them to shift affiliations.

Hybrid interviews were one of many methods I employed. I also conducted participant observation, the lifeblood of anthropology, by attending regular ROCOR church activities, immersing myself in community life, and conducting semi-formal ethnographic interviews with a variety of people from inside and outside of the Orthodox community, from monks to parishioners, to their non-Orthodox neighbors who attend other churches.[20] I volunteered in monastery shops, took part in choirs, baked and cooked for the parish and monastery common meals on a regular basis, and attempted to be a good neighbor. When I first arrived, I was far more interested in iconography and conversion as types of religio-social reproduction than anything else, since I had already filmed a short documentary with the community the year prior on the digital (re)production of Orthodox iconography. I realized very quickly, however, that talking about iconography was not particularly important to those working outside of the small iconography studio. The issues converts were interested in talking about are found in this book: infrastructure, community relations, social and moral politics, the church polity, Vladimir Putin, and the apparent revival of Orthodox Christianity in Russia. From the onset, I let the interests of the Orthodox folks in Woodford guide my research. The earliest interviews, beginning in the winter of 2017, helped me redefine my research model and the questions I asked in later interviews during that twelve-month period and then again in 2020–2021 with former community members.

It is crucial to note how I was given access for interviews with monks. I was free to attend services and volunteer at the monastery under the watchful eye of Clotilde, one of the very few converts who was not so keen on Putin and was seemingly a bit more liberal politically than her convert counterparts. On a typical day at the monastery, I might help Clotilde with soapmaking, chat with monks assigned to run the bookstore, attend a service, and then talk briefly to some of the monks after lunch or dinner on the dining room porch, a public space for visitors to mingle with monks. During periods of free time throughout the day, after Divine Liturgy for example, monks often gathered on the covered porch to chat with each other and visitors. Most conversations were brief and not focused on personal details. Often this would be a time for me to speak with the more reclusive monks in the community, providing a few moments to say hello and exchange niceties. Spontaneous conversations were typically allowable as long as they did not interfere with work schedules or prayers. However, all formal interview requests went through the abbot of the monastery. I would send him a list of names via email; the abbot would reply with names of monks whom I could approach for interviews.

Once I received the finalized list of names, I would then ask each monk if they were comfortable with the process. Most typically replied that they would be happy to be interviewed as long as I had the abbot's blessing. Because monastic life is highly structured, with very little free time, I would often have to schedule interviews with monks several weeks in advance. Many of the monks asked to see a set of questions prior to sitting down with me. Often, they wanted to think about their answers in advance of the interview. This trepidation was largely due to another visitor at the monastery. A few months before I arrived, a non-Orthodox filmmaker, who was interested in becoming a catechumen, and who had social connections to one monk's family, was granted access to shoot a documentary about monastic life. His presence, at first, seemed disruptive to the monks, with several in the community commenting to me that his interview style was very aggressive. Thus, the monks were understandably hesitant to talk with me, and their requests for questions in advance were logical. In a sense, the data gathered from the monks was curated by the abbot, perhaps as an attempt to procure results in line with his vision of how the monastery should be portrayed, or perhaps it was simply a way to reinforce the structures of hegemonic obedience that are so deeply ingrained in ROCOR monasticism. Either way, obtaining interviewees at the monastery proved to be a far more hierarchal endeavor than gathering informants at the parish.

Interviewing parishioners at St. John's was far more straightforward. During the week, save for the Monday evening food pantry hours, the church was quite empty, since services were generally held Saturday evenings (Vigil) and Sunday mornings (Divine Liturgy), unless there was a special feast day service, although the priest generally instructed parishioners to head to the monastery for those types of services. Given the time constraints, and the fact that most parishioners worked full-time jobs, I would typically chat with folks during and after the common meal that followed the Sunday Divine Liturgy, working with them to set up a time we could talk in detail. Some folks invited me into their homes, others wanted to meet at the church during the week, at local restaurants or coffee shops, and a few preferred to be interviewed at my rental cabin. Most parishioners seemed happy to talk with me, and were especially generous with their time, while some others refused, even after numerous attempts to engage them in person and via email. Beyond the thirty-six narrative interviews with Orthodox Christians in Woodford, I also formally interviewed six non-Orthodox area residents.[21] Their interviews consisted of demographic information, questions about their knowledge of and relationship with the Orthodox community in Woodford, and narratives about their own religious experiences. I also interviewed a handful of former members of the Woodford Orthodox community in 2020–2021 via Zoom.

Interviewees, Orthodox and otherwise, gave oral consent, which was recorded along with their interviews in their entirety. Most of these recorded conversations lasted from one to three hours depending on the person. Some Orthodox practitioners were interviewed twice for clarification or additional information. All members of this study, unless stated otherwise, have been given pseudonyms. Additionally, the parish, monastery, and town have all been coded for anonymity. I have, however, selected to maintain the state name, since West Virginia has an important history in Appalachia, and it is the only state considered as wholly in the region. For most of the folks in my study, I use pseudonyms, while others are only alluded to by their role in the parish or monastery.[22] This choice came out of deep consideration for the size of the community and the potential for accidental disclosure. Some of the people mentioned in this book might be obvious to those within the ROCOR community, and are too widely known to be masked in any convincing way, such as the abbot of the monastery and parish priest. Thus, while their names have been replaced by pseudonyms, it is probable that anyone within the community and ROCOR more broadly might be able to decipher who they are with a bit of detective work.

These individuals were briefed about possibility of exposure; all of them still agreed to be interviewed. The views converts expressed to me and each other are not unusual among U.S. ROCOR convert communities, if the social media postings of converts on blogs, Facebook, Twitter, and Instagram that I followed during the course of my digital ethnographic research are any indication.[23] This suggests that their views might be ideologically similar to people who might uncover their identities; thus the risk would be minimal.

Worries in Woodford

From my first few days in Woodford, it was clear that converts had concerns about the social, moral, and political trajectory of the United States. In late September 2017, after a large festal event, I attended a banquet as the guest of the parish priest, Fr. Cyril, and his family. The priest introduced me to one of the more laconic yet politically minded monks whom I had yet to meet. Upon learning that I was from the New York City area, he began to express how "vile" he thought cities were, as places in which one could "change their pronouns at will." Both men went on to joke about LGBTQ+ rights and lament the decline of God-ordained, traditional gender roles in the United States. That encounter was one of many that I had during my first few weeks and months with the community. As converts opened up to me, they began to relay their concerns over what they considered to be the moral decline of the United States, explaining why ROCOR and Russian Orthodoxy were the key to fighting back against the immorality of secularism, and how Vladimir Putin, the Russian president, might be a potential figure for great change in the world.[24] Further comments and interactions produced more questions that guided my research, such as: What makes an American living in Appalachia, who has never been to Russia and who does not speak Russian, profess admiration for Vladimir Putin, and suggest that the increasingly conservative Russian Federation might be America's new political hope? Why Russia? Why now? Why Appalachia?

In asking and answering questions such as those, this book pushes back against the dominant public narratives of both Appalachia and ROCOR as closed, static worlds. This book contributes to scholarship on both topics, but in a way that seeks to understand and contextualize Appalachian conversions in the post-Soviet period of Russian conservative politics and seeming religious re-enchantment. I aim to shift the narrative away from "Trump nation" and show that the moral outrage many rural Christians felt during this period might have been part of their shifting political ideologies and search for religious fulfillment that were transnational in nature.[25] Too often studies of rural

Christians during the late 2010s focused on evangelicals who helped Donald Trump win the presidency.[26] Yet, evangelicals and the Orthodox converts with whom I worked in West Virginia have different intellectual and political world-building projects. At the same time, American conversions to Orthodoxy and the far-right movements found in Evangelicalism during this period speak to the larger, globalized circulations of social, moral conservatism that were springing up in the 2010s. The American Christian nationalism and exceptionalism we saw during this period took on a different formation in the Woodford community, one that looked beyond Protestantism, the GOP, and even the United States in search of religious and political compatriots who might make America holy again.[27]

I became interested in Russian Orthodoxy well before the current attention to Russian influence in American politics, with a particular focus on conversion, religious art, and domestic piety. Yet the legacies of the Cold War since the end of the Soviet Union, the puzzling embrace of Vladimir Putin by Donald Trump, and the signs of Russian interference in America's democratic election processes invite us to consider how some foreign influences rather than others have been and are playing out in distinctive ways on U.S. territory.[28] American religion reflects changing economic, political, and social mores, telling us more about difference and sameness than we sometimes care to know.[29] While considerable scholarly attention has gone to American Christian missions as part of colonial political projects throughout the world, very little attention has gone to the work of overseas religiopolitical projects in the United Sates, which speaks to the need for greater attention to how American religions are caught up in the larger cross-cultural and cross-national currents of social change.[30] The Woodford community—and others potentially like it around the nation that have embraced ROCOR—invites us to make vital connections between local religious beliefs and global politics, allowing us to more fully understand what drives transformations in the structures of ideology and belief in the United States, deconstructing public assumptions about regional, religious, and social stasis in rural America.

Appalachian Intersections

Since the 2016 U.S. presidential election, scholars have begun to take even more seriously the role of Appalachia in American politics, a region long historicized by the media as marginal to the mainstream, a place of religious insularity and nationalism tied tightly to conservative, often Republican, politics.[31] However, as Appalachian scholars note, this region is far more complex than older narratives imply.[32] Over time it became clear to me that Appalachian

ROCOR believers in West Virginia were transforming stereotypical stories of themselves, their political ideologies, and their region through their religious conversions. In doing so, they were not only subverting circumstances and historical notions of place and class thrust upon them; they also spoke to growing ideological trends among rural communities throughout the United States. Appalachian converts to ROCOR expressed their disillusionment with American forms of governance and growing fears over "moral decay."[33] Their nostalgic apocalypticism—a term I use to capture a sense of their desire for a return to a so-called traditional Christian society, combined with their fear of impending social destruction because of increasing liberalism—seemed to be their primary reason for looking beyond the United States to alternative forms of faith and politics. This concept of nostalgic apocalypticism finds a theoretical home under the umbrella of conspiracy theories that seek to both understand and remake the Western world into something relatable to those who feel on the margins of contemporary society.[34] Nostalgia is intimately tied to both a longing for salvation and the belief in a hopeful future through a return to something historical that is often largely fictive. Rather than having apocalyptic fears about a dystopian future, converts seemingly found ways through which to create an alternative Christian utopian future through their Russian Orthodox worldbuilding practices in Appalachia.[35] While scholars of American religion(s) have long been attending to the social economies of rural life in the American South, Appalachia, and the Midwest, they have given less attention to the role of conversion in these regions or what that might mean for larger trends of religiosity, especially in conjunction with the rise of new forms of deep conservatism in the United States and beyond.[36]

This book tells the story of Woodford converts as a community inhabiting Appalachia, living in a globalized, post-Soviet world in which media have become portals for political and social ideologies to flow across time and space. To understand why Americans in West Virginia might convert to ROCOR and seemingly find religious salvation in Russian Orthodoxy and a political savior in its vocal proponent, Vladimir Putin, means attending to the complexities of American rural politics alongside the theologies of ROCOR. The very nature of globalized American Christianity means that along the way, this book will engage with Orthodox political theology, the concept of *symphonia*, and insidious effects of neocolonialism in rural economies.[37] Because my interlocutors' views were deeply shaped by a variety of media, both analog and digital, I also turn to theories within media anthropology and material culture studies in order to think through the implications of the digitally expanding geographical, political, and social networks of Orthodox spirituality.[38] Geography is important, and the Woodford community was and is situated in a region that has long been the topic of research and social mystique; thus I endeavor to provide a contextualized understanding of this Orthodoxy community located deep in storied Appalachia.

Appalachian Studies has a rich and vital history, but often the work was and is historically and folklorically focused. Early accounts, at least in the more southwestern part of Appalachia, explored the history of the area, the impact of the Civil War, arts and craft, geography, and culture broadly construed.[39] More so now than in the early part of the twentieth century, scholars of the region are paying attention to health, economics, and social politics, while drawing out the wide diversity that can be found throughout Appalachia.[40] Appalachian Studies, as a regional subfield in American Studies, came into its own starting mostly in the 1960s and has been highly productive ever since. Scholars of the region from that time forward often suggested that Appalachia was (and perhaps still is) an internal colony of the United States, created by government and big business in order to strip out natural resources and take away power from local residents.[41] The colonization of the area, even the very formation of the region geographically, were ways in which external forces seemingly contoured narratives of incapability and backwardness. Appalachians were often marginalized through public representation as wholly other to mainstream Americans in order to perpetuate these notions of alterity. Poverty, kinship networks, and deep religiosity were weaponized against Appalachians in the creation of the hillbilly stereotype that was so prevalent in media portrayals of the region, especially during President Lyndon B. Johnson's War on Poverty.[42]

Despite these stereotypes, Appalachians have a long history of community-organized resistance work against the oppressive economic and political powers that had contoured both impressions of and landscapes in the region. Mutual aid and relief, unionization, and art/media collectives have been and continue to be ways in which Appalachians seek to subvert the status quo and empower themselves on their own terms.[43] Local literature movements have highlighted works written by Appalachians that emphasizes vernacular oral histories of the region as a way to push back against the academic establishment. bell hooks, Silas House, and Frank X. Walker, among other literary figures, have helped shape new narratives about the region, defying the heteronormative, white-dominated voices that have sought to silence the plurality of life in Appalachia. The long and lasting foundational media work of Appalshop (founded in 1969) and their offshoot, the Appalachian Media Institute (founded in 1988), the socially progressive programs of the Appalachian Southern Folklife Center, and the digital journalism of 100 Days in Appalachia, a program supported by West Virginia University, are a few of the many vital organizations working to reclaim Appalachia from its long history of social marginalization in the American public consciousness. In an effort to support this outstanding cultural activism, I privilege the writings of Appalachian writers who have dismantled and continue to dismantle stereotypes and misconceptions about the region.[44]

Religion is one of Appalachia's sociocultural practices that is highly prone to misrepresentations in popular media and academic writing. Despite early depictions of snake-handling, trancing, glossolalia, and drinking poison as distinctive practices among Appalachians, religious belief and practice are diverse, with cities, towns, hills, and hollers filled with a wide variety of spiritual communities. Certainly Protestantism, as it is broadly understood, is most prevalent in the southern part of the region, and in West Virginia in particular, but there is a more diverse history of religiosity in the area that demands attention. One of the important distinctions to note, is the ongoing tension between mainline Protestantism and mountain religion.[45] Mountain religion is flexible, independent, and often nondenominational.[46] While believers might say they are Baptist or Holiness—two of the most dominant types of Christianity historically found in the region—their churches are often not tied to a particular hierarchal church structure or authority.[47] They often were and are independent congregations. Stemming from Calvinist roots, most mountain churches placed emphasis on expressive worship and being born again spiritually through God's compassion.[48] The emphasis on God's spirit as the transformative power in process of conversion juxtaposes the so-called rational conversions of mainline Protestants who often see salvation as an act of the individual moving toward God.[49]

The emotive, adaptive, and highly personal style of worship and belief in mountain religion was and seemingly still is subject to shallow analysis in which writers, filmmakers, and artists often highlight peculiarities of these communities as spectacle.[50] Given the distinctive and highly individualized variations of mountain religion found throughout the hills and hollers of the region, scholars of Appalachia have pushed for an anthropological approach to understanding these social formations, which have often been misunderstood and misrepresented.[51] Today, scholars of Appalachia are still engaged in the study of Christianity, but they are also taking note of the wide breadth of belief or the refusal thereof in the area.[52] There has also been an emphasis on the relationship between spirituality and ecology in the region, given the ongoing environmental degradation happening because of extractive industry practices.[53] Recent research on social resistance and coal mining highlights stories of religious diversity, showing how nature religion practitioners, Buddhists, and humanists have been coming together to pushback against corporatized exploitation that has often crushed the cultural history, community economics, and physical health and well-being of Appalachians.[54]

Beyond anthropology, religious studies, theology, and Appalachian studies, this book also grapples with the growing literature on far-right communities in the United States. I place great importance on the work of sociologists Andrew Whitehead and Samuel Perry, who explore the idea of what Christian nationalism means in the period when this study was written.[55] I see Christian nationalism as a potential framework for understanding the scaffolding of the religious projects I found in Woodford. I also look to political scientist Cas Mudde's work on the alt-right, in order to show how we need to think of better ways to explain and theorize far-right and ultra-conservative communities in the United States.[56] Studies of far-right communities are few and far between, and those who do attend to the lifeworlds of "unlikeable others" often neglect to engage fully with the religious practices and theological beliefs of the communities they investigate.[57] This may be in part because of the backlash scholars receive—even those, such as ethnomusicologist Benjamin Teitelbaum, who are generally more sensitive or seemingly sympathetic to the subjectivities of the people with whom they work.[58] As someone who has personally experienced this backlash, I am well attuned to the complexities of representing groups who have distinctive social views that they are willing to defend publicly with great vigor.[59]

My fieldwork began nine months after Donald Trump's inauguration and the community, even those who voted for him, which was a very small number, were not thrilled by their new commander-in-chief. Members of the monastery did not vote; by and large members of the parish only voted for Trump because "he wasn't Hillary Clinton." Trump and his potential impact on the United States did not seem to linger on their minds much. Instead, most spoke primarily about Russia's return to morality, the United States' religious decline, and what this might mean for them in the future as converts to Russian Orthodoxy in North America. Starting with one of my first sit-down interviews, I asked what Russia meant to my interlocutors. The stories unfolded. To be sure, most talked at first about their love of ROCOR and Russian spirituality, but they also expressed their deep disillusionment with the United States' political system; most saw the religiously-inclined Vladimir Putin, along with this New Russia, as symbols of morality in a degraded and doomed world.

This study asks why Americans in Appalachia might convert to ROCOR, with all the political complexities of Russian-American relations. What I found in West Virginia across 2017 and 2018 was a community that was keenly aware of stereotypes of Appalachia held by outsiders who assumed them to be "backward" and associate them with certain religiopolitical affiliations. Believers saw their conversions to Orthodoxy as breaking through these stereotypes, for they were not, according to some, "good old boys" or "ignorant hillbillies."

They understood themselves to be taking part in a historical form of Christianity that had deep intellectual ties abroad. In doing so, I argue that they became active participants in a transnational drama that offers access to a form of political affiliation that is not recognized as republican, democrat, or libertarian. Converts used a blending of identifications that included traditionalist, monarchist, and revolutionary. Despite having come from conservative Protestant backgrounds primarily, converts saw themselves as Russian Orthodox warriors for Christ in a nation that they perceived of as dominated by secular liberalism—the antithesis of what they assumed Putin and the Moscow Patriarchate were forming in post-Soviet Russia through a more publicly intimate relationship between church and state.

It is important to note that not all of the Woodford Orthodox Christians converted during Trump's presidency; however, most were received into the Church while Putin was in office. Conversion is not a static event, nor is it apolitical. As the stories of conversion unfold in this book, it is evident that the American political milieu of the late 2010s, of the beginning of the Putin-Trump era, brought with it new dimensions to the converts' understandings of themselves and their religious beliefs. Anthropologist of religion, Kalyani Devaki Menon, in her work on Hindu nationalists and Christian missionaries in India, notes that "conversion is not simply seen as an individual expression of faith, but rather as a political choice that necessarily implicates questions of national allegiance, patriotism, and cultural determination."[60] While Menon is writing in a far different social milieu and political moment in the world, her ideas nonetheless hold salience in the study of Americans converting to Russian Orthodoxy. The looming political issues Menon writes about in her own work came to the fore both theoretically and methodologically for me as my project moved ahead.

In 2020, one of my short public scholarship articles on Orthodox conversion, Russia, and the global culture wars, came under intense debate among many ROCOR and Orthodox believers on Facebook and Twitter. Acknowledging their own beliefs about Putin and the United States, converts with whom I worked in Woodford outed themselves on social media to take issue with the idea that conversion might be political, despite the fact that they, in their own words, expressed this idea repeatedly. They were upset that I wrote about them, even though they sat with me for hours, expressing their theological and political ideologies, and knew I was writing a book about them. One of the most vocal advocates for a return to monarchism and the Russian invasion of the United States messaged me on Facebook to say that "Even if I were not Orthodox, I would admire Putin, but I reject the inference that we are somehow more loyal to him or Russia than our own country." He went on to complain more about my representation of him before ending with, "I am still American, and I do love our country." Representation means something different to each person. As an anthropologist, it is my job to examine the data I gather, process it through the lenses of social science, and try my best to contextualize it within the larger social histories, narratives, trends, and events that form the crucial context for the work. When this convert told me in 2017 that he hoped Putin would invade the United States, he did so seriously, willingly, openly, and without hesitation.

The two statements that this Woodford Orthodox Christian made, roughly three years apart, highlight for me two key issues for many contemporary American converts to the ROCOR: First, it underscores that Putin was a fundamental figure in their ideological concerns for the world. Second, it highlights how fearful Woodford converts were of being portrayed as less than American, despite the fact that most of them saw America as a lost cause morally, politically, and spiritually. Given the unpredictable political moment in which we find ourselves, it is important for me, as a researcher, to incorporate the voices and views of the believers themselves into this work, for each person I talked with, interviewed, and observed had a slightly different take on the larger social issues we discussed. Along the way, I hope for the words of converts to speak for themselves. In doing so, I automatically privilege the voices of people who agreed to be interviewed and audio recorded. This means that some of the more vocal, far/alt-right members of the community will not be heard in this work; concomitantly, it also means that the voices of the small number of less strident converts and Russian-born believers are also missing to some extent. In all, I do my best to draw readers' attention to the widespread positions held by the members of the community across this text.

A Roadmap for the Journey

This book spans seven chapters. By way of a guide, the first chapter is primarily historical in nature; the history of Orthodoxy in the United States is limited in scope, with little work on contemporary expressions of the faith. The lacuna of scholarship on contemporary Orthodoxy in the United States, in either Russian or English, requires me to engage with what exists while seeking to draw out what might be missing from those narratives. Chapter 1 delves into the history of the Russian Orthodox Church Outside of Russia (ROCOR) in the United States and how it evolved over the course of the twentieth and twenty-first centuries. Focusing on converts' conceptions of purity and correct praxis, the opening chapter looks at two important time periods in the formation of the ROCOR: the time prior to the reunification of the ROCOR with the Moscow Patriarchate in 2007, and the time after that unifying event. Along the way, two key figures—St. John Maximovitch of Shanghai and San Francisco and Father Seraphim Rose—for many converts, will come to the fore as pivotal figures in the philosophical opening of ROCOR for Americans without Russian heritage. Finally, the chapter turns to a more detailed introduction to life in Woodford, West Virginia.

Chapter 2 questions the spiritual dimensions of conversion, paying close attention to notions of masculinity, education, and class. Moving beyond the normative language of the American spiritual marketplace, this section explores the motivating factors that might lead to conversion. Drawing out in greater detail the influence of Father Seraphim Rose and his social politics on individual converts in the community, the chapter considers the relationship between conversion and traditionalism for this particular group of believers. As we move into Chapter 3, I begin to open the iris of my theoretical lens a bit more, looking at the political practices of believers within the New Cold War context. Again, I include issues of masculinity and identity in the shifting politics of converts. I also use this space to draw out the implications of labeling this community as alt-right, gesturing at different terminology we might use to talk about how far-right ideologues identify themselves. At the same time, I also ask larger questions about what scholars mean when we use the term "alt-right," suggesting that we might reframe the political conversation in ways that are more productive for understanding the sociopolitical movements emerging around the globe.

Chapter 4 takes up these political complexities through the use of theology, highlighting the impulse toward monarchism in the Woodford community, as expressed in the cultic devotional practices and material culture of honor toward Tsar Nicholas II, who is considered a saintly political martyr in Russian Orthodox hagiography. Exploring the ideas of sovereignty, sacred kingship, and *symphonia*, I tease out the pious politics of the community and how they are related to the affinity many seemed to hold for Vladimir Putin. Continuing the focus on divine kingship, monarchism, and tsarism, Chapter 5 delves into how many in the community understood Vladimir Putin and his relationship to the Russian Orthodox Church. I pay close attention to the moral politics of converts, looking at their ideologies of gender as part of their boundary-making schemas that position them in opposition to liberal secularism. I suggest that— through their stances on gender and sexuality, their apocalyptic politics about secular, Western democracy, and their turn to Russia and Putin—converts were politicizing their conversions, faith, and beliefs.

Chapter 6 also focuses on politics, but on the local level, delving into intra-group conflicts and regional politics. In doing so, I draw out the idea of being a citizen of heaven as a trope that believers use to both reinforce their conversion to Orthodoxy and to dismiss the idea that they need to be involved in local social change in any substantive way. I also highlight the power dynamics between inhabitants of the monastery and the parish, showing how the tumultuous incidents of the past have given way to a complicated sociality between the two institutions that make up the one community. I again return to the figure of Father Seraphim Rose and how his disciple—Father Alexey (Ambrose) Young—had a hand in shaping the early years of the community. Finally, I touch upon economics and missionization, looking at how this community might have been complicit in the long-standing colonization of Appalachia through their presence with and relationship to the impoverished communities surrounding them. The final chapter in this book takes a theoretical look at geographies and temporalities, questioning what the presence of Russian Orthodoxy in Appalachia means for the region, and what roles Orientalism, globalization, and imagination play in the political postures of what I call Reactive Orthodoxy, a far-right Western reimagining of the faith that is deeply tied to the political.

American politics in the late 2010s were fraught, as were the internal politics of global Orthodoxy, especially with the annexation of Crimea by Russia in 2014, the Moscow-Constantinople schism that took place in 2018, and Ecumenical Patriarch Bartholomew's profession of support for the new Ukrainian Orthodox Church that same year.[61] Orthodox social media sites were filled with reactionary, polarizing comments from those with wide-ranging political affiliations after the Moscow Patriarchate unilaterally broke ties with Constantinople in 2018, primarily because of the Ecumenical Patriarch's support of Ukrainian Orthodox autocephaly.[62] In addition, particularly in the United States, there seemed to be a growing number of ultra-conservative converts who were quite vocal politically, both in terms of social politics and the Church. This was not limited to ROCOR. Father Josiah Trenham, a converted priest and a bit of a digital Orthodox celebrity from California, took to the international stage with his speech at the 2016 World Congress of Families in Tbilisi, Georgia, where his highly inflammatory comments about LGBTQ+ communities prompted an investigation by the Southern Poverty Law Center's Hatewatch Staff.[63] Trenham was not the only highly controversial conservative figure in the U.S. Orthodox Church during this period. Rod Dreher, Kh. Frederica Mathewes-Green, and Fr. Peter Heers were all players in the social drama of Reactive Orthodoxy. They, along with other speakers, were part of the March 2019 conference at Holy Trinity Monastery and Seminary in Jordanville, New York, that was titled, "Chastity, Purity, Integrity: Orthodox Anthropology and Secular Culture in the Twenty-First Century."[64] Held in one of the historic

communities of Russian Orthodoxy in the United States, this conference was
created by converts and attended mostly by the same demographic. The conference video proceedings were recorded by Ancient Faith Ministries, one of
the most prominent digital media outlets for Orthodox Christians in the United
States, suggesting that the conservative ideologies present in the lectures might
be welcomed by Orthodox listeners throughout the United States, and perhaps
globally.[65]

The social politics offered by the conference speakers were echoes of what
I heard during my year in Woodford. With the influx of converts from evangelical and fundamentalist Protestant backgrounds, Orthodoxy's social values
are transforming ideologically, shaped by radical conservatives who are creating
Reactive Orthodoxy. The sociocultural baggage of conversion means ideologies
that were not historically found in ROCOR are beginning to emerge as part
of the Church in the United States. The shifting social formations of Orthodox
Christianity are not only found in the United States. Vladimir Putin, along
with Patriarch Kirill and the Russian Orthodox Church, has encouraged a
turn to traditional family values in Russia, a concept that seems to be an American export to Russia, and one that is part of larger ideologies of political and
religious rhetoric about body, family, and country.[66] The rise of these ideologies
in the post-Soviet context is, of course, part of the continuing negotiation of
Russian identity long after *perestroika*, and has as much to do with Vladimir
Putin's desire for autocratic rule as it does with Patriarch Kirill's emphasis on
promoting a post-modern form of Orthodox Christianity on the global stage.
For the conservative believers with whom I have worked in the United States,
Russia's supposed new focus on family values seemed salvific, in a time when
they believed most Western countries were failing to protect the family structure, and morality more broadly. For converts to the Russian Orthodox Church
Outside of Russia, conversion opened the door to an enchanted world of religious and political possibilities that the United States did not seem to afford
them in that particular social moment.

1

Foreign Faith in a Foreign Land

A Discursive History of the Russian Orthodox Church in the United States

Our Church is small but pure as crystal.

—ST. JOHN MAXIMOVITCH

Pollution dangers strike when form has been attacked.

—MARY DOUGLAS, *PURITY AND DANGER*, 1966

"St. John of San Francisco said once that the Russian Church Abroad [ROCOR] has preserved Orthodoxy in crystalline purity," Father Damascene commented as he explained why he converted to and revered the Russian Orthodox Church Outside of Russia.[1] Father Damascene, the guest master at St. Basil's monastery, leaned back in an oversized, puffy chair situated across from me in a small room in the basement of the monastery's library. It was Bright Week, the period of time following Pascha (Easter), and the entire monastery was buzzing with festal joy. Many of the monks were relieved from their typical duties during Bright Week, which provided the perfect time for me to interview them. On this occasion, Fr. Damascene, who had been at the monastery since 2011, was able to procure a secluded spot for our interview in a small confessional room typically reserved for clergy. With warm brown eyes shaded by smudgy glasses, sporting a greying and wiry beard and ponytail, the lanky monk had an easy smile and gentle yet congenial nature. He was easy to talk to and he knew it. My daily interactions with him during services, after lunch, and while working around the monastery grounds were brief, often humorous, and quite casual; they did not prepare me for his staunch beliefs about Russian Orthodoxy. From our prior conversations I knew that he loved being a monk, but sitting down with him in the confessional room that spring afternoon, I began realize that it was not simply being a monk that was important to Fr. Damascene; it was being a monk in ROCOR, and being a part of what he considered to be a pure, undefiled, and thoroughly preserved form of Christianity.

In order to understand, however, why a thirty-something, St. John's College–educated Texan of Sephardic family heritage and evangelical Protestant background would be drawn to Russian Orthodoxy, we must first understand a bit of contextualizing history about the Russian Orthodox Church Outside of Russia. This chapter provides a historical introduction to ROCOR as it has developed in the United States, both in relationship to and distinction from the Metropolia, which ultimately became the Orthodox Church in America (OCA). Drawing on the work of Church historians and oral histories of converts in Woodford, I trace how ROCOR, a community that was founded by refugees and émigrés fleeing communism, and the seemingly Soviet-corrupted Russian Orthodox Church, has become, in recent years, a haven for non-Slavic Americans retreating from what they see as a rising tide of secularism in American culture and politics. Through its assumed crystalline structure, focus on correct practice, and seemingly zealous defense of prerevolutionary Russian Orthodoxy, ROCOR became synonymous for many converts with authenticity, traditionalism, and strident praxis. ROCOR, ultimately, was geo-political gospel truth for many Americans who converted and began to feel as if America was headed toward the same type of political oppression and persecution that Christians in Russia experienced during the Soviet period. By the 2010s, as one former convert monk from Woodford, who is still Orthodox, told me, ROCOR was "preaching the gospel of Old Russia, of prerevolutionary Russia, not the gospel of Christ" and "Putin was the new triumph of Orthodoxy."[2]

Historically, other forms of Orthodoxy in the United States, particularly the Greek Archdiocese, the Antiochian Church, and the Orthodox Church in America, focused on assimilation, social care and justice movements, and, in many ways, the mainstreaming of Orthodoxy. ROCOR, however, perhaps because of its noncanonical status until 2007, created an insular social group that would preserve not only their understanding of Orthodox theology, but also particular cultural expressions of faith in order to re-missionize Russia after the end of the Soviet Union. Despite this containment of sorts, ROCOR did attract converts, and within the past thirty-plus years the numbers of converts have begun to rise, even prior to the religious reunification between ROCOR and the ROC in 2007, when ROCOR was still considered noncanonical in the Eastern Orthodox world.[3] No longer planning to return to Russia to re-missionize the former Soviet Union, members of ROCOR seemingly turned toward the American landscape as a place ripe for spiritual harvest. It is within the context of this new, outward facing moment in ROCOR, particularly in the late 2010s, that we find parishes and monasteries where Slavic peoples make up as little as 0 to 10 percent of the community population. No longer a faith just for cradle-born Orthodox people, ROCOR has become the home of seekers who are looking for a historical Eastern faith born out in the Western world.

Mother Rus', Pray to God for Us

The stories of conversion in Appalachia are, in many respects, linked to the conversion of Rus' by Byzantine Christians, when, according to some Church historians, Prince Vladimir sent his emissaries in search of a unifying religious tradition that could, alongside the monarchic political structure, help forge a cohesive empire.[4] Not finding complementary theologies in Islam and Judaism, Vladimir, who would eventually be glorified (canonized) in the Russian Orthodox Church, turned to Christianity after hearing the stories from scouts arriving back from services at Hagia Sophia, one of the largest Christian churches at the time, located in what is now Istanbul. Christianization took time, and while some scholars argue that it was completed by 988, it was ultimately a process that spanned centuries.[5] As Orthodox Christianity spread throughout the empire of Rus' it became institutionalized over time, and deeply connected to powerful political structures.[6] As scholar of Russian Orthodoxy Zoe Knox writes, "Prince Vladimir's introduction of Eastern Orthodoxy to Kievan Rus' marked the beginning of an intimate link between Church and state, guided by the Byzantine symphonic ideal (*symphonia*) of the dual rule of the ecclesiastical and temporal authorities."[7] The 1589 tomos of autocephaly from the Constantinople Patriarchate meant that the Russian Orthodox Church was canonically independent, although it was still dependent upon the political structures of the transforming empire of Rus'.[8]

This relationship transformed in a variety of social, political, and religious ways under the authority of subsequent monarchs, including Peter I (1672–1725), who reimagined the Church's hierarchical structure, bringing it more directly under the authority of imperial rule through the removal of the Patriarchate in favor of a synod—a way, as Vera Shevzov points out, to remove the patriarch as a singular figure of political competition.[9] Catherine the Great's (1729–1796) further secularization of Russia, despite her encouragement of religious diversity, saw a greater decline in the Orthodox Church's autonomy, as political control of Russia expanded under tsarist rule.[10] While some scholars argue that the ROC was never fully under Russian governmental authority, the relationship was parallel and often mutually beneficial prior to the Soviet era.[11] Most converts with whom I worked never mentioned Peter I, Catherine the Great, or the period of time when the Patriarchate was dismantled. Instead, they move seamlessly from the assumed *symphonia* (a complementary church-state structure) of Kievan Rus' to the reign of Tsar Nicholas II, suggesting that he was a model for true Orthodox governance. Potentially this might be because Prince Vladimir and Tsar Nicholas II are canonized political saints in ROCOR and are thus seemingly more trustworthy as models for the hagiographical rendering of church-state history. This is not to say, of course, that converts were unaware of the history of the Russian Orthodox Church. On the contrary, they were acutely aware of it, with most possessing deep historical knowledge of the Russian Church and Orthodox Christianity more broadly. However, it was clear that they often had specific narratives about Church history that they wanted to convey. More often than not, those histories, or perhaps even hagiographies, of the Russian Church and government leaders left out important issues of religio-political collusion that supported tsarist power and clergy privilege.[12] Furthermore, the narratives about the Russian Church in the twentieth century often failed to mention the priests who tried to incorporate Bolshevik ideologies into the Orthodox Church as a way to reform both the Church and the government.[13]

The conversion of Rus' is still talked about in ROCOR today, especially since the 2018 Ukrainian-Russian schism that caused a great deal of turmoil in global Orthodoxy.[14] Yet the conversion of Rus' itself was not the most important aspect of Russian Orthodox history in the minds of most believers with whom I worked. In the history of the Russian Orthodox Church, according to many of the converts, 1917 proved to be one of the most influential moments. The Russian Revolution(s) of 1917, the focus on atheism, Marxism, and the increased political violence that led to gulag deaths, bans on particular religious practices, and the nationalization of Church properties throughout the Soviet Union became the basis for their narratives about the dangers of secular state power.[15] Sometimes called the catacomb church, the ROC was often portrayed as going underground during the Soviet Union; yet it appears as though a remnant of its former glory remained, for believers suggested that it began to revive after perestroika.[16] Many scholars argue that the holdover Soviet anti-religious policies and practices came to an end in the former U.S.S.R. by 1998 through Mikhail Gorbachev's earlier interventions at the beginning of 1990s that allowed religion to become more acceptable in Russian society and ultimately, it could be argued, helped spur religious freedom legislation, including the 1997 "On Freedom of Conscience and Religious Associations" ('O *svobode sovesti i o religionznykh ob'edineniiakh*) act.[17] While the ending of anti-religious policies helped aid the redevelopment of Orthodox culture throughout Russia, it seems as if the true flourishing, as some scholars call it, of Orthodoxy in post-Soviet Russia came during the multiple tenures of Vladimir Putin.[18] Under Putin's New Russia, many U.S. converts believed that Orthodox Christianity was given place of importance that it was denied under the Soviets and that perhaps it can revitalize world Christianity and defend it with the help of its ROCOR satellites.

ROCOR in North America

This story is not about the early and fiery years of what is now known as the Russian Orthodox Church Outside of Russia (ROCOR) that, according to some of its members, is one of trials and tribulation, preservation at all costs, and a desire to reconvert an entire empire to Christianity.[19] Yet to understand the complexities of American conversions to ROCOR in the twenty-first century, it is imperative to look back at that period briefly. Most of the histories of ROCOR were (and still are) written by male clerics in the Church. A composite origin narrative of ROCOR history focuses on the importance of godly hier-archical leadership, the sequential waves of social transformation Russian Orthodoxy went through during the Soviet Union, and the notion of being in perpetual diaspora. After the 1917 Revolution and the assassinations of Tsar Nicholas II and his family in 1918, it was increasingly clear to leadership in the Russian Orthodox Church that Soviet officials were hostile to their ideological mission.[20] By 1920, fears of the state invading the Church were high and Russian leadership outside of the homeland were growing increasingly worried about what might happen if connections with the Church in Russia were severed by the Soviets. As a way to prevent the total collapse of Church structure, Patriarch Tikhon of Moscow (who was later canonized as a saint) ordered an emergency resolution (*ukaz*) on 20/7 of November 1920 that granted diocesan bishops the ability to reorganize themselves as temporary governing bodies, and to align with other dioceses nearby if they found themselves "completely out of contact with the Supreme Church Administration, or if the Supreme Church Administration itself, headed by His Holiness the Patriarch, for any reason whatsoever cease[d] its activity."[21] Patriarch Tikhon issued *Ukaz No. 362* in an effort to preserve the structural formation of the Church, to keep the global satellites of Russian Orthodoxy attached to the host. On the ground, this decree allowed for more structural flexibility, which is what many hierarchs believed the Church needed to continue, especially in Russia when the Soviet experiment of *Zhivaya Tserkov'*, the Living Church, began in 1922—the same year suggested by some scholars to be the founding date for ROCOR, although 1924 and 1927 are just as equally referenced as the origin years for the organization because of the internal chaos.[22] Overall, the 1920s were decidedly the decade in which ROCOR as autonomous organization emerged in world Christianity. Patriarch Tikhon's emergency resolution played a crucial role in ROCOR's formation and in the historical evolution of the Russian Church in the United States.

Russian religious emigration to and life in the United States in the early to mid–twentieth century were affected by the international political and social complexities of American-Russian relations and the internal canonical chaos of the ROC and ROCOR. The early history of the Russian Church in North America in the twentieth century is one of great turmoil. Depending on which accounts and voices we listen to, we often get two very distinct stories about the eventual creation of ROCOR and the OCA.[23] From most accounts, ROCOR of the 1920s, and even later throughout the twentieth century, did not consider itself to be an autocephalous Church; rather, it believed it was still loyal to the mother Church in Russia and was her voice in the diaspora, even though in 1927 it broke communion with the ROC.[24] There are far too many internal struggles between ROCOR and what would eventually come to be called the Moscow Patriarchate to note here, but it is crucial to understand that once ROCOR became its own entity, as it were, it was canonically separate from the Russian Orthodox Church until it signed documents of reconciliation with the Moscow Patriarchate in 2007.[25] This self-isolation of ROCOR, especially in the United States, was key to forging its distinctive practices and ideas. The focus on monasticism and imperial Russian history were and are two of its defining features, along with deep emphasis on clerical authority. Because ROCOR was not in communion with most of the Orthodox world for almost eight decades, it has seemingly become an echo chamber or perhaps an incubator of prerevolutionary Russian Orthodox thought. Its emphasis on tradition, adherence to the Old Calendar (Julian), submission to spiritual father confessors, and highly structured gender roles have all become concentrated over the years.[26] These distilled ideological distinctions often put them in opposition to their spiritual cousin, the Orthodox Church in America, which embraced, among other things, the New Calendar (Revised Julian), pews, and shorter service rubrics.

The running joke during my time with the Woodford ROCOR community was that the Orthodox Church in America (OCA) was in schism, despite the fact that it received a tomos (decree) of autocephaly (self-governance) from the Moscow Patriarchate (MP) in 1970.[27] Because ROCOR reconciled to the MP in 2007, OCA parishioners, who were properly prepared, could receive Holy Communion at both St. Basil's and St. John's. While community members mostly mentioned the schism in jest, it nods to the tenuous relationship that has historically existed between the two jurisdictions, even after ROCOR's reunification with the rest of the Eastern Orthodox world. The Metropolia, which would eventually become the OCA, ROCOR, and Moscow Patriarchate parishes abroad, possess foundational roots in a common, perhaps even shared faith and history. Indeed, until 1927, the Metropolia participated in ROCOR synodal activity in the United States, even though the former declared itself to be autonomous throughout much of the 1920s. Internal struggles, delayed communication with the ROC, and differing opinions on how American missionization should take place all became linchpins for the divide between the two organizations.[28] Perhaps because of the chaotic circumstances of global politics that created the distinct jurisdictions, there has always been tension between the two groups. The idea that the OCA is a schismatic group and not truly Orthodox is not just found among contemporary converts to ROCOR. Important ROCOR figures throughout the history of the Church have often written about or commented on the tenuous relationship between ROCOR and the OCA.[29]

After Patriarch Tikhon's *ukaz*, the 1920s were a period in which the Metropolia, which was already institutionally separate from what would become ROCOR, struggled to temporarily disentangle itself even further from what they believed was the Soviet-infiltrated Russian Church. Amicable at first, ROCOR (also known as ROCA) eventually proclaimed that the Metropolia was in schism by 1927, the same year they officially broke ties with the ROC. While there was a brief period of short-term ecclesiastical reconciliation between ROCOR and the Metropolia in the 1930s and into the mid-1940s, issues over who was in control led the nascent OCA to once again dissolve canonical ties with ROCOR.[30] As the two emerging institutions embarked on their own canonical paths during the mid–twentieth century, they continued to have quite a hostile relationship. This was made even more contentious when the Moscow Patriarchate granted the OCA the tomos of autocephaly in 1970, a sign to many in ROCOR that OCA was an instrument of Soviet power in North America, even as the icy relations between the two countries were starting to thaw with the détente that lasted for roughly a decade (1969–1979).[31] From 1970 to 2007, the OCA and ROCOR were not in canonical communion with each other. Nor was ROCOR in communion with many of the historic patriarchates of Orthodox Christianity. This is important to note given the fact that many of the older Orthodox folks in Woodford converted to ROCOR prior to the reunification. Those who did so, opted to select an Orthodox body without canonical authority. It seems as if these converts were not looking for an unbroken line of apostolical succession, but rather a religious world built for the purposes of preserving and defending what they saw as traditional Orthodoxy and orthopraxy. Eventually, this insular ethno-religious world foraged in diasporic conditions would be challenged by the social upheaval of reunion with the Church of its forefathers and the political implications of embracing its post-Soviet motherland.

The Reunification

Perhaps the single most important event in the history of ROCOR was the reunification between the organization and the Moscow Patriarchate (MP) in the late spring of 2007. Prior to the signing of canonical communion documents and the concelebration between the two Orthodox communities, both the Muscovite Church and ROCOR lobbed bitter accusations at each other from across the world, with anathemas interspersed.[32] Like any event of global sociopolitical relevance, it had its supporters and naysayers in the media and in private institutional formations. In the summer of 2015, when I visited the historic Holy Trinity Monastery (HTM) in Jordanville, New York, the abbot noted that the reunification was a painful moment for ROCOR in North America. In the wake of the realignment between the two churches, some of the monks at HTM left because they feared the political implications of communion with the MP, especially given how much of an impact the former Soviet Union had on the hierarchical structure of the Russian Orthodox Church. It seems likely that those concerned with reunification were gesturing back to both the Soviet policing of the ROC and the partnership of some clerics with governmental authorities and institutions. Over the course of the Soviet Union's leadership, there were stages of Church suppression, bans on cleric activities, garb, and other aspects of Church life, and, ultimately, some religious officials were imprisoned, persecuted, and even died because of the extraordinary political disagreements between the church and state.[33]

In Woodford, the 2007 reunification was met, according to conversations I had with longtime Orthodox residents, with a bit more of an embrace, since it meant that the parish and the monastery would be able to concelebrate the Divine Liturgy and other services with priests at the nearby Antiochian and Greek parishes. In 2013, during his Paschal address, Metropolitan Hilarion, the first hierarch of the Russian Church Abroad, proclaimed, "It is important that the unity of our Church exist [sic] exclusively on the foundation of Truth and purity. That is why the reestablishment of prayerful communion within the Russian Church, the fifth anniversary of which we celebrated last year, is in our opinion an historic event, and the most important one in recent decades."[34] The reunification, for many in ROCOR, signaled the healing of the painful rift between the disjointed bodies of the Russian Church. It also seemed to herald a transformation in ROCOR's understanding of itself not only in relationship to the ROC (MP) but also the other canonical Orthodox jurisdictions in the United States, including the OCA.[35] While no large data sets have been gathered on the rise of converts after reunification, it seems likely that the event helped spur those interested in the faith to select ROCOR, for it was no longer a separate, noncanonical entity but a fully formed member of the global Orthodox Christian body. At the same time, ROCOR was, and still is, a separatist, nostalgically inclined organization that Rico Monge has noted emphasizes "Orthodox Christianity, the Tsar, and the Russian State as inextricably linked."[36] This tripartite focus, along with the perpetual emphasis on purity and correctness, has created an ideological shadow world of the Moscow Patriarchate, one that is both canonically outward-facing yet far removed socially, ideologically, and perhaps even theologically from other forms of Orthodox Christianity.

Fleeing Communism and Finding Converts

Given its historic focus on maintaining religious and ethnic boundaries, it seems surprising that ROCOR has attracted converts and other religious seekers. Converts, according to Church historians at Holy Trinity Monastery, are not a new phenomenon. Of course, it could be argued that Russian Orthodoxy was and is entirely made up of converts, since the faith only came to the lands of historic Rus' because of Prince Vladimir's desire to find a unifying religion that could help him politically and socially create cohesion among his subjects. The mass baptisms in Kievan Rus' were, perhaps, the start of the convert Church. Yet this is not what ROCOR Studies researchers mean when they talk about conversion to the Russian Church. ROCOR tends to claim many of the indigenous conversions that happen in North America to be under their religious purview (and that of the Russian Orthodox Church more broadly), since most groups were converted by Russian monks in the 1700s.[37] Some, such as public historian Nicholas Chapman, point to early American converts, with Philip Ludwell III, a British colonial solider and public official in Virginia during the mid- to late 1770s, as a prime example of early Russian Orthodox conversions.[38] Indeed, an Orthodox nonprofit dedicated to Ludwell's memory argues that he was the first convert to Orthodoxy in the United States.[39] Beyond figures who can reify the idea of conversion as a historical part of Orthodoxy's presence in North America, ROCOR Studies scholars also look to contemporary mobilizations throughout the global south, particularly in Guatemala, as part of the Church's expanding missionizing efforts.[40]

Because ROCOR possesses a geographically disparate religious structure that seemingly eschews scholastic focus, news and information about the

Church is often only disseminated through Church websites, on social media platforms among believers, and through the digital writings of ROCOR clerics and members. The conversion of indigenous Guatemalans to ROCOR is often documented in this vernacular way. The same holds true for contemporary conversions the United States, where converts tend to share their conversion stories online through social media platforms. This lack of institutional and scholastic focus on conversions as part of public church history might be in part because of the understanding of missionization that developed between ROCOR and the OCA. Historically, ROCOR missionization in the United States was gradual, since most of the Church hierarchs assumed the purpose of the organization was to preserve the teachings and ethos of the community in order to transplant it into the broken and thirsty ground of post-Soviet Russia, with hopes that their seeds of faith and piety would bear a large harvest of souls. In contrast, the OCA's mission was simply that—to be a missionizing force in North America. One of the reasons ROCOR suggests that they have become successful in missionizing the United States more recently is that, unlike the Moscow Patriarchate, they have the authority to plant new churches in the United States. The MP, per the conditions of the tomos of autocephaly with the OCA, seems to be ineligible to expand beyond the parishes that were set at the time autocephaly was granted.[41] While institutional dictates may have contoured the missionizing capabilities of Russian Orthodoxy beyond the borders of its homeland, the transformation of the faith took place and continues to develop in the United States through ROCOR's turn to the American mission field.

One of the crucial aspects that helped conversion spread in the United States was the encouragement of English language usage and resources by St. John Maximovitch and subsequently Father Seraphim (Eugene) Rose, although as American historian Aram Sarkisian points out, there were conversions prior to the latter half of twentieth century, and they were certainly aided by the Russian Church's "English Department."[42] Yet within the mid- to latter part of the twentieth century, it was Maximovitch and Rose who seemed to provide the most public form of influence on converts. Rose in particular helped spur the production of English-language theological materials that have influenced generations of converts, including those with whom I worked in Appalachia. Many of the stories you will find in the pages of this book mention St. John Maximovitch, archbishop of Shanghai and San Francisco, and Father Seraphim Rose, the latter of whom is one of the most understudied yet influential figures in conservative wings of contemporary U.S. Orthodoxy. I spend time in many of the chapters explaining the significance of Rose in the conversion narratives and political ideologies of converts with whom I have worked, but to understand Rose we must first look to Maximovitch, who was a formational force in his life.

Maximovitch (1896–1966) is often considered one of the first contemporary Orthodox saints in the United States. Born in the small village of Adamovka (now part of Ukraine) in 1896, Maximovitch's aristocratic family had deep ties to the Orthodox Church.[43] Hagiographies describe the saint as an almost perfect child who was highly intelligent. The 1917 Revolution pushed the Maximovitch family to flee to Yugoslavia, where the future saint studied theology. Having become a monastic, in 1934 Maximovitch was elevated to the rank of bishop and assigned to Shanghai. There he focused on social projects with the elderly and orphans. At the end of the 1940s, Maximovitch petitioned the U.S. government to allow Russian refugees entry into the United States. In a little more than ten years, he would be made the administrator of ROCOR's Western European Diocese.[44] Then in 1962, Maximovitch arrived in San Francisco, where he worked tirelessly to construct the "largest church of the Russian Church Abroad in America."[45] In the summer of 1966, Maximovitch died. His repose (death) led to a deep focus in ROCOR on his posthumous spiritual influence in Russian-American Orthodoxy through miracles and healings associated with his relics and intersessions.[46] Maximovitch not only had an enormous influence in San Francisco during his life, he also had a great effect on converts in West Virginia long after his death. At St. John's parish, there was a large shrine devoted to the saint, in which part of his relics were housed. Many converts in Woodford had a special affinity for Maximovitch, with ill members of the parish often taking trips to his shrine in San Francisco in order to pray for healing—which believers claimed happened in some instances. It was not only his potential interventions that converts made use of, it was also Maximovitch's translated writings, which were part of the everyday parlance of many believers, including the monks of St. Basil's monastery. For contemporary converts, Maximovitch's authority, hierarchy, and connections to the persecuted Russian Church are not only felt through his writings; his influence on Fr. Seraphim Rose, who's own spiritual son was vital in the early years of shaping St. Basil's and St. John's, has provided human links in the historical and spiritual chain to Russian Orthodoxy prior to and through the transformative moments of the 1917 Revolution and its unfolding history in the diaspora. These links of spiritual kinship and institutional power are important to note, because they allow us to trace the social trajectory of ROCOR in the United States, providing us a backdrop for understanding the potential appeal of hierarchical authority and assumed traditionalism by converts in the United States.

American Conversions to Russian Orthodoxy

Fr. Damascene was one of thirty monks at St. Basil's monastery during my year with the community. He was one of only seven monks whom I was allowed to interview. Along with the abbot, these seven men were the shaping voice of how the monastery was represented to me. All of them professed that they were not only thrilled to have found Orthodoxy, but that they were also grateful that God's providence allowed them to end up in ROCOR, because it was not, from their vantage point, a "modernist" Orthodox community that had allowed aspects of "Western culture" and secularism to creep in. Overall, the monks, clerics, and laity highlighted what they believed to be the traditionalistic nature of ROCOR as one of its most appealing factors. This suggests that Christianity, for the people with whom I worked, was tied intimately to a politics of rigor, often labeled as rigorism in the field of Orthodox Studies.[47] In this instance it seemed as if "rigorism" had seemingly become blurred with social moral political values, leading converts to imaginatively embrace a Church (ROCOR) and its political allies (the contemporary Russian State) as arbiters of true Christian morality.

As I mentioned earlier, statistics do not seem to be a priority for ROCOR. Metrics for converts to ROCOR in the United States are virtually nonexistent, but most Orthodox clergy I spoke with say that converts represent at least 50 percent of the demographics of the Church across the United States. In an article posted to the Russian government–backed news site *Russia Beyond* in the fall of 2018, David, an American convert to Orthodoxy, talked about why he believed U.S. citizens were turning to Russia and the ROC:

> Many American converts admire [Russian president] Vladimir Putin
> . . . and are a little envious of the direction Russia is taking to stand
> up for Christian civilization and Christian virtues in the public square.
> Where you have processions of thousands following the Holy Cross
> and Icons . . . we have to endure yet another flamboyant, often obscene,
> gay-rights parade.[48]

Similar in scope to the comments made to me by converts in West Virginia, David's statement suggests that the preoccupation with Russian Orthodoxy and, by extension, Russian illiberal politics has to do with Putin's well-publicized, or perhaps well-marketed, take on social morality.[49] Drawing on long-standing assumptions about rural spirituality and church attendance, the author of the article notes that "Orthodox churches are growing mainly in the conservative American South and Southwest." Including a quote from David that gestures to the Orthodox decline in "old immigrant home towns in the Northeast and

Upper Midwest," the article concludes with the idea that Orthodoxy was, as of 2018, growing in conservative areas and dying off in liberal parts of the United States.[50] What this article fails to mention is how much of the growth stems from converts.

ROCOR historically was not a convert-friendly group early on in its creation. The insularity and emphasis on heritage preservation meant that ROCOR parishes were often not spaces of inclusion for those who did not automatically read as ethnically Russian *and* pious, or read and write Russian for that matter. Abbot Spyridon, the head of St. Basil's monastery, who never learned to speak or read Russian, recalled how his early encounters with the brotherhood at Holy Trinity Monastery in Jordanville, New York, were quite off-putting to his American convert sensibilities. Other monks at the monastery mentioned how one of the brothers had quite the mental health stamina, since he was able to withstand a year at the monastery in Jordanville as a young convert to the faith with no knowledge of the language and no propensity toward Russian culture. One young monk, Fr. Hubert, recounted how he found a welcoming ROCOR community in San Francisco in the early to mid-2000s, but suggested it was because that parish had been transformed by its connection to Father Seraphim Rose in the 1970s.[51] Fr. Hubert's draw to the Russian ethos was overwhelming, and despite his ventures into the Antiochian and Greek archdioceses for both monastic contemplation and work as an educator, he found his spiritual home in ROCOR at St. Basil's monastery.[52]

Fr. Hubert's affinity for Russian Orthodoxy and culture was not a singular story; it was, in a variety of different voices, expressed by many members of both St. Basil's and St. John's. Surprisingly, the monastery, which housed some of the most ardent yet discreet voices for Russian politics, culture, and theology, was the place in which there was more Americanization. Fr. Damascene believed that it was part of the convert culture of the community coming to bear in their focus on English language use and locally created hymnody (Church music). None of the monks spoke or read Russian, and the only Church Slavonic they knew came from memorized lines from the services. In contrast, the parish seemed to be overtly Russian in its liturgical and social formations, despite the limited number of ethnic Russian members. Much of this seemed to be the work of Fr. Cyril, the parish priest, who was fluent in Russian. A convert, Fr. Cyril encouraged the use of Church Slavonic, Russian festivals, and Russian conservative political ideologies. Many longtime parishioners told me that the church was far less "ethnic" before Fr. Cyril, who was trained at a ROCOR cathedral in the New York City metro area, arrived. I note these differences because they highlight the ways which ROCOR is transforming through the influx of converts. It is expressed in a variety of fashions, but the use or rejection of language is most assuredly one of the primary means for social adoption and transformation. While most converts were seemingly untroubled by their lack of Russian, one of the fathers at the monastery mentioned that he worried about confessing Russian pilgrims, because he had no idea what he was absolving. Most of the clergy at St. John's were fluent in Russian, while a majority of the parishioners were not. The parish's heavy use of Church Slavonic and Russian aesthetics were seemingly linguistic and sensorial properties of the community's worldbuilding project, especially for those who were previously inclined toward Russian sensibilities.

In many respects, the interest of converts and the transformation of ROCOR is almost a chicken-and-egg scenario. As the number of converts increases, ROCOR seemingly becomes more appealing because of its Americanizing sensibilities, which often include the use of English in the divine services, more social outreach programs, and more well-developed social network programs for believers to connect with each other. At the same time, however, converts seem to be interested in preserving aspects of ROCOR that reinforce its Russian identification, especially that of a prerevolutionary church, with all of its sociopolitical trappings, including *symphonia* and tsarism.[53] Whatever the case might be, during the late 2010s, ROCOR saw a steady stream of conversions and converts taking up ranks among their laity and clergy. What might these conversions mean for the future of ROCOR in the United States? The complicated social ideologies that converts with whom I have worked brought into the Church suggests that the relationship between politics and religion might be growing even closer. The ardor with which converts often talked about Vladimir Putin and Russia might indicate that they have lost faith in not only U.S. conservative governmental groups, such as the GOP, but also the idea of democracy, and the separation of church and state. The ritual of religious conversion often belies the sociopolitical values of believers; it also speaks to a different understanding of social reality and one's place in the world. As Mary Douglas wrote, "Social rituals create a reality which would be nothing without them. It is not too much to say that ritual is more to society than words are to thought. For it is very possible to know something and then find words for it. But it is impossible to have social relations without symbolic acts."[54] The ritual of conversion to ROCOR provided, in many respects, a new reality, a new world for disillusioned Americans who desired religious and political communities they could believe in and respect. While many in this book held to deep conservative political ideologies prior to the ritual of conversion, they seemingly, in the vein of Douglas's thinking, found the words for it in ROCOR.

2

Church of God

Traditionalism, Authenticity, and Conversion to Russian Orthodoxy in Appalachia

> When conversion takes place, the process of revelation occurs in a very simple way—a person is in need, he suffers, and then somehow the other world opens up.
> —FATHER SERAPHIM ROSE, *GOD'S REVELATION OF THE HUMAN HEART*, 1988

> This is something I never knew growing up, but it's somewhere in my roots.
> —A CONVERT MONK, 2018

"I didn't have anything to lose. I was a single guy in my late twenties. I could have latched on to anything," Father Romanos said before taking a sip of water and clearing his throat. A wiry, middle-aged redhead, Father Romanos was one of the earliest arrivals to St. Basil's monastery after they broke land in West Virginia in the late spring of 2000. A self-identified curmudgeon, Father Romanos was numbered among the few monks who still opted to live in the small shed-like structures that dotted the heavily wooded mountainsides surrounding the core of the monastery grounds. All the early arrivals to the monastery lived in camp-style conditions until they were able to build a dormitory and a few small monastic cells. Fr. Romanos often suggested that the monastery might benefit spiritually if they went back to less accommodating living conditions. Only the most strident monks, according to some of the younger monastics, still lived in the simple structures without electricity or running water. The difficult life appealed to Fr. Romanos who, prior to his conversion and turn to monasticism, worked in broadcast television and was a drummer in a band. At the monastery, he was in charge of the choir and helped create religious hymnody, much of which could be found on audio streaming websites by the time I arrived in Woodford.

Father Romanos was known in the St. Basil's community for his vagueness, contrarian nature, skepticism, and love of a good quality India Pale Ale, all of which often made for complex conversations. During one of our chats, he offered a cerebral reason for becoming Orthodox:

> Every single group says it's the real thing. So, I had a thing inside of me that needed to be resolved. I knew if I didn't go out and get whatever it was that God wanted me to get, then I would always be thinking I need to resolve this. There was an internal build, those odd coincidences that just sort of made it so that when I heard there was something that was Orthodox Christianity, I just had to resolve that thing.[1]

Most converts in Woodford, especially males, who made up a majority of the Orthodox population, likened their conversion processes to journeys and, more often than not, the ultimate search for the authentic church established by Christ. Their affective desires often became strengthened by autodidactic religious education as they studied the history of Christianity with the hopes of discerning the true faith. Conversion was the means by which these believers located themselves spiritually, ontologically, and, in many cases, temporally. The importance of selective intra-Christian conversion, particularly in the United States, has often been overlooked by anthropologists and scholars of religion, who have historically focused on other forms of Christianization, generally in areas outside of the United States.[2]

Anthropologically, theories of conversion are limited and often address the forced conversion of native and indigenous populations by Christian missionaries.[3] Thus anthropological conceptions of conversion are intimately tied to empire, globalization, colonialism, and white hegemonic Christianity. This is not to say that all forms of Christian conversion are not somewhat tied to these factors. In many respects, the converts of Woodford could be considered not only as members of a minority religion but also complicit in the reproduction of globalizing neo-colonialist Christianity *through* their conversion and, more importantly, their appropriation and transformation of Russian Orthodox religious cultural formations in a way that often subjugated Russians in the community or used them to reinforce their own validity as members of ROCOR. Additionally, conversion is more likely examined outside the context of the United States, or at least current scholarship suggests that to be the case. Yet conversion happens within the confines of the United States. Certainly, scholars take note of this in the historical context, but the lack of contemporary anthropological research on Christian conversions in the United States has left us with a dearth of data. This means that contemporary selective conversions are often analyzed under the same theoretical constructs as historically forced conversions; thus studies often fail to fully contextualize how and why people are selectively converting. If it is true that "to be converted is to reidentify, to learn, reorder, and reorient," then understanding it as part of "interrelated modes" of social transformation is key.[4]

Within the field of religious studies, which often shares theoretical models with anthropology and sociology, conversion is mostly thought of in sociological terms, with many scholars relying on the works of Wade Clark Roof, in the lineage of Rodney Stark, who used the idea of a spiritual marketplace to make sense of why adults switch or find new religious affiliations.[5] While these writings help us begin to explore some of the reasons that surround the adoption of particular religious groups, these theories often assume that the availability of options is one of the primary motivating factors for switching or adopting a religious community. Most assuredly, members of the Woodford community profited spiritually, they would say, from the diversity found within the American religious landscape. However, as I delineate in this chapter, the manifold options available to converts were not the motivating factors that drove their spiritual transformations. Often the impetus for conversion, in most cases, boiled down to a single idea—the quest for true Christianity—and the variety of choices hindered individual searches.[6] Rather than focusing on the economy of the spiritual marketplace, I suggest we can learn more about intent and belief by investigating the thematic elements of conversion to parse out the reasons for fealty.

This chapter highlights the thematic rhetoric believers used to contextualize their place as converts in ROCOR. Crucial to their stories was the idea of maintaining direct connections to the traditional, authentic, and historic Orthodox Church of Mother Rus'. While this chapter touches upon the political implications of conversion, it focuses primarily on the theological and social aspects of converting to ROCOR in order to get at the heart of what it means turn one's self to an "Eastern religion" and away from Western forms of religion and morality. Focusing on themes of spiritual authenticity and traditional conservative values, converts in Woodford provide reasons why they left their familial faith traditions for ROCOR. To understand the themes of conversion, I explore the life of Father Seraphim Rose, a figure of great import to many Orthodox converts. I suggest converts hold up Rose as a model for conversion, as someone who sold out, spiritually speaking, and still, after his untimely death in the 1980s, provided a gateway to the world of Russian Orthodoxy for Americans. The hagiographic stories of Rose's life offer insights into two key aspects of conversion in Woodford—tradition and authenticity—while also offering us a way to better understand the political trends of traditionalism and fundamentalism often present in American far-right religious communities.

Orthodox Conversions

The history of Orthodoxy in the United States, and the North American continent more broadly, is one of conversion and missionization. From the early Greek missions in what are now Louisiana and Florida, to the Russian monks and fur traders who created a creole form of the faith among indigenous populations in what is now Alaska, Orthodoxy has continued to survive and grow in the United States in large part because of conversion, particularly outside of urban areas that are home to ethnic Orthodox communities.[7] ROCOR historian Nicholas Chapman, who also served as the editor for a press working out of the historic Holy Trinity Monastery in upstate New York, suggested that one of the first American converts to the Orthodox Church, Colonel Philip Ludwell III, made his shift from Anglicanism to Orthodoxy before Russians even set foot on Alaskan soil.[8] While Ludwell was received into the Church in London, Chapman argues that Ludwell, who was related by marriage to George Washington, and who was crucial in the shaping of Virginia history, was truly the first American convert to the Orthodox Church.[9] A foundation devoted to the preservation of Ludwell's memory suggests that the colonel's plantation may have included a small chapel for the divine services.[10] Yet, with a lack of data surrounding Ludwell's conversion and no evidence to fully support his practice of Orthodoxy on American soil—beyond the divine services he wrote in English—most scholars tend to focus on well-documented forms of indigenous conversion and monastic missionization in Alaska instead.

Research on contemporary conversions to Eastern Orthodoxy, especially intra-Christian conversion in the context of the United States, is relatively limited. This seems problematic given the notion that conversion is one of the key elements of American religious life. Understanding how and why people chose to transform themselves and their communities through particular faith traditions provides insights not only into conversion as a ritual event but also into the larger sociocultural issues that are complicit in the process.[11] Comparative work on Orthodox conversions does exist, although it is often historically focused, such as Sergei Kan's work with indigenous convert communities in Alaska.[12] Beyond the work of Kan with Russian-Tlingit Orthodox communities, the amount of research on conversion to Orthodoxy in the United States suffers from lack of attention, save a few studies. Fr. Oliver Herbel's historically bent analysis of conversion offers a brief overview of leading convert figures in U.S. Orthodoxy.[13] Phillip Charles Lucas's work offers comparative case studies of different groups that converted en masse to the Orthodox Church. Lucas first looks at the shifting demographics of the Antiochian archdiocese in the 1980s, which experienced an influx of evangelicals into a predominantly Arab Christian organization, before turning his attention to the subsequent conversion histories of both the Holy Order of Mans (HOOM), a mystic Christian community, and Christ the Savior Brotherhood, an offshoot of HOOM.[14] While Amy Slagle's dissertation and eventual monograph employ sociological analyses of converts from a variety of jurisdictions, sociologist Daniel Winchester's article on conversion highlights the process as a lifelong cultivation of continuity with the cultural formations of the Church that inevitably creates or discovers "a latent Orthodox self."[15] Both of these studies make use of convert narratives from a variety of Orthodox jurisdictions in a highly comparative framework.

The intra-Orthodox comparative model, while beneficial, does not allow us to delve deeply into conversions within the context of a particular Orthodox jurisdiction, in a specific space and place, and within a transformative cultural moment in the United States. Narrowing the focus to conversions in one Orthodox jurisdiction allows us to think through the motivating factors that influence believers in the selection of their spiritual home. This is increasingly important given sociopolitical transformations of Orthodox belief and culture in the United States in the past twenty-plus years. In the United States, ROCOR's demographics are not the only thing transformed because of the influx of converts. The very fabric of Orthodox sociality is changing. Cradle Orthodox Christians whom I have interviewed, including several of the Russian-born Orthodox women in Woodford, expressed how troubled they were by how ROCOR culture seemingly has been adopted and transformed by converts. Thus, understanding *why* people convert to ROCOR specifically and what is meaningful to believers during that process can tell us a great deal about not only the ethos of ROCOR, but also the trends among conservative Christian converts more broadly. In doing so, I seek not to highlight the lacuna of research on Orthodoxy and conversion as some have before me; rather, I aim to normalize research on Orthodoxy in the United States. By treating conversion as part of the sociocultural processes of religious belief and practice, we can see how it is related to larger issues locally and globally.

The Techniques of Conversion

Perhaps the best way to understand conversions in context is to track what I see as the techniques of conversion.[16] As a ritual process, in the spirit of work by foundational scholars such as Arnold van Gennep and Victor Turner, the various liturgical and social components of conversion offer personal and institutional forms of meaning-making that are critical markers for the distinctiveness of ROCOR (and other traditionalist Orthodox communities).[17] The process of reception not only serves as a ritual gateway for believers to enter the faith community, it also marks both the community and believers as participants in a church that is theologically authentic with correct religious praxis. It is simultaneously a ritual of worldbuilding and a ritual of entrance into that world. The first hurdle for an inquirer is making their role as a seeker of spiritual information officially recognized by the Church, a service that is called the Reception of a Catechumen. Historically this service was attached to the rite of baptism, but more recently it has been offered as a stand-alone prayer for conferral of the catechumenate upon a person who intends to continue in his or her catechetical studies for a while before becoming an official member of the Church.[18] The Reception of a Catechumen includes the signing of the cross over the body of the person, the priest breathing upon the inquirer, and finally three exorcisms in order to remove the "dark and powerful figure" of the devil that might hinder the process.[19] Once this is complete, the person is officially recognized by the Church as a catechumen, with his or her status acknowledged in the prayers for catechumens chanted during Divine Liturgy. Although many converts begin catechesis well before they become catechumens, the official process begins in earnest after their reception. Catechesis, or theological pedagogy, is not a standardized practice among Orthodox communities. While early Christians often were required to spend three years studying, contemporary Orthodox jurisdictions, particularly those in the United States, generally do not have concrete timelines for catechetical formation. The time that one spends as a catechumen is typically dependent upon their religious background, training, and level of spiritual maturity, all of which are assessed on a case-by-case basis by a parish priest.

In Woodford, there were nineteen catechumens, six of whom were baptized while I was with the community, and seven more a few months after I left. Two remained catechumens. Four, all from the same family, left during their catechetical training because of political differences with the parish priest, who insisted they renounce their white supremacist ideologies. For those who completed their spiritual journeys through reception into the Church, their timelines were influenced greatly by Fr. Cyril's assessment of their spiritual readiness. For some, the length of time as a catechumen was quite short—just a few months—for others it was almost an entire year. Thekla, a middle-aged local, whose husband had converted years before her, officially enrolled as a catechumen in the early spring of 2018 and by that summer was received into the Church. Fr. Cyril mentioned to me that Thekla's faithfulness in helping with the parish food pantry, her declining health, alongside her tenuous, often volatile, relationship with her husband, made it easier for him to decide when she should be baptized. Fr. Cyril was fearful that something might happen to Thekla and she would not be able to receive last rites and burial in the Orthodox Church. Thekla's catechetical training was sparse to say the least, but since the situation seemed dire, Fr. Cyril proceeded toward baptism with haste, and he did so through his discretion and authority as the spiritual head of St. John's.

Other catechumens in Woodford participated in more structured types of catechetical learning, generally in the form of a short class after coffee hour on Sundays. Fr. Cyril would open with a prayer, pick a topic, and then offer a brief lesson before asking for questions and comments. In addition to these classes, catechumens were required to attend liturgical services to the best of their ability, read Orthodox books, and try to adhere to the fasting and feasting cycles of the Church calendar. Even with these requirements, most catechumens only spent a few months in the catechetical process. Angus's wife, Wenna, who was Roman Catholic, along with their three children, spent two and a half months as catechumens. Angus, who had converted the previous year, only spent six months as a catechumen. Both Wenna and Angus described the deep sense of comfort and peace they felt at the parish. It seems as if the affective draw to Orthodoxy, along with the historicity of the Church, motivated them to become catechumens and helped propel the process along at a faster rate. Some catechumens took their time with the process, often opting to meet with Fr. Cyril individually. Once the catechetical phase of conversion was complete, the next step was full reception into the Church through baptism.

ROCOR receives converts through baptism, even if catechumens had been formerly baptized in a Christian church espousing the traditional Trinitarian formula—in the name of the Father, Son, and Holy Spirit (Ghost). In the context of Orthodoxy in the United States, reception by baptism has increasingly become a marker for conservative traditionalism, bound to institutions and people who eschew even the very idea of ecumenism by breaking all ties with former "heterodox" denominations. Within conservative Orthodox communities, other Christian groups are often labeled heterodox as a way to distinguish them as incorrect expressions of Christianity. In the eyes of many in ROCOR, other Orthodox jurisdictions that receive heterodox Christian converts through the rite of chrismation have succumbed to ecumenism by letting *economia* (discretion in the spirit of charity) take over their historic, traditional praxis. Fr. Tryphon, a young monk who entered into the Orthodox Church through the Antiochian jurisdiction in 2007, relayed how he desired to be baptized rather than chrismated. When he told this to his priest, the rector, who was of the same conservative mindset, mentioned that the young seeker might want to lose his old baptismal certificate so there was no documentation to impend reception by immersion. At St. John's parish, catechumens were not given the option of chrismation. In Angus's case, Fr. Cyril told him when he was ready to be baptized; Angus obliged even though he had previously been baptized in a Baptist Church and subsequently received into the Catholic Church through sprinkling. During my time with the community, there were no lay baptisms at St. Basil's monastery. All catechumens who were received at St. John's were baptized—no exceptions—and seemingly all supported this traditionalist form of conversion reception. Baptism is thus not only a corporeal sign of the burial, death, and rising of a new Christian in Christ; it also signifies a form of Orthodox traditionalism, perhaps even fundamentalism.

One rainy spring day I headed to a coffee shop in a small city about forty-five minutes away from Woodford to meet with Fursey, a convert member of St. John's. Fursey, who grew up in the mountains of Tennessee, recounted how he came into the Church through a radical Orthodox parish in his home state, where the normative form of adult baptism took place in front of other parishioners, generally in a creek, with the convert stripped bare. The rector, who was often called the "barefoot priest" around his town, believed that form of baptism to be more authentically true to the process of baptism that early Christians might have taken part in.[20] Fursey's baptism pushed the limits of acceptable contemporary Orthodox praxis; most baptisms in ROCOR, even in convert communities, are performed according to the traditional formula of triple submersion in the name of the Trinity, with the participant fully clothed. While they might not seem extreme, adult convert baptisms are often considered highly controversial among Orthodox Christians who are not part of ROCOR, for they are viewed as material manifestations of the increasingly conservative impulse within the Russian Church abroad, since by requiring baptism they are ignoring the theological idea of *economia* in favor of pushing for a traditionalist and, one could argue, fundamentalist understanding of reception into the Church. The techniques of conversion are thus telling ritual processes that speak to both believers' dedication to authenticity and ROCOR's geopolitical impulse, for intra-Christian conversion baptisms ultimately gesture to larger global issues of fundamentalism and traditionalism tied to ideological worldviews.

Fundamentalism, Tradition, and Far-Right Geopolitics

At first glance, Eastern Orthodoxy does not fit into the historical context of Christian fundamentalism in the United States, which had its beginnings in the early twentieth-century revivalist movement.[21] However, incarnations of Christian fundamentalism that sprung up in the United States during the 2010s have much in common with Orthodox convert ideologies. Sara Moslener and Katherine Stewart, among others, have noted that new forms of Christian fundamentalism, particularly in the 2010s and especially since the 2016 U.S. presidential election, have become increasingly focused on radical forms of purity, tradition, and nationalism.[22] In many respects, this new wave of conservatism seems to be a revision or revival of ongoing culture wars in the United States that came to a head in the 1990s, for religion and politics are once again intimately tied together in social, even mass, displays and affirmations of particular moral ideologies.[23] Shootings in historic Black churches throughout the American South, the 2021 Capitol siege, the Jericho marches, displays of white nationalism on university campuses across the United States, and the digital work of incels (angry young white men without female sexual partners) via social media and meme culture, are just some of the ways far-right, seemingly "Christian" conservatism has begun to emerge in American social spheres.[24] While violent crimes associated with Christian fundamentalists are on the rise, less public, yet still strident forms of this movement are also increasing in the United States and across much of Western Europe, Russia, and parts of the global south. If we take into consideration the variations of Christian fundamentalism, perhaps even fascism, that have and continue to develop in the United States and many parts of Western Europe, often tied to nationalism, far-right politics, and other socially conservative projects, the claims of Orthodoxy as part of this form of fundamentalism can be taken seriously in light of conversion. The growth of converts in conservative forms of Orthodoxy seems to reflect an epistemological shift in how religion is perceived in relationship to the Western, specifically American, cultural body politic.

The foundations of Orthodox fundamentalism rest in the adherence to and preservation of tradition, which makes it virtually impossible to talk about Orthodox fundamentalism without referencing tradition. The protection of tradition, whether defensive or offensive, has become one of the key pillars of convert culture within ROCOR. Fundamentalist Orthodoxy or "Orthodoxism," as Haralambos Ventis describes it, seeks to crystalize tradition in order to remain true to the so-called pure teachings of Christ and the early Christian Church.[25] While the tsarist-supporting White Russians who helped create ROCOR certainly sought to preserve Russian Orthodoxy in diaspora during the decades the Soviets were in power, they did not have the reactionary political vigor that converts in the same jurisdiction possess today.[26] Converts have brought with them the sociocultural baggage of prior affiliation with various American religions and politics, and with Evangelicalism in particular. Early Russian immigrants who helped form ROCOR and sustained it for decades before the convert impulse began, focused on holding fast to the teachings of the Church in order to, in time, take back Russia for Christ.[27] In contrast, contemporary converts to ROCOR, often driven by the revival of religiosity they see in Russia, focus on the moral decay of progressive contemporary Western society. No longer does ROCOR need to re-missionize Russia; instead, for converts, Russia has become a model for creating a better, more Christian, more holy version of the United States; one conversion at a time, converts are building their new, holy America. The desire to return to a time of so-called Christian enchantment, to fossilize both the teachings and practices of the Russian Church before the revolution, to embrace monarchism, a blending of church and state, and imagined, utopian notions of agrarian culture, have become the traditional linchpins of conversion in many respects.

Orthodox Christianity possesses "big-T" and "little-t" traditions. The very theology of the Church is suffused with tradition—big-T tradition—that has shaped the beliefs and practices of the Church for centuries. Big-T traditions might include theologically important ideas and events, such as the Dormition of the Theotokos, the real presence of Christ in the Eucharist, and the all-male priesthood. Small-t traditions are flexible, adaptive aspects of piety that are often influenced by vernacular, collaborative customs.[28] In Woodford, local traditions included a pig roast at the parish on Pascha, fireworks at the monastery for the Paschal celebration, and using repurposed oxygen tanks for bells, among other things. Little-t traditions provide space in the highly structured life of the Church to incorporate important aspects of regional and individual identity (see fig. 1).[29] This aspect of tradition is not limited to convert communities; indeed, scholars have shown that, historically, Orthodox Christianity has had local adaptations and amalgamations, and, as Papanikolaou aptly points out, Orthodoxy possesses a living tradition in both big and little forms.[30] The two types of traditions present in Orthodoxy are not typically in conflict with each other, since they affect different parts of the religious life—namely, theological and practical. However, the desire for correctness among convert communities has often led believers to conflate both types of tradition, drawing them into an ideological stance of traditionalism in order to create and protect a particular way of religious life for themselves and potentially change the cultural formations of their local community and the United States. In doing so, traditionalism then becomes a modality through which converts engage with the living theology of the Church, each other, and secular social formations, with the *Zeitgeist* of everyday life.

Not to be confused with Orthodox "big-T" and "little-T" traditions, traditionalism—particularly within the Russian Orthodox Church (MP) and ROCOR—is as a sociopolitical, perhaps even geopolitical, stance about the Church in relationship to secular and/or liberal culture.[31] In practice, for

Figure 1. Oxygen Bells (Photograph by author, August 2018)

example, a "self-named traditionalist would typically oppose the ordination of women to the diaconate, while a non-traditionalist—usually called, pejoratively, a liberal—might challenge the givenness of the non-ordination of women."[32] In convert ROCOR communities, the traditionalist focus is often on hierarchy, patriarchy, traditional family values, purity, and social morality. In their search for institutions and people who support these political ideologies, American converts typically turn to the leadership of the post-Soviet Russian Orthodox Church, where they find ideological exemplars in figures such as Patriarch Kirill and Metropolitan Hilarion (Alfeyev) of Volokolamsk. Yet this turn to Russia as a geopolitical compass pointing the way to a potential culture teeming with wholesome godly social values is not a one-sided endeavor on the part of Orthodox converts in the United States. In 2000, the MP's Council of Bishops prescribed a "social doctrine," which included a heavy emphasis on so-called traditional, nuclear family values and ideas, and fealty to national geopolitics.[33]

In many respects, that document seemed to signal an institutional shift toward a transnational politics of traditionalism expressed both through religious soft power and through support of policies implemented by the Russian government. Throughout the 2000s and 2010s, the ROC became increasingly concerned with forging a new post-Soviet identity that was tightly linked to both to Putin's platform and to conservative Western, especially American, conceptions of social moral politics. Availing itself of the U.S. Culture Wars rhetoric, the Moscow Patriarchate and other religio-political power actors, such as Aleksandr Dugin, sought to engage with far-right European and American actors. At the same time, the MP was also, officially and unofficially, connected to small radical political groups throughout Russia. While the classical Russian far right was in tatters by the 2000s, the political landscape was dotted with small groups of radicalized ideologues—almost a foreshadow of the United States in the late 2010s.[34] Militias, paramilitary groups, skinheads, fascists, and nationalists were all part of the sociopolitical landscape of Russia in the 2000s, and the Moscow Patriarchate seized the opportunity to engage with these political actors to further its religious soft power. The Sorok Sorokov movement was institutionalized by MP in 2013 in response to the Pussy Riot incident in 2012. Angered by *khramofobii* (churchophobia), the group and its movement focused on "fighting homosexuality and LGBT+ rights."[35]

Other radical, perhaps even fascist, Russian groups such as the Night Wolves and the Russian Imperial movement, (re)emerged at the beginning of the 2010s, bringing with them ideologies of nationalism, whiteness, masculinity, and traditionalism—ideas that were becoming central themes, as Marlene Laruelle points out, to the new far right in Russia, Putin's regime, and the post-Soviet Moscow Patriarchate.[36] These ideas, in many respects, may have been part of Rodina's whitening influence in the 2000s, combined with Moscow Patriarchate's rebranding as the protector of conservative social moral values. Patriarch Kirill and the ROC were key in expanding Russia's interaction with far-right actors in Europe and the United States throughout the 2000s and 2010s. The 2007 reconciliation between the MP and ROCOR meant that the ROC could enlarge its international presence, creating deeper ideological networks in both Europe and the United States through ROCOR. Beyond internal growth, throughout the 2010s, the MP seemed to have found conservative allies among power conservative Christian organizations in the United States, including the American Family Association and the World Congress of Families.[37] These ideological alliances are strategic not only for the MP, but also for the Kremlin; indeed, Moscow has and continues to export political ideologies, particularly illiberal ones, to the West in hopes of creating more networks of political solidarity and expanding their geopolitical grip.

Lauding the conservative mobilization of traditional values in Putin's regime, which have been criticized at the United Nations and by human rights organizations as oppressive, the Moscow Patriarchate has tended to favor preserving the heteronormative family unit over and above equitable human rights.[38] In order to promulgate the traditional values language both in policy and public discourse, the Moscow Patriarchate, Putin's party, and other conservative Russian actors have turned to, and continue to turn to, Western stakeholders, such as the World Congress of Families, in the fight for the preservation of family—the emblem of traditionalism in the midst of rapid social change. Traditionalism links the MP and Putin's conservative base to far-right American actors, such as Steve Bannon, who, in a conversation with Aleksandr Dugin in Rome in 2018, claimed that Russia and the United States are "moving together, towards nationalism, populism, and Traditionalism."[39] The increasingly close connections between far-right American actors and religio-political Russian actors in the late 2010s were made all the more legible during Trump's tenure in office. Bannon himself noted that the Trumpian turn in American politics, the American fight "against globalism and liberalism," was the same fight Russia was taking up in their religious and geopolitical focus on traditional social moral values and nationalism.[40] Benjamin Teitelbaum, in his ethnography of Bannon and other far-right power elites, highlights how the ROC was and is complicit in American far-right political ideas of traditionalism. At the same interview with Bannon and Dugin, the former proclaimed to the latter, "You and the Eastern Orthodox church—you can even teach us to be better versions of ourselves. Our peoples are showing their vitality right now. They can lead this fight."[41]

The ROC is not alone in their social emphasis on traditionalism in the nationalistic and geopolitical sense; ROCOR members, both through institutional formations and via social media, have taken to calling themselves TradOx, meaning traditional Orthodox.[42] TradOx believers, in the whole, tend to be monarchists who are highly supportive of Vladimir Putin, even if they are American citizens. Orthodox Studies scholar Fr. Oliver Herbel suggests that for many converts, the "turn to tradition" is an expression of "Americanness," tying it in many ways to nationalism.[43] Certainly, as I elaborate in Chapter 3, nationalism is a key element in the conversion process, but it is not always a marker for American identification. Nationalism is not simply a form of patriotism. Rather, as Ernest Gellner points out, nationalism is a political ideology that sees both the political and the social as congruent. As a shared cultural expression that is often expressed in micro-groups, according to Gellner, nationalism is, in many respects, a process of sorting, curating smaller communities into the homogeneous, larger social collective.[44] Nationalism, in the context of the Woodford convert community, did not seem to be tied to a particular idea of Americanness or being a good American; rather, it was focused on Russian Orthodoxy and the geopolitical space of Russia by extension.[45] As young Fr. Tryphon expressed, "I feel much more spiritual kinship with Russianness than I do with Americanness."[46] His sentiments mirrored those of

many in Woodford's Orthodox community. The relationship between traditionalism and nationalism did not reinforce the Christian American dream
among converts to ROCOR; instead, it highlights how they viewed the West
as synonymous with modern immorality while Russia, experiencing a religious
revival after the end of the Soviet Union, provided a glimmer of true religious
piety and traditional social structures.[47] In the hearts and minds of many converts I spoke with, ROCOR in the United States, the ROC, and the Russian
government under the authority of Vladimir Putin exude a new form of traditionalism that was and is a key in the expansion of authentic Christianity and
a truly conservative moral social order. The foundation of traditionalism, both
in the ROC and ROCOR, seems to be extreme anti-modernism that sees
progressive secularism as the antithesis of godly conservatism.

Convert Epistemologies and the Christian Quest

The desire to find true, traditional Christianity, combined with a focus on
reclaiming and advancing traditional morality in the public sphere, were two
motivating conversion factors in stories relayed by converts. The epistemological
rhetoric that converts employed when sharing their tales of conversion generally
had two major themes—a focus on the historicity of Orthodoxy through education and affective aesthetic logics. The first, informed by believers' educational histories, focuses on learning (often autodidactic knowledge) that led
the researcher to uncover the theological correctness and historical authenticity
of the Church. The second method of conversion embraces what I consider
"affective logics" in order to legitimize experiential, emotive responses to the
aesthetic, sensorial formations of Orthodoxy.[48] This affective route often includes stories of encountering iconography, liturgical music, and being caught
up both in clouds of incense and heady theologies founded in what they believe
to be ancient Christian mysticism. While these two methodologies sometimes
overlapped, they were often independent of each other. Furthermore, while
each of these methods ultimately led searchers to seek membership in ROCOR,
examining the differences between the two processes of conversion highlights
the motivations that shape subsequent practice and belief. Education-focused
conversion narratives were primarily expressed by two socio-demographic
groups: single white males between 20 and 40, and married white males
between 30 and 55. Many of the monks at St. Basil's would fall into the first
demographic in this type of conversion process. Of the thirty-plus monks at
the monastery, many of whom were 40 years of age or younger had degrees in
history, theology, and linguistics, although there were quite a few autodidacts

in the community as well. Key to their spiritual historiographies were both their own educational experiences and that of Blessed Father Seraphim Rose.

While many converts I spoke with were drawn into the Church by studying the history of Christianity, others were taken by the so-called smells and bells.[49] One of the most popular tropes about the aesthetic draw of Orthodox Christianity among converts was the account of how Prince Vladimir of Rus', who sent out emissaries to investigate the major world religions at the time, selected Orthodoxy because of the splendid beauty of Hagia Sophia in Istanbul (Constantinople).[50] Recalling the words of Prince Myshkin in Fyodor Dostoevsky's *The Idiot*, converts often suggested that "beauty will save the world."[51] Aesthetic beauty, expressed through a variety of sensorial modalities, was often key in the conversion logics believers used to make sense of why Orthodoxy was the right religious choice for them. Within the Woodford community, there seemed to be two avenues of aesthetic logics used in conversion narratives: appreciation for the richly textured sensorial worlds of Orthodox Christianity and/or a love of Russian culture, history, art, and literature.

While some converts came to appreciate the sensorial beauty of Orthodox rituals as part of their aesthetic logics during the process of conversion, there were those who seem to have an innate fondness for Russian sensorial worlds—especially food, history, music, and literature. As a child, Angus, a regional convert, had a deep affinity for the Soviet Union, socialism, and Karl Marx. Enamored with the idea of "utopian communist society" from an early age, Angus devoured the writings of Fyodor Dostoevsky and Leo Tolstoy, and immersed himself in the compositions of Alexander Borodin and Pyotr Tchaikovsky, developing a deep appreciation for Russian artistic expressions. Growing up as the son of a minister in a variety of Baptist denominations in central and southwestern West Virginia, Angus often felt spiritual but not religious. He struggled with the idea of "an angry man in the sky, just wanting to punish people."[52] Throughout high school and college he went through a period of searching, latching on to communism as an early epistemology in his journey to find meaning in the world.

I was a big communist and couldn't wait to bring the social justice and all that nonsense. And, even when I was that, I occasionally tried being an atheist, but always felt that atheists are dishonest with themselves and with other people. I can get an agnostic, who will say, "We don't know." That makes sense. That's fine, but to say, "I know for a fact that there is nothing," I mean, is completely dishonest. So for that reason I never could really latch on to it. And I kinda went through a

pseudo-hippish thing where I wanted everyone to be happy. Peace
and love and all that stuff. And then I started looking into established
religions. I looked into Islam. I really kinda got into Buddhism. I
meditated a whole lot. I went to—one of the best weeks of my life—a
weeklong silent retreat at a Buddhist monastery. Then people started
talking and ruined the whole thing at the end.[53]

Ultimately, Angus did not find the answers to his existential questions in Buddhism, but he continued to value meditation as part of his spiritual
formation.

Angus's shift back to Christianity was prompted by two women in his life—
his wife, who was born and raised Roman Catholic, and a Russian Orthodox
student in the high school history class he taught. His brief foray into Buddhism
was punctured by his conversion to Roman Catholicism in order to marry his
wife. For a time, Angus settled into the Catholic way of life, although he yearned
for a more traditional expression of the faith that was removed from the trappings of modernity; this prompted him to seek out a Latin Rite community
two hours away. Still unhappy with the lack of reverence and piety he found
within this type of Catholicism, Angus began conducting even more research
into the historical roots of Christianity. Eventually, one of his students invited
him to St. John's parish. From his very first visit, Angus was enamored with the
church, especially since it was filled with sensorial markers of Russian spirituality. This was exciting for Angus, but he proceeded with trepidation. Very often,
in Angus's story for example, the combination of aesthetic logics and an educational drive for historicity led converts "astray" in their yearnings for truth; being
led astray for most male converts meant delving into "Eastern, mystical religious
traditions," including Buddhism, Hinduism, Islam, and metaphysics.

One of the key elements that seems to be present in most conversion narratives offered by the male converts in Woodford was a draw to ancient religious
mysticism. Buddhism, Islam, and other "Eastern faiths" were often spiritual
detours for believers as they transitioned from various forms of Christianity
into the Orthodox Church. Angus found temporary solace in the silence of
Zen Buddhism, while many of the fathers and brothers at the monastery looked
to Islam or turned to mystical expressions of Catholicism in hopes of finding
answers to their existential questions. Fr. Tryphon, who was raised "hard-core"
Calvinist in the mountains of North Carolina, began his journey into mysticism
as a teenager and continued searching throughout his college years. A foundational moment in his inquiry occurred when he stumbled across the writings
of Aldous Huxley, particularly *The Perennial Philosophy*.[54] Fr. Tryphon was
intrigued by Huxley's suggestion that "at the heart of every religion is

mysticism."[55] Looking back, Fr. Tryphon noted that he did not feel the same way about the book now as he did during his teenage years of searching, especially once he realized much of the information came from the writings of Joseph Campbell, a religious leader that many of the converts in the community saw as not only an apostate from true Christianity, but also under the influence of demonic forces.

Often when researchers hear about my work with the Woodford community and their struggles to find an authentic form of Christianity, they typically ask me, "Why not Mormonism?" After all, Mormonism is mystical, grounded in American conservative ideologies, and appeals to people looking for a community that has rigid gender norms, hierarchy, patriarchy, and apocalyptic visions of the future.[56] Many converts to Orthodox Christianity, and in particular, to ROCOR, see Mormonism as the antithesis of true Christianity. For them, the very fact that Mormonism is an American religion highlights how invalid it is as form of authentic, historical Christian spirituality. Older is always better when it comes to religious practices, according to many of the converts with whom I spoke. Certainly, during their religious journeys, most Woodford believers were looking for an insular religious community that offered an androcentric hierarchy, so-called traditional gender roles, and a focus on the apocalyptic doom of secularism—combined with mysticism. Yet, they also placed great import on historical authenticity, Trinitarian doctrine, and "traditional" understandings of the Christian afterlife, which they believed Mormonism lacked.[57]

If this is case, then what of believers' detours, as I label them, into Islam, Buddhism, and other ancient religious groups? I suggest these detours were part of their seemingly Orientalist focus on forms of spirituality crafted outside of the confines of the Western religious imagination. Islam often came up in conversations with male members of the Woodford community. It seemed to appeal to male converts because of its traditional gender roles, structured forms of piety, and inclusion of Jesus as a prophet. However, most male converts only briefly investigated Sufi Islam, fearing any complete departure from the tenets of Christianity. For many men, including Angus and Fr. Tryphon, Buddhism also seemed quite appealing as a potential spiritual path because of its focus on suffering, "defeating the passions," and, in many cases, silent meditation practices. In the end, Woodford believers who sought out Buddhism found it to be "ironically empty" or, as one monk suggested bluntly, "vile spiritually."[58] The characteristics of Buddhism that appealed to converts also, in many ways, drew them into the Orthodox Church, particularly those who eventually became monastics. In Orthodox Christianity, they found a similar focus on suffering, denying the passions of the self, and practicing silent humility all situated within a Christian worldview.

The investigation of Eastern mystic religions had little to do with the spiritual marketplace of the United States and the options set before these men; rather, their desire to find ancient, traditional, and authentic Christian spirituality drove their pursuit of religious knowledge into avenues they once frowned upon. It was clear from talking with these male converts that they never considered fully converting to Islam or Buddhism. Their desperation for what they considered to be authentic, mystical spirituality drew them into various communities, but the time they spent with each of these religious groups only solidified their urge to find a traditional form of Christian faith and practice that offered them the "fullness of faith." Along the way, many of the converts, particularly the men in the community, were influenced by a man who experienced many of the same feelings, ideas, and draws during his own journey into the Orthodox Church. Often praised in ROCOR and the ROC for his traditional theological voice, Blessed Father Seraphim Rose of Southern California can be thought of as the model for the conservative American convert who desires a mystical Eastern encounter with the divine.

Seraphim Rose Misunderstood: Cultic Traditionalism and Homophobia

The connections between Orthodox fundamentalism and traditionalism find their home in the unlikely champion of Eugene (Seraphim) Rose—a gay scholar of Asian philosophy from the University of California at Berkeley who became arguably one of the most influential converts to ROCOR in the United States. Born in the mid-1930s in Southern California, Rose grew up in a low- to middle-income white family, did well in school, and eventually enrolled at Pomona College before studying with Alan Watts and completing a graduate degree in Oriental languages at University of California at Berkeley.[59] Rose's official biography indicates that he had a rich life of the mind from an early age, engaging in classical music, art, and poetry that nurtured his artistic and academic pursuits.[60] Growing up in a semi-religious family, with a mother who shopped around in various Protestant denominations and a father who was primarily a lapsed Catholic, Rose took it upon himself to "be baptized and confirmed as a Christian in the Methodist church."[61] While he lost interest in religion during his teen years, Rose's voracity for academics increased exponentially, and he showed promise as a burgeoning polyglot.[62] Rose's biographer, who also happened to be his spiritual disciple later in life, depicts Rose as a young man who was disgusted by the real world, and more focused on important matters of knowledge acquisition.[63] Seeking answers to the large, existential questions in life, Rose delved into philosophy and theology from a wide range of literature, including Classical Greek material and mystical religious ideas from around the globe. Judaism, Hinduism, and many other religious traditions became part of Rose's academic and devotional curiosity. On the "search for reality," Rose became an enamored student of Alan Watts, who drew him into the study of Zen Buddhism.[64] Yet Rose never felt at home during his sojourn in Buddhism despite his love of mystical, Eastern philosophy. Continuing to search for a new spiritual home, Rose eventually encountered Eastern Orthodoxy through both a close friend and the writings of René Guénon, as he explained in a letter to an unnamed acquaintance: "It was René Guénon who taught me to seek and love the Truth above all else, and to be unsatisfied with anything else; this is what finally brought me to the Orthodox Church."[65] While Guénon may have been Rose's philosophical guide to truth, he was also, in all likelihood, the writer who introduced Rose to traditionalism. René Guénon (1886–1951) was a French intellectual and metaphysical theorist who converted to Islam. His philosophical writings, which tackle perennialism and tradition, are widely read in traditionalist circles, and Guénon can be thought of as the father of traditionalism in some respects.[66]

Foreshadowing the opinions of many contemporary Orthodox converts, Rose found Orthodoxy to be mystical, traditional, and true. Rose, an ardent admirer of Russian history and culture soon became involved with Russian Orthodoxy in its West Coast epicenter—San Francisco. A disciple of St. John Maximovitch, bishop of Shanghai and San Francisco, Rose converted and was chrismated into the Russian Orthodox Church Outside of Russia in 1962. Unlike many contemporary converts who have taken up the mantle of traditionalism in the name of Rose, he was not re-baptized upon his reception into the Church. Despite the fact that these "improper" chrismation receptions were seen as "graceless" by many in ROCOR, Rose maintained that he received grace and "the 'fragrance' of Orthodoxy" when he entered the Church.[67] Christensen often suggests that Rose was deeply concerned by the traditionalist impulse that he found lurking in the convert movement of the late 1960s and early 1970s. Indeed, Christensen, drawing on the unpublished writings of Rose, highlights simple faith and unlearnedness as far superior to the pridefulness displayed by conservative and traditionalist converts to the faith who were full of knowledge but lacking in humility.[68]

Shortly before his reception into the Church, Rose wrote a letter to his friend Gleb, who would eventually help Rose found a monastery in Platina, in the mountains of Northern California. Rose's letter offers a glimpse into this quickly shifting worldview. He wrote of "vague morality," "the signs of the spirit of the Antichrist," and his "hatred of this contemporary world."[69] Rose's concerns about rapid social upheaval, combined with his intellect and humility, helped him establish himself as a model convert in San Francisco's elite community of Russian Orthodox émigré intelligentsia. As seeming evidence of his rapid inclusion into the Russian-American sphere of influence in San Francisco at the time, Rose was quickly given missionizing responsibilities.[70] After Rose converted to ROCOR in San Francisco and began a spiritual life as a monastic in Platina, California, at a monastery he helped create, his impact steadily grew within Orthodox circles. Rose, who was tonsured Seraphim, began publishing English-language Orthodox theological works about a variety of topics, including creation, UFOs, and what happens to the soul after death.[71] For Rose, "[the] Orthodox Christian standard was by its very nature radical to modern consciousness."[72] The idea seems to have been taken up by converts and Rose devotees, who use Rose's teaching to help frame a radical world set apart from secularism, ecumenism, and modernity. Rose's conversion process, in terms of socioeconomics, education, and spiritual searching, often mirrored that of young male converts in the Woodford community, particularly at St. Basil's monastery.

At first glance Rose seems far removed from the waves of fundamentalist traditionalism that were spreading through ROCOR in the late 2010s, for he was a product of mid–twentieth-century Southern Californian Anglo-Protestantism and the secular and, one could argue, Orientalist academy at Berkeley. However, he was one of the most referenced Orthodox figures in the conversion narratives of many, if not most, Woodford believers. While Rose's writings might have had a wide variety of topics, they were united by his conservative lens of analysis that focused on understanding contemporary issues through the writings of the Church Fathers. Most convert devotees praised Rose for his historically focused theology that eschewed modern sources or interpretations; this is seen particularly in his writings on environmentalism that aligned belief in evolution with the rise of the Antichrist.[73]

Rose's importance within ROCOR and the ROC has led, in recent years, to the creation of halo-less icons and calls for his canonization. Given his place of prominence in the transformation of Russian-American Orthodoxy, it is curious why Rose is not canonized. Missing from Rose's work, and hardly addressed in his biography by Monk Christensen, was Rose's identification as a gay man. Most Orthodox writers acknowledge that Rose struggled with "homosexual tendencies," but died to himself, to his fleshly desires, in his monastic pursuits of Christ and seemingly struggled no more. Thus, Eugene Rose might be considered a gay intellectual, but Fr. Seraphim Rose was a holy ascetic who devoted himself, body and soul, to the work of the Church and Christ and seemingly thought nothing of his sexuality. Often, converts suggested that Rose has not been canonized because at one point the monastery he was part of was in schism from the rest of the Eastern Orthodox Churches. "Is it because he was gay?" I asked believers in Woodford. They would say no or suggest that he was only gay *before* he converted, as if Rose flipped a switch and was suddenly heterosexual or asexual after taking on the mantle of ascetic practice. Typically, Rose's sexuality was and is straightened to align with heteronormative ideologies of the body that are so prevalent in ROCOR theology. If his sexual orientation is acknowledged by ROCOR adherents, it is generally placed in conversation with repentance, with dying to selfish, carnal desires. Drawing on Rose's written correspondence with family and friends, his niece, crime novelist Cathy Scott, suggests that Rose was indeed gay and struggled to come to terms with spirituality and sexuality. Scott wondered if Rose's internal struggle with his sexuality identity might be why he had such a drastic change in his political and moral worldviews after conversion.[74]

In a 1956 letter to a close friend, Rose acknowledged that he was "homosexual" and wrote that he saw his "sexual inclinations as perfectly 'normal.'"[75] So why might Russian Orthodox converts be negating Rose's sexual identity? I suggest this sanitization, this straightening, might be partly because other aspects of Rose's journey were highly relatable to male converts in Woodford (and elsewhere). Acknowledging Rose's sexuality might have created a crisis of faith in Rose's authenticity as a true monastic or caused them to question their own sexuality in a community in which heterosexuality was and still is the only public option. The focus on heterosexuality was not localized to Woodford. Scholars of Orthodox Christianity in contemporary Russia have pointed out that the rising social and moral conservatism in the Moscow Patriarchate (and Putin's base) have reinforced religiously inspired heteronormative gender roles throughout the ROC, which reverberates in its diasporic forms.[76] The push for heterosexuality, and its seemingly inevitable nuclear family, are not just part of the social doctrines put forth by the MP; most converts in the United States came from post–civil rights Evangelicalism, whatever the institutional label might have been, which, as anthropologist Sophie Bjork-James has pointed out, places divine supremacy on patriarchal heterosexuality.[77] Even in the monastery, the trappings of previous evangelical affiliations, combined with the new politics of the traditional family coming from the Moscow Patriarchate, created a distinct rhetoric regarding chastity, purity, the family, and the self. Much of the understandings of Russian conservatism regarding the family and homosexuality among converts to the ROCOR is part and parcel of their previous affiliation with American Evangelicalism (and post-Vatican II Catholicism). Converts' desire for the Russia to restore moral order in the United States is in many ways a projection of American Evangelicalism's complicated history with not only conservatism but also secularism onto Russia's own difficult political past.

Within the context of convert ROCOR culture, Rose, stripped of his sexual identity, robed in the holiness of strict asceticism, offered a modern, conservative view of embodied religiosity that hit home with young male converts. In ROCOR, to become a monastic is as salvific as becoming a spouse in a heteronormative marriage, for each takes up vows of martyrdom that aid them on the ladder of divine ascent to salvation. Homosexuality does not enter into this ontological worldmaking scheme for salvation. Thus Rose's sexuality, if acknowledged, could have created a theological and, perhaps, psychological stumbling block for many converts. Rose's focus on traditional forms of spirituality, his devotion to the Russian *typicon*, and his seemingly prophetic apocalyptic concerns about the end of days painted him as a relatable figure for male converts to ROCOR in Woodford and Orthodox Christians in Russia it would seem. "Father Seraphim Rose is a man known and loved today all over Russia," reads the opening line of the preface to his biography, written by one of his early disciples. The deep devotion to Rose throughout the former Soviet Union is something his parents might have balked at, especially considering their fear of Russia. Included in the first edition of Rose's biography are letters that his father Frank wrote to him during his conversion process. In one letter, Frank wrote: "Mom has a complex fear of Russia and all things Russian."[78] Yet, Rose seemed to have little to no problem accepting Russian Orthodoxy wholeheartedly, something that seemed to endear him to contemporary conservative converts with whom I worked.

For believers in Woodford, Rose's seemingly strident teachings offered a guide to navigating secularism, providing a conservative intellectual haven for those who felt uneasy engaging with more progressive Orthodox theologians. Rose's allure, among many converts I have encountered, stems in part from a lecture he gave at his monastery in Platina, California, the summer before his death in 1982, in which he talked about a traditional Orthodox worldview, drawing on prerevolutionary Russian Orthodoxy as a model for how to have a truly Christian state supporting the Church.[79] This idea was appealing for most converts I spoke with in Woodford, who expressed the desire for traditional Christianity, which they often believed was theocratic in nature. Yet, in many respects, at least per the writings of Rose's closest disciple, the convert monk might have been taken aback by the radical ways in which contemporary converts read his writings, which suggests by the late 2010s Rose had become a soft-power figurehead for a movement he may not have agreed with if he had lived.

Fr. Theodosius, one of the younger monks at the monastery, became a deacon and then a priest while I was living in the community. With an upper Midwest accent and a curly auburn beard, Fr. Theodosius was a jovial man in his mid-twenties. The assigned monastery baker, Fr. Theodosius grew up in what he called a "traditional [and] simple" branch of Reformed Calvinist Protestantism, but even his family focus on affirming the historical accuracies of the Virgin birth and the resurrection of Christ, and a daily commitment to scriptural reading, was not enough for him as he approached adulthood.[80] The youngest of four, and the only son in his family, Fr. Theodosius remembered the relief he felt as a child when during his the confirmation process his Sunday school teacher held up a copy of the Heidelberg catechism and proclaimed that they had to use this text but the Church did not adhere to it strictly. During his teenage years, Fr. Theodosius "read a lot" about various religious traditions, seeking something more traditional and authentic than the faith he was born into.[81] In a similar fashion to many young male converts I spoke with, Fr. Theodosius began to pull away from committed religious belief and practice during his college years, but continued to search textually for some form of traditional Christianity.

During his third year at the local state university, Fr. Theodosius took a leave of absence from his studies, left home, and moved in with group of life-long friends who were college students. The odd man out, he worked a full-time job with extended hours at a print shop and bindery. During his days off he began reading about different religious traditions, while at the same time being deeply introspective, "taking a look at his life."[82] Through a textual journey, Fr. Theodosius started to have "an awareness of Christian practice" and believed "the Lord was beginning to wake" him.[83] The long hours of wearing earplugs at the print shop were, according to Fr. Theodosius, "providential" for they allowed him time to "inspect his thoughts."[84] Solitary reflection combined with voracious reading during his off days formed the basis of his spiritual journey toward Orthodoxy. Most of the educational information Fr. Theodosius gleaned was from the writings of Catholic mystics, for in the same vein as many other converts in this community, he was first attracted to Western mystical expressions of Christianity. As he talked about the importance of mysticism in the search for real Christianity, Fr. Theodosius held up Rose as an example of how converts journey toward Orthodoxy: "There's something deep that they realize—like Father Seraphim Rose—that what they've been looking for, this depth, this mystic east, is Christian. Fully Christian."[85]

Through Catholic contemplative writers such as Thomas Merton, who often wrote about the *Philokalia*, the primary text of the mystical hesychastic (meditative) tradition within Orthodoxy, Fr. Theodosius began to uncover "the desert fathers and the practice of the Jesus prayer."[86] Along the way, he was also drawn to the writings of St. Ignatius of Loyola, specifically his spiritual exercises. Around this time, Fr. Theodosius decided to take a self-guided retreat at his parents' cabin in the upper Midwest, in order to engage more fully with

Christian mysticism. This was a self-described crossroads for him: "I was there with these two traditions [Catholic and Orthodox]; the texts about them."[87] As Fr. Theodosius began to delve into the Catholic texts he had brought with him, St. Ignatius of Loyola's emphasis on mental imagery did not resonate with him. "I didn't, for the life of me, have any faculty of imagination," Fr. Theodosius exclaimed.[88] At first, he felt as if this mental block, this lack of imagination, meant something was wrong with him. Yet when he turned to the set of Orthodox writings that he had also brought on the retreat, he seemed to find the answers he was looking for: "I opened the *Philokalia* and it was talking about the Jesus Prayer. Pray to Christ! Don't be whisked about by your thoughts, by imagination, [by] these images. Focus on Christ. So it looked like the Lord was saying, 'No, no.' And he was allowing me to see that this simpler path, this more deep path, that's not just limited to the realm of imagination and emotion, this is the path I want you to go on."[89]

Fr. Theodosius continued, elaborating on the aspects of Orthodox that drew in him:

I was really attracted to the Jesus Prayer, like a lot of people are, and I discovered that it existed in the tradition of Church called the Eastern Orthodox Church, so I started looking into it and at the same time, I guess providentially, I had a very, very strong desire to be baptized. Fully immersed to start my life fresh and I realized this Church [the Eastern Orthodox Church] does full baptisms. Even though I was sprinkled as an infant, I had this great desire to be baptized. I started looking around and I realized that there was an Eastern Orthodox Church, a mission, ten minutes away in the hometown I grew up in. I very quickly took to it. I recognized it immediately, as most people do, as home. Before checking out the church, I went through the period of learning about Orthodoxy mostly through Protestant critical remarks about it. Of course, raised as Protestant you have aversions to anything that looks or smells Catholic. But thank God, I wasn't so rooted in Protestant understanding. Soon, by the grace of God, I knew that this is the Church. This is the Orthodox Church. I believe what they say and I understand it.[90]

In a similar vein to that of Rose, Fr. Theodosius's conversion narrative is steeped in autodidactic religious education and affective desire for something authentically Christian and truly mystical.[91] Fr. Theodosius was one of many monks at St. Basil's monastery to acknowledge Rose's appeal during the conversion journey. Yet this influence on young male converts was and is not limited to the wilds of West Virginia. Rose is praised in his biography, which was written by Monk Damascene Christensen, who himself led a good deal of youth from the California punk scene into the Orthodox Church, as someone within "American Orthodoxy" who cultivated a traditional form of Orthodox spirituality by emphasizing Russian ascetic practices as the antithesis of nihilism—something that often seems to appeal to young white males seeking religious paths.[92]

Not all converts in Woodford felt the same affinity for Rose. Angus, for example, appreciated Rose, but worried that his writings were still tainted by modernism and the culture of the United States; he was automatically suspicious of "anything new."[93] The identification with Rose also seemed limited to male converts, with virtually none of the female parishioners mentioning him as an influence in their spiritual journeys. Rose's impact within the lives of male converts highlights another crucial aspect of the turn to ROCOR in the United States—namely, its gendered nature and demographics. Certainly, Woodford skewed heavily toward Caucasian cis-male converts because of St. Basil's monastery. However, this seems to be a common demographic trend in ROCOR conversions more broadly based on conversations with church leaders and field research. Issues of conservative family values, authenticity, and historicity are important to the typical male ROCOR convert, many of whom hail from evangelical backgrounds, suggesting they have more in common with the so-called heterodox conservative Christian counterparts than they would like to imagine.[94] These ideologies are expressed in their conversion narratives through their emphasis on understanding historicity through self-education and aesthetic logics—both of which are tied to draw to so-called Eastern mysticism and the legacy of American-born Fr. Seraphim Rose.

Head, Heart, and Bias

In many ways, the affective logics and education-focused narratives found in conversion stories are expressions of the larger issues of traditionalism and fundamentalism that have, in some respects, seeped into ROCOR from Protestantism, especially Evangelicalism. Rod Dreher, a columnist and political pundit, who is an Orthodox Christian convert by way of Methodism and then Roman Catholicism, suggests that traditionalism is the fundamental way conservative Christians understand themselves in relationship to "the sneaky kind of secularism" that has invaded the public sphere of the United States.[95] Turning to Orthodoxy, whether because of its aesthetic, sensorial qualities or its place in the history of Christianity, expresses the individual contouring of conversion and its motivating factors. These two types of conversion rhetoric parallel, in many respects, Dreher's notion of conversion as an experience of the head and the heart.[96] While both schools of conversion—head and heart—in Woodford emphasized different ways of approaching ROCOR, the focus on feeling or being in the right or correct form of Christianity was expressed repeatedly by converts. Dreher suggests that converts are drawn in because, "in this time and place, the Orthodox vision helps modern people to see divine truths more clearly than Westerners (like me) whose inner eye is occluded by 700 years of teaching ourselves not to see the things that are."[97] Perhaps this was what Rose was looking for when he left behind secular academia for the wilds of California, and this might have been what one convert was alluding to when he proclaimed, "I've done Catholic churches in the city, and I've done Protestant churches out in the holler with only four people. It [ROCOR] is just Christianity the way it's meant to be, I think."[98]

The Woodford convert focus on correctness was, in many respects, also tied to ideas of purity. This search for correctness was not only about the crystalline purity of ROCOR as an expression of stalwart faithfulness to historical Christianity; it was also seemingly connected to American constructions of masculinity, gender, sexuality, and whiteness, perhaps even "muscular Christianity."[99] Orthodox Christianity is often thought of by converts with whom I have worked as a hard faith—one that attracts men because it is physically difficult and often spiritually grueling. Long services, hours of standing, strict fasting calendars, and intense submission to one's spiritual father create an almost militarized spiritual ethos. This, it seems, is often attractive to males looking for place to amplify both their spiritual commitment and their notions of gender complementarianism through a church steeped in patriarchal practice.[100] By and large, Orthodoxy has a high density of males among its ranks, primarily because serving the Church in an ordained capacity is limited to men. The patriarchal nature of the Church is not only acknowledged in traditional Orthodox communities, it is also celebrated as the correct structure of religious authority. Some conservative Orthodox clerics and laity take to their digital communities to express the support for keeping the androcentric focus of the Church alive. Websites such as goodguyswearblack.org, which was tied to a cleric training program and a blog, were quite popular among the Orthodox men I encountered.[101] Run by two convert priests in different jurisdictions, the site offered vocational information for men serious about becoming deacons and priests. The goodguyswearblack.org website was filled with Orthodox news from around the world, with articles ranging from the growth of small church communities in the United States, to the revival of churches and priesthood in Russia, to question and answer columns. The latter was often a section that reinforced the gendered structures of Orthodox Christianity.

One such article from December 2018 answered questions from a new Matushka (priest or deacon's wife) about her obligations to her husband and her parish family. The reply, written by a priest, instructed the Matushka to understand her "new duty" and to "make some effort," for her role was only in "helping the priest."[102] The instructions continue, suggesting that the wife "shouldn't whine or complain," nor should she let the devil break up her family.[103] Rather, the priest asked her to "feel that you're a wife and begin to build up your family and your inner self, which is so pathetic right now. Work hard!"[104] The priest reinforced the wife's role as a helpmate, belittling her internal turmoil as not significant, urging her instead to focus on her job as a wife and mother. The dominant masculine roles in traditional Orthodox cultures are not only part of partitioning gender work used to reinscribe proper notions of the family (even a monastic family); they are also part of the broader focus on purity and separation, both institutionally and socially that can be found in many far-right Orthodox convert communities. An emphasis on purity, separation, and preservation is present in constructions of the self, the family, and the nation, which may be why believers both convert to the Church and seem to gravitate toward radicalized understandings of social moral politics.

3

America the Beautiful

Of Guns, God, and Vodka

> All power has its derivation from God; the Russian tsar, however, was
> granted a special significance distinguishing him from the rest of the
> world's rulers. . . . Herein lies the mystery of the deep distinction
> between Russia and all the nations of the world.
>
> —MIKHAIL NIKIFOROVICH KATKOV, 1882

> In the West, we have been withdrawing from our tradition-, religion-,
> and even nation-centered cultures.
>
> —JORDAN PETERSON, *12 RULES FOR LIFE: AN ANTIDOTE TO CHAOS*, 2018

"There's a threat. It's coming. It seems like it's coming from the inside," Fursey
said as he stared intently at the rain pouring down outside of the small coffee
shop not far from the banks of the Ohio River. He drew his steaming mug of
coffee closer and tugged at his gray hoodie, as if he were cold despite the humid
early summer weather. "Why does Orthodoxy attract all the weirdos?" he asked,
referencing a radical nationalist who recently had been attending St. John's
parish. Fursey's question gestures to the larger sociopolitical transformations
that are happening in U.S. ROCOR, and in Russia and the United States more
broadly. This chapter addresses the transforming social politics of ROCOR in
the United States through the lens of the Woodford community, drawing out
how ROCOR political ideologies and social moralities were transformed by
both the influx of converts and the broader context of American religion and
politics in the late 2010s. To make sense of why the political beliefs of this
community were both distinct from and in line with the larger social setting
around them, I examine ROCOR political ideologies in the United States,

assumptions about rural American political participation, the new global culture wars, and the increased focus on populism. In other words, this chapter looks at the sociopolitical mechanisms of secularism and American exceptionalism, tied to notions of democracy and complacent nationalism, suggesting that they might have influenced conversions to ROCOR.[1] To do so means to return to the looming historical relationship between the United States and Russia, the influence of Evangelicalism in American religion and politics, and the controversial United States presidential election of 2016. Through these larger conversations happening in the study of religion and politics, I draw out why converting to ROCOR was potentially a product of U.S. and Russian relations, the (New) Cold War, and the global rise of nationalistic (moral) conservatism—the new global culture wars—that were expressed in other religious communities around the world during the 2010s.[2]

Because politics are often influenced by religious philosophies, I also attend to ROCOR theological beliefs and social ideologies, showing how those, particularly in the context of the United States, have created an environment in which ideas such as the traditionalist "trad" motive, white nationalism, and the alt-right have the potential to flourish. Concomitantly, I suggest that the concept of the alt-right must be reframed, expanded to understand ideologies that are not always associated with this genre of politics but are now being incorporated into it quickly. In doing so, we can better understand people who see themselves as devout, pious, nonviolent, and loving American Christians while ascribing to radical ideologies that have damning connotations for those outside of their particular communities of affiliation. Looking at the broader political setting for these conversions allows us to contextualize them as part of the larger social processes at work, rather than just isolated events in the hollers of West Virginia. In doing so, it provides a more nuanced way to think about converts as political actors in the social drama of religious change that is locally situated and globally connected.

The Exceptional Convert

As we chatted over coffee on that stormy summer day, Fursey reached into the pocket of his dark gray hoodie and pulled out his cell phone. Scrolling through his Facebook feed, he arrived at a post from Benny, who was a current catechumen at the parish. Thrusting his phone close to my face, he pointed out several Nazi memes in Benny's feed.[3] "See? He's a blatant white supremacist. It's this kind of stuff that gives us a bad name."[4] While he clung to a deep moral conservatism, Fursey also feared the growing right-wing convert demographic in Orthodoxy, worrying that they could be the harbinger of more sinister transformations for the future of ROCOR. Fursey was an early Appalachian convert to ROCOR. Interested in monasticism, he moved from Tennessee to West Virginia, giving up a prestigious educational opportunity with the Navy in order to live near St. Basil's monastery. When he first arrived, he lived in an apartment with several other men from around the region who had moved to a city near Woodford. There they hoped to find employment to pay off student loans and other debts before becoming novices at the monastery. Most of the original group members were attached to the monastery in some formal capacity for different periods of time. However, of the early cohort of single males who moved to the area, only one was still at the monastery. The rest either moved away and got married or still lived in the area and were single. Fursey fell into the latter category. In his early forties by the time we met, Fursey often expressed his frustrations about his own life trajectory and that of ROCOR in the United States because of the "crazy converts."

Fursey fits the vernacular convert demographic: single or married male between the ages of 20 and 60, typically with a college degree and, more often than not, an advanced degree from a seminary or graduate training in theology, philosophy, or history.[5] Typical male converts have conservative to radical political leanings, including but not limited to far- and alt-right affiliations and monarchist inclinations.[6] Religious backgrounds of male converts in Woodford often ran the gamut from nondenominational to Southern Baptist to Pentecostal to Catholic, but the largest number generally hailed from evangelical communities. Crucial to the political concerns converts had were fears over social moral issues, such as abortion, same-sex marriage, human rights (gay, trans, and women's rights, primarily), and restricted access to legal firearms. These fears were not new, but they were an embedded part of Religious Right's platform that emerged in the early years of the Cold War and grew throughout the latter half of the twentieth and beginning of the twenty-first century. It is difficult to talk about conversion to ROCOR in North America without nodding to the Cold War, the changing politics of the twentieth century, and the complicated relationship the United States and Russia have had with each other, seemingly because of their different understandings of national exceptionalism.

Exceptionalism in the Russian context was and is often focused on the collective, with an authoritarian bent.[7] Former U.S. Secretary of State Henry Kissinger once noted that Russia and the United States have something in common when it comes to ideas of exceptionalism—the open frontier and expansion.[8] Certainly Russia's conceptions of exceptionalism fall into this category, but expansion was often framed in the rhetoric of expanding empire for the sake of the country and its inhabitants by extension. This was seen not only in tsarist rhetoric, but also during the Soviet period. One of its defining features, it seems, was, and perhaps still is, Russian exceptionalism's emphasis on messianism. This idea of being a salvific figure on the stage of global politics is not only felt in early iterations of Third Rome ideology, but also in Eurasianism, and Vladimir Putin's drive to preserve and expand *Russkii mir*, the Russian World, as a global concept in the early 2000s.[9] Looking at *Russkii mir* through the lens of messianism suggests that Russia suffered, survived, and now believes it has the potential capacity to transform, perhaps even save, the world through the cultural expansion of empire via the drivers of language, religion, and social solidarity in diaspora.[10]

Within the history of the United States, exceptionalism was and is primarily caught up with the notion of expansion and the idea that America was and is truly distinct.[11] Manifest destiny, westward expansion, and colonization became expressions of the individualism, democracy, and morality found within American exceptionalism rhetoric. Infused with dominant Christian ideologies, exceptionalism in the United States also took on a reform focus that was expressed in missionization, the penal system, Prohibition, and the spread of the moral empire through the colonization of indigenous populations.[12] Rather than utilizing a collective cultural form of salvific exceptionalism, the American formation emphasized the moral order of individuals as members of an exceptional state, one graced by God's divine providence.[13] These differences are particularly important when thinking about the ongoing tensions between the United States and Russia and how each country understands their roles as actors in global politics, and how individual conservative actors understand themselves in relationship to the east/west binary and ideas of social morality, providence, and reform. Exceptionalism is critical in analyzing the new turn to morality that we see in Putin's conservative policies and the Russian Orthodox Church's public decrees of social order that have seemingly created a new type of global culture wars in which ROCOR converts often find themselves ideologically aligning with Russia.

The (New) Cold War

Social/moral conservatism in the United States is often associated with the Religious Right, evangelicals, and Protestant fundamentalists. Scholars of American religion show how the rise of a dominant religious voice in the GOP was fueled by discontent "kitchen-table" activists of the 1960s.[14] This shift allowed conservative ideologies to take hold, especially during the late 1970s through the early 2000s. Since its early formations, Evangelicalism in the United States has been caught up with political systems of power, particularly within the various levels of the state and federal government.[15] The expansion of conservative politics in the United States came at a time of shifting social formations, gender norms, and quickening globalization.[16] Early corporate capitalistic concerns over socialism and New Deal liberalism influenced companies to fund Christian activists, ultimately leading to the 1952 election of Dwight Eisenhower.[17] These grassroots efforts expanded in the 1960s, when white conservatives became even more vocal in their communities and active in politics in a decade that saw immense social transformation.[18] Although, in this period, conservatives failed to fully take back power until the late 1960s; that decade was instrumental in helping them shape the right-wing movement that set up their increasing dominion for years to come.

In spite of Richard Nixon's resignation in light of the Watergate scandal, the conservative movement still maintained momentum during Gerald Ford's presidency, despite the fact that Ford was often considered a moderate and did not use his office as much as others to spread the GOP's agenda.[19] Indeed, Jerry Falwell endorsed Ford over and against Jimmy Carter, an evangelical, in the 1976 presidential election cycle.[20] Carter's moderate conservatism did not endear him to the evangelical and religious conservative base of the GOP, and they helped vote in Ronald Regan in 1980. During this period in American religion and politics, evangelical conservatism ascended, expressed in influential organizations such as Focus on the Family and the Moral Majority, emboldened by social moral perfectionism tied to American exceptionalism.[21] The ideologies of boundary making that religious conservatives deployed during the late 1940s into the early 1990s, also help shape the ways in which the American government and media outlets depicted the Soviet Union.[22] Through these decades, American political rhetoric and conservative Christianity were infused with concerns over the intentions and position of the Soviet Union. While WWII brought the two countries together as allies against the Nazi threat spreading through Europe, United States government officials were still uneasy with the socialist country, and by the late 1940s and early 1950s they were seeking ways to contain the Red threat.[23] Wisconsin senator Joseph McCarthy's speech in Wheeling, West Virginia, on February 9, 1950, increased fears that the so-called godless threat of communism had invaded the United States, infiltrating the structures of American democracy.[24]

In subsequent years, fears over freedom of speech were juxtaposed by public rhetoric that reinforced the weaponized threat of socialism and communism.[25] The 1950s proved to be a period of intense social scrutiny and boundary-making ideologies, where the media image of the ideal family living the American dream was promoted on television and in advertising, an image that was once again taken up in the late 2010s by traditionalist movements. During the 1950s, the American dream, with its white, heteronormative, capitalistic family, was juxtaposed with Cold War propaganda that sought to vilify the atheistic inhabitants of the Soviet Union.[26] The Cuban Missile Crisis, followed by Soviet and U.S. negotiations, John F. Kennedy's assassination, and Lyndon B. Johnson's subsequent ascendency to the presidency in the 1960s shifted the dynamics of the Cold War, and the ensuing détente provided a period of brief stability in the relationship of the two countries.[27] Johnson's expansion of American governmental power and influence was not only felt in the U.S.S.R., but it was also present in attempts to perfect the global image of the United States and its inhabitants, imaging the country and its citizens as bearers of morality, power, and stability despite persistent internal issues of gender inequality, racial discrimination, and class struggles.

The Appeal of Russia

In 1977, around the time Jimmy Carter was sworn in as the thirty-ninth president of the United States, when the Cold War was going strong and socialism was still spreading throughout the Eastern Bloc, citizens of Vulcan, West Virginia, decided to appeal to the Soviet Union for financial assistance. Located in Mingo County, one of the areas with the most public coverage during Lyndon B. Johnson's "War on Poverty" in the 1960s, Vulcan was about two hours southeast of Woodford.[28] In the 1970s, access to the town of around two hundred inhabitants, located between a river and a mountain, was via a footbridge built by miners; it had been renovated over time to accommodate vehicles. During the summer of 1975, the bridge collapsed, leaving the town without connection to the rest of the region. No word of aid or bridge reconstruction came from the state or federal government. So John Robinette, a local who worked various jobs, including a stint as a carnival barker, appointed himself mayor and, over the next few years, worked tirelessly toward getting the bridge back in working order.[29] While Robinette persuaded the then governor to agree to have the bridge rebuilt, nothing came of it. Tired of waiting, Robinette decided to contact the Soviet Union for project funding. Even aides to West Virginia's Governor Rockefeller suggested that Robinette might "have to go to the Russians" for assistance.[30]

While the two letters Robinette wrote to Leonid Brezhnev went unanswered, a reporter from *Literaturnaya Gazeta* arrived in town to cover the bridge collapse and the mayor's plea for Soviet aid.[31] In a strange twist of events, the very day that the Soviet reporter arrived in Vulcan, state officials announced that they would rebuild the bridge. Despite the positive report, residents of the town, who were interviewed by Gregory Jaynes reporting for the *New York*

Times, did not seem to believe the state government would follow through with the actual construction.[32] As one reporter noted, "Vulcan may be one of the only towns in the nation that is keeping its fingers crossed that the Russians are coming."[33] Russian aid fell through, however, and eventually the state of West Virginia made good on its promise to rebuild the bridge. On July 4, 1980, surrounded by townsfolk, Robinette dedicated the new bridge, smashing two bottles of vodka onto the railing. A reporter for the *New York Times* was on hand to witness the event, during which Robinette and Russian reporter Mr. Andronov passed around shots of vodka.[34] Robinette used vodka to christen the bridge since, according to the news release, "if it weren't for them [the Soviets] the bridge wouldn't be here."[35] This event was seen as an embarrassment not only for the state of West Virginia but also for the United States, with an infrastructure official commenting that "it was an international incident."[36] At a time of political upheaval and social transformation within the United States, and specifically Appalachia, where community labor activists were often accused of socialist collusion, Robinette and his neighbors reached out to Russia as their singular hope of regaining the stability of the town's infrastructure.[37] The Vulcan bridge incident came during a period of great tension between the United States and Russia politically, not unlike the tension felt during the concurrency of the Putin and Trump administrations. The events in West Virginia in 1975 stirred up questions of nationalism, political loyalty, and security, just as the media rhetoric in the coverage of Russia's potential interference with the 2016 (and then the 2020) U.S. presidential election brought concerns about the influence of a foreign power in American politics and life.

Until recently, the Red Scare, the McCarthy Hearings, and the Cold War were often seen as the apex of tension between the two countries, but the 2016 U.S. presidential election brought renewed interests in and fears of Russian influence in American politics and social lifeways. In many respects, the American ethos during the Trump administration mirrors that of the Cold War era, when reactionary Christians tried to grapple with an increasingly diversifying and modernizing religious landscape.[38] The language of moral evil that came to prominence among conservative Christians during the Cold War, that helped spawn the beginnings of the Religious Right and the eventual Moral Majority, reemerged with unabashed vigor among many far-right Christians during the Trump administration.[39] As Jason Stevens aptly points out, the Cold War period became a moment in which Christians in the United States were grappling with a so-called lost innocence that accompanied the fast-moving changes of modernity, pushing back with fierce conservative ideologies.[40] History, as always, repeats itself.

Scholars have become increasingly interested in the potential social and religious trends that may account for the surprising victory of the Republican party with Trump's win in 2016.[41] Certainly, there seems to be a correlation between the increasing forms of nationalism and conservativism that are emerging across the United States, Europe, and parts of the global south with a tendency to elect right-wing, populist candidates to national positions of power.[42] Within the American context however, the nationalistic impulse, which from my vantage point is linked tightly to Christianity, is also intimately tied to the rhetoric of the Cold War era that pitted the holy United States against not only the Soviet Union, but also other foreign powers that did not align with the democratizing and moralizing force of American domination.[43] In other words, fears over the Red Empire were often a means through which the United States solidified its identity in opposition to the other. The emerging forms of nationalism that are tied to the new Christian Right are products of Cold War conservative fears and propaganda in some respects. The powerful ideological rifts that were formed during the Red Scare of the early twentieth century and that were solidified during the Cold War helped create a public framing (most often through media) of conservativism in the American consciousness that disassociated Marxism and the Soviet state with morality.

Since perestroika, but especially within the last twenty-plus years, however, that framing has changed. No longer is Russia viewed by American conservatives as a regime of godless, socialists; rather, in many circles, Russia has become the new authoritarian champion for conservative ideologues. The increasingly close relationship between the Moscow Patriarchate and the Russian government, under the watchful eye of Vladimir Putin and other officials who have ties to conservative Russian religious organizations, has seemingly shifted the perceptions of Russia such that American conservative Christians, by media and academic accounts, now see it as a guardian of "traditional, social moral values."[44] This new American emphasis on Russia as a geopolitical beacon of morality is primarily a twenty-first-century phenomenon, and seems to be a reactionary move on the part of the far-right movement that is largely based in a political reimagining of conservative coalition building projects. In the 1980s and 1990s, conservative Protestant organizations, such as the Billy Graham family, Focus on the Family, and others who had ties to Russia and the Russian Orthodox Church, were complicit in the moral panic over both secularism in the United States and socialism in Russia, as historian Bethany Moreton points out.[45] However, since the 2000s, America's new generation of conservative Christian warriors, who continue to fight back over overt public displays of sexuality, the fluidity of gender, and abortion, are engaging not only with

American groups, such as World Congress of Families, America First, and the GOP, but they are also collaborating with Russian conservative actors in their fight to redefine moral ethics in the United States.[46] Russia has become, for many Western conservatives, a moral ally.

Among conservative American Christians with whom I have worked, there was a deliberate moral outrage focused on the human rights afforded to LGBTQ+ communities, with special attention placed on transgendered people as a sign that the United States and the Western world more broadly are trying to play God in rethinking what gendered bodies should look like. For conservative converts, who fear the "LGBTQ+ agenda in the US" and the "lavender mafia," Russian president Vladimir Putin's signing of "anti-gay" propaganda laws in 2013 signaled a very public stand for the traditional family and, by extension, a traditional public or society.[47] This moral outrage over gender and sexuality is tied to other issues surrounding bodies that are steeped in anti-science and anti-intellectualism rhetoric. Fears over these issues were quite palpable in Woodford, where talk of the liberal gay agenda and the deconstruction of biological gender differences were raised consistently in conversations. Some have suggested that the increased transphobia and homophobia in American conservative religious discourses and the negative pushback against LGBTQ+ rights seems to be part of the forms of far-right populism that have been developing anew since the 2010s.[48] I agree with the far-right part of this assessment, but I also suggest that these fears over social transformation were, among ROCOR converts, part of the reactionary understanding of postmodern values that was not just about feeling disenfranchised as Christians; rather, their fears over LGBTQ+ agendas were and are part of broader discourses of alterity, whiteness, and domination that have long been part of the imperialistic expansion and colonizing intentions of both Russia and the United States.[49] Populism was not at the heart of their reactive pushback against LGBTQ+ rights. Nor was it part of their embrace of Vladimir Putin.

Populism, Evangelicalism, and Their Reactionary Discontents

The election of Donald Trump in 2016 brought with it an increased focus on populism, highlighting how the social, geographical, and ethical divides between people are manifested in voting booth actions. Scholars have argued that events such as Brexit and the election of authoritarian leaders globally were part of the rise of "authoritarian populism" in which a rhetoric of fear was used to garner the loyalties of disaffected communities.[50] Certainly this idea seems to ring true in terms of Trump's language, which used xenophobic ideology to reinforce arguable fascist boundary-making schemas of "us versus

OF GUNS, GOD, AND VODKA

them."[51] Trump's appeal, particularly in socioeconomically disadvantaged areas, was partly because of his assurances that he, as an outsider to Washington, would shake things up in the governmental structures of power, while also reminding his base that he would carry their issues and needs with him into the White House. Reynolds, a middle-aged Woodford convert who considered himself a staunch conservative, was one of the few converts who was openly enamored with Trump. While Reynolds recognized that the majority of Trump's promises were probably lies, he still proclaimed heartily, "He actually cares about us, he's one of us. Maybe he is a goddamn asshole; he's still one of us."[52]

"He is one of us" was a turn of phrase that I heard many converts in Woodford use to describe Trump, even though most did not vote for him. This notion of likeness seems to be caught up in deep issues of whiteness that are part of the larger xenophobic, homogenizing discourses of fear that are embedded in populism and reactionary politics more broadly.[53] Populism does indeed, as Cas Mudde notes, focus on creating distinct camps of purity and corruption in order to reinforce boundary-making schemas. Yet, populism is a thin ideology that is often used when scholars are unsure what to call a hybrid political form. The fact that populism, at least fourth wave populism, so easily absorbs nationalism and other political ideologies, such as finding the sovereign (in some form), suggests that it lacks the robust theoretical scaffolding we need to make sense of what might draw American converts to contemporary illiberal Russian politics in hopes of resurrecting monarchic authority.[54] This apocalyptic vision of American politics does not align with the normative populist impulse to flatten political structures of hierarchy by letting the people—the populace—reclaim their country from the outside forces of difference; rather the apocalyptic vision of American politics that I found in Woodford was interested in hierarchal intervention from abroad that was far removed from the hands of everyday Americans. To be sure, there were rural Americans, and Orthodox Christians, who shared the same or similar sentiments as Reynolds regarding Trump. Yet there is also great diversity of religious and political opinions throughout the American South, Appalachia, and the Midwest that is often missed in the critical assessments of rural societies that immediately label voters as populists. I suggest that the political phenomenon I encountered in Appalachia can be understood through the lens of reactionary, perhaps even fascist, nationalism—one that is most assuredly Christian but, by no means, focused on a vision of America that many conservative Christian nationalists rally around.[55] In order to understand how this type of hybrid ideological formation emerged in Woodford, we must look briefly at the Christian environment of West Virginia, the transnational efforts of evangelicals (and Orthodox) to find moral allies abroad, and, finally, the ideological anxieties and theo-political hopes of Orthodox converts.

Snakes, Sex, and Sovereigns:
Understanding the Politics of Converts

Evangelical culture in Appalachia often does that not have the same political force that it does in other places. In popular media, Appalachian Christianity, often called mountain religion, is seemingly synonymous with groups radical enough to handle venomous snakes and drink poison in order to prove their holiness.[56] To be sure, these groups do exist, although not only in Appalachia, but also in other parts of the American South and the Midwest, including the Ozarks. These religious communities are just one segment of the widely diverse forms of Christianity present in Appalachia. Historically, religion has been an important aspect of sociocultural structures in the region. While Holiness-Pentecostal movements are most widely associated with mountain religion, many of the Christian communities in Appalachia historically have not claimed a denominational affiliation, which American religions scholar Catherine Albanese suggested represents the essence or "the fruit of the mountain spirit."[57] The focus on mountain religion, even as a method for reshaping our under-standing of the so-called wild spirituality of some communities in Appalachia, fails to fully develop the image of the vibrant forms of Christianity found there. Appalachia, as a constructed geo-cultural region, spreads, by the standards of most scholars, from the northeastern corner of Mississippi to the southwest section of New York State.[58] Along the way, it encompasses the entirety of West Virginia and sections of its neighboring states. Often considered part of the American South, it also overlaps with the Rust Belt and shares many similarities with other defined regions nearby, including the Ozarks.[59] The geographical spread of the region brings with it a wide variety of religious practices and communities. Woodford happened to be located in a portion of West Virginia that expressed less religious diversity than other, more urbanized parts of the state. Yet, within the small town of Woodford there were a wide variety of Protestant churches. Church of God, Church of God in Christ, Canadian Christian, Old Baptist, American Baptist, Southern Baptist, Holiness, Pente-costal, and Assemblies of God. All of those denominations were found right off the main highway that split through the town. Driving up into the moun-tains and down into the hollers meant encountering many nondenominational churches. Often small, white clapboard or log-style buildings, they dotted the landscape, and on any given Sunday morning or Wednesday night, the gravel or dirt parking lots would be filled with cars and pick-up trucks (see fig. 2).

At many of the non-Orthodox services I attended, congregants would pub-licly ask for prayer regarding their personal lives or issues friends and family were facing. Occasionally, someone might request prayer for political leaders,

Figure 2. Church at the Crossroads (Photograph by author, August 2018)

but that was rare, and that speaks the idea that Appalachian Christianity, by and large, was not as politically minded as other forms of Christian faith found throughout the United States. Most non-Orthodox congregants I talked with, even those who were affiliated with nondenominational Christianity, considered themselves evangelical. The majority of Woodford converts to ROCOR also consider themselves previously attached to various forms of Evangelicalism found throughout Appalachia, the American South, and the Midwest. To say the evangelical movement has been influential in the shaping of both U.S. and regional politics is an understatement. Scholarship focused on the Moral Majority, the Reagan years, and the Tea Party as the main narratives in the conservative Christian networks of influence in the United States the past twenty years, and even more so since the 2016 presidential election, has pushed Evangelicalism to the fore in our understanding of American religion. Orthodox conservative converts, however, seemed hesitant to engage actively with thinkers who helped shape their former evangelical values—such as Focus on the Family, Trinity Broadcast Network, or the GOP. Perhaps this was because any whiff of affiliation with Protestant groups smacked of ecumenism to them. Or perhaps it was because they were seemingly done with American conservative politics and the Republican party—there was nothing left for it to offer them, they claimed. Instead, they looked to Russian Orthodoxy and Putin's new Russia as a salvific haven in the fight over global moral politics. However, during the late 2010s, ROCOR converts were not the only American Christians and social conservatives looking to Russian politicians and religious institutions for moral support.

While questions were still swirling in the media around the Russian influence in the 2016 presidential election, U.S. evangelicals broadly seemed eager to embrace Russian conservative figures and ideologies, especially those focused on so-called traditional family values. These values often play out in the adoption of homeschool methods in order to protect the ideological purity of the family structure.[60] The growing focus of international conservatives on a so-called nuclear family of one man with one woman and multiple children seems to be at the heart of these emerging relationships. Anthropologist Sophie Bjork-James notes in her study of white hegemonic Christian heterosexuality that conservative evangelicals, such as Franklin Graham, are beginning to turn to Putin's Russia as a model for supporting the moral family.[61] This increasingly cozy relationship between moral conservatives in Putin's Russia and conservative Christians in the United States—Orthodox and Evangelical—has also been facilitated through far-right organizations such as the World Congress of Families (WCF), which have often hosted their international meetings in predominately Orthodox countries.[62] The WCF also drew a large international Orthodox presence throughout the years. Patriarch Ilia of Georgia, who provided a blessing to the 2016 World Congress of Families, has promoted radical forms of conservatism and traditionalism that have seemingly led to assaults on LGBTQ+ rights in Georgia, alongside an increased social focus on family purity that is expressed in the annual Family Purity Day on May 17, which is often held in conjunction with mass weddings to promote heterosexual Christian marriage in the public sphere.[63] Father Josiah Trenham, a convert to Eastern Orthodoxy and priest at a California parish in the Antiochian Archdiocese, who became a conservative celebrity but also contentious figure in many Orthodox communities in the late 2010s, offered highly inflammatory comments about LGBTQ+ communities at the 2016 World Congress of Families X in Tbilisi, Georgia, even catching the attention of the Southern Poverty Law Center's Hatewatch Staff.[64]

By the late 2010s, Christian conservatives in the United States, perhaps spurred on by the image of Billy Graham's engagement with Russia, looked eastward in an effort to curry favor with Russian conservative intellectuals, officials, and clerics. In a July 2018 op-ed for the *New York Times*, American journalist Katherine Stewart noted how Maria (Mariia) Butina, a Russian citizen who was eventually indicted in the U.S. federal courts for numerous charges including conspiracy, was at the National Prayer Breakfast.[65] A known connection-building event for global networks of conservatism, this was just one of many events in which Russian actors were present and ready to create ties between conservative Russian political leaders and American evangelicals. Along with the WCF, the Heritage Foundation, and others, leaders from the breakfast were courting Russian actors in an effort to promote a shared platform of conservative social moral values. As Stewart noted in her op-ed, "It turns out that anti-L.G.B.T. politics are an effective tool in mobilizing religious nationalists everywhere, which is in turn an excellent way to destabilize the Western alliance and advance Russia's geopolitical interests."[66] In a *Newsweek* article that same month, Tom Porter wrote, "Russia has reinvented itself as a bastion of Christian values in a world beset by relativism and godlessness. As a result, conservative Christians gathering at the World Congress of Families are looking to Putin to protect Christianity from the West."[67] At the same time as the ardor for Russia reached a fever pitch among evangelicals, Orthodox converts in the United States were also looking to Putin as a political savior from secularism.

While far-right Orthodox Christians and Evangelical Christians tend to be theologically estranged from each other, they do have a close and consistent understanding of social moral politics and so-called family values, perhaps better thought of as theology or politics of the family. With the influx of converts from evangelical and fundamentalist Protestant backgrounds, the social moral values of ROCOR and Orthodox Christianity more broadly are transforming ideologically. The sociocultural baggage of conversion means ideologies that were not historically found in Orthodoxy are beginning to emerge as part of the Church in the United States, the United Kingdom, Europe, and other areas around the globe. Scholars of Orthodox Christianity in Russia have pointed out that the rhetoric of family values is somewhat foreign to the faith, suggesting that it is perhaps a Western, mainly American, import from the culture wars of the 1990s.[68] Putin's focus on "national pride" as a unifying factor that could help support the flourishing of traditional Russian culture, is reminiscent of the Moral Majority's emphasis on Christian America. At the same time, Putin's encouragement of the increasingly conservative and expansive Russian Orthodox Church highlights the religiously-inflected notions of values and identity that are caught up in the idea of national pride expressed by the Russian president and his supporters.[69] In the Russian context, scholars have suggested that the increase in values rhetoric combined with the focus on national identity has not only led to heightened xenophobia, it is also creating a space in which free speech and human rights are not only undervalued but also at risk of being obstructed by forcible and enforceable means.[70] The dark underbelly of increasing social interactions between conservative citizens of

Russia and the United States is troubling given the stances both groups have on human rights and equality.

In the context of the United States, rapid secularization and a turn toward inclusivity have created widespread fears among conservative religious communities that often nostalgically lament the loss of what they see as a "Christian Nation."[71] Nationhood, personhood, and belief are seemingly bound up together in the vision of family values set forth by conservative Christians. This rhetoric of belonging, of nation and religion as co-sharers in the creation of new Eden, was part of, at least in the late 2010s, what sociologists Samuel Perry and Andrew Whitehead labeled Christian nationalism. Although, by 2020 and early 2021, it could be argued that Christian nationalism was on the brink of becoming blatant fascism.[72] A bedfellow of white nationalism in many respects, Christian nationalism is tied to issues of race, class, and patriarchal expressions of traditional gender ideology conveyed by many conservative Christians in the United States. [73] The push for traditional marriage—that of one woman and one man—is one foundational article for this movement; its expressions are manifested in homophobic fights against same-sex marriage and adoption, the civil encroachment on reproductive rights, and a trend toward anti-intellectualism, from which the homeschooling fever seems to emerge.[74]

The emphasis on homeschooling and moral values that united American and Russian conservatives indicates two important issues undergirding the rapid expansion of far-right cultural politics in the United States—namely, moral panic over gender/sexual diversity and what I call *nostalgic apocalypticism*. At least in the Woodford community, nostalgic apocalypticism—an attempt to return to what they saw as a traditional Christian national ethos for fear that secular liberal agendas in the United States will create an apocalyptic scenario—was a key aspect of the conversion process. Apocalyptic politics are part nostalgia, part conservative political ideology, part Russian Orthodox theology. Nostalgia, ideology, and theology create the building blocks of both nostalgic apocalypticism and their new social reality—their new world. Each piece affects the other; nostalgia and theology are mapped onto politics, social issues, and current events, while politics is understood through the writings of Russian saints, monks, and other figures in the history of Russian Orthodoxy. ROCOR then becomes the vehicle through which these apocalyptical politics have traction in the world. Converts' understandings of ROCOR as a safe ideological haven were bound up with issues of church and state, with surveillance of the body, with the erasure of gender diversity, with the remaking of the world into something it never was—heaven. In order to fulfill this spiritual and ideological terraforming of the current political reality, they looked to both politicians and personalities who could reinforce their ideologies and potentially give rise to a new, conservative world.

Praising Peterson

From inside my log cabin, I heard a horn honk. It was Fr. Cyril. During the fall of 2017 and early spring of 2018, he would often pick me up on the way to his house, where he also ran a religious products business. I was happy to get away from my molding abode that seemed plagued with continual wasp invasions, bats, and wolf spiders the size of softballs. Along with almost daily power outages and virtually nonexistent Internet access, it was not a comfortable situation to say the least. There were very few rentals in Woodford, and locals told me I somehow managed to snag one of the prime pieces of property, although it certainly did not feel that way from my perspective. Hearing Fr. Cyril's horn meant I would have a welcomed respite. I hopped into his dusty green SUV, the same one he had generously let me borrow when I first moved to West Virginia, and noticed immediately that he was in what seemed to be a terrific mood. "What's going on?" I asked. He replied that he had just watched a clip from a debate between controversial Canadian psychologist and academic Jordan Peterson, who had a large following among young conservative males, and a "feminist" reporter who had "tried to take him down." As we passed the sign for the monastery and drove down the pothole-pocked one-lane road to his house, he insisted I watch the interview in its entirety once we arrived at our destination. Within the next twenty minutes, I found myself seated on the brown leather sectional in Fr. Cyril's spacious living room next to his daughter and oldest son as he proceeded to act as master of ceremonies for our YouTube clip screening. Throughout the interview, Fr. Cyril paused the video and offered commentary about Peterson and women's rights, suggesting that Peterson had won the argument over wage inequality fair and square.

During the screening, Parson, a local convert, arrived with his children in tow; they were there to pick up Fr. Cyril's daughter to attend a Russian ballet production in the state capital. "Thank God it's Russian; otherwise I don't think I could stand it," Parson quipped. Parson noticed Jordan Peterson on Fr. Cyril's flat screen and mentioned how much he respected him and his traditional views about modern society. Fr. Cyril and Parson's enthusiasm over Peterson was also expressed by other male members of the Woodford Orthodox community. Peterson's emphasis on masculine strength, traditional gender roles, and his loose social ties to ROCOR converts in Canada made him somewhat of a superstar both in Woodford and in the social media worlds of

conservative Orthodox, predominantly ROCOR, converts. Peterson rose to
international recognition in 2016 when he argued against ideas of political
correctness found in a Canadian bill that would protect gender identity and
expression under the banner of human rights. Peterson's calm and seemingly
unflappable demeanor during public debates, and his sympathies toward right-
wing ideologies, made him a champion of traditional gender norms in the eyes
of many Orthodox converts.

With his emphasis on traditional archetypes for social values and his dismissal of female leadership, Peterson seemed to have struck a chord with many
Orthodox males in Woodford, for he was seemingly a strong, cogent, learned
voice, with the authority of the secular academy behind him, that could suc-
cessfully argue against the trappings of feminism and modernity. Throughout
the Orthodox blogosphere, writers, the majority of whom were male, affirmed
how important Peterson's voice was in this particular cultural moment of conservative resistance to secularism and progressive liberalism. Despite the fact
that Peterson self-identified as an atheist, many converts suggested he was
highly interested in the Orthodox Church and might even convert at some
point. These ideas were reinforced when Jonathan Pageau, a close friend of
Peterson, who also happened to be a convert to the Orthodox Church, was
interviewed on Peterson's YouTube channel in a two-part event.[75] Peterson, in
a similar fashion to Father Seraphim Rose, offered converts an option that
seemed focused on ancient beliefs and archetypes that could reclaim a traditional world before it was too late.

What draws converts specifically to the Russian Orthodox Church Outside
of Russia? The narratives of conversion in the previous chapter indicate a deep
longing among believers to find an authentic form of traditional religiosity
steeped in history. From a spiritual standpoint, their reasons for selecting
ROCOR seemed to be the preservation of and adherence to religious purity.
Yet it is not simply the liturgical rites, mystical theology, and the abundant
sensorial practices of ROCOR that have shifted the faith of converts. In the
next two chapters, I look at the influence of monarchism in the appeal of
ROCOR and Russian Orthodoxy more broadly for many converts I encountered in Woodford; while I argue that the disdain for the separation of church
and state is part of their turn to Putin's illiberal and seeming autocratic Russia
and the monarchically focused ROC, it is also about the role of democracy
and American politics. Monarchism's appeal for many converts was the very
idea that a God-ordained king bridged the gap between church and state,
providing them with a salvific form of governance that they believed was lacking in Western democracy and social politics.[76]

Donald Trump's election, for most in the community, was a hopeful event that they believed would squelch the liberal left's agenda, despite the fact that most of the converts did not vote for Trump or vote at all. The deliberate moral outrage over trans rights, abortion, and vaccines led converts to focus on nostalgic apocalypticism. Many believers expressed fears that one more Democratic president might cause the rise of the Antichrist and the ultimate destruction of the United States and other Western countries. The relationship between moral outrage and apocalyptic politics among converts to ROCOR was made all the more evident to me when one convert spoke of the revolutionary day when Vladimir Putin would invade the United States and restore moral order to avoid God's wrath. War between Russia and the United States was often on the minds of converts, especially males, many of whom own guns (or arsenals of weapons in some cases) and talk about their potential positionality in the coming war. They highlighted Putin as a God-inspired leader, who not only would fight for moral, religious values, but would also embody the ideas of someone like Tsar Nicholas II and bring back the glory of the Third Rome. Crucial to understanding the attraction converts had to Putin's conservative form of Russian government is the Russian Orthodox emphasis on Russia as the holy heir of Byzantium, the historical centrality of monarchic government in Russia, and canonic veneration of the Romanovs, particularly Tsar Nicholas II—the last godly global leader in the eyes of many Orthodox converts.

4

Port of the Tsar

Material Monarchism and the End of Days

Hell is a democracy, but heaven is a kingdom.

—ST. JOHN OF KRONSTADT

O pure one, who ever intercedeth for us together with the pious
Tsar Nicholas and all the saints, grant us peace under the invincible
dominion of the heavenly kingdom, keeping us from all subtle
deception and blatant apostasy. For though the seal hath been
removed, do thou thyself restrain the Antichrist by the might of the
Heavenly King.

—A WEST VIRGINIA MONK, SESSIONAL HYMN TO THE PORT ARTHUR ICON

On a warm summer morning, I drove up the gravel mountain road that led to
St. Basil's monastery. Cresting the top of the hill, I gazed through my bug-
splattered windshield down into the holler where a majority of the monastery's
buildings were grouped at that time. Something different caught my attention
that morning. Across the porch railing of the *trapeza* (refectory) building was
a large banner. On the left side was the coat of arms of the Russian empire
with the phrase *Slava Rusi* (glory of Russia or Rus') at the bottom; on the right
side was an image of Tsar Nicholas II. These images were superimposed on a
background made up of the black, yellow, and white Russian imperial flag.[1] As
I hiked up the trail from the parking lot to the refectory, Br. Patrick, a young
monk with a long auburn ponytail, appeared behind the sign, leaning over the
railing. "Isn't it great? *S prazdnikom* (Happy Holiday)!" he asked and answered
joyfully. "Happy feast day, Brother Patrick," I replied as he ran into the church
to avoid being late for the Divine Liturgy. That Tuesday in midsummer was

the feast day of Tsar Nicholas II, but it was more than just the yearly commemoration of the saint; it also happened to be the one hundredth anniversary of the assassination of the last Russian tsar and his family. One century after the Bolsheviks slaughtered the ruler, his wife, and his children in the basement of a house in Ekaterinburg before unceremoniously dumping their bodies into unmarked graves, believers in Appalachia reverently celebrated them as political martyrs for the faith, and the memory of their martyrdom occupied an important place in the creation of Russian-American Orthodox political theology.

Historically Russian Orthodoxy has been caught up in political economies of imperialism and the state, and it continues to be so, even in its diasporic and convert incarnations in the contemporary United States. This is seen readily in the controversial glorification (canonization) of Tsar Nicholas II, his wife, and his children by ROCOR in 1981, when the jurisdiction was still separated canonically from the Moscow Patriarchate (MP).[2] This chapter explores the political importance of the Romanovs' canonization in both ROCOR and the Russian Orthodox Church, questioning why a political figure who died a century ago and thousands of miles away from the mountains of West Virginia has such an influential presence there. I suggest that through his supposed posthumous transtemporal intervention in matters of church polity and global politics, Tsar Nicholas II became a key figure in the nostalgic, reactive ideologies of convert practitioners, providing them with a guiding example of how a country and its leader should function in relationship to Christianity, thereby fueling their monarchic sympathies. Focusing specifically on the ROCOR veneration of Tsar Nicholas II and his sovereign connection to the cult of the American-Russian version of the "Port Arthur" icon of the Mother of God housed at St. Basil's, this chapter highlights how Orthodox religious belief and materiality in Appalachia were entangled with pre-1917 tsarist ideologies that affected practitioners' understandings of contemporary Russian-American politics. Setting these canonizations and subsequent practitioner veneration within the context of Orthodox political theology, and the historic complexities that surround the idea of church-state relations within Byzantine and Russian Orthodoxy, I tease out the reasons why many converts found monarchism so appealing, and how the materiality and sensory cultures of ROCOR reinforce the importance of a monarchic figurehead.

Political Theologies: The Return of the King and His Tsar

When I inquired where the monks found the banner of Tsar Nicholas, they brushed my curious questions aside. Undaunted, I kept asking members of the community the same question over the course the summer, mentioning the banner in passing conversations to see what I could uncover. Eventually one of the monks told me they found it "on the Internet," although he could not remember what site or when they purchased it. During a conversation with the abbot, I asked him about the banner, and he replied, "Oh, isn't it great? We got it on the Internet. It's just wonderful." Again, the abbot failed to remember what site they purchased the banner from or who recommended the website. During a volunteer day making candles and soaps, I asked Clotilde if she knew anything about the banner. She replied, "Isn't it fun? I think I know who bought it." When I asked her who bought it, she grinned and said, "One of the monks!" Yet again, my efforts to find out about the banner seemed only to falter as people surely felt uncomfortable with my asking because of its extremist transnational connections. Indeed, a cursory Internet search of the image ties it to Russian fringe nationalist groups such as Union of Orthodox Banner Bearers, who were highlighted in a Reuters article in the summer of 2018. While the sight of the banner in the holler that morning was visually striking, what went unsaid and was avoided around the image of the tsar speaks much more to the relationship between theology and global politics in this convert community.[3]

The American political imagination is imbued with faith, which makes it crucial to look at both theology and politics in order to understand church-state formations. This, of course, is particularly critical when we approach a community such as the one in Woodford that is focused on forms of religious and state exceptionalism that fall outside the boundaries of American democracy. Since this Russian Orthodox convert community had a predilection toward a political imaginary that situates sovereignty or sovereign power transtemporally, it is only fitting that we analyze their practices and beliefs through the framework of political theology. By political theology, I am referring to interdisciplinary conversations that have brought religion into dialogue with other fields of thought in an effort to address complex issues surrounding religious practice and spiritual belief in everyday life. Drawing on continental philosophy, political science, anthropology, and theology, among other fields, political theology provides frameworks for thinking through larger issues, such as liberalism, capitalism, and globalization in ways that are sensitive to the subjectivities of individuals.

Within the Russian Orthodox context, sovereignty is situated transtemporally in two spheres—the celestial kingdom and earth—that are not separate but commingled. Russian Orthodox culture possesses a long history of understanding the tsar as God's anointed intermediary on earth, not just in Russia. Indeed, as Abbot Filofey of the Pskov Monastery wrote in a 1528 document to Tsar Vasily III, "Let us say a few words of the present state of the Orthodox realm of our most illustrious and most high Tsar and Sovereign, who is the only tsar for Christians in the whole world and the guardian of the holy and divine altars of the Holy Apostolic Church."[4] The idea of the tsar being the global guardian of holiness, in various formations, has found its way into the writings of numerous Orthodox monastics, clergy, and lay scholars over the centuries. Believers with whom I have worked drew upon these writings, such as those written by St. John of Kronstadt, to highlight how Christ, the sovereign of heaven, was for so many a model for an earthly sovereign—a king who would give up his life for his people.

Both types of sovereignty, heavenly and earthly, are thought to intermingle with each other within this particular Russian Orthodox worldview, thus breaking through normative notions of temporalities. If we draw upon political theologies that assume a fallen created world is in need of a salvific sovereign alongside an eschatological messiah, then some strands of Russian Orthodoxy, wherever it is found geographically, falls within its purview.[5] The figure of the sovereign, for many traditionalist Orthodox Christians, is part of their "anti-democratic anti-modernism" paradigm that focuses on the imperial past of Christianity as the model for contemporary church-state relations.[6] In a way, *symphonia* also expresses a version of this antidemocratic spiritual and political entanglement. Sovereignty is not typically understood in relationship to divine kingship in the social sciences, especially in political science and legal studies, where scholars conceptualize the idea as part of self-governance, independence, and autonomy bound to the notion of the modern nation-state.[7] Thus legal and social science paradigms do little work in helping make sense of why contemporary American citizen converts to Russian Orthodoxy often desire the return of a Russian tsar and monarchic authority.

Strikingly, anthropologists David Graeber and Marshall Sahlins, in their work on the history of kings, take a more holistic approach to this type of leadership by focusing on the divine or sacred aspects of kingship.[8] However, the issue with Graeber and Sahlins's framework for divine kingship, at least in the Orthodox context, emerges in their understanding of temporality, presence, and power: "Sacred kingship . . . would appear to be largely a means of containing sovereign power in space. The king, it is almost always asserted, has total power over the lives and possessions of his subjects; but only when he is physically present."[9] Divine kingship in the Orthodox context is not contingent upon space—it envelops the heavenly and earthly temporalities—nor is it contingent upon physical presence as the marker for power. At the same time, Sahlins is correct in stating that, "A lot of social intercourse goes on between humans and the metahuman persons with whom they share the earth, as well as with those who people the heavens and the underworld."[10] Within Russian

Orthodoxy, interactions between humans and metahumans is part of their transtemporal understanding of world; it is, what we would call in the field of religious studies, their ontological understanding of the universe. Not confined to the Western scholastic concepts of separate spiritual and earthly spheres, Orthodoxy possesses a permeable theological cosmology that allows for fluid temporalities. Heaven, according to one contemporary conservative American Orthodox theologian, is not upstairs from earth—it is on earth, with earth, in earth.[11] This theological distinction is essential in understanding both the Orthodox preoccupation with divine kingship and the ability of celestial figures, what Sahlins would call metahumans, to affect the politics of the world through their agentive presence in the Orthodox sensorium.[12] Understanding Orthodox theological conceptions of leadership, the state, and politics in general requires an interdisciplinary approach. Looking at monarchic veneration only through the lens of the social sciences leaves these phenomena unexplained, for Orthodox Christianity, particularly ROCOR, possesses theologies that are historically tied to geopolitics.

While political theology within the fields of religious studies and anthropology often seems to be the academic production of continental philosophers such as Giorgio Agamben, it is found in theology more readily in the writings of Christian theologians and philosophers, particularly in the United States with the work of Stanley Hauerwas, Reinhold Niebuhr, and Richard H. Niebuhr.[13] Within the Russian context, religio-political philosophers such as Nikolai Berdyaev, Vladimir Solov'yev, Pavel Florensky, Sergei Bulgakov, Aleksandr Dugin, and many others have influenced theological understandings of the relationships between church and state in writings that could easily be covered by the umbrella of political theology.[14] Many members of the Woodford Orthodox community had a deep appreciation for Russian political philosophy, although their focus was primarily on the writings of saints from Russian or very conservative Greek traditions.[15] Converts often addressed contemporary issues through the writings of the holy fathers of the Church. "What do the fathers say about this issue? What does the church say? What does St. John of Kronstadt say regarding this matter? What do the writings of Russian monastics offer in relation to these issues?" were common questions I overheard in the community. The emphasis on the "fullness of the faith" as it was passed down by the religious institution historically combined with a focus on individual humility—one that considers personal theological opinions to be reserved for startsy (elders)—created an environment in which all of the theological texts of the Church became prophetic utterances for the future; they were relied upon to understand what might come about socially, culturally, and politically.[16]

While practitioners in Woodford saw their political ideas as deeply contoured by the teachings of the Church, they were also keenly interested in contemporary socio-political events, for they believed that both historical writings and current affairs were aligned to understand the end of days, which most assumed was close at hand. From an anthropological perspective, this poses a curious form of anachronistic social practice that superimposes historical figures and ideas onto the current geopolitical situation in a prophetic formulation that creates new political ideologies about the United States and Russia, perhaps without even intending to. Theologically, this seems to reinforce the idea of temporal permeability, creating a social space in which the voices of departed elders are not only present in the lives of believers, they also possess a special role in shaping the future of the world. If the departed are still speaking, then it seems only natural that the converts in Woodford wanted to diligently follow their ideas and examples in order to preserve and perpetuate the correct form of the faith. On the whole, practitioners at St. Basil's (monastery) and St. John's (parish) saw themselves as adhering strictly to the traditions and teachings of ROCOR. Abbot Spyridon told me on more than one occasion that while the monastery might create new service hymnody for icons and festal days, they always received the blessings of hierarchs to do so. More importantly, they ascribed, in daily practice, to the Russian *typicon* (a rubric book for daily divine services), in order to remain in solidarity with their spiritual legacy and their contemporary brothers at the Optina Pustyn monastery, where monks from St. Basil's often visited on pilgrimage to reinforce their spiritual kinship with the community. Thus while Abbot Spyridon might have blessed his monks to write music, he was always mindful of being faithful to the Russian Orthodox tradition, lest the brothers fall prey to notions of modernity through the idea that individuals can change the services or structure of the Church to accommodate themselves or even influence the future.

Traditional Transformations

Often when I was at the monastery, monks would make backhanded comments about another ROCOR monastery in the United States—St. Aidan's—that was seen as liberal because it was not firmly in line with the Russian *typicon*. One sunny afternoon while I was sitting on the refectory porch after lunch, a young monk, who was often quite shy, began chatting with me about how much he loved St. Basil's. As a way to explain why he found St. Basil's to be the right place for him, he offered up a story about St. Aidan's monastery. A few years prior, St. Basil's hosted some of the fathers from St. Aidan's. "They [church hierarchs] sent some of those monks here to learn how to do things right," the young monk told me. Another monk, who was sitting nearby and sipping a cup of coffee, overheard the conversation and interjected, "They [the monks from St. Aidan's] told us that on Saturday nights sometimes they would skip the services and go into town to have Chinese food. Can you believe that?! They're really different." On a separate occasion, another monk told me that he was glad he was at St. Basil's rather than St. Aidan's because it was too modern for his tastes: "We do things the right way here." In ROCOR, change as a marker of modernism, perhaps even an acceptance of secularism to some extent, is countered by overwhelming emphasis on traditionalism, which shapes everything from piety to politics in conservative convert communities.[17]

What is curious about the training mission for the St. Aidan's brotherhood is the fact that the hierarchs selected to send the monks to St. Basil's rather than the historic home of Russian monasticism in the United States—Holy Trinity Monastery (HTM). This decision seemed to mark a shift in monastic tradition in U.S. ROCOR, which traditionally assumed that all monks would, at some point during their lifetime, spend time at HTM learning the rubrics of services and appropriate monastic conduct. Historically, HTM was seen in convert communities as quite severe in its Russian asceticism. There was a general consensus among those at St. Basil's that only converts with a God-given grace could endure long periods of time at HTM. Abbot Spyridon, during a conversation about his entrance into the monastic life, explained how he felt about visiting HTM as a younger monk: "I . . . didn't like it at all because it was all Russian in those days. Totally Russian. There wasn't a word of English anywhere and I felt like I was in a foreign country."[18] Despite this sentiment, Abbot Spyridon, once he became the head of St. Basil's, requested that the community be a *podvor'e* (dependency) of HTM, which it was for quite some time. Abbot Spyridon seemed to believe that the time spent under the authoritative mantle of HTM accounted for their "solidly traditional" status in ROCOR. At St. Basil's "nothing experimental" goes, he told me firmly.

A couple of years before I arrived at St. Basil's, I took an extended research trip to HTM, where I met with Fr. Luke, the abbot of the monastery. A Carpatho-Russian, his parents had him baptized as an infant in a historic church located in the Rust Belt region of Pennsylvania. While Abbot Luke was influential in creating a more linguistically open seminary and monastery for converts, he was, at the time of my visit, still quite leery of outsiders and those who refused to submit to the mantle of ROCOR or the MP, since my visit took place after the reunification. Despite his unwillingness to have me stay for a longer period of time with the community, Abbot Luke took me on a tour of the monastery and seminary, proudly showed me icons that were donated by Vladimir Putin, and ultimately provided me with a way to think about the different formations of Russian Orthodoxy in the United States. He suggested that if I liked HTM, I would not care for St. Basil's, and the reverse. For Abbot Luke, St. Basil's represented a departure from the stalwart old guard of ROCOR in the United States. The irony, of course, is that convert communities such as St. Basil's and the parish of St. John's ascribe to the idea that they are safeguarding the crystallized prerevolutionary traditions, ideas, and mechanisms that have historically made ROCOR a distinct religious community within Russian Orthodoxy—they are, in many respects, the gatekeepers of ROCOR's ethnonational traditionalism.

Unlike many Christians in the United States (and elsewhere) who are often focused on recovering or restoring the social formations of the early church as a way to return to the faith of their forefathers, converts in the Woodford community were focused on the Russian *typicon*, traditions, and beliefs that were historically associated with prerevolutionary Russian Orthodoxy as part of their process of nostalgically collapsing time and geography to somehow get closer to a pure type of orthopraxy.[19] The services of the Church, particularly vigil, matins, and the Divine Liturgy, were crucial ritual and material forms of orthopraxy that reinforced, through readings, hymnody, and kinetic oblations, a roadmap to guide believers through the turmoil of life in the secular United States. Thus, adhering strictly to the canon of ROCOR services was key, for it provided a homogeneity of ideology and standardized forms of devotion and belief. One of the most beloved figures in Russian-American Orthodoxy, St. John Maximovitch, in his 1951 essay on how to preserve the uniformity of the Church, wrote:

> Our Church typicon is not a compilation of dead rules and it is not the fruit of some abstract desk work, it was imprinted on the spiritual experience of holy ascetics who came to fully understand the depths of the human spirit and the laws of the spiritual life. . . . The divine services in their composition contain all the fullness of the dogmatic teaching of the Church and set forth the path to salvation.[20]

At the heart of ROCOR theology, according to converts with whom I worked, is the idea that every doctrinal teaching passed down by the Church is for the spiritual edification of believers and should not be tampered with by the laity. This includes ideologies and theologies about gender, sexuality, human rights, and politics to name a few. Furthermore, because the theology of the Church is manifested in its services, the words prayed and chanted by practitioners should form and inform their political outlooks and social practices.

Because the services express the theo-social dogmas of ROCOR, believers in Woodford saw it as imperative that theological praxis in text and verse stay traditional. One Monday afternoon when Fr. Cyril, the priest at St. John's, picked me up to help out at the weekly food pantry, he railed against the "modern, liberal theologians" and "service innovations" in the Greek Orthodox Church in the United States, explaining that Orthodox Christianity did not need new theologies or pews to make sense of the world; rather believers needed to focus on the traditional teachings handed down to them over the centuries, for they would sustain the Church in the uncertain future. Political theology offers a helpful way to understand what religio-political philosopher Vincent Lloyd calls the "social practice" of a community, using it as a lens through which we can more substantively understand the complexities of theology and politics at play in a community such as Woodford.[21] If we think of political theology as the relationship between religion, politics, and the social—in its various constructions—political theology is a fundamental, lived aspect of Orthodox theology and praxis in Woodford that is borne out in the cycle of services. Within the context of anthropological research, scholars have recently been grappling with the importance of addressing political theology ethnographically rather than theoretically, for in doing so the substrata of geopolitics and religion that systematically support social projects are made more visible.[22] It is exigent to see how the political ideologies borne out in this community are not only shaped by the ethos of American politics; they are also fundamentally formulated through theological ideas that were convinced of in wildly different social-economic and religious contexts than that of twenty-first-century Appalachia.

Of God and Kings: The Role of *Symphonia*

If we take political theology as part and parcel of the social practices that have historically contoured the religio-political formations that comprise Russian Orthodoxy, then the centrality of Byzantium in the creative idea of *symphonia* (*simfoniia* in Russian)—the equality of leadership between church and state— must be examined.[23] The theological importance of symphonia has its roots in the Byzantine Empire, with its definition attributed generally, in its earliest incarnations, to Eusebius first, and then to Emperor Justinian I, who suggested that God gifted humanity with the priesthood and sovereign imperial powers in order to minister to both human and divine affairs on earth.[24] The emperor went on to note that if both parties—priests and imperial officials—do their jobs with dignity and care then the result will be harmony for the community at large.[25] This idea is a form of political theology in active practice. Indeed, Orthodox theologian Aristotle Papanikolaou notes that the creation of symphonia was in fact a political move that was manifested out of the ontological theology of divine-human connections during the Byzantine period.[26] While contemporary converts' conceptions of the relationship between God and humanity might be different from those expressed in Byzantium, although their ideas tend to align with Eusebius's image of the sovereign and his critique of democratic rule, their focus on theocratic forms of governance seems politically motivated.[27]

Converts often seemed taken by a model of church-state relations that Zoe Knox, a historian of modern Russian history and religion, would suggest is spherical but also intermeshed, with church principles shaping "state policies to the same extent that they guided the church."[28] Papanikolaou notes that for early Christian political ontologies, "The whole of societal space was destined to be infused with God's presence in all its constitutive parts so as to realize a mode of being that reflects communion with God and, hence, the active presence of the Word."[29] Thus as Knox aptly points out, while imperial power was an ideological link that united together church and state within the social construct of Byzantine Christianity, its effects are still felt through Orthodox worlds today, particularly in Russia, which historically saw itself as a crucial center of religio-political power, and perhaps the only true holder of Christianity, after the fall of Byzantium. Within the Russian context, the notion of symphonia took on a distinctive political meaning relative to tsarist rule. Despite the often strained relationship between the Russian Orthodox Church and the Russian government—in its various incarnations—there has been, historically, a link between church (the Orthodox Church) and state that is somehow founded in the idea of symphonia.[30] Therefore, while the Russian Orthodox Church is not a formalized state church, it, in many ways, has been and currently functions as one. Symphonia is key to understanding why the Woodford community tended to place so much emphasis on the importance of Tsar Nicholas II as both a saint and prophetic figure regarding global politics, and why his repositories of holy materialities are venerated with such ardor.[31] Through believers' liturgical celebrations of the saint and their pious venerations, the socio-political transtemporal interventions of the king who was glorified take shape in Appalachia.

Political Martyr, Saintly Tsar

On any given day at St. Basil's, pilgrims were milling around the grounds; volunteering in the garden, soap room, and graveyard; or perusing the small gift shop located near the parking lot. Stocked with baked goods fresh from the monastery kitchen, frankincense and myrrh goat-milk soaps, beeswax candles, rose incense crafted in the workroom upstairs from the gift shop, icons from both Russia and the studio right down the road, and religious texts and prayer books, the small space provided pilgrims with a wide variety of purchasable goods. Beyond items for sale, there were often blessed oils from the shrine of one of the monastery's patron saints, paper icons, and other images offered free of charge. Located on the bottom shelf of a bookcase filled with candles and icons were copies of charcoal sketches, created by an anonymous monk, of important saints and figures in ROCOR. Alongside the images of twentieth-century American figures such as St. John Maximovitch and Father Seraphim Rose, there were depictions of the Romanovs, with a portrait of Tsar Nicholas II front and center on the shelf. A popular item among pilgrims, the gift shop employees made sure to keep the tsar's image in stock, especially in the days leading up to the one hundredth anniversary of his assassination in midsummer of 2018 (see fig. 3).

The hagiography of Tsar Nicholas II was fundamental to ROCOR political theology in Woodford, which placed primacy on the role the tsar fulfilled as a God-ordained leader shepherding his empire and church through the trials of secularism and socialism. In the late 1960s, St. John Maximovitch wrote regarding Nicholas:

> Why was Tsar Nicholas II persecuted, slandered, and killed? Because he was tsar, tsar by the Grace of God. He was the bearer and incarnation of the Orthodox world-view that the tsar is the servant of God, the

Figure 3. Charcoal Portrait of Tsar Nicholas II (Anonymous)

Anointed of God, and that to Him he must give an account for the people entrusted to him by destiny, for all his deeds and actions, not only those done personally, but also as tsar.[32]

St. John Maximovitch goes on to say that Tsar Nicholas II "was a living incarnation of faith in the Divine Providence."[33] For many monarchists, Nicholas II was and is God's imperial emissary. In contrast to the historic narratives that highlight Nicholas II as an ineffectual autocrat who could not withstand the sweeping tide of social change that ultimately led to his forced abdication in 1917, Orthodox devotees saw him as both an influential figure in Russian history and the preserver of the contemporary world from demonic forces. Not only did Nicholas II perpetually extend time through his heavenly interventions as a canonized (glorified) saint, but he also provided a model for a future tsar, who many in the Woodford community were praying would come to power.[34] As I point to in the next chapter, Russian President Vladimir Putin was often seen as a successor to Tsar Nicholas II, whose relics can be found, in part, at St. Basil's; this idea seems to be fundamentally a symptom of the monarchic political theology found in St. Basil's and St. John's. The figure of Nicholas II, whether it was on a banner, in a sketch, portrayed in a painted icon, or his physical remains fixed in beeswax in a West Virginia reliquary, was a corporeal site through which political theology and ideologies were both reified and reinvented in ROCOR convert culture (see fig. 4).

Believers in Woodford, on the whole, refused to engage with historical accounts of Tsar Nicholas that would paint him in a negative light. Thus, the leader's relationship with Rasputin, his failures in the Russo-Japanese War, and speculations about affairs were muted by community members who saw these ideas as modernist, secular allegations by academics and the media who they believed spewed slanderous anti-Russian propaganda in an effort to mar the image of the holy sovereign. Often believers evoked tropes of family life and divine kingship to justify the canonization of Nicholas II. One self-proclaimed monarchist parishioner at St. John's parish explained why he had an icon of the tsar in his home icon corner:

> I have [icons of] Tsar Nicholas and the New Martyrs of Russia, and the Royal Family or Royal Martyrs. I've always had a big affinity for Nicholas II, and I have a real soft spot in my heart for him . . . because he and his family were murdered in such a gruesome way. But again, as somebody who's given up on democracy and sees monarchy as the hope, he was the last tsar and they killed him. I think a lot of misinformation has been spread about him. No matter whether he was a

Figure 4. Icon and Reliquary of the Royal Martyrs (Photograph by author, August 2018)

good or bad tsar, there's no disputing that he loved his wife and he loved his family and he was very devoted to them. Often, I pray to that icon or to him to pray for me to be half the father and half the husband he was.[35]

The language of Tsar Nicholas as a family man is not foreign to the hagiographies that help aid his glorification (canonization) in ROCOR and subsequently in the Russian Orthodox Church nearly twenty years later, and his continued veneration among the Russian faithful in the federation and the diaspora.[36] This language of family was also employed by converts as a way to emphasize a correct model for the nuclear, heterosexual, patriarchal family structure— something that was noticeable both in Woodford and in the social media conversations about the saint.

Because the cultic following of Nicholas II proliferated concomitantly with the advance of digital technology, a good deal of tributes to or arguments for the tsar's sainthood are often found on Orthodox websites.[37] It is fair to say that Orthodox Christianity in the twenty-first century is one that is connected, by and large, through digital means given the size and diffuse geographical nature of the communities. Believers connect via church websites, religious news outlets, personal blogs, and, of course, social media. The "Orthonet," as it is often affectionately dubbed by believers, is seen as both a great benefit as well as a pitfall to intra-Orthodox relations and personal spirituality. Through digital networks, believers send prayer requests to various shrines, swap PDFs of liturgical texts, and connect to current affairs going on in regions considered to be traditionally Orthodox, such as Russia, Greece, Romania, and Serbia. In Woodford, the Internet was *the* resource to find and connect with Orthodox materials. Matushka Emilia, the choir director at St. John's, scoured the web weekly to find appropriate ROCOR liturgical sheet music for each feast day. Clovis, a married lay member of the monastery, was enrolled in a digital Orthodox Studies graduate program and spent time daily combing through open source texts in order to create PDFs of Orthodox study material for himself and members of the monastery who had spiritually imposed restrictions on Internet usage. Fr. Cyril, the rector of St. John's, used digital software to manipulate high-resolution photos for his icon reproduction studio. For the believers in Woodford, the Internet, despite its dial-up speeds, was a crucial assistive device utilized in their religious practices and belief. In contrast, however, officials in the Russian Orthodox Church, in recent years, have publicly decried the use of the Internet, with Patriarch Kirill, during an interview given on the television station Russia 1, a state-sponsored outlet, suggesting that technological gadgets might be part of the control mechanisms that signal the *"prishestviye antikhrista"* (the coming of the Antichrist).[38] Ironically, believers in Woodford used the Internet to find prayers and hymns to the last tsar, who they believed was holding back the Antichrist and persevering the world through his intercessions.

Popular American convert blogger Jesse Dominick, who moved to Russia, worked for various Orthodox news outlets as a translator and columnist, and ultimately married a Russian woman before returning with his family to the United States, was one of Nicholas II's ardent advocates online. In a 2015 article for pravoslavie.ru, Dominick tied together Orthodox traditional ideas about the family with the notion of a sacred monarchy in the honor bestowed upon tsar by the Orthodox faithful, noting that "The tsar was a man of great conviction. His sense of duty and faith was unwavering, his family values impeccable."[39] Elsewhere in the article, Dominick explained that the God-ordained tsar "was undoubtedly a man of deep faith. As we have seen he was keenly sensitive to the lives of his people, and especially in times of disaster and suffering his first instinct was to find solace in the stillness of a monastery."[40] For Orthodox Christians, particularly in Russia, Dominick believed that the tsar and his family represented humble examples of how to live out the Christian faith, and that they, through the prayers of believers, posthumously and transtemporally provided "a bulwark, a firm wall of protection for the Russian people and land."[41] It seems somewhat normative to see Orthodox Christians in Russia embrace the glorified tsar, but it seems curious that converts in Appalachia might feel deep devotion to a leader whose platform was the antithesis, in many ways, of American democracy. I suggest that converts found Nicholas II appealing for two reasons: First, he offered them an idealized moral guardian of the relationship between church and state; and second, he provided a way to existentially yet hopefully make sense of the end of days. I assert that we can understand more about these political ideologies and eschatological concerns through the materiality and sensorial practices of ROCOR converts surrounding the departed tsar.

Finding a Port to Weather the Apocalypse

"We are at the end of days," was one of the constant refrains echoed by Orthodox believers in Woodford. While this phrase was sometimes attached to an apocalyptic fear of a global doomsday event, it was more often associated with God's judgement because of increasing secularization in the post-modern period. Converts believed that homosexuality, abortion, and the destruction of Christian ideals were all complicit in the downfall of Western civilization. Secularism and liberalism were not only the harbingers of destruction, but also the bearers of it. These ideas were not unique to Appalachian ROCOR. In 2013, Patriarch Kirill, during a speech a Moscow's Kazan Cathedral, suggested that same-sex marriage was a "very dangerous sign of the apocalypse."[42] Four years later, the His All Holiness again brought up apocalyptic ideas, suggesting that humans are "priblizhayeti k kontsu sveta" (approaching the end of the world) because of the 1917 Revolution, which fueled individualistic human passions and artistic sinful endeavors that have shaped the course of world politics.[43] In many respects, this is the language of political theology used to understand the social politics of the public sphere, something believers in West Virginia engaged in regularly. I arrived in Woodford nine months after Donald Trump's January 2017 inauguration as the 45th president of the United States. Members of the community did not seem interested in talking about the new president; rather, they were far more interested in talking about the hundredth anniversary of the Romanov murders, which, at that point, was almost a year away. The Romanovs—Tsar Nicholas II, Tsarina Alexandra, and their five children, often labeled the Royal Martyrs, New Martyrs, or Passion-Bearers—are canonized saints.[44] While the Royal Martyrs are beloved in Russian Orthodoxy, it is Tsar Nicholas who seems to hold a prominent place among converts, often because of his office rather than his beliefs.

Within Russian Orthodoxy, the tsar is sometimes identified as "he who restrains," an idea that is derived from the New Testament epistle of Second Thessalonians: "For the mystery of lawlessness is already at work, but only until the one who now restrains it is removed."[45] Most converts I spoke with used this particular verse in prophetic reference to Tsar Nicholas II restraining the Antichrist. Fr. Tryphon, a young monk at St. Basil's, explained a bit of the prophecy:

> The only reason why this world is still existing is because of the New Martyrs. In particular, of course, the Royal Family being at the forefront of those. So basically, after he [Tsar Martyr Nicholas] was assassinated the world should have ended, but because of the intercessions of the New Martyrs, God has granted more time for repentance.[46]

When questioned why the prophecy was interrupted, Fr. Tryphon explained further, drawing on the teachings of a popular web-based English convert clergymen to ROCOR, and the Hebrew Bible story of Jonah and the city of Nineveh:

> Fr. Andrew Phillips . . . gives the example of Jonah preaching to Nineveh. He preached that Nineveh would be destroyed, but they repented so it wasn't destroyed. Does that mean that it was a false prophecy? No, it was a true prophecy. So, he [Fr. Andrew] says it's been like that several times in the history of the world and the two millennia of Christianity. There have been points where things really

are at the point where they could have ended then, but because there was repentance, then things were allowed to continue. Because that's the only point why any of this is happening anyway. If no one else is going to repent, then this whole thing becomes a noxious farce.[47]

Fr. Tryphon's commentary is important for two reasons: First, it provides an example of how deeply entrenched the tsar and, by extension, the concept of the monarchy are in the theology of ROCOR; and, second, it points to one of the key differences between Russian Orthodoxy and other forms of Christianity—namely, the focus on eschatological transformation through continual repentance or purification. Repentance and hierarchy are both foundational to the lives of Orthodox convert Christians, for each provides a form of structure that perpetuates the belief system. In Nicholas II, both of these ideas were seemingly manifested, showing forth a model of governance that fulfilled converts' notions of what it means to be a true Christian leader. The question then arises: How did believers contact their salvific departed tsar? The primary means believers used to engage with Nicholas II was material cultic devotions that offered sensorial, transtemporal channels through which to summon the canonized sovereign into the hills and hollers of West Virginia.

Sensing the Sacred: Holy Materiality and Pious Politics

Orthodox culture is resplendent with material and sensorial experiences that evoke sacred spirituality for believers through theologically rich rituals, drawing them into the history and presence of Christianity.[48] Incense, bells, icons, prayer books, music, candles, oils, water, bread, and wine were just some of the material culture used by ROCOR converts in their daily devotional lives. Materiality was a means through which Woodford believers not only encountered Christ, they also found ways to participate in transtemporal political structures of belief and practice. Thinking through the sensorial aspects of Orthodox ritual and piety as they are related to political theology helps flesh out the intersubjective experiences of converts. The writing and chant of a supplicatory canon to Tsar Nicholas II takes on much more complexity if we approach it through the lens of sensory studies, asking what believers experience through their participation in calling forth the saving prayers of a king so far removed from them. Furthermore, focusing on the mediated forms of transtemporal social connectivity might tell us more about how the politics of Russian Orthodoxy are reimagined in the U.S. context. Both of these ideas were tangibly manifested in many believers' devotion to one particular image: the Port Arthur Triumph of the Theotokos, a special Russian-American icon housed at St. Basil's monastery (see fig. 5).

Figure 5. Port Arthur Triumph of the Theotokos icon (Photograph by author, August 2018)

The building used for the temple (church) at St. Basil's monastery was one of the first structures built on the property that the monks acquired back in 2000. A small building, it was divided by a short wall used as a barrier to separate the monks from the laity during services. The entrance to the building was a set of red double doors, with oval, decorative glass inserts. Upon entering the temple, a large icon of the Mother of God was located immediately to the right. Secured in a wooden-rimmed glass case with handles (for ease of carrying during processions), the icon measured approximately three feet wide by five feet high. The shrine surrounding the icon was simple but well kept, with monks charged to look after it daily. A candle stand was located to the left of the icon, with a vase holding fresh flowers mounted on the right side of the icon. Draped over the top of the icon frame was an embroidered towel, an item that is often placed around icons or reliquaries to provide an extra material form of reverence. This central icon at the entrance of the building was called the Port Arthur Triumph of the Theotokos. A special copy of an original icon of the Theotokos that was part of the history of the Russo-Japanese War, this image was created to represent the sacred bond between Russia and the United States; to reinforce Tsar Nicholas's prophetic role in the salvation world; and emphasize the importance of divine, monarchic leadership.

The hagiographic narrative of the original Port Arthur icon presented by most of the monks at St. Basil's was one of divine foretelling, war, and global travel. Within Orthodox circles, icons are often referred to as theology in color or pictures. This was most assuredly the case with the Port Arthur Triumph of the Theotokos. The original icon, which was, according to Orthodox tradition, commissioned by the Mother of God herself through a vision to a Russian Crimean war veteran in late 1903, depicted the Theotokos standing upon two broken swords at the edge of body of water.[49] The story goes that icon, which was produced in Vladivostok and blessed by religious and state dignitaries, never made it to Port Arthur, thereby causing Russia's military defeat.[50] Eventually the icon was lost and then found, as oral tradition goes, at an antiques store in Jerusalem, then transported back to Russia, and then taken to its intended home in Port Arthur, Manchuria. Given the political importance of the icon in the lackluster military efforts of Russia in the Russo-Japanese war, it seems strange at first glance that a giant wonder-working copy of the icon would be housed in West Virginia. How that icon found its way to St. Basil's monastery is part of the story of how ROCOR is changing in the United States. The shift from émigré to convert culture that I traced in previous chapters has moved the locus of power from the historical and well-established institutions founded by White Russians fleeing Soviet persecution to newer locations such St. Basil's, that are reimagining the faith in ways that are still caught up with the trappings of conversion from American Protestantism(s). The geographical journey of the Port Arthur icon in North America shows how ROCOR is transforming politically, for the icon not only reinforces monarchic ideologies and prerevolutionary tsarist veneration, it also provides a material form of Russian-American Orthodox political theology, one that is sensorially accompanied by American-written hymnody and devotional prayers that express those same ideas.

The monks at St. Basil's were quite proud of the fact that the Mother of God chose to grace them with her presence in the Port Arthur icon, with many of the monks telling me this fact on numerous occasions. In his narrative of how the icon ended up in West Virginia, Abbot Spyridon suggested that the success the monastery had experienced in recent years was probably attributable to the presence of the icon in the community: "We had twelve monks for a long time. When that icon came, suddenly we started getting more and more men coming. We had all these candidates come, and all of that started happening when the Port Arthur icon came here."[51] The success of the monastery seemed indebted to a Russian organization that considered itself nonreligious but promoted religious activities that encouraged traditional forms of Russian cultural morality in the Far East, and renewed relations between the United States and the motherland. Originally created in an icon armory near Port Arthur, the Russian-American icon was brought to North America in 2006 by a Canadian missionizing foundation. Worried by the lack of authentic Russian piety they found in some of the parishes, the organization traveled to the United States in order to bring the icon to HTM. They arrived, as Abbot Spyridon relayed, in time for the funeral of Metropolitan Laurus:

> They came right at Metropolitan Laurus's funeral, and what they saw
> there really pleased them, because they . . . saw Russian piety, and they
> hadn't seen that in Canada. And they saw it on a big scale, because
> there were lots of bishops and lots of people. The church was packed
> for this funeral and the whole service was in Slavonic. It pleased
> them very much, so they decided to leave the Port Arthur icon in
> Jordanville.[52]

According to Abbot Spyridon, the abbot of HTM claimed there was no room in the church for the icon, so he kept it in his office. Abbot Spyridon mentioned to Abbot Luke that he would like to have the icon at St. Basil's for their patronal feast day, a major pilgrimage event for the monastery. Abbot Luke agreed, but only on the condition that the monks from St. Basil's would transport the icon to West Virginia. Once the pilgrimage was over, Abbot Spyridon called Abbot Luke and asked if he could keep the icon for a bit longer. Abbot Luke obliged, saying, "Yeah, you can keep it for as long as you want, but just remember, it really belongs here."[53]

Ten years later, the icon was still at St. Basil's, and the monks had no intention of giving it back. For the community, the icon had become a symbol of hope in what they saw as a world darkened by sin. Abbot Spyridon conveyed a story that offered insight into how the icon was viewed by many among the Woodford faithful:

There was an old man who used to live here, and he told me, "You know, I had a dream last night. It was a strange dream." I always remember this [story]. He said, "In this dream, I was like floating up in the air somewhere very high and everything was dark. It was very dark. And I knew I was up above the earth, and as I came down to the earth, I saw everything was black, our whole country, the whole world was black." And he said, "But there was one light, and as I came down closer and closer, I saw that light and sparks were coming out of this light and going in different directions. Then I got closer and closer and I realized it was the Port Arthur icon." I always remember that story.[54]

The abbot's sensorial recounting of the man's affective experience with the image uniquely illustrated its socio-theological relevance. The icon served as a beacon in a world marred by sin and evil. This same type of evocative affect and relevance was also expressed in the stories around and the words of the accompanying festal texts written by a monk at St. Basil's for their treasured image of the Theotokos.[55]

It was at St. Basil's in 2014 that Fr. Theodosius, the young monk who had previously wrestled with a lack of imagination, wrote the first services for the feast day of the icon.[56] Fr. Theodosius was considered by many in the community to be a truly gifted hymnographer. Because the monks believed humility was an ultimate virtue, Fr. Theodosius always refused to talk about writing the texts. I received most of the information about Fr. Theodosius's pivotal role in the creation of monastery services through second-hand conversations, especially with Clotilde, who often provided me with common knowledge information that went unsaid by the monks. Through conversations with Clotilde and Fr. Romanos, the choir director at the monastery, it was evident that Fr. Theodosius was the central figure in a new wave of Orthodox liturgical hymnody and hymnography in U.S. ROCOR. One hot day in the late summer of 2018, I sat down to chat with Fr. Theodosius after he finished baking bread in the monastery's new industrial kitchen. We convened in his tiny office, filled with icons, stacks of papers, and liturgical books. As a sign of goodwill, he gifted me some of the sand he had gathered at the shrine of his patron saint earlier that year. Fr. Theodosius was, by nature, quite gentle, kind, and a bit nervous. Despite being in his late twenties, he had a lot of responsibility at the monastery. This was not uncommon in terms of the community's management style and the fact that the demographics of novices and monks skewed young.

About halfway through our conversation, Fr. Theodosius acknowledged shyly that he had written services for several feast days and had been deeply involved with the Russian-to-English translation of the akathist (hymn) for Tsar Nicholas II, which took place at the monastery while I was in Woodford. While the celebratory services including vespers and the Divine Liturgy were open to visitors, the brotherhood planned to assemble together in the temple to chant the akathist in front of the tsar's relics and icon when the clock struck midnight on the feast day. However, as several monks confided in me later, the service did not take place until well after midnight because Fr. Theodosius, along with another monk, and Lyudmila, a friend of the monastery who helped with Russian-language translation, had not finished translating the Russian version of the akathist into English. Despite the fact the monk was willing to talk with me about his more recent hymnody, he always refused to explain why and how he wrote the services to the Port Arthur icon. Thus, I look to the words of the service to express Fr. Theodosius's views of the icon and its political significance in the late 2010s.

One of most important functions of the Port Arthur icon services was to denote the fall of Russia to Soviet power and the potential for the United States to experience that same type of persecution if they did not recognize looming political oppression and ask for the intercessions of Tsar Nicholas II. Right-believing Christians, those intimately tied to Russian Orthodoxy and those who honored the icon, had nothing to fear, however, as text from the Great Vespers service to the icon read, "And, gathered into the ark of thy mediation, Orthodox Russia and North America, as two united noetic flocks, are led to worship Christ the Chief Shepherd with fear and joy."[57] Elsewhere in the same service, Fr. Theodosius highlighted the role of a sovereign in the unification of both countries, suggesting that the "image sealeth peace between Russia and North America."[58] The entirety of the service to the Port Arthur icon was filled with vivid proclamations of sovereign salvation for the United States and Russia through the transtemporal iconographic interventions of the Theotokos and Tsar Nicholas II. Mapping the divine aid of the Theotokos onto North America, specifically Appalachia, the service called for the queen of heaven to "fill every hollow with divine exaltation."[59]

It is clear from the service to the icon that Fr. Theodosius believed the relationship between Russia and the United States was somehow sensorially manifested through the physical image of the Mother of God. During the

Great Vespers services held the evening before the liturgy, when the *litiya* (breaking of the bread) took place, the following words were chanted: "In heaven, with his troops, the godly Tsar Nicholas exults today, for all Russia is glorified by the radiance of thine icon, O Lady, which, with the meek Herman as its forerunner, also graces North America."[60] The eighth ode of the canon to the icon suggests that the image is the victorious boast of holy Russia, before going on to express the importance of the icon not only in North America generally, but West Virginia specifically: "Falling down before thine icon, O blessed Mother of God—who walketh even amongst us in triumphant glory— we honor it as Freedom of North America, Mediation of Alaska, Surety of Canada, Royal Diadem of New York, Glory of West Virginia, and Intercession for all the world!"[61]

North America, in the words of Fr. Theodosius, became the place through which the faithfulness of Orthodoxy that was not kept at Port Arthur was preserved and defended:

> Today, O Mother of God, the city of Vladivostok rejoices, and with it all the reaches of the earth, in beholding thine icon, which bears the historic name of Port Arthur, for blessed and glorious provision, was offered to the devout forces of the far Russian realm, and is offered to us today, as we gaze on thy holy image and cry, "O Orthodox Christians of North America, preserve the Orthodox Faith, for this Faith is your firm foundation."[62]

The troparion (a hymn formed of complex stanzas) above highlights one of the most crucial elements of the icon and Fr. Theodosius's accompanying service—namely, that of using the spiritual history of the icon to map a salvific, monarchic political future onto the Russian-American Orthodox Church in North America. Another sessional hymn in the service proclaims:

> O pure one, who ever intercedeth for us together with the pious Tsar Nicholas and all the saints, grant us peace under the invincible dominion of the heavenly kingdom, keeping us from all subtle deception and blatant apostasy. For though the seal hath been removed, do thou thyself restrain Antichrist by the might of the Heavenly King, confirming us in the sacred Tradition, that we may obtain the eternal glory of our Lord Jesus Christ.

As words and hymns were chanted on a cool Thursday evening in late May of 2018, monks and laity lit candles and made prostrations in front of the icons and relics of the tsar and his family, which had recently been moved into a custom-carved wooden shrine funded by an anonymous benefactor. Their low-sweeping bows and reverent postures were reflective of subjects meeting a monarch. Indeed, many there that evening believed not only that the tsar heard their petitions, but that he was also present that evening in the church as part of the "great cloud of witnesses."[63] Within the text of the service, and the devotions of the community, time and space seemed to be collapsed in a nostalgic attempt to preserve the past in order to affect the future. At the end of the service for Great Vespers, the following doxasticon (a type of hymn) was chanted before the icon:

> When thou, O heavenly ladder, didst reveal thine icon to the Russian people, on it they beheld angels above thee, holding a crown, thereby prophesying the loss of the tsarist dynasty when Tsar Nicholas would abdicate, becoming a sacrifice for our sins. But today, we behold thee as the reigning Queen, who hath taken thy people under thine own rule. Thus, falling down before thee in tears, we beg pardon for our sins; raise up Holy Rus' and, in God's time, crown her last tsar, who will be the fear of Antichrist and the guardian of the Church, against which the gates of hell shall never prevail. By Her true hierarchs, pastor us to heaven amongst the one flock of the One Shepherd thrice-glorious: Father, Son and Holy Spirit.[64]

The hymn calls upon the Theotokos to help renew the holiness of Rus', imbuing the language of monarchic salvation into their apocalyptic vision of the end of days. These words were not theoretical; they were part of the everyday devotional belief systems of converts in Woodford, who were seeking a sovereign for the end of the world.

Abbot Spyridon told me that he not only saw the icon as a powerful image of religious solidarity between the United States and Russia; he also believed that it had political implications as well, particularly given the tensions between the two countries that were occurring in 2017–2018:

> I think it's very wonderful that the Mother of God wanted to be here in that form of that icon, because it symbolizes the two countries and their peaceful union, which we want very much to happen—have peace between us and Russia. Unfortunately, the way things are going in America and the liberal press, there's just this terrible renewal of anti-Russian feeling. I think Mr. Trump made a big mistake when he was running for president, or after he became president—I don't know when it was—but he said, "I would like to make friends with Russia. There's no reason why the two most powerful countries in the world can't work together to fight some of the issues that we have in common,

to work together on these issues." Well, the Democrats used that against
him, and they really exploited that and from that came the whole accusation that Russians affected the election, that Trump talks to Putin all
the time, that Trump is really a puppet of Putin.[65]

Despite the negative media, Abbot Spyridon believed in the religious and political unity of Russia and the United States. He hoped, as did most believers
in the Woodford community, for peaceful, close relations that would allow the
proliferation of Christianity and social conservatism in both countries. The
icon, thus, served as an imaged prayer for the future, one that believers hoped
would triumph over the secular progressivism of the Western world.

Sensorially the Port Arthur icon was not only a visually important reminder
of the link between Russia and the United States, but it also served as another
bulwark in the hagiography of Tsar Nicholas II. The importance of sovereign
leadership as an ark of safety from secularism was found throughout Fr. Theodosius's service to the Port Arthur icon. Veneration of the icon through the
divine services allowed believers to imaginatively look for a savior and social
safety in their current situation. Thus, it is no wonder that words such as those
below, taken from a sessional hymn during the vigil to the Port Arthur Icon of
the Mother of God, had such relevance in contemporary political ideologies
of believers:

> Having passed through the flood of the revolution, the Russian Church,
> now as another Noah, beholdeth the reappeared icon of our Lady as an
> all-beauteous rainbow, the manifest promise that such devastation will
> never again overtake Holy Rus'. O North America, forsake not the
> Holy Faith lest that which began in Russia end in thee; but let us all
> rend our hearts in repentance, crying: "O Lord, save Thy people and
> all Thy world!"[66]

The icon offered a pictorial expression of future transformations, provided that
the faithful remain true to the teachings of ROCOR and preserve the faith
undefiled. Within the context of their current political situation, believers,
such as Abbot Spyridon, started looking to international figures who might fill
the monarchic void left in the wake of the murder of Tsar Nicholas II, with
him and others in the community suggesting that Vladimir Vladimirovich
Putin might be the heir apparent.

5

Palace of Putin

Political Ideologies in Orthodox Appalachia

The Orthodox Christian is called to love his fatherland, which has a
territorial dimension, and his brothers by blood who live everywhere
in the world.

                       —FOUNDATIONS OF THE SOCIAL CONCEPTIONS
                            OF THE RUSSIAN ORTHODOX CHURCH, 2000

In late December of 2017, I sat with Angus in St. John's parish, a log church
located just off the highway in the heart of Woodford. The Sunday Divine
Liturgy had just wrapped up. As parishioners shared a common meal in the
parish basement, we adjourned upstairs to talk privately. Children, including
some of Angus's family, practiced carols for Old Calendar Nativity in a nearby
room, while we sat in the empty priest's office to have a conversation about
why he converted. Angus talked about his pride in being from West Virginia,
his complex spiritual path to Orthodox Christianity that included traditionalist
Anglo-Catholicism, and sojourning in silence with Zen Buddhists. Toward the
end of our conversation, Angus began to focus on his political leanings, con-
fiding in me that he held a "much higher opinion of Vladimir Putin" than he
did any contemporary American political figure, and that he would not mind
at all if Putin somehow could manage to influence, even forcibly, the political
trajectory of the United States.[1] He positively evaluated the relationship the
Russian leader had with the Orthodox Church, questioning what might happen
if the United States were to become "a Christian nation," akin to modern Russia.[2] Although Angus understood he was member of a Christian minority group
in the American religious landscape, he also believed, or hoped at least, that
he was part of a community embedded in the broader movement of increasing

religiopolitical conservatism that was springing up in the United States and around the globe in the late 2010s.

This chapter examines the political ideologies of the Woodford Orthodox community, suggesting that their religious conversions are not only caught up with new incarnations of the religious far right emerging throughout the United States, but also with the increasingly nationalistic conservatism expressed in Russia by the Moscow Patriarchate in conjunction with President Vladimir Putin, a shared church-state ideological framework that often draws on the imperial history of Holy Rus' in shaping new trajectories for the Federation.[3] While media portrayals of alt-right and far-right actors are burgeoning, as are books exploring the sociological roots of the right-wing base that supported Donald Trump in 2016 and 2020, scholarship has yet to catch up with the philosophical turn to Russia in American religion, and what it tells us about the changing dynamics of religiopolitical patterns in the United States, especially with the unanticipated attraction to the Orthodox Church and Putin. By aligning themselves with Putin's conservative ideologies, the Russian Orthodox Church, and ROCOR, Appalachians are finding a form of political salvation that they believe has vanished from American politics, while also resurrecting notions of monarchism as a vital form of governance both at home and abroad. In doing so, they become actors in reimagining the drama of religiously tinged right-wing nationalism that sees progressive secularism as not only the antithesis of traditional morality and family values but also as part of an ultimate apocalyptic spiral toward the end of days.

Scholars have noted that Russian Orthodoxy's political ideologies in the 2000s and 2010s created an environment in which ideas such as traditionalist movements, nationalism, and the alt-right could flourish. Indeed, Cyril Hovorun suggests that the antidemocratic movement in post-Soviet Russian Orthodoxy is appealing to traditionalist Western actors who hold to the same ideological trinity—anti-modernism, monarchism, and conservatism—with its accompanying emphasis on nationalism.[4] Converts in Woodford praised Putin's example of Christian leadership that seemed to encourage the unification of church and state and conservative nationalism, while drawing on Russian political history as a portent of things to come for Christian inhabitants of the United States, unless they looked to the model of Putin's new Russia for salvation.[5] Focusing on believers' conversations, actions, and critical media engagement, I analyze conversions to ROCOR in Appalachia as a means through which we can understand the transnational project of conservative Christian moral outrage, perhaps even radicalization, toward the assumed expansion of progressive secularism in the United States.[6] Strikingly, these new religiopolitical projects allow us to see unanticipated shifts in national loyalties among growing traditionalist, fundamentalist, Christian communities in the United States, a country that historically pushed for the American-led Christianization of the Soviet Union.[7] For ROCOR convert practitioners in Appalachia, conservatism in the United States was no longer synonymous with Christian American Republicanism, and nationalism was no longer tied to American exceptionalism. Their conversions then can be seen as almost subversive acts that were deployed for larger theo-political means.[8]

Politicizing Faith

The late 2010s was a crucial political juncture in the ever-unfolding relationship between Russia and the United States, and conversion to Russian Orthodoxy provides a window into how Vladimir Putin's vision of *Russkii mir* (Russian world)—namely, his support of traditional religio-cultural organizations at home and abroad—was influencing Christians in United States, particularly in rural areas.[9] While much can be said about the reasons why rural communities swung heavily for Donald Trump in the 2016 presidential election, particularly because of legitimate grievances about regional inequalities in the United States, I suggest that the concurrent draw to Putin tells us far more about theo-political ideologies, which are manifested not only in converts' unexpected attraction to monarchism, but also in their nostalgically influenced desires for an alternative conservative cultural project, an alternative world. Thus, converts often narrated their reasons for supporting Putin through their versions of Soviet history, relating it to the political climate of the United States in the late 2010s, when they believed secularism was triumphing and it was only a matter of time before Marxism was rampant throughout the country. While the Orthodox faithful in Woodford, such as Angus, expressed support for Vladimir Putin and his seemingly pro-Christian, pro-Orthodox platform, many also offered accounts of why Putin's role was not only important on the global political stage, but also, perhaps, God-inspired or ordained. Often, these validations of Putin's religious devotion and political correctness drew on royal religious figures, events, and ideologies of prerevolutionary Russia in order to show how Putin was bringing back the glory of the Third Rome. For this very reason, the transnational political dimensions of conversion must be analyzed in order to have a fuller understanding of what it meant for rural American Christians to turn to Russian Orthodoxy.

In a previous chapter, I discussed believers' spiritual reasons for conversion while suggesting that conversion to Russian Orthodoxy as a political act—one that is wedded to theology *and* global cultural politics. This allows space for understanding how American Christianity is being transformed through import rather than export missionization, while also being reconfigured through current political events and sociocultural shifts.[10] The act of willing conversion in the contemporary context pushes us to ask more questions, including: What does it mean to join a religious community that is often in philosophical dissonance with the sociopolitical structure of one's homeland? I suggest that an example of these import interventions is evident in the beliefs and actions of Appalachian converts who sought out ROCOR because they understood it to be an anti-Western, authentic, traditional form of ancient Christian spirituality that had the power to withstand and perhaps shape political institutions. Russian Orthodoxy offered converts a stalwart type of Christianity—one that could undergo the trials of both Russian socialism and American secularism, emerging on the other side as a bastion of religious purity, traditional piety, and conservative morality. Through conversion, not only were their spiritual needs met, but converts, most of whom were already deeply conservative, also found a political haven that provided them with a historical model of church-state relations and contemporary theo-political projects they could map onto the United States.

Between 2017 and 2018, less than 10 percent of the St. John's parish members were ethnic Russians, while all, save one of St. Basil's inhabitants, were non-Russian.[11] In spite of this, these converts were not only dedicated to Russian Orthodoxy, they are also highly supportive, on the whole, of a political framework, perhaps alt-right to varying degrees, through which they believed their ultra-conservative, Christian worldviews could be expanded in the United States and beyond. New forms of deep political conservatism in the United States are most readily seen in their large-scale public forms, such as in the 2016 presidential election, where religious conservatives in rural areas helped Trump win the White House, in the support for Brexit across the Atlantic, and even in the January 6th Capitol Siege. Pundits and analysts have offered reasons for why the United States is experiencing a growing tide of religiopolitical conservatism, or what might be better termed traditionalism, through reinforcing long-held stereotypes about what it means to be an American conservative Christian. Yet, just as a digital photograph is composed of individual pixels, the macro form of conservatism is, at the micro level, made up of actors, social structures, and systems of power that together comprise not only a new political trajectory for many parts of Western society, but also a shift in national loyalties.[12] While my research is in the United States, specifically rural Appalachia, the trends that are present in this area are part of a larger network of political movements around the world. The upswing in ideologies of conservative, often Christian-based, nationalism globally allows for scholars of American religion(s) to think more broadly about cross-cultural issues in a way that positions the

POLITICAL IDEOLOGIES IN ORTHODOX APPALACHIA

United States as one site among many that is continually transforming through religiopolitical changes.

From the culture wars of the Reagan administration to Sarah Palin's Tea Party–supported 2008 vice-presidential bid, scholars are quick to point out how the 1970s Moral Majority impact can still be felt in the New Christian Right.[13] However, the new forms of conservatism, emboldened during the 2016 presidential election, are different in many ways from the ideologies of Jerry Falwell, Pat Robertson, and Billy Graham. With the increasingly quick shift from the right to the far right, and even the alt-right, Christians are often anything but conservative in terms of their political ideologies. Furthermore, scholarship on anti-Semitism, racism, homophobia, and transphobia attached to this new religious right suggests that the internal politics of the ultra-conservative base is shifting away from a rhetoric of boundary making to active, sometimes violent, forms of social separation.[14] While the language of converts to ROCOR was peppered with a rhetoric of alterity regarding the secular Western world and its sinful liberal ways, there tended to be a lack of physical violence attached to their verbal and written beliefs. Given their far-right political leanings, the Woodford community could be considered under the umbrella of the alt-right, a movement that is one of the new right-wing political forms gaining traction globally. To say that believers in this community were alt-right might be pejoratively accurate, yet it does a disservice to understanding the distinct forms of political ideologies springing up around the religious traditions and values these believers held dear; doing so flattens the layered history and cultural complexities of both Appalachia and the Russian Orthodox Church.[15]

One Sunday afternoon in late summer, I sat down for a chat with Fr. Basil, the parish deacon, and his wife, Matushka Emilia, in their home just a short walk from the monastery. When they first became Orthodox Christians in the early 2000s, they attended an Antiochian parish in a neighboring state. As their spiritual journeys evolved, so too did their political beliefs, which ultimately led to their move to Woodford to become part of the ROCOR community. Between brief power outages caused by daily summer thunderstorms, they explained how their political leanings were related to their religious worldviews. Fr. Basil considered himself a reactionary monarchist, while his wife, when thinking about politics on a spectrum of right (conservative) to left (liberal), believed she was "as far right as it gets."[16] "Very right" or "very conservative" were often identification markers that converts used to explain how they saw themselves in relationship to the American political system. There were quite a few political ideologies floating around within the Russian-Appalachian Orthodox community: paleoconservatism, monarchism, populism, nationalism (for the adopted Russian father/motherland), traditionalism, and even fascism.[17]

While all of these beliefs are found in clustered formations that seem to constitute the alt-right, the Orthodox group in Woodford rarely indicated the overt
racist or supremacist tendencies of those typically associated with alt-right
movements, although there were outliers.

At St. John's parish, two men—Albert and Benny—became catechumens;
they both ascribed to either white supremacy or white nationalism. Often, they
could be found at parish social gatherings talking openly about white power,
their fears of becoming minorities in the United States, and their disdain for
"the Jews." A perusal of Benny's Facebook feed found scores of Nazi, alt-right,
and white nationalism propaganda, often in memes, which seems to be the
preferred form of digital output by the alt-right, scattered among quotes from
Russian Orthodox elders and Vladimir Putin. Once the parish priest, Fr. Cyril,
became aware of their ideological beliefs, he talked extensively with both men
and their wives in order to explain that ROCOR does not subscribe to hate
beliefs or actions.[18] Albert, who seemed to have a public change of heart, stayed,
while Benny left, never to return during the time I was in Woodford. Most
assuredly there were members of the Appalachian ROCOR community who
would self-identify as alt-right. Furthermore, most, aligning ideologically with
one of the core tenets of the alt-right, saw little to no value in the American
conservative project, which they believed had become too liberal and corrupt
to possess the moral standards needed to save the United States. Thus, they
looked to Russia for an alternative political model that could alleviate their
apocalyptic worries about social and moral decay by an assumed unification
of church with state.[19]

Third Rome and Tsar Putin

Many converts living in Appalachia found in Russian President Vladimir Putin
the strong embodiment of their theo-political ideas—someone who, through
his political office, was supporting the expansion of socially conservative Christianity and morality throughout the former Soviet Union, perhaps even the
world. Yet Orthodox Appalachians' glorification of Putin as the "last true
statesman" was symptomatic of something larger than a desire to link themselves politically with their adopted religious homeland. It was part of their
apocalyptic politics fueled by moral panic. Russia, then, became a salvific
figure on the global religiopolitical scene, offering believers an example of how
to avoid the impending doom brought on by secularism. This was made evident
to me when one member of the Woodford community spoke of crowning
Vladimir Putin tsar and letting him rule for life. The idea of Russia as a messianic figure in global politics is not a new concept, and certainly not a quiet

one in Russian conservative thought. Aleksandr Dugin, seemingly a favorite thinker among many young male ROCOR converts I have encountered, suggested in the early 2000s that Russia could save the world from a moral apocalypse.[20] While Putin's popularity among Russian Orthodox Christians and conservative Russian ideologues in his home country is to be expected, it is the unexpected embrace of the leader, particularly among American converts to ROCOR, that offers us a glimpse into the changing forms of a transnational religion and the global flows of political ideology.[21] Especially since the reunification of ROCOR with the Moscow Patriarchate, during Putin's tenure, converts seemingly shifted away from fears of a cozy church-state relationship that prompted the historical origins of ROCOR, choosing instead to enthusiastically endorse the public fondness Patriarch Kirill seemed to have for Putin.[22] Crucial to understanding the attraction converts had to Putin's new conservative form of Russian government is the Russian Orthodox emphasis on Russia as the holy heir of Byzantium.

Russian Orthodox Christian converts with whom I worked were seemingly drawn to Vladimir Putin because of the theo-political teachings of ROCOR, particularly the idea that Moscow is the "Third Rome."[23] While scholars debate the actual meaning behind the term—whether it was meant to convey the historical downfall of both empires or give credence to Russia's place in Orthodox Christianity—it is a vital theological idea in the hearts and minds of many converts.[24] Theologically, Moscow as a Third Rome belies the imperialistic notions of dominance that accompany this title, something that is crucial in understanding the power dynamics of the relationship between the monarchy and the Church.[25] Outside of religious connotations, research on Moscow as the "Third Rome" abounds, for it has proved to be a vital component of Russian political philosophy regarding empire, expansion, and culture.[26] As Dmitri Sidorov points out, the term unites eschatology with imperial geopolitics; with the title came a message that the Third Rome would be the last, a key idea in the formulation of Russian messianic ideology and expansion.[27] The geopolitics attached to Moscow as the Third Rome is not limited to the age of the tsars; indeed it had very little influence during the late eighteenth and nineteenth centuries.[28] Rather, as Justyna Doroszczyk notes, it came into vogue in the nineteenth century and is currently a very present tool of a Russian political mission to separate "the 'rotting' western world and the Russian world, which manifests as a cradle of traditional, conservative values that individualistic, materialistic Western civilisation has rejected."[29]

Despite its historical complexities, Moscow as the Third and/or final Rome is not limited to the realm of philosophical queries; it is alive in the ideological beliefs of many Russian Orthodox Christians. In Appalachian Russian

Orthodox circles, Moscow was often referred to as the "Third Rome" in off-the-cuff, everyday conversations. Converts would mention this idea as more than just a political paradigm; they would see it as an apocalyptic prophecy—one that held special significance since the murder of the Romanovs and the end of the U.S.S.R. Fr. Tryphon at St. Basil's monastery, stressed how this idea, which might be controversial in other Orthodox jurisdictions, was vital in understanding the hagiography of Tsar-Martyr Nicholas II and believers' conceptions of religion, politics, and hierarchy on a global scale.[30] Throughout my year in Appalachia, I witnessed numerous events during which references were made to the holy, God-pleasing Orthodox kings, queens, and other monarchs. Every Saturday night vigil made reference to Tsar-Martyr Nicholas II and the rest of the Russian royal family murdered by the Bolsheviks; they were commemorated not because of their life and death, but because of their office, their status as monarchic rulers. With these invocations came the assumption that political authority, when correctly constructed, was created by God to promote a society in which there was no separation between church and state, between God and civil authorities.

For many in the Woodford community, Putin was seen as the natural political successor to Tsar Nicholas II. As one convert exclaimed when explaining why he supported Putin's political maneuvers, "He's an echo of something that used to exist in the person of Tsar Nicholas." This statement highlights how believers mapped historical people, ideas, and narratives onto the current Russian political administration in an imaginative effort to unite the imperial structure of prerevolutionary Orthodoxy with Putin's dwindling *Russkii mir* project.[31] Founded in 2007, the foundation seeks to promote the development of Russian culture and language around the globe. While the foundation is not directly linked to the Moscow Patriarchate, it is indicative of an ideological framework in Russia that emphasizes traditionalist notions of nation and conservative understandings of personhood. In the post-Soviet period, both the Russian Orthodox Church and the Putin administration seem to use conservatism as a modern worldbuilding project in order to defend Russia's mythic cultural status as a unique civilization that possesses distinct anti-Western ideologies.[32] The negative propaganda used by the Russian Orthodox Church toward the Western world, particularly Europe and the United States, emphasizes the traditional morals of Russian society, juxtaposing them with the vulgarity of secularism. With Orthodoxy's resurgence or rebirth after the end of communism, missionization became bedfellows with flourishing state-approved projects of nostalgic nationalism, such as *Russkii mir*, creating an ethos that allowed for the Church and the state to become ever closer ideologically.[33]

Marlene Laruelle, in her research on monarchist leanings in contemporary Russia, drawing on quantitative data, showed that by 2018, Nicholas II was one of the most popular historical figures in Russian contemporary history, with Stalin and Lenin following closely behind.[34] Despite the fact that the Russian government has little concern for Nicholas II or support for tsarist ideologies, they are deeply connected to the ROC, which has an ideological bent toward monarchist ideas. As Mikhail Suslov aptly notes, the post-Soviet ROC is creating a monarchist ideology "from scratch," drawing on theological paradigms to help shape both political movements in Russia and a religiopolitical image of the homeland as Holy Rus' in the post-Soviet imagination.[35] The close relationship between the ROC and Vladimir Putin's regime during the 2010s signaled for many in ROCOR convert communities that Russia was once again becoming a beacon of Christian fortitude. It also seemed to signal that the ROC was ready to embrace the more traditional, prerevolutionary spiritual ethos—one that ROCOR had built its identity on in the early part of the twentieth century. The embrace of tsarist nostalgia by the ROC after perestroika, particularly through their focus on the Royal Martyrs, found appeal among converts who were already tied spiritually to Russia, and who were living at the fringes of American politics.

While American conversions to ROCOR, like that of Father Seraphim Rose, occurred prior to perestroika, it was after that, particularly starting in the 1990s, that non-Russians who strongly identified with or were part of the Russian Church, such as Nun Nectaria McLees, were beginning to write about the socioreligious trajectory of Russia with a nostalgic bent:

> Today, with the advent of reform and the resulting break-up of Communist rule many Russians have begun looking to the past for a key to their future. A rising tide of monarchist sentiment has become the symbol of a nationwide rejection of communism. As much as it represents a return to traditional religious values and the reawakening of cultural integrity it is useful.[36]

Looking to the past, particularly prerevolutionary, tsarist Russia was key for converts, for in it they found a much closer relationship between the Church and governmental leaders. Viewing the Church through a nostalgic lens, converts in Woodford and other ROCOR converts who took to social media platforms, drew on the language of monarchy and divinely influenced governance to narrate a new vision, a new world for both themselves and Russia. Converts' "practices of memorializing" were ethically charged forms of collective memory that reinterpreted the tsar's martyrdom through the current political situation, collapsing time to authenticate somehow the new world, the new reality they constructed and continued to build.[37]

The Byzantine idea of *symphonia* that converts so deeply desired—"the dual role of temporal and ecclesiastical authorities"—was exemplified in their oral hagiographies of Prince Vladimir of Kiev, Tsar Nicholas II, and other seemingly holy officials who served at divine behest in tandem with their patriarchic contemporaries.[38] Grappling with the current lack of any monarchic, God-ordained figurehead in traditionally Orthodox countries, many converts in the North American Orthodox diaspora have begun constructing ways through which they sensorially encountered kingship within a democracy—through the legitimization of Tsar-Martyr Nicholas's relics, their cyber celebrations for the feast of St. Vladimir, the Prince of ancient Rus', and their oral ardor for the seemingly newest heir to the Third Rome, Vladimir Putin.[39] Given the diasporic nature of ROCOR and Russian Orthodoxy it is no wonder that believers, cradle and convert, turned to the Internet to find fellow travelers. This is one of the ways in which narratives and ideas about monarchism and Vladimir Putin were and still are disseminated and reinforced by convert clergy and laity. I draw on these sources, since the men and women with whom I worked often referenced them during conversations with me and each other.

The Two Vladimirs

In the summer of 2018, two important milestones in Russian Orthodox history occurred: the 100th anniversary of the murder of the Romanovs and the 1,030th anniversary of the Christianization of Kievan Rus' in 888. Both events held deep significance for Orthodox Christians in Russia and in the United States. As the abbot of St. Basil's monastery explained in his luncheon address on the feast of the Royal Martyrs, while the Romanovs might not seem that significant to most people in Western societies, they were very important in the Orthodox hollers of West Virginia, where their examples of repentance showed God-pleasing leadership. Just over two weeks later, the feast of St. Vladimir, Prince of Rus', was celebrated with great fanfare. While Tsar-Martyr Nicholas II held a special place in this community, St. Vladimir was seen as the key through which the pagan lands of Rus' became united as the powerful Holy Mother Russia. Hours before the monastic community in Woodford gathered to celebrate the festal Divine Liturgy of St. Vladimir, the Russian president, accompanied by His Holiness Patriarch Kirill, processed to a highly contested monument of Vladimir the Great in Moscow.[40] On the feast day of St. Vladimir, Putin, flanked by two patriarchs, standing in the shadow of his namesake, gazed up at the face of the statue.[41] Erected in 2016, the monument, which is almost sixty feet high, was met with a great deal of outcry given not only its size but also its original intended location—on one of the hills overlooking the Moscow River in remembrance of the mass baptisms that took place in the Dnieper River during the reign of Prince Vladimir. The opposition, which included an online petition on change.org, may have led to the shift in statue size and location. Smaller in stature after the pushback, and now situated closer to the Kremlin, news outlets hinted that the statue might be a tribute for a different Vladimir than the one it depicts. Over the course of the festal weekend, parishioners made note of the procession in passing and in conversations. Fr. Cyril said longingly, "You definitely wouldn't see that here," referring to the United States.

Patriarch Kirill, in his address in front of the statue, which is not far from the gates of the Kremlin, linked the prince to the current president of the Federation, proclaiming that it was no coincidence that Putin bore the prince's name and that he was creating or even cultivating social change in the world.[42] This cultivation was felt not only in Russia, but in the United States, where converts focused on nationalism and conservatism as part of the traditional way of life they wish to ascribe to fully. For converts, the festal celebration of St. Vladimir was part of their imaginative worldbuilding process through which they constructed their varied social realities. The holy leadership of Prince St. Vladimir seemed to invigorate their monarchic desires even more despite concerns over mixing of religion and politics. Father Tryphon elaborated:

> Maybe we are grasping at straws with Putin and Russia and everything like that, and maybe it's, you know, this is still just the prelude to the catastrophic end of all things, but there's still a glimmer. Anyone who is Orthodox, that part of their heart has been awaked to some extent.
> . . . Orthodoxy is directly talking to that part of us. And Russia is the only thing that you can look at in the outside world that corresponds in any sense to this hunger that we all of a sudden feel—and we all feel it. There has to be something I can love and bow down to for the sake of God, because this is who Christ gave to us. We don't choose who our fathers are. We don't choose who our kings are. It's something that is given by God and for that reason, because it's an icon of him, it's intrinsically worthy of love, even if they do a bad job of it.

Father Tryphon's words highlighted the importance of position rather than person. Thus, it is not Putin himself that believers desired; it was someone who could return Russia to its prerevolutionary state by bringing back the monarchy, and thereby affect sociopolitical change on a global scale. Because of his affiliation with the Russian Orthodox Church and his well-marketed piety, Putin seemed to be an answer to believers' prayers, for he had the potential to not only make Russia great again, but also make America, by extension, *holy* again. Many in the community were disappointed to see that this was something that Donald Trump did not promise citizens of the United States during his presidential campaign.

Putin Saves the World

"The only thing that can save the world is Russia," Father Tryphon said to me as he stroked his curly black beard. At 31, his self-guesstimated age, since those inside the monastery did not celebrate birthdays, Father Tryphon was one of the younger priest-monks in residence. He had the further distinction of being the dean, ensuring that the monastery ran smoothly so that the abbot could tend to the spiritual rather than administrative needs of the community. A convert from fundamentalist, Calvinist Evangelicalism by way of Eastern esoteric mysticism, Father Tryphon tended to be one of the most outspoken Putin supporters in the brotherhood, where public discussion of politics was frowned upon typically. Besides his work as a priest, dean, and treasurer at the monastery, Father Tryphon also wrote a semi-anonymous blog about spirituality and culture that was shared readily across the social media platforms of ROCOR believers. During our conversations, and through an exploration of his digital scholarship, it became quite evident that the notion of a holy or righteous leader was crucial to Father Tryphon's understanding of traditional Orthodox Christianity.

In a similar fashion to many of the believers in this community, Father Tryphon lamented the moral decline of the West, which he believed had brought with it a supposed dismissal of authority, hierarchy, and patriarchy, something that created a void in the hearts of people:

> We don't have fathers. We don't have leaders. We have bureaucrats.
> We have people at the DMV—those are the people who rule over us
> now. Who can love that? So, you see, Putin, he's just a man, he's not
> any kind of savior or hero, he's an okay political leader, but he's a man
> of faith. And he's an echo of something that used to exist in the person of Tsar Nicholas—Tsar-*Martyr* Nicholas. And even that glimmer—
> we can't help but love that and wish that there were more of that in
> the world. Kids know this stuff. You don't open up children's books
> and read about the minister of transportation; you read about princes
> and kings.[43]

Fr. Tryphon's words echo that of Nun Nectaria McLees, an Orthodox author whom the hieromonk recommended to me several times during our conversations. In her writings about the Royal Martyr, Empress Alexandra Romanov, McLees stresses the importance of a monarch as a father figure:

> The hunger of the modern world for personal and political freedom has all but abolished monarchy, especially Christian monarchy, and is now "liberating" us from the strictures of traditional moral standards and family ties. Perhaps it is time to ask whether if in ridding ourselves of monarchical "tyrants" we haven't also thrown overboard a natural longing in man to have a national father as well as a personal one; that even an incompetent father feeds a hunger in the soul of men and nations that will never be satisfied by the wholesale acquisition of personal freedoms. Perhaps in some deep way we have orphaned ourselves.[44]

The notion of a monarch as a father figure is pervasive in ROCOR, a hierarchical, gender-stratified form of Christianity seemingly preoccupied with traditional gender roles, the divine expressions of the family, and correct patriarchal forms of authority.

Many laity at the parish also expressed hopeful desires for godly monarchic powers to return to Russia and perhaps spread to the United States. A majority of converts I interviewed considered themselves monarchists, although they stressed that ideology without application is pointless. They wanted monarchism not only in theory but also in practice. One Monday afternoon, as the volunteer hours at St. John's food pantry came to an end, Angus stepped back into the church after carrying groceries to the car for a client. Heading down the stairs to the kitchen, he turned and said, "You know, I found this group the other day on Facebook that sums up my beliefs perfectly and they have regional chapters. It's called the Russian Imperial Union. I'm so excited! This is great." A cursory examination of the group's Facebook "About" page in 2018 offered up the following information in both prerevolutionary Russian and modern English: "The Russian Imperial Union-Order is the oldest and largest organization of Russian legitimist monarchists. It was founded in 1929 in Paris by monarchist White Army officers."[45] The group honors the legacy of Tsar Nicholas and seeks to legitimate the foundation's patron HIH Grand Duchess Maria of Russia. A divorcée, descendant of the House of Romanov, and a distant cousin of Tsar Nicholas II, she resides in Spain with her son. Supporters, including many within the ROCOR community, viewed Duchess Maria as the "current Head of the Imperial House of Russia" and legitimate heir to the imperial throne that was once the seat of the Royal Martyr:

RIUO works toward the restoration of Russian Orthodox Monarchy; for the restoration of the legitimate Romanoff Dynasty to which the Russian people swore fidelity at the All-Land Council (Zemsky Sobor) in 1613, headed by the Dynastic Head the Sovereign Grand Duchess Maria Vladimirovna and her heir, Grand Duke Georgii Mikhailovich; for the preeminent position of the Orthodox Church in the life of Russian society and government; for the territorial wholeness and sovereignty of the Russian Empire; for the restoration of the Russian people in national development. The ideology of RIUO is based on the Holy Orthodox Christian Faith.[46]

This group, which was founded to manifest the fidelity of Russian people to the Orthodox monarchy, has become one among many digital havens for converts, particularly young males, to express their support of Russian nationalism, desire for a Christian monarchy, and the need to infuse the West with traditional, conservative values. In other words, it is part of the growing traditionalism expressed in Russian Orthodox culture. Thus, while some see Duchess Maria as the heir apparent to a new Orthodox-friendly monarchy, many simply want a strong leader, whatever his or her pedigree might be.

Putin as a Symptom: Diagnosing New Conservatism

Despite the differences in how the monastery and parish inhabitants understood the role of Vladimir Putin in church/state politics, both factions of the Orthodox community in Woodford tended to see Putin as figurehead who embodied their spiritual angst about the rapidly changing social fabric of American life. One of the overarching themes converts continually brought up was the idea that Vladimir Putin was one of very few politicians in the world who was not trying to actively destroy his country or people through liberal ideas associated with secularism. Finian was a middle-aged family man and a historian who converted to ROCOR shortly before I arrived in Woodford. Born and raised in West Virginia, he firmly supported Putin, going so far as to suggest that Russia should "crown him tsar and let him rule for life." For Finian, Putin was a strong political figure who had the moral backbone to align himself with Christianity through his increasing connectedness to Patriarch Kirill and the Russian Orthodox Church. The agenda of believers seemed to be one of reviving the so-called traditional influences of conservative Christianity in cultural formations in order to push back against Western values and secularism. In contemporary Russian theo-politics, Western secularism has also become a paradigm through which Russian alt-right philosophers, such as traditionalist Aleksandr Dugin, portray the United States as a land of hedonism, without strong, traditional moral values—a place that has lost its guiding compass of faith.

Alongside political philosophers, Orthodox leaders in Russia have also decried what they see as the social and moral decline of national culture. In 2014, Metropolitan Hilarion of Volokolamsk, chairman of the Department of External Church Relations, in an address regarding the theology of freedom, noted that "moral relativism and the all-is-permitted attitude are raised up as the basic principle of life" in "secularization under the guise of democracy."[47] As Dugin suggests in his primer on his projected fourth political theory, modernism is "the rot which conservatism seeks to reject."[48] For Dugin, liberalism (from both the left and right), communism, and fascism are three political trajectories that have all failed in some way or another; however, the fourth political theory is a struggle against the status quo that pushes back against all forms of modernity, industrialization, and globalization, seeking a return to tradition and theology as part of its Heideggerian-influenced ontological effort to save the world from a moral apocalypse.[49]

In late summer of 2018, while I was still in Appalachia, Dugin was interviewed by self-proclaimed Canadian traditionalist Lauren Southern, who asked him questions about reviving religion in the secular West. Dugin suggested that Western Christianity was suffering the effects of secularism, something that was felt far less by its Eastern cousins. Continuing, Dugin provocatively offered up the idea that the "Orthodox Church could play an important role in helping this Christian revival in the West."[50] "Religion is deep . . . ideologies are shallow," Dugin added during the same interview.[51] For many convert members of ROCOR, support for the Russian Orthodox Church was not simply devotion to a cultural form of Christianity; rather, it was a political stance, and one that aligned believers with Putin's push to Russianize the world through religion, culture, and traditional values. The Putin-supported reunification of the Moscow Patriarchate and ROCOR not only signaled the strengthening of global Orthodoxy in 2007; it also brought with it an expansion of Russian influence and power in the diasporic church, especially throughout North America and Europe.[52] Convert believers in Appalachia found Putin's support of Russian Orthodoxy encouraging; for they believed it signaled something larger than a tightening of relationship between the ROC and the Russian government; it opened the way for the potential return of the monarchy and the rise of a new tsar.

From West Virginia with Love

Only ten miles separate the parish and the monastery, but in terms of support for Vladimir Putin, their reasons were often light-years apart. While inhabitants of the monastery by and large seemed reticent, apart from Fr. Tryphon, to express political fealty to Putin, they often portrayed his role as almost apocalyptic in the future of global Christianity. Many monks drew upon the language of the Third Rome and the figure of Tsar-Martyr Nicholas II to portend what could happen in the face of growing secularism, and how Putin's push for Christianity in the public sphere might be the only thing that saves the world. In contrast, to some extent, members of St. John's parish viewed the president of the Russian Federation ideologically as a good candidate to promote Christian values globally. They tended to focus on current events that they heard about through various Russian government–sponsored media outlets or via word of mouth from ROCOR clergy who frequently visited Russia. On the whole, both sets of converts supported Putin, but for different ideological reasons. Beyond the Orthodox convert community, most of the Woodford residents I spoke with were in no way aligned with Vladimir Putin or Russian political ideologies, yet they often spoke of him with fondness or, at the very least, admiration.

The town mayor, who moved to the area as a child from the Pennsylvania Rustbelt, was from an Orthodox Hungarian background. One afternoon I sat down with him to chat about the area. He greeted me at the Woodford City Hall in a T-shirt and jeans with grease-covered hands: "I'd shake your hand, but I've been out back changing the oil in the fire truck."[53] A tall man, balding, with a dark tan, he was a former small business owner who worked for a nickel plant in the largest city nearby. At just over a year in office, the mayor stumped door-to-door during his campaign to get to know the residents, stressing a platform of economic stimulation and increased focus on fixing the aging infrastructure of the town. Not just a man of words, the mayor went right to work after the election, meeting with the city council to cut spending and create a budget that took the town from red to black by targeting the out-of-date water pipeline system. The mayor, in a similar fashion to many folks in town, believed the infrastructure and economy in Woodford were symptomatic of a decline in American standards and progress. While Vladimir Putin was not a key political figure for non-Orthodox Christians in the town, the mayor, who noted that most of the citizens of Woodford voted for Donald Trump in the 2016 presidential election, believed that both politicians share values that people in the community, and in the region more broadly, desired in their elected officials. "They're a lot alike, ya know?" the mayor said to me, "Trump and Putin. They're strong leaders. We need that. They get the job done. I don't care what they do in their free time."[54]

The mayor's statements echoed that of another elected official—at the state level—who was also from Woodford. A historian and member of the legislature,

Edward lived in the area his entire life, growing up just down the road from the current location of the monastery. On a rainy spring day, we met at a local diner, one of the few that had signs out touting that their employees had received Hep-A vaccinations, a virus that was running rampant throughout the region at the time. In his early thirties, Edward's buzzed black hair and large, round blue eyes gave him a youthful appearance. Over chili dogs, onion rings, and sweet tea we talked about the history of the county, particularly his publications about the formation of the towns and local government in the area, his job as a high school history teacher, the steady economic decline in West Virginia, and the sociality of mountain culture. As he fiddled with his high school ring and looked at the rain beating against the window, he recalled how regional views regarding the former Soviet Union were starting to change. During his youth, Russia was thought of in Cold War terms, with fear and apprehension surrounding anything to do with godless communism. In recent years, however, especially since the 2016 United States presidential election, as Edward specifically noted, the vocabulary regarding Russia was beginning to change. "My high school students say we should give him a chance," Edward said in reference to Putin. "They're getting that from someone, and it's probably their parents."[55] Raised in the Church of Christ denomination, in a community not far from the diner, Edward noted that the region had always skewed conservative at the presidential level, but that right and alt-right ideologies were on the rise among youth. Harkening back to sociologist Robert Wuthnow's study of moral rage in rural America, Edward's stories indicated that the combination of poverty and isolation may have led to an increasingly politicized lifestyle.[56]

Dean, a West Virginian ex-military convert to Russian Orthodoxy, husband to a Russian-born wife, and local schoolteacher, indicated that he had also seen a spike in conversations—both inside and outside of the classroom—about the importance of Vladimir Putin in global politics. Unlike his wife, Photini, who seemed reticent to support Putin wholeheartedly, Dean believed Putin might change the world for the better. Echoing the sentiments of Woodford's mayor, Dean, who was a slender man in his early fifties with graying hair and glasses, suggested Putin provided a new form of conservative moral governance that would not back down in the face of modern secularism. Shy and uncomfortable with crowds, Dean tended to stand at the periphery during social occasions at the parish, talking with male congregants or simply people watching. One-on-one, however, he was a different man altogether. "I'm angry," he yelled at me. "Do you want to know why?" Sitting at his dining room table in a craftsman-style two-story house about forty minutes from the parish, he expressed his outrage at not being heard, being looked over as a white male in what he saw

as an American progressive society too focused on minority rights. He was
worried about the increased "diversity" in his neighborhood, and he was fed
up with liberals. "I'm sick of it," he said. "Do you know what I have upstairs?
It might surprise you," Dean smiled. Pointing to the ceiling right above the
dining room table, he proudly proclaimed, "I have a safe full of weapons.
There's a war coming you know, and I want to be on the right side." For Dean,
who voted for Donald Trump in the 2016 election, Russia and Putin were the
right side, for they represented a return of traditional masculinity to the political world, one that would bring with it Christian values and morality to the
public sphere. While Dean was ready to take up arms for his adopted motherland, others seemed to have deep existential issues with understanding their
place in the world. One parishioner mentioned that he would not know which
side to fight for if a war broke out between Russia and the United States. Converts felt caught between two worlds in a tide of increasing political turmoil.
Were they Russian? American?

It was not only laypeople (non-clergy) who wrestled with these questions.
One of the main figureheads of the Orthodox community was the abbot of the
monastery, Fr. Spyridon. A midwestern convert by way of Catholicism, he was
a Benedictine monk before he converted to Russian Orthodoxy. Fr. Spyridon
drew on Cold War themes, noting how he believed that much of the issue
surrounding Russia and Putin was Western liberal bias at play. I cite him here
at length given the way in which he captured the sentiments of so many I spoke
with over the course of my time in the community:

> It used to be in the past it was the conservatives who were anti-Russian
> and the liberals who were pro-Russian; now it's all switched. A lot of it,
> as far as I'm concerned, is on a spiritual level. The two roles of our
> countries, as I knew as a child in the fifties, have completely reversed.
> Our country now represents anti-Christianity and Russia represents
> Christianity. It's really a complete reversal of roles. Russia is trying
> with all of its might to hold up Christian morality and Christian belief
> and defend Christians. President Putin is personally rebuilding all the
> churches in Syria that were destroyed. Not just Orthodox but Catholic
> and Uniates. He's rebuilding all of the churches there. There's no offer
> like that from America. There's no one speaking up for persecuted
> Christians except for Russia. There really isn't. But if Putin says some-
> thing or Patriarch Kirill says something, the liberal press tears them
> apart: *Who do you think you're fooling? No one believes you. You're just
> saying these things because you want to impress people. You want Amer-
> ican evangelicals to support you.* So, it's a kinda of a no-win situation.

No matter what Russia does, they'll still tear them apart. If they do something good, they'll say they're fake. That's the way the situation is now. We want to hear what they have to say, and if you're really listening to what they are saying, and if you look at the evidence in their country, I don't see how you can believe all these accusations against the Patriarch and against the president of Russia. I don't see how you can believe it, because you look at how their country is living and how they're turning their country away from . . . trying to turn it away from abortion, and sensuality, and immorality. You know, they're trying very much to do all that. No one else is at all, but part of these issues that Russia stands for in terms of morality are issues that the liberal press holds very dear—transgender rights, gay marriages, women priests, and women bishops—these are all issues that are very important to the liberals and to liberal Christianity in the West. Russia is the opposite of that. It stands for traditional morality and traditional beliefs, and so they just don't like Russia and they don't like the Russian Church—not at all. They think the Russian Church is simply a tool of Putin's government. They don't see any sincerity at all. They look at our church and they look at our services and they don't recognize anything, so they dismiss it. I don't know what the future is gonna hold, if this thing doesn't change and it keeps getting worse, I don't know what that's going to mean for us as Russian Orthodox Christians, as American converts to the Russian Church.[57]

Fr. Spyridon's apocalyptic worries of persecution echoed that of most converts in Woodford, where it seemed as if the only Orthodox people not caught up in the grip of Putin fever were Russians themselves.

While communities of like-minded people often have overarching beliefs and ideologies, there are always dissenting opinions.[58] With the case of Appalachian Russian Orthodox Christians, the dissenters came in the form of Russian-born believers. Photini—Dean's wife—who immigrated to the United States in the early 2000s after receiving her doctorate, worried that Putin's relationship with the Church was not as picturesque as religious leaders and Russian media outlets let on. Two other Russian women in the parish—Veronica and Masha—also worried that converts to the Russian Orthodox Church were too eager in their embrace of President Vladimir Putin and his political ideologies. Both women saw a turn for the worse in Russian economics, culture, and society since perestroika.[59] Veronica, a former schoolteacher, moved from a small village in Russia to the United States for the sake of economic survival during Boris Yeltsin's tenure. "I hate Yeltsin," she said. "What he did to our country. . . ." In her late fifties, Veronica was a spry woman with short curly ash-blonde hair, who favored turquoise jewelry and white lace outfits. At one of the biweekly summer gatherings of women at Masha's house, I was the only other attendee besides the two women, since most of the female parishioners were either on vacation or attending a ROCOR summer camp with their children. Veronica and Masha decided to talk with me about their feelings surrounding convert beliefs, the relationship between Russia and the United States, and how they felt about Putin.

"It's kind of weird," Veronica chuckled in reference to Americans converting to Russian Orthodoxy. "Maybe it's because it is just in our blood, in our bones."[60] Both women found, in some respects, a totalizing conversion—that of complete enculturation, political and otherwise—to be off-putting. Masha's partner, Reynolds, converted to Orthodoxy after falling in love with her. However, his attraction to Russian political ideologies did not stem from his relationship with Masha, but rather his dedication to conservative values—political, moral, social, and economic. Whereas Reynolds saw Putin and, to a lesser extent, Trump, as strong figures with positive transformative social capabilities, Masha saw both leaders creating downward spirals for otherwise open, democratic cultures. For both Masha and Veronica, the Soviet Union was imperfect but supportive. "Things were so much better during the Soviet Union. I'm very disappointed in Putin," Veronica sighed. The idea that converts could support monarchic theories and desire the return of tsarist Russia, even Tsar Putin, was appalling to both women. As Veronica poured rose-scented tea, she shook her head violently and said loudly, "The tsar is never coming back. Ridiculous."[61] One of the few Russians in the community who openly supported tsarist tendencies and Vladimir Putin's ideologies was the parish priest's wife—Matushka Olga—who immigrated from Kazakhstan as a young adult. After spending a year conversing with Matushka Olga, it was evident that her ideas about the Russian government and Putin were deeply affected by Father Cyril, a convert. Given the overall leeriness with which many Russian-born ROCOR members in this community approached Russia's political regime, it begs the question as to why converts were so attracted to Vladimir Putin, his seemingly illiberal and or autocratic politics, and the potential return of kingship to Holy (adopted) Mother Russia.

Reactionary Politics as Heavenly Ontologies

It seems curious that American converts to ROCOR would support a government that is not their own, since church and state are popularly projected and understood as separate entities within the United States. The convert support of Putin seemed to be part of a reactionary move that was bound up with the politics of conversion. This presses at a puzzle. Most members of the Orthodox community in Woodford considered themselves to be quite conservative in terms of American politics. Yet their notions of monarchism, emphasis on illiberal political ideologies, and a potential return of tsarist rule to a place thousands of miles from them was far from conservative. These ideas lend themselves quite readily to the label of far-right reactionary politics. As historian of American politics Mark Lilla writes, "Reactionaries are not conservatives. This is the first thing to be understood about them. They are, in their own way, just as radical as revolutionaries and just as firmly in the grip of historical imaginings."[62] In this case, the reactionary movement among the Appalachian convert community highlighted issues of purity and patriarchy, expressed through their ultra-conservative understandings of gender, sexuality, and the roles women and men should have in the Church, the domestic sphere, and society more broadly.

Despite the lack of moral panic over race that is often associated with far- or alt-right communities, there was a great deal of disdain surrounding secular understandings of gender and sexuality in the community. The fear stemmed from the "liberal" disruption of the gender binary in Western culture, which they believed was the work of feminists, homosexuals, and the transgender movement.[63] Outrage over gender and body positivity, the increasing usage of gender neutral pronouns, and the "abomination" of transgender "propaganda" were part of conversations at the food pantry, during *trapeza* (lunch in the refectory), at events and outings where converts gathered together, such as potlucks, open houses, and movie nights, while also being found in the social media of believers and the blog writings of Fr. Tryphon. In one popular post, he wrote, "Men are men. Women are women. And there is no pronoun nor bodily disfigurement in the world that can change that basic fact of life. To go to war with reality is always a losing proposition, and to encourage your child to fight that war is neither love nor compassion, but only a tragedy waiting to unfold."[64]

Outrage over the shifting gender and sexual dynamics in the United States was part of the reactionary political process by which ROCOR converts created dichotomous boundary-making binaries—us versus them, conservative versus liberal, Christian versus secular, traditional versus progressive. In this way, they formed the structure of their social world. These taxonomies of ideology create, in the Bourdieuian sense, limits "commonly called the *sense of reality*, that is, the correspondence between the objective classes and the internalized classes, social structures and mental structures, which is the basis of the most ineradicable adherence to the established order."[65] One could also argue, that by extension, these boundary-building projects are the basis of religio-social fascism. At its core, the community's focus on heterosexuality seemed to be linked not only to boundary-making schemes, but also to monarchism, patriarchy, and hierarchy as traditional markers for correct belief and practice.

One of the more popular blogs for traditional Orthodox Christians in the late 2010s was called *The Sobornost*, a term that defies easy translation, but which generally has the connotation of spiritual community within ROCOR. It was an anonymous blog, with authors located somewhere in the so-called Western world. In 2018, the "About Us" page proclaimed: "We are at a turning point with the resurgence of Holy Russia, and so we believe this is a fine opportunity to express and promote the bond of unity that has carried us through some of the most difficult times in the history of the Church: The Traditional Orthodox Worldview!"[66] The notion of a worldview was bound up with familial and ecclesial structures, as the author stated:

> We create community beginning with the nuclear family as well as
> ecclesial family (Church), helping one another around our nuclear
> and ecclesial family. Gender identity is important in these families to
> retain the structural integrity of the community at large. With gender
> confusion comes community confusion. The husband and wife are
> "king and queen" of the nuclear family in that the divinity is managed
> through them to build the family "kingdom." This man and woman
> take up the royalty of Christ in that we use his power in humility and
> great sacrifice as Christ did for us.[67]

The coupling of a man and woman in the sacrament of Holy Matrimony in the Orthodox Church is considered an example of royal martyrdom in many respects. At the beginning of the ceremony, the holy God-ordained kings and queens are commemorated, foreshadowing the crowning of the couple that will happen toward the end of the ceremony. Thus marriage, in the Orthodox worldview, encapsulates both social insularity and monarchic political ideologies.

Among adherents to ROCOR, creating exclusionary social boundaries was not only present in the United States. Igumen Phillip (Ryabykh), one of the most prominent clerics in the Moscow Patriarchate, who also happened to be the church's representative to the European Union, in an interview with pravoslavie.ru, a Russian Orthodox digital media site, provided key ways in which societies, even countries, should address the relationship between church and state.[68] Drawing examples from Russian and Byzantine history, Igumen Phillip focused on the idea of *symphonia*, the importance of Godly governmental structures, and Christian practices of piety and power that create cultures of morality.[69] Opposition to abortion, euthanasia, and homosexuality, which were three of the main issues raised by Orthodox converts in Appalachia, were at the heart of the two-part article.[70] He explained that societies should be built on traditional Christian values of morality, which he did not believe were oppressive:

> I don't believe that Christian values are restrictive or limiting. They give a positive foundation to society and they orient people to the good. In a country where a majority of people are either practicing or culturally Christian, and where it is possible for religious or moral minorities to live out their differing beliefs in the private sphere, Christian society can legitimately promote these positive norms— a spiritually oriented life, creativity, family, constructive work, and useful civic and social activities.

Here the sense of limits, the power of belief, and the organization of classes constitute what Bourdieu might consider a *habitus*, for these create a "construction of reality" that helps believers reproduce distinctive, constrictive social formations that aid their worldbuilding projects.[71] These formations were adhered to tightly by many conservative Orthodox Christians in Woodford, for they believed that it was dangerous "to confuse the borders between the Church's teaching and a worldly outlook."[72] Social partitioning seemed to create spiritual safety.

Configurations of the external world are, within Orthodox theology, expressions of the inner state—that of the soul. As Igumen Phillip writes:

> If you have the inner state of an Orthodox Christian, you won't feel the need to be modern, and if, for example, you are a woman and your head is uncovered or you are wearing trousers in church, you will find yourself uncomfortable. If you are a man wearing an earring, you know that you have stepped out of the stream of tradition, and you eventually will feel that you have gone against God's grace by adopting these fashions. It will be the prompting of your own conscience to have a traditional appearance, the imperative of your soul.[73]

The priority in the preceding passage is placed on being traditional as a sign of one's spiritual health and devotion to God. Tradition is vital for correct belief and practice, for those are two social expressions of true religiosity and political positionality that would allow one to be part of ROCOR convert worlds. This was most assuredly the case in ROCOR Appalachia, where a bowl of scarves and skirts could be found by the door in the *narthex*, or lobby, in order to "cover up" women who did not follow protocol. However, in terms of women, it was more than just their garments that should be traditional; it was also their behavior and their understanding of their divinely ordered gender roles in both liturgical spaces and the domestic sphere.

In the late spring of 2018, the parish hosted a Russian festival in order to raise money for the food pantry, which provided groceries to roughly thirty non-Orthodox families on a weekly basis. During the event, Fr. Cyril offered church tours to guests, many of whom had never stepped foot in an Orthodox parish before that day. Several days after the event, I was teaching a parishioner how to film documentary footage and he mentioned that a visitor, a woman, had walked through the royal doors of the iconostasis. "What happened?" I asked. He relayed that the priest had "pulled her out and then blessed the altar with holy water to get rid of anything bad." "Why? Is that what you do when non-Orthodox people enter the altar area?" "No," he countered, "it's because she was a woman." The conservative views and treatment of women in many ROCOR convert communities was often seen to be spiritually positive, for the strict segregation of the sexes highlighted their fervent traditionalism. The narrative of securing boundaries for female participation was an ongoing theme in Russian Orthodox literature, the blogosphere, and daily conversations with parishioners. In his article on church and state, Father Artemy described one of his visits to an Orthodox community in France, where he notes that the degree of liberalism there is "not only astonishing but frightful."[74] In this case, the liberalism stemmed from the priests' lack of teaching regarding the role of women in the church and when they should abstain from communion. Fr. Artemy was appalled that "some Orthodox priests in France consider it *de mauvais ton* [bad taste] to mention abstaining from Holy Communion during women's "critical days."[75] One female pilgrim at St. Basil's recalled that during a prior visit she had been questioned by the monks regarding menstruation while she was in line to receive Holy Communion. It took that visitor a good deal of time to get over that event and return to the monastery.

Within ROCOR, it is the job of spiritual fathers to monitor how and in what ways men and especially women participate in the church, just as it should be the job of a monarch to guide a country. However, where I worked, women often monitored each other and themselves in public and semi-public ways. Often, I had women who did not partake in Communion tell me the reason was their monthly cycle, as if I was keeping tabs on them and would report back to the priest. At the monastery, where the boundaries for the sexes were rigid and highly enforced, women could only receive Communion after all the monks, laymen, and the nuns went through the line. As soon as Mother (Nun) Magdalena went through the line, Matushka Emilia would rush to get behind her, for she believed that the wives of clergy ranked above other women.

If a woman who was not married to a clergyman got in line before her, Matushka Emilia would correct her immediately. Another matushka told me that this was a pious Russian custom, but she found it quite silly. Enforcement of these "rough divisions between the male and female world" enable participants to more readily "grasp the dialectic of objectification and embodiment" within the spaces of a community.[76]

Certainly, this type of purity partitioning was not the worldbuilding work of ROCOR convert Christians alone.[77] Often within a wide variety of conservative forms of Christianity, this type of rhetoric appears.[78] Yet Russian Orthodoxy, even outside of Russia, has created structural realities that are not enmeshed in the fabric of modernity. Nor are they wholly focused on New Testament–era beliefs and practices in ways that many Protestant denominations desire to recreate the ancient or "original" form of Christianity. ROCOR converts' lives were not affected by this form of Christianity; their lives *were* Russian Orthodox Christianity lived out, expressed in their ritualized embodied practices, participation in the liturgical calendar, and socio-spiritual ideologies. It was an imagined nostalgia for prerevolutionary Russian Orthodox morality and traditionalism that was manifest in the community's material and symbolic language and beliefs.[79] Gendered boundaries were one of the main ways these nostalgic structures of religious purity, of morally traditional conservatism were reinforced as the building blocks of their social world. Yet it was also present in the devotion to God-ordained leadership, whether it was in the form of St. Vladimir, Tsar-Martyr Nicholas II, or President Putin. These beliefs were not ethereal; rather they were concrete and expressed in material ways, from headscarves to the four-by-six-foot banner of Tsar-Martyr Nicholas II with the phrase *Slava Rusi* ("Glory to Russia") which the monks joyfully affixed to the porch of the refectory on the feast day of the saint (see fig. 6).

If ROCOR and Russian Orthodoxy more broadly were the structural foundation of their worldview(s) (often talked about in Orthodox writings as theological anthropology—how humans relate to God and each other), it makes sense that ROCOR believers in West Virginia were, by and large, monarchists, for their theology teaches that God appoints kings to rule over nations and peoples.[80] Often during sit-down conversations, questions about politics seemed to confuse converts, or at the very least agitate them. Numerous times they would employ a similar phrase: "I don't like to talk about politics." While their reasons for feeling uneasy about political conversations varied, they often emphasized how they preferred to keep their minds on religious ideas, rather than worldly ones. Matushka Emilia explained that it was hard for her to talk about politics because the basis of modern, secular political cultures were so far removed from her religiously tinted worldview. Her statement echoed that of

Figure 6. Tsar Holler (Photograph by author, July 2018)

others in the community who believed that politics and religion were separate
value systems that should not be thought about tandem. Converts would quote
a phrase from the antiphons sung during the Divine Liturgy, which is translated
generally as, "Put not your trust in princes and sons of men in whom there is
no salvation," although it depends on the jurisdiction. At the same time, while
believers noted that worldly salvation was based in God alone, they also placed
great stock in political leaders who would promote their social policies, religious
ideologies, and moral viewpoints. In a sense, religion was political belief.
ROCOR was the standard by which all their social, moral, and economic decisions were made.[81] As Blessed Fr. Seraphim Rose said, "Orthodoxy is life. If
we don't live Orthodoxy, we simply are not Orthodox, no matter what formal
beliefs we might hold."[82]

Praxis Makes Perfect

Life outside of the church was, in some respects, meaningless for converts to
the Russian Orthodox Church Outside of Russia with whom I worked. This is
not to say that the Orthodox Christians in Appalachia, outside of the monastery,

were not employed in secular positions, did not go on vacations, and avoided taking part in the fabric of everyday American life. They had active lives, worked, traveled, and went to the movies. Yet the focus of their lives was ultimately salvation, and for many of them, that only came through a society totally transformed by holiness and focused on traditional forms of morality constructed in ways that would support their deeply held religious beliefs. Praise of Vladimir Putin, moral reforms pushed by the Russian government, and the intimate relationship between the ROC and the Federation were part of their desire for this social transfiguration through political means. Conversations in the community were always tinged with political ideologies formulated as Orthodox belief. On the Fourth of July, I attended a fireworks event at the parish. As the humid night's sky filled with a dazzling array of colors, Fr. Cyril turned to the parishioners seated on the lawn and proclaimed, "God bless the red, white, and blue, and by that, I mean Russia!"[83]

An ardent supporter of Vladimir Putin in our private conversations, Fr. Cyril tried to be a tad more diplomatic about his fervor in public. Sometimes he could not contain himself, however. A couple of weeks after the fireworks display, I went to the movies with his family to celebrate his daughter's patron saint's feast day. Her patron saint happened to be a member of the Romanov royal family who was canonized by ROCOR in the 1980s. As we drove almost an hour to the nearest movie theater, we talked about the summit between Trump and Putin that took place just days earlier. Fr. Cyril noted how calm and collected Putin was in the face of sheer American belligerence. "Of course, the Western media portrayed him in a negative light; he's brilliant and they are scared of that," he said. Conversations such as these were not few and far between; rather they were part of the embedded discourse of the community, from hushed conversations between male congregants at the weekly food pantry, to jokes among clergy at the monastery as they gathered on the porch after lunch, to women lamenting the lack of traditional culture in the United States and praising the government-backed push for more children in Russia.

Outside of the ROCOR community in Appalachia, other Orthodox believers in the area did not seem to share the same ultra-conservative beliefs or an affinity for Putin. Indeed, many consider themselves progressive in terms of American politics, decrying not only the current Trump administration, but also what they saw as the growing alt-right presence in the United States and abroad. ROCOR converts in Appalachia often created boundaries between themselves and other converts to Orthodoxy who chose to attend the "modernist, new calendar" Antiochian and Greek parishes in the nearest city. These terms are derived from multiple conversations with a wide variety of ROCOR community members. Because the word "modern" came up so frequently, I began adding a question to my survey during formal interviews: *What does that word [modern] mean to you?* Within the community, modern was equated with two things: religious innovation and secularism. When "modern" was used in reference to other Orthodox communities, such as the Orthodox Church in America, the Greek Archdiocese, and the Antiochian Archdiocese, most ROCOR members were referring to innovation. Any form of assimilation, from the use of the Revised Julian Calendar to pews, was considered an injection of modernity into Orthodoxy. When "modern" was used abstractly or in regard to Western culture, it was almost always in reference to secularism. "America has become modern. The decay of modern society, etc." These types of phrases were part and parcel of converts' everyday conversations. The way in which believers used the word "modern" speaks to how they understood themselves in relationship to the world around them. As historian Frederick Cooper suggests, these definitions of modernity flatten social dynamics, thereby reinforcing partitioning categories.[84]

Appalachian converts to the ROCOR seemed to express who they were apophatically. In other words, they set themselves apart by showing what the world was rather than who or what they were. This was an important part of their ideological worldbuilding process. Converts created distinctive ways of constructing and participating in the world, and by saying what they could not do, they reinforce notions of what was on the outside of their ideological home rather that what was on the inside. The same seems to hold true for Putin's administration, which prides itself on not being Western or modernist. As religiopolitical conservatism in Russia increases, it seems very likely that Americans holding to fundamentalist ideologies of social traditionalism will continue to convert. Indeed, some are even leaving the United States for Russia, in hopes of sparing themselves from a secular apocalypse. Most believers I talked to in Woodford, however, believed they were warriors for Christ, hoping to transform themselves, Appalachia, and the political system of the United States through their beliefs and actions. While they are more likely to be the moral minority rather than the moral majority, they are an important gauge for understanding the powerful shifts occurring in the late 2010s political climate among Christians in the United States, for in a region historically noted for its emphasis on Americana, we find, unexpectedly, growing fealty to Russia's contrasting political project.

6

A People Set Apart

Intra-Community Politics and Regionalism

Appalachia is a region apart—both geographically and statistically.
—PRESIDENT'S APPALACHIAN REGIONAL COMMISSION, 1964

The Church was an "outpost of heaven" on earth, or a "colony of
heaven."
—GEORGES FLOROVSKY, 1959

The Orthodox Christian converts with whom I worked in Appalachia were
truly a people set apart, not just because of their support for Vladimir Putin
and their wholesale devotion to ROCOR, the ROC, and Patriarch Kirill, but
also because of their social insularity and intragroup conflicts that pushed
non-Orthodox Christians, even their close neighbors, to the fringes.[1] Despite
the ROCOR community's struggles and apprehension over non-Orthodox
West Virginians, most Woodford citizens I talked with knew of the group and
many respected them. "They're good people. They're good, Christian people,"
was a common response when I would ask townsfolk in Woodford what they
knew of or thought about the Orthodox community. Theories that the monks
might be Russian spies or that the parish was involved in cult activity had long
fallen away by the time I got to Woodford, although Orthodox and non-Orthodox
alike told me that many narratives of suspicion swirled around the monks when
they first arrived. Were they Catholic? Cult members? A Muslim or radicalized
terrorist cell? After almost two decades of living with the monks and the rest of
the Orthodox community, most locals either knew or assumed that the Orthodox of Woodford were Christians, but that was not always the case.

Sartorial Concerns

Orthodox and non-Orthodox would often bring up attire as the primary reason for suspicion. Russian Orthodox formal monastic garb consists of long, flowing black robes and a black *klobuk* (a type of clerical hat) that has a veil attached to the back of it. During the day, when monks were working, they typically wore black habits and small circular, fitted, black hats. Many of the monks suggested that their clothes looked similar to traditional attire often worn by Muslim men and that the similarities between clothing and grooming (long beards, in particular) might have caused some in Woodford to believe the monks were part of a Muslim extremist group. Upon first glance, one might see some similarities between a *thobe* (a traditional long outer garment worn by some Muslim men) and a cassock worn by Orthodox clerics, but they are not identical pieces of clothing. This suggestion on the part of the monks seemed to be more of product of post-9/11 rhetoric than anything substantive. When I chatted with non-Orthodox locals about the monks, they often tended to see their clothing as "funny" or "odd." Some would call their robes "dresses." Most assuredly, there were some locals who mentioned that the monks looked "like Muslims," but they immediately followed that with a disclaimer that indicated they knew they were Christians.

One of the issues related to dress that the monks consistently brought up to me was the date of their move to West Virginia from Missouri. They settled into the holler in Woodford in the late spring of 2000. While their reception was not festive, the monks were accepted by the community. Many of the fathers, including Abbot Spyridon, noted that if their arrival had taken place after September 11, 2001, the reception might have been quite different. By the time of the attack, people had grown accustomed to the monks, seeing them at the local hardware store, post office, and Walmart. In contrast to the monks' fears of being associated with Islamic converts, non-Orthodox people often mentioned their garb in relation to so-called cultic practices of New Religious Movements. Whatever the case may be, the ideas on both sides reflect the post-9/11 discourse of religious practice. As historian of religion Bruce Lincoln notes, "Even seemingly trivial differences—those of diet and dress, for example—can assume enormous import in the construction of alterity."[2] Fortunately, it would seem, for the monks, townsfolk in Woodford were more concerned with other material religious practices beyond the sartorial.

When non-Orthodox townsfolk described the ROCOR community, "good" and "Christian" seemed to always be used together, since, of course, there was the possibility of being a bad Christian.[3] Abbot Spyridon offered me a glimpse into what might make a bad Christian in terms of Woodford social politics when he relayed a story from their first few months in the region. Shortly after their arrival, the monks lived in tents in the holler, often sleeping in the mud, since there were limited structures already on the property and they had yet to start their long-term building project. They had limited finances, no clean running water, and very little food. One afternoon, a Lincoln Town Car was spotted by the monks as it made its way down the side of the steep mountain into the densely wooded ravine where the church and monastery buildings would eventually stand. Inside the car were two men. The driver got out and asked to speak to the leader. Abbot Spyridon stepped up and greeted the man, who asked if the monks were Christians. The father replied that they were indeed Christians—Orthodox Christians. Then the man asked what translation of the Bible the monks used. Fr. Spyridon explained that they used the King James Version. The man turned to the car passenger who nodded at him. The driver walked behind the vehicle and opened up the trunk, revealing bags of groceries and other essential supplies. Using the correct version of the Bible marked the monks as good Christians for these unnamed Samaritans. Several weeks after that incident, one of the fathers was in town and mentioned the goodwill event to a local, who proclaimed that the passenger was surely Garland Franks, one of the wealthiest men in the area and a very devout Christian. Many at the monastery believed that Garland's acceptance of the new community was potentially influential in shaping how folks in the county came to view the monks over the years. If the abbot had mentioned a different translation of the Bible, they many have not been accepted as good Christians. Even with that identifier, locals still seemed hesitant to interact with the Orthodox community; if they did so, it was almost always at a distance. Woodford locals who did convert were seen as a social anomalies and often considered with suspicion by many of the townsfolk. When I talked with pastors of other Christian churches in Woodford, they almost always brought up the idea of social insularity, noting that the "Orthodox stuck to themselves."[4]

This penultimate chapter looks at group conflicts within the Woodford Orthodox community and how believers were engaged with and separated from socioreligious and political networks in this part of Appalachia. ROCOR converts in Woodford valued distinctive practices and ideologies, which came through not only in their relationships with each other, but also with the larger, non-Orthodox community around them. Focusing first on the tense social history between the monastery and the parish, this chapter explores the community's own sociopolitical agendas and how those have affected its development and expansion since the early 2000s, offering a glimpse into how the community has both embraced and rejected Appalachia in their efforts to missionize the region. Bringing this community into conversation with larger issues of the Christian colonization and missionization of Appalachia, I suggest that ROCOR converts are both complicit in and yet seeming outside of the goodwill missionizing efforts historically found in Christianity throughout this region. Through interviews with politicians and religious leaders in the region, I explore how St. Basil's and St. John's were viewed by those outside of the community. Converts created isolating boundaries as part of their worldbuilding project of defending and preserving particular social and religious traditions; concomitantly, however, they reached out through social projects as a way to both fulfill their theological ideologies and grow their community through conversions. Highlighting ritual expressions of religiosity and community outreach as markers for difference and assimilation, this chapter draws out the theological importance of lifelong pilgrimage and touches upon long-held anthropological questions of what role socioeconomic status plays in notions of belonging, heritage, enculturation, and social justice.

Citizens of Heaven

Throughout the history of Christianity, the idea of being an earthly pilgrim headed for the celestial kingdom has often been part of theological orienting philosophies developed in order for believers to make sense of things cosmologically.[5] These ideas seemingly had their start in the early Christian communities, where an eschatological focus, combined with distinctive notions of the body and spirit, pushed believers to seek their ultimate homeland in heavenly temporalities. Drawing on Jewish apocalyptic literature, early Christians often saw themselves as citizens of the heavenly Jerusalem, rendering their earthly life but a pilgrimage to the city on the hill.[6] As Christianity transformed throughout the centuries, the idea of perpetual pilgrimage underwent metamorphoses. Within Eastern Orthodoxy, it took on two important aspects: individual struggle and communal return. The image of the Christian pilgrim is often one of asceticism and struggle in Orthodox Christianity, for through askesis (self-discipline), theosis (divine union or deification) and heaven might be attainable. As a community concept, pilgrimage became politicized, often tied to diasporic communities who were separated from their historical Orthodox homelands and longing for return.

In a 1981 address on the future of Russia and the end of days at an Orthodox youth conference, Fr. Seraphim Rose highlighted the importance of being a perpetual pilgrim:

Every Orthodox Christian is placed between two worlds: this fallen world where we try to work out our salvation, and the other world,

heaven, the homeland toward which we are striving and which, if we
are leading a truly Christian life, gives us the inspiration to live from
day to day in Christian virtue and love.[7]

Rose's ideas seemed to have resonated with the Orthodox converts in Woodford. Being "citizens of heaven" was important for them because it offered the
necessary ideological framework to devote themselves to ROCOR, Russian
Orthodoxy, and Putin's foreign political platform, while also giving them the
necessary social clearance to maintain a sense of distance from the surrounding
community, for they were, after all, migrants on their way to the celestial kingdom.[8] Where converts lived, worked, and owned property in this corner of
West Virginia was not their homeland. This idea was present in the material
expressions of faith in the community, even in the previously mentioned service to the Port Arthur icon of the Mother of God. An *aposticha* (hymn) from
the Port Arthur Great Vespers service written by Fr. Theodosius highlights
American Orthodox Christians as strangers dwelling the United States: "As
ones in a foreign land, our hearts are ever fixed on that city above, wherein
alone is life everlasting. Dying daily upon this earth, we unworthy soldiers of
Christ entreat thee, our Heavenly Leader: grant us to press on—fighting the
good fight, ending our earthly service honorably—and enlist us amongst the
eternal hosts of heaven."[9] Despite their social solidarity in the fight for the
kingdom, and their common celestial destination, intragroup squabbles in the
Woodford Orthodox community often created distance between travelers,
especially between those at St. Basil's and St. John's.

Kings of the Mountain

The monastery and the parish have a long and complicated history, one that
was often difficult to broach with believers, since for many the emotional
wounds were still fresh and had yet to scar. Because the early years of the community were so fraught with intragroup turmoil, it took quite a while for longtime members to open up to me about that period of their lives. Several months
into my stay, after my involvement with the food pantry, baking, volunteering
in the soap house, and singing in the parish choir, I began broaching the subject with interviewees. Some approached the issues abstractly, others straight
on, while some openly sobbed over the chaos and pain that ill-mannered leadership had caused for many of the founding members. It was difficult for most
to talk about the early years, because by 2017 the community was seemingly
in a solid social and emotional space. During the time I was there, it appeared
as if there was a lull in disputes, and I understood people's natural caution in

broaching subjects like this with an outsider. When they did open up, however, I often felt as though I was in the middle of a tug-of-war, with both sides vying for my time and approval.

Since the monastery and the parish had the same set of services on the weekend, I typically spent a majority of my Saturdays and Sundays at St. John's parish, leaving the week free to volunteer, attend services, and talk with monks at St. Basil's. While I appeared to spend more time at the monastery than I did the parish, the social mores and religious codes at the monastery meant that I had less face-to-face time with community members. Spending my weekends at the parish proved difficult, since I missed out on the fellowship time after *trapeza* (communal lunch) for the monastic community on Sundays—one of few times during the week when the monks could freely chat with visitors and seemed more open and relaxed, often sharing a beer on the porch with traveling clergy. However, in order to ingratiate myself into the parish community, I needed to attend Sunday services at the very least. First, as a way to enmesh myself into the parish structure, I joined the choir at the behest of Fr. Cyril. The parish needed a soprano and I happened to fit the bill. Second, while most parishioners lived in West Virginia, they often traveled over an hour each way to attend services. Some had even longer commuting times from Eastern Kentucky and Southeastern Ohio. Between work and family life, most people were busy during the week, so I often scheduled conversations after coffee hour on Sunday, although I did visit parishioners in their homes as well, and some selected to meet with me at my rental cabin.

Orthodox liturgical days run from sunset to sunset, so for feast days that occurred during the week, I would often attend evening vespers at the monastery and then head to the parish for the morning services. As time progressed, and I interviewed more parishioners, I began taking a weekend or two a month to attend services at the monastery. At first, this did not go over well. Fr. Cyril asked me if I was "converting" to the monastery, suggesting that parishioners felt neglected, even though most of them would see me at the parish food pantry every Monday evening. I found out along the way that some parishioners over the years had defected to the monastery, an issue that created deep chasms of insecurity and pain in the parish. Eventually, after explaining the situation multiple times, parishioners and clergy at the parish understood that I was not leaving them behind but trying to find a holistic view of the community at large. Ironically, my positionality in both worlds—the monastery and the parish—often helped converts open up about the long-standing tensions between the two groups.

When the early monastery inhabitants arrived in the late spring of 2000, there were but a few laypeople who would help out and attend services. The convert and his Russian wife who donated the land for the monastery were already senior citizens by the time the monks arrived. The few converts, and even less cradles, who were living in the area at the time wanted a full-time Orthodox community. While the monastery seemed to fit that bill at first, it was quite evident that it could not provide the social networks and religious life that families needed. As the monastic brotherhood grew, so did the need for a parish that could directly minister to families, especially those with children. During their tenure in the Midwest, the monks had a monastery attached to a parish; the close proximity proved to be challenging for their spiritual life, since they were constantly inundated with visitors and pilgrims, making a solitary religious vocation virtually impossible. Thus, when the laity in West Virginia began to rally around the monastery, Fr. Spyridon knew it was time to help them form their own parish. St. John's was built to be an almost auxiliary arm of the monastery. Just as St. Basil's was once a dependency of historic Holy Trinity Monastery and Seminary in Jordanville, New York, the parish was to become, in many respects, a lay dependency of the St. Basil's. It was clear to parishioners at the beginning of the parish building phase in the early 2000s, that they would need the support of the monastery. Perhaps not financially, but spiritually and socially, within both West Virginia and the ROCOR global community. Dependencies are not only about financials. In fact, it is often more about spiritual legacy or kinship than anything else. To be under the spiritual mantle of a particular community is key, for it signals to the broader Church network the canonical structures of hierarchy present, something that is key to ROCOR sociality. The relationship between St. John's and St. Basil's was from the outset, it seems, unequal in terms of support, with the monastery clearly being the institution that could provide more in the relationship.

Clergy from both the monastery and the parish explained that over the years this relationship was tested, especially during multiple phases of leadership at the parish and because of tensions with benefactors. Historian of religion Bruce Lincoln notes that intragroup conflict is often a defining characteristic of the "sentiments of affinity" that helps shape boundary-making schemes, while providing an outlet for figuring out change and social transformation within a community that believes they hold to an unchangeable, eternal truth.[10] Certainly, this could be said of the Orthodox community in Woodford, where divisions between the monastery and the parish often served to reinforce notions of correct praxis, while also highlighting the individual social and political positionalities in each organization. When I first arrived at the parish in Woodford, I noticed two large *analoys* (icon stands) with icons of saints who are not typically the most popular or traditional to have at the front of the nave; these would be the primary icons venerated by the faithful when they arrive for services.[11] Later I found out these icons were in honor of the couple who owned the church building and land around it. They— Coleman and Mildred—would be an excellent source of information about the early years of the community, Fr. Cyril told me. After chatting with the couple at the parish for a couple of weeks, I emailed the husband and asked if we might have a conversation about their role in helping build the parish. His immediate response was negative; he indicated that he did not want to stir up old hostilities. Eventually, he conceded to a brief interview; the couple brought with them lots of photos from the early years of the parish, showing me how they themselves dug the foundation of the church building. A local, who lived in Appalachia for most of his life, Coleman was a politician of sorts. He, along with his wife, converted to Orthodoxy while he was in graduate school in the Midwest.

At first, Coleman and Mildred attended the monastery, but as a couple with children it was clear to them that they needed to have a parish with Sunday School and other social activities geared toward families. They, along with other families who were visiting the monastery and converting around that period, started the process of building a parish from the ground up. Coleman bought a piece of property in the middle of Woodford that seemed ideal for a church community. He paid for all the costs to design and construct the building, opting to be the parish landlord for the next eighteen and a half years.[12] While I was there, Fr. Cyril asked Coleman to think about selling the building and land to the Church because they hoped to make the parish more ADA compliant and create a new structure to house the expanding food bank. At that point, Coleman refused, indicating that he wanted the property to stay in his family, even after his death. "Is there any way to change his mind?" I asked Fr. Cyril. The priest replied that it was not very likely since Coleman was from "mountain folk" and had very insular ideas about ownership.

The local/regional divide between the monastery and the parish was one that stood out immediately. Converts who joined the monastery tended to be from various parts of the South, Midwest, and the outer edges of Appalachia, with smaller numbers from other parts of the United States and a few monks from outside of North America over the years. Beyond the workers, who were employed by the monastery, there were no locals who attended the monastery full time, and most assuredly, none were numbered among the brotherhood.[13] Unlike the monastery, the parish had a much more local demographic among its membership. Most converts hailed from small towns and midsize cities in West Virginia, small towns just across the Ohio border, and a few from Woodford proper. This distinction complicated the ways in which both communities relate to each other. This conflict emerged distinctively in two ways: language and economics, both of which were embedded in the social transformations occurring in each of these institutions in the late 2010s.

While the number of Russian parishioners was quite small at the parish (less than 10 percent), Fr. Cyril focused on embedding Church Slavonic (CS) into the liturgy. Often, he would instruct one of the deacons to read the gospel in both English and CS. Many times, the litanies and Cherubic Hymn (the hymn sung during the Great Entrance procession prior to the consecration of the Eucharist) would also be chanted in CS. I asked Fr. Cyril why this was important, and he joked that it was training for heaven, where everyone would have to be familiar with CS. Often parishioners would comment that the parish was a bit more traditional in their linguistic liturgical approach than the monastery, where CS was rarely used. In fact, St. Basil's focused on producing Orthodox hymnody and prayers in English, specifically for ROCOR convert believers in the United States. That, combined with their own distinctive tonal compositions, a melding of Byzantine, Obikhod, Kievan, and Znamenny chant styles, influenced by traditional Appalachian shape-note music, according to the monastery's choir director, seemingly made their community a bit more modern and adaptive to the needs of American converts who might not be as comfortable with Russian and CS language chant primarily in Znamenny style, the preferred musical system in St. John's.[14] The parish's emphasis on CS and Znamenny seemed to be part of the community's efforts to emphasize their Russianness, despite the fact that upward of 90 percent of regularly attending members of St. John's were not Russian. This embrace of what some scholars term as "ethnodoxy" is an attempt to merge nationalism and religious ideology with ethnicity.[15]

This ethno-nationalistic focus was also present in the parish's annual Russian Bazaar, through which the community raised funds for their food pantry. Strikingly, it was largely the non-Russian members who hosted and were the public face of the event, while most of the Russians, primarily women, were tasked with kitchen duties in the parish basement. Through Fr. Cyril's charismatic push for media attention, the local newspapers generally covered the event, which meant that the Bazaar was typically well attended by the local community. Most events that were open to the community, beyond the weekly food pantry, emphasized the Russianness of the parish. Converts mentioned to me that the increased focus on the Russian heritage of the community arose, in many respects, with the placement of Fr. Cyril as rector. One longtime parishioner pointed to the sign in front of the church building and said to me, "You'll notice it doesn't say Russian Orthodox. It only says Orthodox Church." According to him, that was an intentional act by the early parish community in order to be more homogeneous with the other churches in the area. This act of not noting Russian connections was also present on the signage for the monastery as well.

The ideological shift at the parish certainly led to more strained relations, with monastery attendees often rolling their eyes or grumbling about the "Russia and Putin fever" at the parish. At the same time, however, it was clear that despite their emphasis on English-language services and new religious hymnody, the monastery was deeply centered on their ROCOR and Russian Orthodox heritage. The issue between the two institutions, it seems, was the parish's public interest by and large in Russian politics. Those who professed allegiance to Vladimir Putin at St. Basil's did so far more discreetly. In many respects, the social differences, however they were manifested—culturally or linguistically—were not as difficult to overcome for believers as the socioeconomic differences that plague both institutions in unique ways. On the whole, as a community, Orthodox Christians in this part of Appalachia lived well above the poverty line. The county that was home to both the parish and the monastery saw a high rate of poverty. Transplant converts—those from other parts of Appalachia, the American South, the Rust Belt, and the Midwest, were more likely to have a higher socioeconomic status than those born and raised in the county, and the monastery faired far better than the parish on the whole economically. Fr. Cyril was known for making public pleas to the parish to be generous givers. After talking with the rector and the treasurer, it became clear that the parish was almost always at a tenuous point financially. Because of the depressed economics of the area, six families had left in the years leading up to my arrival, families who were generous benefactors to the community. While the parish was struggling for its very survival every month, the monastery seemed to be flourishing financially.

Orthodox monastics are called individually to vows of self-imposed poverty, yet that does not mean that the monastic organization itself should be impoverished. The various business operations that St. Basil's had—the bookstore, incense, honey, soap, and music—were not enough to create wealth for the community. Rather they looked outward to benefactors who might see the community as a spiritual garden in need of cultivation. While I was there, several anonymous donors contributed generously to St. Basil's infrastructure and beautification projects, with one benefactor donating a six-figure amount in order to help the monastery procure high-speed fiber optic broadband, something that was not available to the residents in the surrounding area, including myself, who had to make do with dial-up speeds. The addition of new shrines for the Holy Elders of Optina and the Royal Martyrs were also completed through private donations. The frugality of everyday living, raising animals for milk and eggs, and keeping a large garden, meant that all

nonessential funds were immediately devoted to building projects. Abbot Spyridon mentioned more than once that many men were on the waiting list to
come to the monastery as novices, but they did not have adequate space in
which to house them. Rather than embedding themselves into the social fiber
of the community through active charity outreach work, St. Basil's sought to
build up the Orthodox presence in Woodford, creating a space that allowed
for pilgrims from around the world to participate in their community, thereby
changing the sociality of the town in many respects. While issues of heritage
and economics were often at the center of the intragroup differences in Woodford, it was the dynamics of globalization and the subsequent easements of
mobility that allowed for the further diversification of the area.[16] A town that
once comprised only small families from the county was now home to a wide
range of inhabitants from around the United States and the world. The increase
in Orthodox Christians in Woodford also brought with it more economic complexities to a region struggling with poverty. Beyond the permanent Orthodox
residents, the influx of pilgrims for holy days throughout the year also points to
how mobility and class are playing a part in changing nature of rurality. The
movement of Orthodox Christians to the small town of Woodford has changed
both the social and physical geography of the area, which I discuss in the final
chapter. These changes seem to have occurred in spite of the internal squabbles
the Orthodox community had since their move to Woodford.

    While the typical narrative that swirled around the community seemed to
indicate that the monastery was the first to claim the area for ROCOR, this
does not hold up after examining historical church documents and talking
with Peter and Fevronia, the elderly couple who originally donated the land
for St. Basil's and who were essential in forming a Russian Orthodox community in this part of West Virginia. By the time I arrived in Woodford, Peter and
Fevronia's health was in decline. I talked with Fevronia first in 2016 when I
stayed with Fr. Cyril's family one summer, but given her advanced dementia
at that time, it seemed unethical to ask her any questions about the community.
When I returned in September of 2017, she did not remember me, although I
spent time visiting with her and Peter regularly. One of the primary reasons
the couple donated the land to St. Basil's was their desire to have a Russian
Orthodox community in the area. Fevronia was Russian, the daughter of an
Orthodox priest. While she was working as a diplomat, she met and fell in love
with Peter, who was, at the time, a Baptist minister. According to Peter, Fevronia never pushed him to convert, but eventually he found his spiritual home
in the Orthodox Church. When Peter took an academic position at a local university, they moved to Woodford. Folkloric tales from Orthodox and non-Orthodox
alike paint Peter as quite a character, who used to land his airplane on the top
of a mountain close to the monastery property.

After Peter's conversion, the couple began to focus on building an Orthodox community in the area. They formed a small chapel in their home, where they would conduct reader services. Documents that Fevronia and Peter provided me from that time period indicate that the couple were financially and emotionally invested in building an active parish of Orthodox Christians in their small corner of West Virginia, engaging in correspondence with church hierarchs in various Orthodox jurisdictions to facilitate the process. At one point, the couple, along with their growing group of believers, which included converts and Russian immigrants, rented property in the closest city and had a priest from the next state over serve occasional Divine Liturgies. I asked Peter if they originally set out to form a ROCOR parish. He replied that they were simply trying to form an Orthodox community. The documentation he provided backed up his story; it showed that the community was reaching out to any canonical Orthodox jurisdiction that could help them get up and running. Yet Fevronia's deep ties to Russian Orthodoxy meant that she was still drawn to having a Slavic-influenced community around her. Eventually the couple heard through the Orthodox grapevine that a ROCOR monastery in the Midwest was in need of land to build a full-scale compound. The couple invited some of the monks to assess the property and tour the area.

When Fr. Spyridon first arrived in 2000, it was spring—the dogwoods were in bloom and the holler was alive, green, and lush with foliage. It looked to be the perfect spot for the monastery, he told me. Fevronia and Peter donated the land to the community with the agreement that they could live on the land until they were unable to take care of themselves. Eventually, the aging couple moved to a nearby town so they could have better access to health care. In doing so, they also moved from the monastery to the parish full time. While the parish had Coleman to thank for the physical space, Fevronia seemed to be the person who was responsible for the development of ROCOR in West Virginia. Without the couple's donation of land, St. Basil's might have remained rooted in the Midwest and the parish would have never come to fruition. Peter, in a similar fashion to many of the early founders of the parish, disliked talking about the moment of animosity between St. John's and St. Basil's. Fr. Cyril's tenure since 2011 seemed to bring about the longest period of amiability between the two organizations, although even he was complicit in some of the hostility that reared its head during my year in Woodford.

The Father Alexey Effect

On the surface, the monastery and the parish seemed to be cohesive halves of a whole community. Monks from St. Basil's often helped out at St. John's weekly food pantry, parishioners and clergy attended special feast days and services at the monastery, monk priests filled in for Fr. Cyril when he was out of town, and the list goes on. To be sure, longtime parishioners still remembered when Fr. Spyridon sent monks to the parish to remove the *antimins* from the altar, indicating that they were no longer canonically eligible to serve the liturgy, but by 2017 there seemed to be a mutual understanding, if not respect, in place.[17] While most community members were reticent to talk about the past turmoil, Fr. Cyril, the current rector of the parish, opened up more than others. This seemed to be, in part, because he was not present when most of the early conflicts took place and he seemed to feel as though he was a bit of an outsider. Fr. Cyril was fourth or fifth, depending on whom you asked, in a long line of priests who were assigned to the parish. At first, monk priests were assigned to serve the parish, but the ROCOR hierarchy of the Eastern American Diocese quickly realized that was not an excellent idea for a parish full of families. Short-term priests, some coming from out of state once a month to serve liturgy, were then assigned. Finally, Fr. Cyril and his family took up placement in 2011. As someone who was born and raised in the American South—the Carolinas— and who went to a Pentecostal university in the Midwest before converting, Fr. Cyril seemed to be the ideal candidate to lead a group of Appalachian converts. Indeed, Fr. Cyril realized it was the right place for him after his first visit to the community. What he did not realize when he first arrived, he told me, is that he would be dealing with ideological baggage stemming from the influence of one monk—Fr. Alexey (Ambrose) Young.[18]

As I mentioned earlier, Fr. Seraphim Rose was an influential figure for many of the males in the community—among both monastics and laity. The presence of Fr. Seraphim Rose was not simply felt in the literature and recordings that believers used in their religious media practices; it was also expressed through the person of Fr. Alexey Young—a spiritual son of Rose and, eventually, a monk, for a time, at St. Basil's. Though they met for the first time in the late 1960s in San Francisco, the relationship between the two men started in the 1970s, when Rose was already in the mountains of Northern California creating a monastic community and Young, a former Catholic and Orthodox catechu- men, wrote to Rose for spiritual advice.[19] Young was instrumental in helping Rose with his print media projects, including *Orthodox Word*, a periodical dedicated to Orthodox culture and life globally. Young went on to help establish a parish in the wilds of Northern California but found his true spiritual home after his wife reposed (died). He became a monastic, taking the name Ambrose and settling at St. Basil's in Woodford. Fr. Ambrose, according to many of the clerics and fathers in the community, was instrumental in shaping the Ortho- dox ethos of both the monastery and parish.

Whenever conversations veered toward the nascent stages of the community, Young's name would inevitably come up. For many, his influence as the monk priest serving the parish was formational. Much as Rose had guided him on his path to Orthodoxy, Young seemed to see it as his mission to help shape the spiritual lives of new Appalachian converts and neophyte monks to the faith. Families who had been in the parish the longest, including the founders themselves, tended to become quite emotional when Young's name was mentioned. The strict, almost ascetic praxis that Young required was quite demanding on many in those early years. Despite Young's strident form of the faith, he was much beloved in the community by many of the laity and monastics. Eventually, however, he left the monastery and moved to a Greek monastic community in Ohio. By the time I arrived in West Virginia, Young had been gone for years. I found out through conversations with Fr. Spyridon and the monks at St. Basil's that Young had been diagnosed with dementia and was living with a caregiver. Young's departure took a toll on many in the community, especially among the monks, for Young was in the spiritual lineage of Fr. Seraphim Rose, whom many saw as a holy guide for monastic life in the United States.

One of the most important issues to come out of Young's departure was an understanding of how the monastery and the parish related to each other spiritually. Young, who had served as the rector of the parish, shaped the spirituality of the laity in a fashion that was monastic in nature. Yet as Frs. Spyridon and Cyril pointed out, the parish was meant to be a space in which laity could learn about lay spirituality. It was never intended to function as a monastery—that was the role of St. Basil's. In many ways, through his spiritual grooming, Young was trying to create monastic laity, which blurred the lines of organizational structure that Fr. Spyridon and the early monks tried so hard to enforce. The issues surrounding Young point to larger structural problems that seem to be complicit in the complexities of two communities trying to function as one. More often than not, these issues were a result of questions regarding the institutional membership of new Orthodox believers, many of whom had children, who moved to the area to be close to the monastery.

My Place or Yours?

One of the largest sources of disagreement between the monastery and the parish surrounded the placement of new families. During my time in Woodford, several new Orthodox families moved into the area. These tended to be Orthodox converts from the United States who had heard about the community through Orthodox acquaintances or on the Internet. Many of them often visited for short periods of time before finally deciding to move to the area

permanently. One such family was the Gardeners. Aiden, a computer program-
mer who had spent time at St. Basil's as a novice when he was younger, along
with his wife and child, decided to move to Woodford about a year before I
arrived, but it took them until late 2018 to complete their journey. After a lengthy
battle with health problems, the family felt that it was time to move closer to
a spiritual community, one where they could attend church daily. Since Aiden
was familiar with the area and the monastery, Judith thought it might be a
good fit. From the onset, according to the Gardeners, they intended to have
their spiritual home base be the monastery, with occasional visits to the parish.
However, before the family arrived, this idea was already being contested by
Fr. Cyril.

One afternoon in the fall of 2017, I was helping Fr. Cyril at his printshop
and he relayed to me, somewhat excitedly, that an Orthodox family was planning to move to the area. He told me the Gardeners had a desire to be in a
place with a strong Orthodox ethos. I asked him if they planned to attend the
parish. He replied, "Of course. They have a child. People with children attend
the parish. That's just the way it is." However, once the Gardeners arrived, it
became evident that they planned to attend the monastery instead. I would
often see them on the grounds of St. Basil's while I was working in the soap
house. They were visiting to make confession with Abbot Spyridon, a practice
that is typically associated with a believer's spiritual father. If the Gardeners
planned on attending the parish full time, Fr. Cyril would have been their
confessor. Once the family settled in, Clotilde, who worked at the monastery,
had a small party, attended by monks and a few single laypeople from the
monastery, to welcome the Gardeners to the area. As I chatted with Judith, she
noted that they did not plan to attend the parish full time; it was too hard on
her to keep up socially and be expected to participate in group activities. She
also worried that this move might cause issues with Fr. Cyril, who often seemed
anxious to acquire parishioners who could contribute to the economic and
labor endeavors of St. John's.

Some believers, especially those with children, came with the purpose of
attending the parish but visiting the monastery regularly. Those folks saw
themselves as parish members. However, some came because they were more
focused on following the rhythms of monastic life, even if they were married
couples with children. These new arrivals caused a bit of turmoil in the delicate
balance that had been established between the two factions of the community.
Fr. Cyril would often comment that it seemed as if the monastery was neglect-
ing the unspoken rule between the two communities that families, especially
those with children, should be attached to the parish, not to the monastery.
Yet those at the monastery explained that there was a rigorous screening process

for non-monastic believers permanently attached to monastery. At the same time, however, they did not want to turn anyone away from the monastery or try to persuade them not to attend services there. Part of this conflict over family placements seemed to have stemmed from a few shifts that occurred in the community just a couple of years before I arrived.

Two couples, both of whom did not have children, seemingly swapped organizational affiliations. The first couple arrived with the intent of attending the monastery full time, but still wanted to help with the parish. They originally moved to West Virginia to work at and be near the monastery, after converting at Holy Trinity Monastery in Jordanville, New York, where the abbot encouraged them to live near a ROCOR monastery. The husband, who worked in the health care industry, was able to procure a job in a small city about an hour from Woodford, and the couple rented a small house less than a five-minute drive from St. Basil's. The wife found employment at the monastery and the couple was content to attend services regularly with the monks. Yet their desire to make sure the parish succeeded led them to consistently visit St. John's in order to help out. The wife would sing in the choir, while her husband would assist Fr. Cyril in the altar. Eventually parish tensions and personalities caused a rift and the couple moved their affiliation back to the monastery, recognizing it as the primary place for their spiritual development. In contrast, Fr. Basil and Matushka Emilia, who had been at the monastery from the day they arrived, found that Fr. Basil, as a deacon, had no clerical mobility at the monastery and thus they decided to transfer their membership to the parish. The movement of parishioners was key; it changed the economic structures of the community in a way that pushed the pendulum of power and influence one way or the other.

Generally, however, the pendulum swung in favor of the monastery. St. Basil's resources far surpassed that of St. John's, although the individual monks themselves did not seem to benefit from their financial security. Focused on building initiatives that would provide a larger church, more dormitories, and a bigger common area for guests, the monastery was investing in their own infrastructure rather than that of the larger community. In contrast, the parish, which was seemingly on the brink of closure at a moment's notice, consistently pursued outreach programs as a way to both assist those in the area and gain more adherents. Interestingly, the conflicts between the parish and the monastery seemed to be centered on Orthodox converts who moved into the area, not locals. From the onset, this seemed to stem from class and economics, something that was confirmed when I talked with Fr. Cyril. He lamented the lack of more financially secure parishioners. He would often bring up the departure of Clotilde and her husband, noting that they "were major contributors to the parish." Fr. Cyril seemed pleased to have new parishioners, but he also worried about their economic ability to contribute to the parish's livelihood. While most of the parishioners were well above the poverty line, many of them were not as economically stable as those who had left to pursue employment in other states. Despite the financial struggles of the parish, it was, as a community, focused on providing benevolent care to citizens of Woodford as part of their communal almsgiving and missionizing efforts.

Missions and Money

Appalachia has often been seen as a mission field for many Christian organizations. Much of the missionization started with the Moravians, German Protestants, who came to the region in the eighteenth century, but other, mostly Protestant, religious organizations also saw the hills and hollers as ripe areas for a spiritual harvest starting in the eighteenth century going forward.[20] One of the main forms of missionization in Appalachia came as part of the benevolence work that various denominations sponsored in the region. Christian charity missions in this area of the United States highlight two main issues that scholars of Appalachia often bring to the fore as critical for better understanding the region: the fetishization of poverty and poor whites in need of a savior. Loyal Jones, one of the foremost local Appalachian scholars, has noted that Appalachian Christians, often because of their varied religious traditions, were scrutinized by other Christians who assumed they needed salvation.[21] In addition to potentially claiming the region for God, religious benevolence workers also brought a disproportional amount of attention to the rural poor in the area. Combined with government and media attention, poverty and its accompanying images became fetishized in popular culture.[22]

Lyndon B. Johnson's efforts to eradicate poverty in the United States led to a great deal of public interest in Appalachia, with photographers, journalists, and other media personalities traveling to the region to feature public interest stories and images.[23] The focus on poverty and lack of resources generally placed the blame on Appalachians, highlighting them as "hillbillies" who were often portrayed in the media as lower on the evolutionary scale, incapable of helping themselves rise above their circumstances. The rhetoric of poverty typically used in media about Appalachians failed to critically assess the colonizing and extractive forces of capitalism that were often to blame for the entrenched wealth disparities and suspicion of outsiders.[24] Mineral and other natural resources abound in many parts of Appalachia, but the most prominent resource was, and to some extent still is, coal. The lore and allure of coal is a vital aspect of Appalachian life. Coal often seems a ubiquitous part of what it means to be an Appalachian. Yet as the coal veins began to run out, the companies, who had long dominated the region, moved from shaft mining to mountain top removal for easier and more affordable access to the last dusty traces of combustible carbon.

The shift in extraction methodology meant that miners, who were already beholden to companies for housing and food, among other things, were left entirely out in the cold. The county that Woodford was part of used to be a player in the local mining community, but by the time I arrived there in the late summer of 2017, mining was no longer a feasible financial option unless miners wanted to travel several counties away for work. I met quite a few former miners, but only one actively employed, who was beginning to seek alternative job options in the steel industry because of both the financial and health issues associated with coal. Some scholars have suggested that capitalism was the colonizing force that shaped the region, creating an internal American colony that has persisted, in part, because of the continuous, extractive nature of capitalism, wealth distribution, and classism in the region.[25] While it is evident that economics have greatly impacted regional socioeconomics and education, religion has also had a substantial colonizing effect on the everyday lives of locals. The desire to provide charity to the impoverished people of Appalachia meant that religious communities from all over the United States began sending home missionaries to the region as part of their missionization through relief aid efforts.[26]

In many respects, the Orthodox community in Woodford can be seen in this same vein of colonizing Christian missions focused on saving poor whites from poverty. However, social justice, among the Woodford Orthodox, was labeled a liberal ideology entirely incompatible with Russian Orthodox theology. Indeed, as Elena Namli points out, social justice does not seem to have any "theological significance" in contemporary, post-Soviet Russian Orthodoxy.[27] As many of the volunteers at the parish's weekly food pantry made clear to me, social justice was a code word for liberal politics. Thus, they framed their outreach work in terms of religious obligation rather than equality, equity, and human rights. Any outreach or charity that the parish or monastery participated in was always focused on fulfilling Orthodox Christians' obligations to follow Christ's commandments regarding help for the helpless. Much like the early forms of Christian charity work in the region, the parish focused on missionization through community aid. Every Monday afternoon, the parish hosted a food pantry that was part of a larger regional nonprofit food insecurity network. The pantry drew in locals from throughout the county, many of whom were regulars while I was there. Parishioners and sometimes monks would gather early on Monday afternoons to unpack and set up fresh produce, bread, and other staples for the pantry customers. The St. John's pantry was a local partner with a larger nonprofit food bank in a nearby city. This partnership, which was funded in part by the state and federal governments, allowed the parish pantry to service a larger number of those in need. While there were a couple of other smaller food banks and pantries in Woodford, customers who came to St. John's food pantry indicated that there was a much larger and more stable selection of food and supplies at the parish (see figs. 7 and 8).

Before customers signed in and were directed downstairs to the parish hall where breads and produce were displayed for selection, Fr. Cyril would say "a quick prayer" and remind customers why the parish was choosing to host a food pantry. Every week, as twenty to thirty locals gathered just inside the parish *narthex* (vestibule), the priest would recite a variation of the same phrase: "By helping you, we are helping Christ." This phrase highlights why the community participated in this type of outreach. Unlike many Christian social justice endeavors that place the priority on care of the recipients as part of their missionizing outreach, this project focused particularly on helping Christ.[28] Thus the customers themselves served as a means to an end for the parish, through which they could fulfill their spiritual calling or, perhaps, obligation. This was part of their Orthodox worldview that promoted almsgiving and charity work as a way to aid one on the path of righteousness.[29] Through providing food to Woodford residents, parishioners were saving themselves and

Figure 7. First Come, First Served (Photograph by author, August 2018)

Figure 8. The Lord's Larder (Photograph by author, August 2018)

participating in a soft form of missionization. The use of food assistance as part of the parish's almsgiving to Christ was not only part of the larger project of Christian missionization of Appalachia, it was also caught up in broader discourses surrounding poverty and aid in the state. Although members of the monastery sometimes helped out with the parish's food pantry, the monks were more focused on creating employment opportunities and providing financial aid, rather than addressing food insecurity. Locals in need of employment often found part-time, temporary jobs at the monastery, working in landscaping, gardening, or infrastructure projects. While the monks encouraged underemployed individuals living around the monastery to ask for work, they were also skeptical of locals, worried that they might have ulterior motives.

Abbot Spyridon and the monks would often tell me stories about theft and drug addiction. As St. Basil's sought to help those around them, they did so with trepidation and at a bit of distance. At St. John's parish, the fear of drug users and addicts caused volunteers to close access to restrooms and surveil customers heavily. The Orthodox were not alone in their moral panic over narcotics. In recent years, the broader media rhetoric surrounding Appalachia has shifted from poverty to addiction, but the impulse, the desire to paint the region with broad strokes that image it as a land teeming with welfare recipients in trailer parks is still alive. Now the media emphasizes opioid use and narcotics as material expressions of how Appalachians are complicit in sustaining their own poverty.[30] For the Orthodox, the prevalence of opioid use and overdoses signified a symptom of Appalachia being part of the fallen, created world, of which they did not want to take part in, even if that area was somewhat less corrupted than others.

Almost Heaven, but Not Quite

In 2018, the West Virginia board of tourism started a campaign using a line about the state from John Denver's "Country Roads, Take Me Home." Released in 1971, the song contains lyrics that describe West Virginia as "almost heaven."[31] This descriptor was often heralded in the local media as the unofficial motto of the state.[32] In everyday parlance, locals also used this turn of phrase to express their love for the state, and even the region more broadly. While the Orthodox faithful in Woodford often found themselves uncomfortable with the community around them and even the United States in general, they often noted that the state of West Virginia was idyllic in many respects; it was almost heaven. Indeed, many, especially those born and raised in the state, used that turn of phrase to describe the natural environs of the area. The mountains, rivers, caves, and abundant wildlife were all part the glory of West Virginia for them. It was humans who had tainted God's creation through their economic and infrastructure endeavors. The monks told me often that cities, as urban prisons, were an abomination; God intended for people to live off of the land. The economic circumstances and the lack of infrastructure was certainly irritating at the least and debilitating at the worst for believers, but the lack of urbanization and secularization, in many respects, also made the area somewhat of a haven for them while on their spiritual journeys.

Capitalist colonialism contoured not only the topography of West Virginia through extractive resource mining, but it also created systems of power—political and otherwise—that have stunted expansion efforts and squelched Appalachian visions of developing and sustaining a vital regional economy that would keep revenue local.[33] The combination of these forces seemingly created a vacuum of globalization and, more importantly to the Orthodox community, secularization. Complicit with media assumptions about the region, the nostalgic lens through which Orthodox Christians would talk about Appalachia belied the wealth of diversity and cultural formations that were, and still are, abundant in the area. Certainly, the twentieth-century popular images of Appalachia's poor whites, along with the increasingly predatory national companies that pushed families in the state to become dependent on them for food and housing, restricted access to networks of modernization and concomitantly helped create false narratives that portrayed the region as an incubator of low-brow static Americana lacking vibrant diversity.[34] Of course, this is far from the truth of life as Appalachians know it. The region has always been home to diverse populations with distinctive religious and cultural beliefs, practices, and ways of being in the world.[35] From the historically Eastern European–dominated coalfields of West Virginia, to the underrepresented, self-identified Affrilachians (Black Appalachians), to the Serbian enclaves in the north of the state, not to mention the Scotch-Irish groups that helped found much of the area early in American history, the region was, and still is, home to groups from around the world. Appalachia has a long history of Russian presence, particularly in the coalfields and steel mill areas of the northern part of the region.[36] Thus Russian immigrants and Russian Orthodoxy seemingly should be familiar to Appalachians. Yet this often seemed not to be the case in Woodford, where the insularity that stereotyped most of the region was present among the Orthodox and often noted by inhabitants.[37]

Late in the summer of 2018, after the main roads were cleared of water and debris from a dangerous summer thunderstorm, I made my way to a small town about thirty-five minutes northwest of Woodford. Sliding into a high-back wooden booth at one of the longest-running drugstores and confectionaries in the state, I waited for Frank Wilson, a West Virginian businessman and local politician. I first met Frank at the icon print business run by Fr. Cyril, who often asked me to sit in on his work meetings in order to learn more about his company and the business infrastructure in the area. During the meeting, Frank mentioned he was sympathetic to the convert Orthodox community because he was a new Catholic. This news piqued my interest, given the fact that the singular Catholic Church in Woodford had been suppressed by the local diocese in November of 2017 and there were a limited number of Catholics in the county. I contacted Frank in early 2018, but he was running for reelection and did not want to be interviewed at that time. Finally, in the summer, after the local elections were complete, he agreed to sit down with me for a chat.

The bell over the door of the drugstore jingled merrily as Frank entered. Immediately he was waved over to a large table where a group of local officials from the county courthouse were having lunch. Eventually Frank broke free and made his way to my booth. Over fountain drinks and chicken tenders, per Frank's recommendation, we chatted about his role in the political structure of the area and the importance of religion in mountain sociality. Frank grew up Baptist and remained in the faith until the year prior. His wife was Catholic, and they had been happily married for many years before he converted. I asked him why he converted; he replied that he was drawn to the faith after watching his wife, attending services with her, and reading. "It's why I lost the election this year," he said as he ended his conversion narrative.[38] Frank lost a seat in his home county that he had held for years. The only change to account for the failed campaign was, according to him, the fact that he was a Catholic. I questioned why that would matter; Frank explained that while political flexibility was socially accepted in the area, religious transformation was generally frowned up; area residents typically adhered to their family's historic church affiliation. In fact, subtle political transformation was a fundamental part of the region according to most of the politicians and community leaders I spoke with. As I mentioned in Chapter 3, while the state skewed Republican at the national level, local and regional politicians were often left-leaning on most issues. Political plasticity was acceptable to some degree. Yet changing one's religious affiliation, something many had had since childhood, was not quite as palatable.

Cut Off by Faith

The small Protestant churches of varying denominations, which dotted the mountainsides, filled the hollers, and lined the streets of Woodford, were all relatively historic in the community, even if their physical venues had changed over the years. Despite being in the area for more than seventeen years, the Orthodox community was still considered to be new in town at the close of the 2010s. By far, they were not the youngest religious organization in Woodford. When I first began looking for a place to live near the monastery, I contacted a staff member at a local university to see if they had any recommendations for real estate agencies or brokers. One of the faculty members connected me with Hattie, a local businesswoman who, along with her husband, flipped houses and rented properties. While Hattie did not have properties available during my anticipated stay, I decided to keep in contact with her, since she had lived in the area for a majority of her life. In the fall of 2017, Hattie, along with her husband Leonard, was in the process of building a nondenominational church in the heart of Woodford. Situated right across the highway from the local bar, the historic society, and the post office, the new church was meant to reach out to un-churched people who felt like they were without a Christian community. Hattie asked me to attend their Sunday night services, which I did, since it was one of the few times during the week when the Orthodox community did not hold services.

It was easy to see why people had quickly started gathering at the new church. Members were warm and welcoming to each visitor, Leonard was a passionate public speaker, and the church had multiple outreach programs and social groups. It was, in many respects, the opposite of what a visitor might have encountered upon entering St. Basil's or St. John's. Leonard and Hattie, who were quite well-off, funded the church building and endeavor themselves. One night they invited me to their compound for dinner. Driving south out of Woodford, I turned onto a small dirt road that climbed its way circuitously around the side of a mountain. At the top, I reached an elaborate wrought-iron gate with a speakerphone. Hattie buzzed me in and told me to park near the main garage. Standing on the front porch of an imposing chalet-style log home, Hattie welcomed me warmly and said Leonard was stuck at work but would be joining us shortly. Over a steak dinner and dessert, the couple talked with me about their calling to minister to an area that has succumbed to addiction and how they saw themselves as warriors for Christ, along with their God-given leader—Donald J. Trump.

In the vein of Orthodox sentiments, the couple expressed fears of growing secularism, but they also worried about the Russian influence in American and foreign affairs and feared for the safety of Israel. These sentiments were also expressed in their social media posts and in other public forums. Hattie and Leonard were focused on making America holy again, but not through a Russian invasion as some of the Orthodox in Woodford hoped for. Rather, they were part of the subsect of Christian nationalism that focused on the "protection of symbolic boundaries, including which religious or ethnic groups should be considered 'American.'"[39] Hattie and Leonard's social emphasis on America as a Christian nation seemed influenced by notions of belonging, whiteness, and fears about immigration. Their concerns over the Orthodox community stemmed mostly from their concerns over their assumed political allegiance. The couple worried that the Orthodox community might have insidious designs for the area. Hattie mentioned that the lack of Orthodox socialization with locals, even after all of these years, made people talk about them. While Hattie and Leonard knew that some of their parishioners used the food pantry at St. John's, they wondered aloud why the parish would not partner with other churches in the area that were focused on local community outreach. Hattie's parting comment of "they just seem like Catholics" helped contextualize the local views of the Orthodox converts in Woodford. The materiality of Orthodoxy, their veneration of saints, talk of feast days, and focus on hierarchal, patriarchal religious formations did not seem familiar in a region where forms of democratized Christianity, often with female leadership, were not sacramentally focused.[40]

Views from both the Orthodox and non-Orthodox seem like a given, since both groups possess forms of insularity that lead them to see alterity in the other.

Yet it seems strange on the part of Orthodox converts to eschew socialization with members of their own local community. In a 1966 article for *The Orthodox Word*, an English-language periodical that Rose started along with fellow monastic Gleb Podmoshensky the year prior, the monk wrote that "Orthodox Christians know the living God and dwell within in the saving enclosure of His True Church."[41] Rose continued, "It is here, in the faithful and fervent following of the unchanging Orthodox path—and not in the dazzling 'ecumenical' union with the new infidels that is pursued by Orthodox modernists—that our salvation is to be found."[42] Rose's emphasis on living, dwelling in the Church, removed from ideas and individuals who might corrupt the faith, is key to understanding why converts to ROCOR see themselves as faithful followers of truth in a world gone mad. Being an Orthodox Christian, from the perspective of Rose, was a life dedicated to the "narrow, hard, and dangerous path" of truth, for the "Orthodox mission" opens the door to a world that manifests "the right (ortho) teaching (dox)" and "eternal life in the kingdom."[43]

The actions of the converts in Woodford, in some ways, were summed up in Rose's statement. More often than not, individuals would tell me they were trying to work out their salvation in and with the ROCOR community as they all completed their individual journeys toward theosis. Perhaps intra-community conflict and outsider avoidance were part of their ascetical process of becoming like God. Certainly, the complicated ways in which converts interacted with each other and non-Orthodox Christians in the area often led to struggles that affected how their social networks functioned, but most of the members seemed to believe it was for their spiritual betterment. Often when parishioners went through traumatic events, they viewed it as part of their ascetic labor or *podvig* (lit. feat or achievement) to bear better spiritual fruit.[44] Within the community, it seemed as if each layer of conflict, despite creating tensions, often resolved in such a way that both institutions became cohesively functional and more socially intimate. This seemed to happen in the case of Aiden and Judith, who worked out an amenable solution with both the monastery and the parish by the time I left West Virginia.

The Orthodox community's tepid involvement in the local social scene seemed to be part of converts' larger ontological worldview as pilgrims journeying on the narrow and correct path through a foreign land on their way home. Furthermore, the way in which the community approached benevolence works also served to reinforce their ideological concerns. As Alexander Agadjanian notes in his interrogation of the Moscow Patriarchate's social vision document of 2000, "The church is represented as being an exclusive locus that retains the purity that the world has lost; it is juxtaposed to the world as another reality, thus restoring the breach between the divine it claims exclusively to represent, and the profane, which is by itself inexorably doomed."[45] Living in this liminal position of retaining and restoring the divine, ROCOR converts seemingly created their own form of strident *communitas* with the goal of re-mapping not just Appalachia but the world in the image of Orthodoxy.[46]

In a letter to Young in June of 1972, Rose discussed the proposed layout for *Nikodemos*, an Orthodox periodical the two men were working on at the time. In doing so, he drew upon apocalyptic concerns of the Antichrist, noting that they needed a stronger Orthodox community.[47] Rose believed their work was "opening up a 'dimension' of Orthodox life" in North America.[48] This form of lay Orthodoxy, according to Rose, "searches for deeper roots and feels that it cannot 'fit in' with the world."[49] This type of community, he wrote, "looks to the Fathers for answers, not on academic questions or theology, but on how to live."[50] In doing so, this form of the faith was one that, according to Rose, "transform[s] life, that makes Orthodox people something of a scandal to the world, that grows up with its own principles quite apart from the world around it, and yet that is quite sound and normal in itself."[51] In alignment with Rose's vision of Orthodoxy in the United States, missionizing outreach and social mistrust were part of the Orthodox worldbuilding project in Woodford. The social and religious infrastructures of the St. Basil's and St. John's were shaped by the bounded yet timeless nature of Orthodox theology, and so, too, were their history, memories, and understandings of belonging. Inside and outside of time, place, and space, these believers in West Virginia seemingly found a spot in which they could imaginatively create an anticipatory "outpost of heaven," a place "where the righteous souls reside" uneasily.[52]

7

The "Holler Feast"

Spiritual Geographies and Temporalities

East is East and West is West, and never the twain shall meet.
—RUDYARD KIPLING, 1889

The Russian Diaspora is an archipelago of salvation amidst a new
planet and world far removed from Christian morality.
—ARCHPRIEST ARTEMY VLADIMIROV, 2010

West by God Virginia.
—REGIONAL IDIOM, 1926

"We call it the holler feast," a monk mentioned to me as he talked about the
Presentation of the Theotokos, a religious holiday dedicated to the story of the
young Virgin Mary being given by her elderly parents to priests at the Jewish
temple in order to serve God.[1] While the high holy day is considered to be one
of the twelve Great Feasts of the Orthodox Church, often it does not draw as
much attention as other larger feasts that are either devoted to or predominantly
include Mary, such as the Nativity and Dormition of the Theotokos.[2] I asked
the monk why that feast day was tied to holler and he replied that the Theotokos saved the monastery from a fire on that feast day. Dotting the grounds of
St. Basil's compound were older structures built by their predecessors, one of
which was a traditional log cabin with white chinking, a popular architectural
style throughout the region. Somehow a fire of unknown origins started in or
near the log building that would eventually become part of the monastery's
library, a place where I spent hours reading and talking with the monks. At the
time, the monastery did not have reserve tanks of water or long-range sprinkler

systems for emergencies; there was also limited route access, because of narrow, dangerous roads that fed into the compound, which meant the local fire department would not have been able to reach them in time to help or even at all. The fire spread quickly through the leftover dry grasses of late summer and the fall leaves of early autumn that lay in piles around the building, causing the monks to question whether or not the monastery would collapse that day, leaving them homeless. The monk recalled that the abbot had asked for someone to bring him the festal icon of the Mother of God. Fashioning himself in the style of Moses during the battle between the Israelites and the Amalekites in the Hebrew Bible, the abbot lifted the icon high, with two young monks supporting his arms. Praying that the Theotokos would spare them, the monks threw buckets of water at the fire to no avail. As the abbot continued to hold the icon of Mary high, the skies darkened, the rains fell heavy, and the fires were assuaged before the clouds cleared and a rainbow emerged. Since that day, the monks hold entry feast of the Theotokos in high regard, making sure that their festal celebrations are elaborate. In their hagiographic recollections, Mary became the guardian of their holler that day. She stopped the fires. Because of her spiritual intervention, it seemed as if Orthodoxy was allowed to take root and grow deep in the hills of West Virginia, changing both the physical and spiritual topography of Appalachia.

In the previous chapter, I touched upon how class and economics might factor into the relationships Orthodox Christians in Woodford had with each other and with non-Orthodox townsfolk. This chapter nods briefly to those issues but focuses predominantly on how spirituality shaped particular political geographies and religious temporalities that converts took part in and created. In doing so, I return to the idea of conversion, looking at how religion, politics, and notions of the secular are entangled in Woodford converts' gestures toward Russia. As the hills and hollers of West Virginia became dwellings for Orthodox Christians, they transfigured their corner of Appalachia into an image of Holy Rus', while also bemoaning the American political infrastructures that allowed them freedom of religion and political affiliation. In a region that has reached out to Russia in the past for economic assistance, American converts looked abroad for salvific connections that could rescue them from what they saw as the destructive and demonic forces of Western progressive democracy. The Woodford ROCOR community highlights how immigration gave way to conversion, nationalism became tied to morality, and democracy was traded in for monarchism in the shifting spiritual geography of American religion.

By embracing the Russian Orthodox social vision of life in this world and the next, converts not only reconfigured their personal subjectivities, but were also complicit in the geopolitical deployment of Russian conservative ideologies of morality that were propagated by the Putin administration and his compatriots in the MP during the new global culture wars of the 2010s. In much of the same vein as the culture wars of the late twentieth century, the new global culture wars—that seemingly began with the 2016 U.S. presidential election—also possessed "polarizing impulses" with actors emphasizing their own understanding of moral truth and right belief about sociocultural issues.[3] Not surprisingly, Russia figured into the narratives about American morality during the twentieth-century culture wars, but for seemingly dialectically opposed reasons to the ones given by conservatives in the late 2010s. In the 1980s and 1990s, American citizens worried that "communist Russia" might be the end of "Western civilization."[4] Americans viewed the quickly ending Soviet Union apocalyptically, fearing that it would spread secular humanism to the Western world. In the culture wars of the 2010s, however, Russia, in far-right and conservative communities, took on a new image—that of the moral champion of conservative social moral values. In both eras of the culture wars, Russia held a significant position in the protection of and quest for social morality and authentic Americanness. This fear or embrace of Russia seemingly has its roots in the (neo)colonialist, Orientalist constructions of East and West, and what it means to be modern.[5]

Orthodoxy as Other

The everyday life of Appalachian Orthodox Christians in Woodford was oriented religiously and politically toward Russia, toward the East as a conceptual framework that rejected Western modernity.[6] The emphasis on orienting oneself eastward in Orthodoxy is embedded into the theology of the Church and the everyday spiritual practices that believers take part in. Churches are constructed so that the priest and parishioners face eastward as they celebrate the Divine Liturgy and the consecration of the Eucharist.[7] Icon corners, where believers chant their morning and evening prayers, are intended to be in an east-facing corner.[8] The East, as physically tied to holiness, is also present in the baptismal and chrismation rites of initiation for converts, when they are asked by the priest to face the west and spit on the devil three times. In American Orthodox convert culture, there are popular phrases such as "to the east," "eastward," or even "facing east," the latter of which was included in the title of a highly popular convert autobiography; these phrases are part of the worldbuilding rhetoric of conversion.[9] In Woodford, converts often talked about being drawn to "Eastern mysticism," or "Eastern spirituality," suggesting that religions and practices of "the East" held more spiritual validity or authenticity than those found in the Western world. This predilection to turn toward Eastern religions, mysticism, and philosophy is not new in the history of American religious belief and practice.[10] U.S. conversions to ROCOR are part of the historical transnational movements of migration, religious belief, and cultural practices that were and are part of the spiritual strands of Eastern mysticism in American religion, which included early followers of Swami Vivekananda and the more contemporary embrace of Vedic health trends that have popularized various forms of yoga.[11] It is pressing to see how the notion of Russia as the East, which seems to be a (neo)colonialist construction, is complicit in and reproduces the matrices of economics, class, and political ideology that are part of Orientalism and globalization more broadly.

Social scientist of Russian Orthodoxy Victor Roudometof highlights how, in the study of global Christianity, Orthodoxy "is still cast in the role of the 'subaltern Other' and falls victim to latent yet widespread Orientalism."[12] More often than not, this seems to be the case, particularly in the context of the United States, where American religious history has pushed the study of Orthodoxy to the margins. Within research on Orthodox Christianity, Orientalism functions in two ways—as a form of secularism and as a rhetoric of alterity.[13] Orientalism, in the Saidian tradition, is part of the binary schemes of Western domination that seek to categorize and marginalize specific communities.[14] In the context of Orthodox Christianity, its deep ties to ideas and geographies beyond those of the Western world have seemingly led to its dismissal in academe, where the focus tends to be on Protestantism (adherence to and rejection of), because of its relationship to secularism and power.[15] Yet these issues of secularism and power were often the main agitators that sparked Orthodox converts' shift to ROCOR, for they saw both as intimately tied to liberal democracy. Furthermore, secularism and power have deep, complicated geopolitical relationships with the various forms of Orthodox Christianity, most of which are intimately tied to Orientalism.

It is difficult to parse out the dimensions of Orientalism that are present in conversations regarding Orthodox Christianity, because often Orientalist scholarly assessments point out how the faith's embedded emic discourses are Orientalist in nature.[16] Sabrina Ramet suggests that, in terms of the European context, "the Orthodox Church refuses, for the most part, to accommodate itself to change, standing fixed in time, its bishops' gaze riveted on an 'idyllic past' which serves as their beacon."[17] Often the Orthodox traditionalist focus is analyzed through the lens of Orientalism, which simply serves to reinforce the essentialist perpetuation of Orthodoxy as the primitive form of Christianity clinging to the traditions of the ancient past in a way that is far more entrenched than Protestantism and Catholicism. Concomitantly, Orthodox Christianity does seem to possess deterministic theological ideas about secularism, religion, and politics that often lend themselves easily to labels of both fundamentalism and traditionalism.[18] Yet there must be a different, better way of understanding the social work of Orthodoxy without furthering notions of alterity. This is especially important when we talk about Orthodoxy in the United States, where it is a minority religious community. In order to overcome the academic forms of Orientalism that plague Orthodox Studies, we must acknowledge how attuned contemporary Orthodox—convert and cradle—are to the various machinations and mechanisms of historical, political, and cultural power. In the case of converts, it is imperative to understand how their conceptions of the East are intelligently attuned to the theologies of ROCOR and, at the same time, beholden to American Orientalist concepts of the exotic other. Placing these two aspects in relationship with each other provides us with an understanding of traditionalism that does not foist our own academic presuppositions upon it; nor does it see traditionalism as other. In analyzing the philosophical constructions of ROCOR and Russia that believers hold, we can gain a better understanding of what their conversions mean in the history of American religion and what they mean for believers themselves.

In the U.S. convert context, Oliver Herbel believes the emphasis on tradition among converts is part of the Restorationist Movement that has been taken up in many areas of American religion.[19] Certainly, the fact that many converts to Orthodoxy in the United States were once part of Protestant communities that emphasized a Christian restoration of sorts potentially had a trickle-down effect on the way American Orthodoxy developed.[20] Yet if the primary impulse for converts was to return to the pristine roots of Christianity, their regard for prerevolutionary Russian Orthodoxy and their venture into ROCOR would be quite a historical and spiritual detour. Many converts to ROCOR whom I interviewed and worked with often came from communities with Restorationist roots. If their goal was to continue on the Restorationist path, their shift to Orthodoxy seems philosophically jarring, especially given its political overtones, since primitive Restorationism was, and still is, mostly concerned with reclaiming ancient Christian polity with very little regard for social politics. Much in the vein of early structural functionalist approaches to culture, Herbel's assessment of conversion, which is a cultural phenomenon, is isolated from the larger sociocultural issues of (in)equality, power, privilege, and mobility that are complicit in and spring out of attachments to an identification with Orthodox Christianity in the American context. Most importantly, from my perspective, Herbel fails to fully think through issues of secularism and globalization that have impacted the ways in which U.S. citizens engage with religious values and practices.[21] Theoretically, Herbel's contention that conversions are processed through "a very American way (by means of Restorationism)" with an end result that "may seem to be a very unAmerican conclusion (the Eastern Orthodox tradition)," only serves to reinforce a binary of what is American and what is not, continuing the legacy of Orientalist approaches to Orthodoxy that peg it as the Christianity of alterity.[22]

Certainly, Eastern Orthodoxy is often seen as one of the last holdouts to secularism and (post)modernity; its rich sensorial structures of religiosity, combined with its seemingly ultra-conservative stances on social moral issues, has given it the public image of being steeped in ancient history, a primitive form of Christianity that lacks the post–Vatican II scholastic nature of Roman Catholicism and the flexible individualism of Protestantism, while shunning ecumenical dialogue that might help bridge their social differences. However, to highlight the turn to Orthodoxy as a search for the so-called primitive is at the least essentializing, and at the worst subjugating, and serves to reinforce the long-standing assumptions scholars often hold not only about conservative religious communities, but political ones as well. Most assuredly, many factions of Eastern Orthodoxy do hold deeply traditional values and ideas. The swelling voice of political conservatism manifests in the Russian Orthodox Church's proclamations about morality that have come to the fore in the global culture wars.[23] Scholars of the ROC would argue that it is not only the Church's public image but also their everyday doctrines that are seemingly cemented in bygone eras and ideas, particularly those found in Russian Orthodoxy prior to 1917.[24] Yet, simply seeing this nostalgic attitude as purely as theological move, as Herbel might, denies the intellectual politics of Orthodoxy that are far more ideologically sophisticated and socially attuned than its naysayers often realize.

Perhaps a way to gain more traction in understanding conversion as something besides some sort of primitive impulse, is to view it through the lens of fundamentalism in order parse out how and why the notion of tradition was and is so important to many Orthodox Christians, particularly converts. Papanikolaou and Demacopoulos, who have taken up the issues surrounding traditionalism, fundamentalism, and secularism, highlight how Orthodox Tradition is neither fundamentalist nor traditionalist. Tradition, in the very Orthodox sense of the word, is a living, transforming part of the faith that has evolved over time.[25] Tradition and traditionalism are not equals; the latter, from my vantage point, is part of the ever-evolving negotiation that Orthodoxy has with Christian fundamentalism, by way of its convert population predominantly, and its struggle with secularism. R. Scott Appleby suggests that fundamentalism seems to be spreading into Orthodoxy, merging with traditionalism, its close ideological cousin.[26] For Appleby, fundamentalism is often an orientation of being that is "reactive and selective" and sees the marginalization of religion in the post-secular world as indicative of a sort of violence toward belief.[27] In their resistance to the modern implications of secularism, fundamentalists, according to Appleby, react as "quintessentially modern people."[28]

In other words, fundamentalists "are not the Amish, seeking a cultural return to premodern purity, or Restorationists, hoping to rebuild the kingdom or return to the golden age."[29] Rather, as Appleby aptly points out, these well-educated ideologues, who have very little patience for the ambiguities of secular modernity and its effects on religion, are "looking ahead, not backward."[30] Fundamentalists' anxieties are based on the fears over what ambiguities might bring, such as a moral or environmental apocalypse. Thus they "attempt to eliminate ambiguity, bleach out complexity, and make the 'Tradition' politically expedient."[31] Appleby notes that Orthodoxy should seemingly be immune to fundamentalism, since it has a strong tradition as its basis. Yet given its apocalyptic eschatology and focus on rigorism that have emerged in the contemporary context, Orthodox was and is affected by fundamentalism. Orthodox fundamentalism is specifically expressed by those who, according to Appleby, were and are "trying to protect the Orthodox Christian faith from the corruption of modernity."[32] Appleby suggests that there are a lot of questions about whether or not Orthodoxy is capable of being a haven for fundamentalists and those who adhere to tradition. By nature, the definition of being an Orthodox Christian is to be one who ascribes to tradition, since that is the very structure of the Church. Certainly not all of those who are members of the Orthodox Church have a fundamentalist outlook. Many do, however. If we take Appleby's ideas of fundamentalism as a lens through which to think about the Woodford convert community, the ideas that believers offered up about the future of the United States, the angst over moral secularism, and their desire for political transformation begin to make much more sense.

Travelogues, Tradition, and Tariffs

One Sunday evening in early July of 2018, I headed to Clotilde's house for a dinner party for Fr. Damascene and Fr. Theodosius, who had just returned from a two-week trip to Russia. They went first to Moscow and then on to Optina Pustyn near Kozelsk, the spiritual sibling community of St. Basil's. Fr. Spyridon often sent monks to Optina, as it was known colloquially, for liturgical formation and periods of restful reflection. With friends of the monastery as guides, Moscow was their first stop, since they needed to acquire more liturgical vestments for the community, and they wanted to reconnect with their old friend, Fr. Artemy Vladimirov.[33] Throughout the course of the evening, over beers and homemade delicacies from Clotilde's kitchen, the fathers offered a PowerPoint presentation of their travels, interspersing stories with images of the places they visited and the people they had met. During the presentation, one of the guests asked how the monks were received by people in Moscow, since they were Americans traveling to Russia at a very unstable political moment between the two countries. Fr. Damascene, the elder of the two monks in terms of spiritual formation, answered the questions, drawing on the Trump administration's foreign policies to explain interactions the two had with people on the streets of Moscow. "They loved us!" Fr. Damascene said joyously as he adjusted the laptop he had balanced on his knees. "They were so happy about the tariffs," he continued. Someone in the group asked why that might be the case and Fr. Damascene elaborated, explaining that Russians he encountered appreciated the tariffs, for they believed in the long run that tariffs would strengthen the internal financial and political stability of Russia, even if it meant economic setbacks at first.

Fr. Damascene also relayed that most Orthodox believers he encountered were encouraged that Trump won the 2016 presidential election given his seemingly warm relationship with Vladimir Putin at the time. The presentation given by the fathers that evening seemed to be a multimedia travelogue, one that highlighted the sociocultural differences and similarities between Russia and the United States. Visiting with Fr. Artemy was the final stop for the fathers before heading on to Optina. Most of the fathers and many of the clergy and parishioners at St. John's believed Vladimirov was clairvoyant; throughout ROCOR there were mentions of Fr. Artemy being a living saint. Vladimirov's work in Russia was and is primarily among English-speaking expats (mostly converts). In 2010, as part of his whirlwind tour of American ROCOR communities, Vladimirov visited St. Basil's monastery, staying with the monks. In Russian Orthodox media outlets, Vladimirov often decried the secular nature of America life, and one of the monks at St. Basil's noted to that Vladimirov refused to return to the United States after his last visit, for he was concerned, they claimed, with the devolving American political system under President Barack Obama.

While some Russians the monks encountered wanted to talk about U.S. politics, most preferred to talk about Orthodoxy in the United States, asking the fathers if they knew about or had met Father Seraphim Rose. "He's so popular there. They loved him," both fathers proclaimed. The monks recalled how many Orthodox believers they encountered, ranging from laity to clergy, were quite devoted to the spiritual legacy of Rose, who is often portrayed in Russian Orthodox media as an international conservative icon for true piety and devotion to Holy Rus'. Rose can thus be seen as a linking figure, aligning American conservative converts with Orthodox Christians in Russia through their adoration of conservatism. As the monks finished their presentation, Clotilde beamed with joy and commented how she would love to visit Russia again. "What a grace-filled place," she said with a sigh. The idealization of Russia as an enchanted land filled with Orthodox Christians and churches was often part of the rhetoric used by converts to denote the difference between Russia and the United States. It was this type of Edenic haven that the converts sought to create in West Virginia.

They Came, They Stayed, and They Might Go

Most converts who moved to Woodford did so because they saw it as a spiritual haven in the tradition of communities that sprung up in the countryside around rural Russian Orthodox monasteries.[34] The steady migration of converts brought socioeconomic transformations to the region. When I first started searching for property to rent in the area, a local real estate agent warned me that rental prices would be high because of the elevated cost of homes in the area. After talking with her and several homeowners in the community, I found out that the migration of Orthodox Christians seemed to be potentially responsible for the increase in housing prices, with Fr. Basil and Mat. Emilia's home purchase being the impetus for this increase. The typical narrative conveyed by disgruntled property seekers centered on the couple's quick purchase of a small home within walking distance of monastery grounds at a price disproportionately high for the area. That property purchase, which coincided with other Orthodox Christians moving to the area, meant that the housing prices kept going up. The influx of Orthodox Christians from areas outside of Appalachia seemingly brought about a form of "rural gentrification" to Woodford, one that saw locals being outpriced by those moving in to be near the monastery and the parish.[35] Most Orthodox converts who moved to the area were happy to finally find a place in which they could be themselves. While the community was not isolated from the outside world, it was steeped in a particular calendar of lengthy services and numerous feasts that created an almost alternative reality or world. As one monk said to me, "Time moves differently here." Living in a seemingly idyllic natural environment, among like-minded believers, with less influence from the outside world, these converts seemed to believe they had created an intentional Orthodox refuge almost outside of time and space.[36]

While most of the Orthodox of Woodford were content to stay in the United States, there were a few, including Angus, who wondered what life might be like in Russia. He, along, with a few other members of St. John's, was part of a popular public Facebook group focused on resettling in Russia.[37] Founded in 2016, a month prior to the presidential election, the group's description identified the key foci: "faith, family, farming." Within the description for the group,

the administrators also expressed their Orthodox ideological impetus for creating the group: "Some people call us brave. Some people call us 'The Benedict
Option on Steroids.' And some people call us crazy! :-) Whatever you call us,
if you are interested in helping build a healthy community of Christian families
in the heart of ancient Russia, you are welcome in this group!"[38] The language
used in the group description draws on Orthodox writer Rod Dreher's separation ideology to reinforce how Russia was a safe space for morally healthy
people.[39] The image of Russia as a moral, ideological, and even biologically
safe haven for Orthodox (and other) Christians was an idea that was repeatedly
emphasized in the group's feed through postings from its members. Amid posts
of church music, videos of divine services in Church Slavonic, and practical
questions about resettlement, members often posted content that emphasized
what they saw as the immorality of Western society in contradistinction to the
traditional, Christian milieu of post-Soviet Russia. Fears over "equal rights for
homosexuals" were rampant, with one administrator posting a link to an article
about Christian schools being threatened with a loss of financial aid if they
did not "support LGBT," and commenting: "The rainbow mafia won't stop
until every child in the country is forcibly indoctrinated into the demonic ways
of the homosexuals. It has to stop now. . . ."[40] Posts of that nature were prevalent
in the public group of almost two thousand members, who saw the United
States as a sort of battleground for Christian morality. Equal rights for same-sex
couples and transgendered people pushed members to think about moving
away from their homeland in hopes of finding a place that might support and
champion their ideological beliefs.

The desperation of American Orthodox converts in the group to find a
spiritual oasis of some sort was evident throughout the history of the feed. In
the spring of 2017, one member posted a *pravmir.com* article about the importance of American converts learning Russian history, noting that "Russia becomes like a lode stone for the compass of my soul."[41] The magnetic draw of
Holy Mother Russia was part of the geopolitical migration rhetoric of many
Orthodox converts in the United States that seemingly finds its basis in the
ideas of empire and collapse. Scholar of Russian Orthodoxy in the post-Soviet
context, Mikhail Suslov, explains that Holy Rus' is a geopolitical idea that does
have a distinct history in religious belief, but in the contemporary period, it
has taken on a far more political bent, especially through actions of Patriarch
Kirill.[42] Suslov notes that within the last few decades the concept has become
an ideological way of "remembering the past."[43] The ideology, which looks to
Prince Vladimir and the conversion of Rus' as the beginning of the holy
empire, tries to remap pre-1917 Orthodoxy onto new global terrains and communities. This idea became especially salient in Woodford, where the sensorial

festivals of commemoration for Tsar Nicholas II and the Port Arthur icon of the Mother of God not only altered the spiritual topography of Appalachia, but also collapsed the distance in the geographies of belief, allowing converts to participate in geopolitical remembrance and all its possibilities. During the Trump presidency, a political moment in which believers felt trepidatious hope for social change, some viewed their future with great apprehension, with converts wondering when their nation would turn on them and if their Russian Orthodox compatriots abroad would welcome them as legitimate heirs of the holy Slavic kingdom. At the same time, many converts remained staunchly devoted to breaking down the barriers between the Christian church and state at home; they seemingly understood themselves as Americans on a quest to reclaim their Christian nation. For the latter, place did not matter as much as time, since they participated in the heavenly kingdom through liturgical drama and through their digital encounters with Orthodox Rus'.

Mediated Migrations and Digitally Deconstructed Democracy

Anthropologist Webb Keane notes that "if globalization means more than the objective circulation of people and money, it is not merely a matter of imagination. Ideas, like everything else, circulate insofar as they have some medium."[44] The ideological beliefs that were present in the Woodford community are part of the larger circulations of knowledge that have become more legible around the world through processes of globalization. Media have become mechanisms through which social connectivity becomes easier, with the distance being covered through a few simple keystrokes. Space and time seemingly collapse within the ethernet. The prominence of digital media technologies as a means through which Christians build and sustain religious worlds cannot be underestimated. Technology is the link through which they find information, friendship, and spiritual purpose—through which they build out their world.

Many of the posts in the Russia resettlement Facebook group were from the popular website russian-faith.com, which was founded by David Curry, a well-known American member of ROCOR. As of 2020, the site was jointly run by him and Charles Bausman, the founder of *Russian Insider*, both of whom lived as ex-pats in Russia for a time. The site description, which was written by Curry, states, "We created this website in August of 2017 to more fully report on a major global cultural, social, and political shift which affects not just Russia, but indeed the whole world—the rebirth of Christianity in Russia, the attacks on, and decline of Christian values in Western Europe and America, and the profound subsequent effects in society, culture, and government."[45] Launched around the same time I was moving to Woodford, the site sought to promote Orthodox social values, while highlighting how "modern Russia" rejects the "most sacred of modern Western beliefs"—the separation of church and state.[46] In 2018, after a health crisis, Curry handed over editorial reins to Bausman for *Russian Faith* but stayed on at *Russian Insider* as the operations director.[47] *Russian Faith* functions much like most private media clearinghouses, providing articles and information with a specific agenda. Topics include "Explaining Orthodoxy," "Christian Persecution," "Anti-Ecumenism," "Family Values," and "Church Politics," interspersed among articles about homeschooling, Russian language acquisition, economics, and guides for those interested in moving to Russia.

Curry was the son of a convert who lived near the historic ROCOR monastery in Jordanville, New York, and he had deep ties to the community in Woodford. One of his siblings attended St. John's and his mother used to own a home near St. Basil's. Ideologically, his public views on social media were quite in line with what I encountered among converts to ROCOR throughout the United States, and especially in Appalachia. His public Facebook feed was littered with reposts from Ben Shapiro, the far-right media outlet *OAN* (One America Network), and memes about Alex Jones. Curry's focus, as expressed through his social media posts and his work at both *Russian Faith* and *Russian Insider*, seemed to be on reinforcing the dualistic binary of Western secularism and depravity against the salvific forms of Russian Orthodoxy in the Eastern world. In order to "give Christianity" a voice, Curry's *Russian Faith* had private funders while also being crowdfunded. The site also served as a form of income for posters who have moved to Russia, including Fr. Joseph Gleason, an Orthodox convert and American expat in Russia, who was a frequent contributor in the resettlement group. Fr. Joseph rose to fame among ROCOR convert communities when he moved to Rostov the Great in 2017 with his wife and eight children.[48] An American convert from Protestantism, Fr. Joseph was the rector of an Orthodox parish in the Midwest before moving to Russia. During an interview with Artemy Schmidt, a Russian sociologist, Fr. Joseph highlighted the two primary reasons he decided it was time for his family to resettle in Russia: homosexuality and American foreign policy. Certainly, the political nature of *Russian Faith* was not limited to Curry's influence or Fr. Joseph's. Charles Bausman's role as the editor beginning in late 2018 meant that the religiously focused site would become even more sensitive to issues of global politics and even far/alt-right ideologies.

In 2019, Bausman had an interview on the *Info Wars* set with digital and radio media pundit Alex Jones while he was there filming a documentary about

Jones. In the interview, Bausman talked about living in Russia as a child, when his father was the bureau chief for the Associated Press, and moving in far-right and alt-right media and social networks during the later 2010s.[49] The connections of David Curry with Jones and Bausman are not to be overlooked, for each has networks that are deeply entrenched in both Putin's government and far-right American conservative communities. Jones and Bausman were fearful of "liberal globalists" who might take down the United States through open borders and progressive politics.[50] "They are coming for your children," Jones said of the globalists in the interview, claiming progressive secularism to be a satanic force in world politics.[51] The main issue for both men was freedom—of the press, of religion, and, above all, of the moral family.

Freedom was an idea that came up regularly among Orthodox Christians in Woodford. Members feared that their religious civil liberties, their freedom to practice, preach, and spread their beliefs would be denied them. I suggest that this focus on individual choice and freedom, in the vein of personal liberties, is part of the long history of American religious practice and belief. Unlike Herbel and Slagle, however, who emphasize the true Americanness of the spiritual marketplace of choice, I see this focus on freedom as part of the heritage of Christian nationalism combined with the technological affordances of globalization that have allowed for more flexibility in selecting not only one's faith, but also one's political alignment.[52] While Orthodox converts claim themselves to be Russian Orthodox Christians, they were and are still American citizens who are enmeshed in the fabric of both American democracy and religious life. The political structures of the United States that converts feared might take away their civil liberties, compromise the moral integrity of their children, and perhaps even incarcerate them for their beliefs, were in fact the mechanisms through which their freedoms were made possible. Often, believers drew on the origin stories of ROCOR to show how bishops and other Russian Orthodox Church leaders, fearing Soviet influence in religious practice, left Russia to find religious freedom elsewhere. Whether they stayed in the United States, lamenting its potential decline, or hoped to move to Russia in order to save themselves and future generations, converts I spoke with in Woodford are exemplary of what fundamentalist traditionalist adherents to ROCOR and Russian Orthodoxy often looked like sociopolitically in the 2010s. These Appalachian converts, along with their compatriots in other parts of the United States, are part of the new face of Orthodoxy, or what I have termed "Reactive Orthodoxy." This new, hybridized form of religiosity is a worldbuilding form of the faith that finds it roots in an imagined nostalgia for ancient Rus', American Christian nationalism, and an apocalyptic disenchantment with democracy.[53]

Political Postures of Reactive Orthodoxy

Reactive Orthodoxy is not American Orthodoxy, which is understood by scholars to be expressed in the pan-ethnic attempts in the late-nineteenth and
twentieth centuries to create a truly homegrown form of Orthodoxy in the
United States. While American Orthodoxy was and is found in different formations given the time period and the jurisdiction, historically it has not been
tied to Christian nationalism, disillusionment with American political structures, or extreme social and moral positionalities. As mentioned previously,
the OCA considers itself to be an American Orthodox Church, but it is just
one of many jurisdictions that falls under the umbrella of this terminology.[54]
Other jurisdictions, such as the Greek Orthodox Archdiocese (GOA), used
their ethnic identification as part of social solidarity building projects and as
outreach in their promotion of foodways and festivals; at the same time, however, the GOA and the Antiochian Archdiocese did take part in American
enculturation and assimilation processes, including the embrace of cleric collars
rather than robes, the use of pipe organs and pews, and the creation of phil-
anthropic organizations.[55] The Antiochian Archdiocese also took on a different
form of Americanization through the influx of evangelical converts from
Campus Crusade and the noncanonical Evangelical Orthodox Church in the
mid-1980s, the effects of which are still surfacing today.[56]

Russian Orthodox parishes (MP) and ROCOR (both during and after reconciliation) preserved much of their heritage through language and practice,
although within the twenty-first century, English-language use in parishes and
seminaries skyrocketed. However these jurisdictions chose to express themselves,
they were still part of the larger umbrella of American Orthodoxy that was synonymous with diaspora and mission. On the whole, American Orthodoxy in
the nineteenth and twentieth centuries was far too concerned, it seems, with
interchurch politics and creating a cohesive community in the United States to
be deeply caught up in American social politics more broadly—although the
GOA was instrumental in supporting the civil rights movement.[57] More recent
formations of Orthodoxy in the United States, especially ones rich with convert
populations, are far more invested in finding or creating ways in which their
political ideologies, often framed by converts as theologies, are not only supported by state policies, but perhaps also enforced by them. This politically
assertive strain of Orthodoxy in the United States is the foundation of the Reactive Orthodox movement. It is fair to say that the contemporary political
preoccupations of many converts—in ROCOR and in other jurisdictions—have
brought about the rise of Reactive Orthodoxy, which has become a theo-political

home for a wide range of ideologies not found widely in most of American Orthodoxy during the twentieth century.

Many converts in Woodford were professed monarchists, praying for the reintegration of Christian church with the state in a new type of Orthodox *symphonia*. Reactive Orthodoxy's preoccupation with tsarist Russia is tightly linked to both their fears and appreciation of the separation of church and state. Many of the monks I interviewed at St. Basil's told me they would support the unification of church and state in the United States, provided that the church—in their case the Orthodox Church—was able to guide the government, rather than the state controlling religious practices and beliefs. This understanding of a holy nation, guided by both the church and state, is reminiscent of symphonia in Orthodox tradition, but it is also a major tenet of belief among American Christian nationalists. Scholars of Christian nationalism, an ideology found most explicitly in evangelical Protestantism, note that it focuses on creating and preserving a strong, perhaps even overlapping, relationship between Christianity and governmental institutions.[58] In some respects, Christian nationalism seems to be a contemporary American form of symphonia, which, at its core, emphasizes strong, unified leadership that is religiously influenced.[59] Perhaps this why Woodford converts like Fr. Damascene felt "more patriotic" as Orthodox Christians.[60]

Fr. Damascene, who emphasized repeatedly that he considered himself a Russian Orthodox Christian, believed that in ROCOR he found not only "spiritual freedom," but also a way to be a more productive member of American society.[61] Converts often expressed how being Orthodox made them better Americans, for in their minds it seemed as if Christianity and Americanness were tightly linked. As Fr. Damascene pointed out, "We pray for America during the liturgy." Most assuredly, the ROCOR liturgy does include a petition for God to have mercy on the United States and its authorities, but it also has the same plea for the God-preserved land of Russia. This dual spiritual citizenship is one that seemed to help practitioners make sense of their place in the world. By and large, they certainly felt as though they were part of a disaffected, perhaps even persecuted, Christian community in the United States that was in desperate need of advocates for their values, beliefs, and lifestyles that seemed to be vanishing amid growing secularism. Yet, at the same time, they feared the liberty and equality of democracy that gave them ready access to those advocates in the public sphere, looking at Russia's illiberal regime of conservatism as a much more ideologically safe nation.

Nationalism is not a stranger to Orthodox Christianity given how its structural formations have been historically tied to state identity politics and pride in distinct ethno-religious practices. However, nationalism in the context of American converts to ROCOR is far more complicated than loyal affinity to one's homeland. The nationalism expressed by converts I worked with was not tied to the dream of American exceptionalism. America was not exceptional. America was a social failure in the eyes of Woodford converts. National pride had fallen by the wayside. American nationalism gave way to Christian nationalism that often took the form of fealty to Russian Orthodoxy, heritage, monarchy, and conversative politics. The loss of their patriotic attachment to the United States or finding it to be enhanced is part of their negotiation of nationalism, but it also speaks to their understanding of being citizens of the heavenly kingdom. Perhaps this negotiation is, in part, because of the social doctrine of the Russian Orthodox Church, which emphasizes a world-affirming view of estrangement from the terrestrial.[62] Whatever the case may be, it was clear from my encounters with Woodford Orthodox Christians that they held deep pride in being Americans, even if they decried it as a broken country on the brink of destruction and believed their best chance of finding a country that was not spiritually bankrupt was to look to Russia.

A superficial analysis of these conversions might assume they are simply part of the new populism that has reemerged in more vigorously active formations since the 2016 election, but that would not provide a contextualized picture of this community in the global context.[63] As scholars have noted, populism in the context of the United States is typically not antidemocratic. Indeed, populists tend to want a more extensive form of democracy that pulls power away from the elites and delivers it into the hands of the citizens.[64] Nor are these conversions part of movements of national populism that were present in the push for Brexit in the United Kingdom and communities that mobilized for Marine Le Pen in her 2017 French presidential bid. To be sure, converts in Woodford did share many of the ideological fears that have been attached to nationalist populists—concerns about the government, xenophobic immigration fears, Western (white) marginalization, and the loss of tradition. While the issues Russian Orthodox converts talked about often mirrored those of populists, their approach to combating or solving these issues seemed to be antithetical to methods employed by those seeking more diffused governmental powers. Rather than wishing to increase the promotion of citizen liberties, many converts in Appalachia sought to give up their inalienable rights to reconstruct an autocratic, perhaps even fascist, regime that would save them from the hellish freedom of democracy.

For most converts I spoke with, submitting to hierarchical, God-given governance, both spiritually and politically, was the only way to find salvation. Proper governance without Christianity would be, for many, a failure, not only for them, but also for society more broadly. Fr. Tryphon elaborated on this during a conversation in the spring of 2018:

> It doesn't matter if you have the best society with the best king, and you live in the bosom of nature 24/7 and you don't have God; it doesn't mean anything. So, for Orthodox people to be monarchists, I think it can be good and beneficial; and maybe someday Russia will have a tsar again, I don't know. If it's [monarchism] not in the context of your love for Christ, then it's just another "-ism." I would say that objectively speaking it's an "-ism" that has much more to recommend it than democracy does.[65]

This type of language was employed by many in the community. In a similar fashion to Christian nationalists, converts drew on the importance of placing Christ at the center of their political decisions.[66] Given the fact that most converts were former evangelicals, this type of rhetoric might have been a continuation of their American ideologies, refashioned through the lens of their new faith. Through their turn to ROCOR, converts seemed to believe they found a system through which their conceptions of Christianity and politics could flourish. In doing so, they may have unwittingly created a new form of Orthodoxy.

Conclusion

In Soviet America, Russia Converts You!

Reactive Orthodoxy was and is political. Its figurehead is not Vladimir Putin, but the American, homegrown Father Seraphim Rose. Rose's writings were taught and revered in the Woodford community by most, especially at St. Basil's monastery. A blending of political ideology and Russian mysticism, Rose's philosophy was not only important for converts' journeys to Orthodoxy; he was also vital in helping Woodford Orthodox Christians make sense of modernity and life at the imagined end of the world—through his works and Fr. Ambrose, his spiritual son. Rose was a product of his social environments, which included training at the University of California at Berkeley, but also the Russian Orthodox community in the Bay Area. Ideologically, Rose was influenced not only by Chinese philosophy and the teachings of his mentor Alan Watts, but also by Evangelical Zionist Hal Lindsey, for he mentioned both in his various works on the Antichrist, secularism, and a future apocalypse. Drawing on the latter, Rose created a particular political theology in his writings that encapsulated what he saw as mystical "Eastern" piety, Russian monastic conceptions of the afterlife, and evangelical moral politics. Additionally, Rose's entry point into the Russian Orthodox Church was traditionalist René Guénon, and his presence is especially felt in Rose's emphasis on the existence of a universal truth. Through all of these influences, Rose seems to have formulated a reflexive type of traditionalist theology that was not only influenced by politics, but also served as a lens through which adherents analyze current events for their apocalyptic value (fig. 9).

Rose's influence in the lives of ROCOR converts is not to be underestimated. His works were and are sold by most, if not all, ROCOR seminary and monastery bookstores in the United States. Rose's influence is not limited to the

Figure 9. Gifted Icon of Seraphim Rose
(Anonymous)

United States, as the monks indicated during my time in Woodford—he was
and is much beloved in Russia. In Rose's biography, Christensen writes:

> For just as Russia once brought the fullness of Truth—Orthodoxy—
> to America, so now is America, through Fr. Seraphim, bringing the
> Truth back in whence it came. Through this man who was a pivot of
> the American conscience, modern America brings forth, out of its own
> soil, a fruit of ancient, mystical Christianity. It is a depth of Christian-
> ity that America as yet scarcely knows; formed in the silent heart of the
> catacombs, hidden from all earthly tumult and vanity, and by nature
> *not of this world.*[1]

Just a few pages earlier, his biographer, recounting the words of a Russian monk,
notes that "without Fr. Seraphim Rose, we'd all be dead."[2] Rose is indeed a
global figurehead for Reactive Orthodoxy. The digital world is rife with the
religious materiality of Rose—memes, photographs, quotes, stories of people
who were affected by his life and teachings, and PDFs of *The Orthodox Word,*
the periodical he founded and edited together with Gleb Podmoshensky.

Countless websites, in English and Russian, offer personal stories about Rose, his connections to John Maximovitch, and his desire to promote traditional Orthodoxy in the United States and abroad. Converts in Woodford often looked to Rose to make sense of what they saw as "revolutions" in global politics. This ranged from the French Revolution to the 1917 Russian Revolution, and what they saw as the moral revolution happening in twenty-first-century America.

Over coffee one spring morning, Clovis, Clotilde's husband, explained to me that Rose was essential in understanding how world politics are tied to the spiritual realm. Revolutions, according to Clovis's reading of Rose, are demonic, for they end in democracy, which he believed was ultimately "the oppression of the monarchy."[3] For Clovis, Rose understood the significance of monarchism as a way to suppress evil forces and the inevitable destruction of the world. Drawing on American attempts to spread democracy throughout the world, especially the Middle East, Clovis tried to explain why bringing a monarchy to the United States might not be a good idea socially, despite its substantial theological benefits:

> It might be a bit extreme in the same way that democracy doesn't
> work in Iraq. Yes, it sounds like a great idea. We want democracy
> everywhere. Freedom for the women. You want to be able to have
> your Coca-Cola and your McDonald's. The freedom for education
> and stuff like that. But you can't just invade, topple things and then
> just say, okay, we just need to make it stable for long enough. It'll just
> grow out of the ashes to do it. Not necessarily. So, monarchy? Yes.
> There's lots and lots of reasons . . . that it is a good thing. Do I think
> it should be restored here, there, and everywhere? Not necessarily.

Often the desire for a monarchic nation is tempered by the realities of contemporary American life. In spite of this, the converts I spoke with did not give up their longing to reclaim a type of governance they believed would save not only their souls but their country, governance seemingly composed of both ROCOR theological values and Christian nationalism.

A Nation under Something Else

The members of St. Basil's and St. John's were one community among many burgeoning ideological groups that were carving out new political realities beyond U.S. democracy at the end of the 2010s. Certainly, the alternative sociopolitical imaginaries of this community were on the far right of the American political system, but around the same time in Appalachia, there were also far-left Marxist collectives who also espoused radically different ideas about what the U.S. government should look like.[4] Rural progressives and socialists living and working in West Virginia were also frustrated with the old "hierarchies and systems of power" that were complicit in negating the experiences and values of those living in Appalachia.[5] They did not believe their voices were heard, but unlike their Orthodox counterparts, they dug deep into the history of American politics and used grassroots activism and labor organization to reformulate the system in hopes of creating a revolution that would be more attuned to their needs and ideas. In contrast, far-right Orthodox Christians in Appalachia, who also felt oppressed and dismissed by those with political power, reacted with fearful dismay at the advancing front of progressivism, perhaps becoming radicalized in the process by Russian propaganda they saw as truth in what they perceived of as a post-truth era for Western media outlets.[6] At roughly the same political moment in American history, two ideological networks were spreading throughout West Virginia, trying to reconfigure the social landscape of the Appalachia for radically different agendas.

Scholars of the region have long tried to express the social diversity that has sprung forth historically in Appalachian spaces that are often framed by the media (and academia) in terms of capitalism and neocolonialism. These lenses often reinforce and perpetuate the long-standing public assumptions about the people and practices found in this area of the United States. In many respects, conversions to Russian Orthodoxy in Appalachia were part of a geospatial disruption of class, economics, and politics that shatters our normative assumptions about religion and politics in the region. Perhaps the ideological conversations that converts took part in were not engaged with the larger leftist endeavors that historically fought systems of corruptive power in the region; yet, nevertheless, they were, in their own ways pushing back in a reactionary move against what they saw as oppressive hegemonic political formations. In a period of American history when rural populations were heavily marginalized in the media—portrayed as uncouth, uneducated Republican hillbillies who voted for Trump because he was a populist, a man of the people—there were communities throughout Appalachia, on the left and the right, who did not fall into this category.[7] Appalachian public scholar Elizabeth Catte askes, "So, how do we define change?"[8] Catte's question is one that surely comes to bear in the stories of Orthodox Christians in Woodford, who feared social change, while trying to create it for themselves.

For the believers I worked with on a daily basis, the political, social, and religious change that they desired did not prompt them to flee the area or even the United States; rather, they sought their freedom through religious rites and rituals, through the creation of intentional communities, through their intellectual engagement with political systems beyond their physical reach, and often through ideas linked to Seraphim Rose. Change, whether positive or negative, is subjective. For some converts, change meant dismantling American structures of democracy through a Russian invasion, while for others it meant supporting the MP and Putin's ideologies from the security of the United States, with varying levels of ideological support found in between. At the base of most of their opinions was the desire to pushback against secularism by looking outside of the Western world. While they considered themselves to be far-right but not Republican, these Appalachian discontents could not abide by the tenets of libertarianism, for they did not want to settle for states being individual arbitrators or "laboratories of democracy"; instead they looked beyond the normative American political system to find solutions that could allay their fears.[9] These solutions, it would appear, first came in the form of religion that allowed converts to join and perpetuate a community of like-minded believers who would share their ideological fears over the future.

Spiritual conversion then served as a gateway to enter a world where religion and politics were not housed in distinct spheres but were part of everyday systems and languages of belief. Regarding secular politics as devilry, these converts found in religion a way to engage with the political that used a rhetoric of spirituality to make sense of their ideologies. At the end of the day, the praise of Putin, the focus on Russia, and the desire for a king were simply new symptoms of the long-standing fears conservative Christians in the United States have had over progressive liberalism since the nineteenth century. Haunted by the influence of Christian (evangelical) nationalism, the remnants of Cold War rhetoric about East and West, and influences of Orientalism and secularism, these converts reinvented what it meant to be a far-right Christian during the 2010s. Well-educated, philosophically inclined, and focused on ritual religions that could make sense of modern life for them, converts reached out to a national leader who seemingly had their best interests at heart, or so he claimed. In doing so, they engaged the freedom of religion that democracy afforded them, while they decried the system as broken.

The truth of American conversions to Russian Orthodoxy is complicated. It is messy and does not fit neatly into the historical, anthropological, and theological categories academia has constructed for the study of Appalachia, American religion, and Russian Orthodoxy more broadly. This is just as much a story about secularism as it is religion, about history as it is anthropology, about the connective implications of digital technology as it is conservative theology. This is a story about Orthodox Christianity, one that moves away from post-Soviet countries to look at Orthodoxy as a minority religion in a spiritual geography that is steeped in far different notions of nationalism and Christianity than we often find it. This is a story about people whose views were far from mine, often found in the spiritual writings of Russian elders from the snowy Northern Thebiad, but who embraced me, nonetheless. This is a story about Appalachia, but it is not the typical narrative we often read or hear about the region. In the end, the largest figures, Trump, Putin, and the liberal populations that converts feared, fall away. They are not what this story is about. In the end, this is a story about everyday Americans who found a home and, in doing so, defied the temporal and geopolitical boundaries of what it means to be a conservative Christian in the United States.

Epilogue

The idea of being at home often has connotations of being with family and loved ones, being safe, being secure. This sentiment held true for the Orthodox Christians in Woodford. Their community was a home, a haven, where their ideas about theology and social politics were safe to profess, and where the emic and etic boundaries were clearly demarcated through daily belief and practice. In thinking back to the early stages of the community, it is hard to imagine how a pan-Orthodox group of converts and cradles from around the United States seemingly transformed into a community deeply invested in ideological ideas associated with far-right radicalism. In the years since living in Woodford, I have begun working on a new project that explores how self-professed radicalized Orthodox Christians create digital networks of political solidarity. Found throughout the United States and connected via social media, these individuals galvanize one another to create social change in a way that I did not see in the Woodford community. As I reflect on views from the monks and laity in Appalachia and those espoused by online far-right Orthodox believers, I return to questions about motivation, questions that ultimately bring us back to the rhetoric of purity and panic and the centrality of nostalgia as a reactive motivator for worldbuilding.

In its early years, the Woodford community focused by and large on infrastructure building and creating networks with both ROCOR in the United States and the Russian Orthodox Church, particularly after the reunification in 2007. Politics, at least the kind that were espoused in the late 2010s, were not as central to the social mechanisms of St. Basil's or St. John's. While the ethos of St. John's in the late 2010s seemed to be, in large part, a product of Fr. Cyril's making, the monastery's transformation took place a bit prior to his arrival in

2011. In 2008, a shift began to occur at St. Basil's. The election of Barack Obama and changes in leadership at the monastery were part of that turning point according to Benedict, a former and much beloved monk at St. Basil's, who worked intimately with monastery leadership and the hierarchs of ROCOR. Benedict was one of several Woodford defectors I interviewed in 2020–2021. A born-and-bred Texan who spent sixteen years at St. Basil's, helping build the community from the ground up, Benedict was no longer a monk. When we spoke in the fall of 2020, he was married, living in Paris, and working as a writer. Well-educated and from an affluent background, Benedict had been taken with Russian Orthodoxy and monastic life in Appalachia until it became too demanding and highly politicized. Benedict's story is typical of the narratives I heard from others who had left the community, all of whom were longtime members and left in the waning years of the 2010s.

The shift toward far-right political ideologies at St. Basil's, it seems, began with the arrival of a hierarch who not only created social angst but ideological anxiety through his enthusiastic embrace of conspiracy theories. Benedict recounted how the bishop would spend hours surfing the Internet, watching videos from conspiratorial sources, sending links to monks in order to share his findings. Enamored with this "early QAnon type of stuff," the bishop's digital media consumption began to transform the social ethos of the monastery.[1] A pro-Russia convert, the hierarch's influence seemed to "trickle down" to the younger monks, who could be found watching exposé documentaries about a wide range of topics like 9/11 late at night—something that was generally not allowed.[2] At the same time, two elderly monks in the community began listening to conservative talk shows during their weekly shopping trips; fairly soon, they began talking about Obama as the Antichrist, focusing on the birther conspiracy as evidence.[3] Benedict noted that by 2008, politics, as a topic of conversation among the monks, "became ubiquitous."[4] After living through the social transformations at the monastery, Benedict left in 2016, frustrated by increasing politicization of ROCOR through the MP, the intense clericalism that pushed laity to believe conspiracy theories spread by hierarchs, and the ideological partitioning work he saw expanding in Woodford and throughout ROCOR.

As we neared the end of our conversation, Benedict offered the following reflection about the sociopolitical ethos of the Woodford community:

> Can you imagine living in the monastery or going to the monastery or
> the parish . . . and not revering the tsars or believing they are God's
> anointed, or accepting the Holy Russia ideal? You'd definitely be on
> the fringes if you said, "No, I'll just stick with the creed and with some

early Christian writings, the Didache, but I'm not really into the whole God's anointed tsar and all that." You'd really have trouble fitting in. So the question is: *What really makes a person Orthodox?* That's what I think a lot about now. There's really a high bar for all the stuff that you have to accept.[5]

This book, in many respects, is an attempt to wrestle with Benedict's deeply profound and reflexive question: *What really makes a person Orthodox?* At the heart of Benedict's question are the long-standing issues of philosophical, anthropological, and theological import—identity, community, belonging, difference, and sameness—that are often expressed among far-right Orthodox Christians in the United States through a rhetoric of purity and panic tied to nostalgic apocalypticism.

All social groups—religious, cultural, political—are created in order to unite particular communities of people around certain tenets, ideals, and goals. Conversion is part of that self-sorting, self-selection process of finding a community of mutual comradery, of solidarity and trust. The process, always in tension with time and reality, in most cases, rests upon the assumption that one's group holds to right, correct, and authentic principles and aims. This is not new, of course, since history is recycler of themes and movements. However, in the late 2010s, the sharp intersection of the Putin-Trump era, the rise of the America First nationalist movement, new traditionalists, the Black Lives Matter protests that reached a new apex in 2020, the COVID-19 pandemic, and the new global culture wars seem to have made the process of finding and maintaining social group affiliation—an ideological home—a radically charged, often digitally attuned endeavor of nostalgia in its various temporal formations.

When I returned home from West Virginia in 2018, I launched more fully into the digital ethnographic portion of my research, since I was no longer beholden to dial-up speeds. Transcribing audio interviews, reading Orthodox blogs and social media accounts, and watching the increasingly despotic actions of both Putin and the MP with Ukraine and elsewhere, it became clear that ROCOR in the United States, despite its small size, was a far more integral part of the religio-political networks of the far/alt-right than I had imagined when I first arrived in Appalachia. The community in Woodford were certainly part of the online social discourses attached to Reactive Orthodoxy, taking part in the Russian resettlement group, reposting Russian propaganda as news, blogging, in Fr. Tryphon's case, and sharing ideas, fears, and anxieties with their online compatriots. At the same time, the basis for their ontological and social understanding of Orthodoxy, history, and contemporary politics may have been supported online, but it was produced, on the whole, through autodidactic or scholastic engagement with religious and philosophical texts. Digital networks allowed them to connect, share, and be a part of the broader Orthodox community across the globe, but their ideas were not wholly gained or transmitted through the ethernet since they also lived in and with like-minded community members. Being too deeply entrenched in online Orthodox culture was often a red flag for Woodford believers, as it was for Benedict before he left St. Basil's.

Before Benny, the white nationalist inquirer, left St. John's in the early summer of 2018, several members, including the parish priest, brought his social media output up as a marker for extremism. Benny's social media postings were filled with far/alt-right news sources, Nazi memes, conspiracy theories, misogynistic rants, and anti-Semitism. While the Woodford Orthodox community skewed far right, with radicalized political and social ideologies, they still were not comfortable with hate speech and violence. Benny's social media postings were not indicative of the status quo in Woodford; however, they were representative of the younger generation of Reactive Orthodoxy that are primarily found online. The closing years of the 2010s and the beginning of the 2020s brought to the fore more publicly engaged, social-media-focused members of Reactive Orthodoxy, who skew much younger in terms of age and, often, engagement with Orthodox Christianity. The story of these social media movements—under names like America First, Groyper, nationalist, and trad—is one unto itself; at the same time, this younger generation is part of the broader digital and social networks of far-right Orthodoxy that shares religious belief, political ideologies, and nostalgically inclined fears with the community in Woodford. Perhaps the easiest way to understand them is to think of them as overlapping nodes in the network of Reactive Orthodoxy, and political conservatism more broadly.

United via social media, particularly alt-media platforms like Gab and Telegram, far-right, reactionary converts and cradles, most of whom were young males, often proudly bearing the incel mantle, were outraged by the shifting social norms in the United States, fearful of the potential political and religious persecution of American conservative Christians, and concerned by threats to white hegemony. One Orthodox candidate for the U.S. House of Representatives called for a "ten-year moratorium on immigration."[6] Throughout the social media worlds of these far-right Orthodox believers, the themes of purity and panic are legible in their writings, memes, and comments; however, their social logics were often far more politically diverse and less theologically and historically nuanced than those expressed at the local level in Woodford. The Reactive Orthodox believers I encountered among the community in Appalachia were steeped in history, philosophy, and theology. While their ideologies were reactive, perhaps even religio-fascist to some extent, their worldbuilding project was articulate, shaped by well-read and well-educated people, with a deep appreciation for history, art, and culture. But this new generation of geographically diffuse, digitally connected Reactive Orthodoxy—shaped by meme culture and social media discourse, emboldened by the waning years of the Trump administration, and steeped in conspiratorial ideas about science, religion, and the body—offer a more galvanized and yet far less nuanced expression of far-right Orthodoxy. At the same time, these digital fellow travelers of the Woodford community are important to note, for their discourses surrounding Nicholas II, the MP, and (often) Putin, are complementary to those expressed throughout this book. Benedict questioned what ROCOR might offer this younger generation of traditionalists, suggesting that in the end their religious practice might be more about geopolitics than anything else: "I don't know what relevance it has unless you're excited about Russia, holy Russia, the revival of holy Russia, and have some dream of maybe moving there someday when the apocalypse comes."[7] Benedict's comments surely pertain to many of the far-right social media personalities who consider themselves Orthodox; at the same time, however, there are also those Russophiles, monarchists-in-training, and devotees of Tsar Nicholas II who nonetheless espouse the language of the America First movement, claiming that MAGA and Trump nation are not finished.

Despite their political differences, online and local Reactive Orthodox believers focused on purity and worried about persecution typically selected ROCOR as their spiritual home. Indeed, a ROCOR convert cleric, during an interview in 2021, noted that in recent years even the historic Holy Trinity Monastery seems to have become a "traditionalist alternative" for Orthodox seminarians from the United States nostalgically looking for the most pure, undiluted form of Russian Orthodox theological training.[8] Both the monarchic idealists in Appalachia and the more inflammatory and conspiratorial online Reactive Orthodox community provide us another way to understand the radicalization of religious belief and the growing far right in the United States, which has, since the 2010s, accelerated and become strikingly close to a mainstream movement.[9] Globally connected through social media, influenced by Russian propaganda and far-right ideologues both at home and internationally, Reactive Orthodoxy, both on and offline, is filled with actors who employ nostalgic, conspiratorial language about the deep state, globalism, Critical Race Theory, and LGBTQ+ groups in order to highlight both why they have turned to Orthodoxy—because they view ROCOR as a refuge from them—and why they are looking for alternative political projects, whether it be America First, monarchism, or a melding of both.[10]

Reactive Orthodoxy, in its Woodford incarnation and its online formations, is a worldbuilding project founded in nostalgia. Certainly, Reactive Orthodox Christians look to history to reclaim what they believe is lost. However, that is only one aspect of their collective nostalgia. Fears about the future, concerns over progress, and apocalyptic anxieties are all part of their struggle with time, reality, and secularism. It is the longing to return to a home that never was; it is, quite simply, nostalgia. As the masterful and late Svetlana Boym pointed out, nostalgia is "a defense mechanism in a time of accelerated rhythms of life and historical upheavals."[11] Too often, we think only of the historical dimensions of nostalgia, the longing for a mythic past, not realizing that it is most often temporally oriented to reclaim the future—Donald Trump's Make America Great Again campaign is a striking example of nostalgia in action. Yet the nostalgic apocalypticism, fears, and desires expressed by Reactive Orthodox Christians were not only about reclaiming the future, but perhaps rewriting it too. Boym wrote:

> In a broader sense, nostalgia is a rebellion against the modern idea of time, the time of history and progress. The nostalgic desires to obliterate history and turn it into private or collective mythology, to revisit time like space, refusing to surrender to the irreversibility of time that plagues the human condition.[12]

This impulse to crystalize the teachings of Russian Orthodoxy from the pre-revolutionary period is certainly part of that attempt to mythologize the past in order to fight for the future. Yet nostalgia among Reactive Orthodox Christians goes beyond Russia. In 1994, Orthodoxy was labeled "the last true rebellion" by Monk Damascene Christensen, Fr. Seraphim Rose's spiritual son and biographer, in the inaugural issue of the *Death to the World* periodical.[13] Christensen's framing of Orthodox Christianity as a radical alternative to Western society and secularism was a nostalgic extension of Rose's teachings about the Orthodox reality in the United States.

In 1972 (the year of the historic Moscow Summit that featured the signing of the Anti-Ballistic Missile Treaty between the United States and the Soviet Union), while ROCOR was still canonically separated from the Moscow Patriarchate, Rose wrote in a letter to Fr. Alexey (Ambrose) Young:

> There is a glimpse here of an Orthodoxy not merely "added to" the American way of life and then apologized for and made understandable to non-Orthodox, "fitting in" as the fourth major faith—but something rather that transforms life, that makes Orthodox people something of a scandal to the world, that grows up on its own principles quite apart

from the world around it, and yet that is quite sound and normal in itself.[14]

Rose believed that Orthodoxy in the United States had to be different than its historical counterparts abroad. He also believed, as he wrote to a friend several years before his letter to Young, that there was "a distinct feeling in the air in America" and that Orthodox Christians at that point were, in a similar fashion to the Church in Russia, about to "enter into the 'catacomb times.'"[15] Rose's nostalgic emphasis on the persecuted Church, its need to be wholly outside of American society, and the conspiratorial ideas found in his audio and written legacy, such as his posthumously compiled *Orthodox Survival Guide*, is an attempt to rebellion against modernity, against reality, something that resonated with many of the reactionary Orthodox Christians with whom I have worked.

As I mentioned in the opening of this book, Orthodoxy is thought to be inside and outside of time, perhaps even timeless, while at the same time rigorously marked by participation in both liturgical time and history itself. As a religion, Orthodoxy is a human production of the social that gathers ideas, philosophies, and practices into itself and becomes a culture unto itself—a culture that strives for a reimagining of reality in the image of divinity. The exceptional Alexander Schmemann once wrote that the Church expresses "the kingdom that is to come," and that "[t]he unique—I repeat, unique—function of worship in the life of the Church and in theology is to convey a sense of this eschatological reality."[16] This goal, of understanding life and one's life in relationship to God and to the end of time, has been, historically, a part of not only Orthodoxy, but Christianity more broadly. In the case of Reactive Orthodoxy, however, this goal is infused with nostalgia, traditionalism, and the language of the culture wars—it longs for the Christian past "that is remade in the image of the present or a desired future."[17] The allure of traditionalism and Orthodoxy—the melding of which is highly reactive, even potentially volatile—might, in the end, stem from Father Seraphim Rose.

In Rose's biography, Christensen writes that seekers of mystical traditionalism "like Guénon" will see Rose as a "living link" to the catacomb church that can fortify Christians against the Antichrist.[18] In Woodford, Rose's works—read by many of the male converts and on the reading list for novices at the monastery—were essential guides for spiritual warfare in the age of modernity. Among online Reactive Orthodox, believers tweeted about Rose, offered reviews of his most popular works, and shared photographs of him in order to spread his prophetic worldview, suggesting that he understood both the nihilism of modernity and the mystical salvation of Orthodoxy. One could argue that this Rose-inflected nostalgic form of Orthodoxy is not inside and outside of time, but rather attempting to transform time and reality itself. This happens not only through participants' engagement with the correct liturgical cycles of the Church, but also through their continual intercessions to Tsar Nicholas II to save the world from an apocalyptic doom brought about by the future Antichrist. Each prayer, each invocation, each akathist, each service to the deceased tsar reverently pushes through the fabric of time and space, calling out for his intercessions on behalf of the world, the nation, and the family, and his assistance in shaping the realities of the future.

In their American homeland, Reactive Orthodox Christians are building their own world, their own home. This is not Dreher's Benedict Option, an American Orthodox communal living project that draws influence from ancient monasticism and American self-contained religious communities such as the Oneida colony, Shakers, and various Brethren groups.[19] Rather, this world marshals theological and political structures far removed from ancient Christian monasticism and American religion and politics, yet continually in tension with both. This is primarily because religion is a social production, a humanly developed understanding of metaphysics that is just as much about divinity as it is about social connectivity, belonging, and defining the self and the other. Furthermore, religion has always been, as Elizabeth Shakman Hurd and Winnifred Fallers Sullivan wrote, "central to American self-understanding."[20] Perhaps Reactive Orthodoxy, as a religio-political project, is part of the American theologies of exceptionalism that Hurd and Sullivan link to globalized, dynamic assumptions about the self and others.[21] Anthropologist Marshall Sahlins may have been right when he suggested that history is the assumption that "men and women are suffering beings because they act at once in relationship to each other and in a world that has its own relationships."[22] This world of Reactive Orthodoxy, this nostalgic, ideological reality unto itself, one of simultaneous spiritual liberation and potential persecution, is, it seems, a reactionary form of both American exceptionalism and self-loathing, in which America First adherents, tsarist ideologues, and fearful (potential) expats find safety, a nostalgic home as it were, to weather the storms of secularism.

In his philosophical treatise on liberative worldbuilding, Jarret Zigon suggests that the political act of building a world reveals openings and potentials.[23] Indeed, it does. In the same turn, reactive or reactionary worldbuilding, whether digital or analog, affords us opportunities to see how the political act of creating a world rests in ideological terraforming, foundational tenets, strict statutes for inclusion, and salvific sanctions. One could, and perhaps should, argue that this is the basis of fascism or, at the very least, a hybrid type of fascism that unites religion with the political. Fears over purity—sexual, spiritual, and, in many cases, racial—are part of the larger discourses swirling throughout the social media platforms and conversations of Reactive Orthodoxy. Online, this also takes the form of anti-Semitism with crossover rhetoric from QAnon conspiracy theories and traditionalist ideologies of globalism.[24] This is the reactive language of exclusion, of partitioning, of purity that does the caustic work of ideological terraforming, of building a nostalgic world from the ground up. Panic over social norms and potential persecution are part and parcel of the historical layers of the long American project of far-right, fundamentalist Christian domination focused on the control and subordination of others while decrying assumed persecution.[25] Combined with a fervent turn to traditionalism, including ideas from Seraphim Rose, René Guénon, Julius Evola, Aleksandr Dugin, and others, Reactive Orthodox Christians in the United States, at the rising crest of a new decade, were seemingly complicit in both the American politicization of Russian Orthodoxy and the radical reimagining of American democracy.

Acknowledgments

The anthropological pursuit, the ethnographic method, and the process of writing a book all take time. I was especially fortunate to have my time as a researcher and a writer supported by so many excellent institutions, organizations, and people. This project started while I was at New York University, a place where I found immense institutional support. My initial fieldwork research for this book was funded by NYU's Jordan Center for the Advanced Study of Russia, a Patricia Dunn Lehrman Fellowship in American art, along with the Department of Anthropology's Annette Weiner Fieldwork Grant, which I considered a great honor. I had the good fortune to receive three writing fellowships. A fellowship from the Louisville Institute not only supported my first year of writing, but it also brought me into contact with a diverse group of scholars who were influential in helping me think through the early stages of my project. In 2019–2020, my writing was supported by both the National Endowment for the Humanities in conjunction with the Orthodox Christian Studies Center (Fordham University) and the Charlotte W. Newcombe Fellowship in religion and ethics from the Institute for Citizens and Scholars (formerly the Woodrow Wilson National Fellowship Foundation). These two fellowships allowed me the luxury of time to sit with my field notes, recordings, and writings in order to craft many of the paragraphs you find in this book. In 2020–2021, the final stages of research and writing were supported by the Social Science Research Council's fellowship in Religion, Spirituality, and Democratic Renewal in partnership with the Fetzer Institute. This book was also supported by my participation as a Senior Fellow in the "Orthodoxy and Human Rights" project, sponsored by Fordham University's Orthodox Christian Studies Center, and generously funded by the Henry Luce Foundation and Leadership 100.

I finished writing this book as a Postdoctoral Fellow in the Luce-funded Recovering Truth: Religion, Journalism, and Democracy in a Post-Truth Era project in the Center for the Study of Religion and Conflict at Arizona State University. I am forever grateful that the Recovering Truth project brought me into contact with such an excellent community of scholars, journalists, and administrators. Project co-directors John Carlson and Tracy Fessenden's vision for public scholarship, civic education, and bridging the growing truth divide in the United States through academic intervention is one I align with and seek to promote in my own work. While the final incarnation of this book was shaped by the simulating cohort conversations in the Recovering Truth project, it began with the critical support of the brilliant and generous scholars in NYU's Department of Anthropology. I am not a classic Russianist, yet I had the exceptional luck to work with one of the very best—Bruce Grant. His impeccable advice, constructive commentary, and clarity of vision have helped shape my work in ways still to be revealed. I would be hard pressed to find a more generous, warm, and intellectually thoughtful mentor than Faye Ginsburg. Every time I pick up a camera to film, I am reminded how grateful I am that Faye encouraged me to be part of the Culture and Media program. Each time I sit down to write, I think about the meticulous and capacious writings of Fred Myers, whose expansive knowledge and intellectual curiosity have challenged me not only to be an interdisciplinary thinker and writer, but also a thorough, thoughtful, and critical one. My time at NYU was also enriched by the solidarity I found with co-travelers, especially human rights lawyer and anthropologist Nathan Madson.

Throughout this writing project, I received critical feedback at several of the annual American Academy of Religion conferences. I am also indebted to the following people who provided insights or have informed my work along the way: Alexandra Antohin, Fr. John Behr, my dear godfather Fr. Moses Berry, James Bielo, Thomas Bremer, Shaun Casey, Simon Coleman, Jerome Copulsky, Regina Elsner, Ayala Fader, Jason Fox, Gerald FitzGerald, Hannah Gais, Philip Gorski, Nic Hartmann, Angie Heo, Fr. John Jillions, Christopher D. L. Johnson, Marlene Laruelle, Inga Leonova, Fr. David Lowell, Emily Martin, Rico Monge, Kristy Nabhan-Warren, Elayne Oliphant, Bradley Onishi, Michael Ossorgin, the late and marvelous Leonard Primiano, Teva Regule, Bryce Rich, Robert Saler, Kerry San Chirco, John Schmalzbauer, Vera Shevzov, Daniel Silliman, Kristina Stoeckl, Dmitry Uzlaner, Catherine Wanner, and Jared Warren.

Of course, my work would not have been possible without the participation of the Orthodox Christians in my field site. From 2015 to 2019, I shared many deep conversations, drinks, meals, laughs, and frustrations with the community featured in this book. Though my research time with that community has come to an end, I am appreciative of their willingness to talk about matters of faith and politics.

As I close the chapter on this research project and look to the next, I am mindful of two more groups of people who must be praised. I am immensely grateful for the support and work of everyone at Fordham University Press, including Will Cerbone and Fredric Nachbaur. It is a privilege to have my book housed in the Orthodox Christianity and Contemporary Thought series, guided by the inimitable Aristotle Papanikolaou and masterful Ashley Pupura, visionaries in the field of Orthodox Studies. I also must pause here to thank the exceptionally generous and intellectually adroit George Demacopoulos who, along with Aristotle Papanikolaou, founded the Orthodox Christian Studies Center at Fordham University. Orthodox Studies is a small but highly productive community of scholars, and one of the best is the stylish and erudite Nadieszda Kizenko, who provided me with critical insights into the history of the Russian Orthodox Church Outside of Russia. Orthodox Studies has afforded me an exceptional set of interlocutors and friends—far too many to list here— and among them I am forever indebted to Timothy Carroll, Phil Dorroll, Jacob Lassin, Sarah Livick-Moses, Petre Maican, Elena Romashko, Aram Sarkisian, Christopher Sheklian, Aaron Sokoll, Gayle Woloschak, and, especially, Candace Lukasik.

This research would not have been possible without the support of my friends and family. Many thanks to Andrew Boyd, Jayne Everson, Michael Kazmeirczak, Benjamin Wilson, Lauren White, and so many others. A special note of thanksgiving I leave here for my mother and mother-in-law, both of whom provided excellent childcare over the years. Finally, I will never be able to fully articulate my overflowing gratitude to my husband for his unwavering support. JD, you are the incandescent southern star guiding my way home.

Notes

Preface

1. Catherine Bell, *Ritual: Perspectives and Dimensions* (New York: Oxford University Press, 1997), 108. One aspect of ritual timing that unites all Eastern Orthodox Christians is Pascha (Easter), a common (immovable) feast day celebrated on the same day by those on the Old and New Calendars.

Introduction. East of Appalachia:
The New Russian Turn in American Christianity

1. I lived in Woodford for twelve months. The area was rural, with a lack of rental properties. Through a real estate agent, I was able to secure a twelve-month lease on a log cabin located on one of the main roads in town. Most of the citizens of Woodford with whom I spoke asked me where I lived. Once I gave them the particulars of the house, they often proclaimed it to be an excellent piece of property. Given the other options in the area, it was quite a luxury. However, it was not without downfalls. Cabins, as I found out through conversations with my local pest control sprayer, are notoriously subject to pest infestations. The first infestation to plague the cabin was wasps. Autumn brought with it a daily average of ten to twenty wasps buzzing wildly through the rafters of the cabin. Eventually the property manager found a wasp nest in the furnace and proclaimed that the infestation was done. Sadly, that turned out not to be the case. The cracks in the log home meant that wasps found any and all sorts of entry points. After months of battling the winged terrors, the landlord consented to have the cabin sprayed on a monthly basis. Pest control kept the wasp population to a minimum throughout the spring and summer of 2018, but the wasps never fully left the premises. Mice were also my constant companions as well; and birds would often fly down the mountain breaking their necks as they crash-landed

into the sides and windows of the cabin. One night in July of 2018, I thought a bird had somehow managed to get into the cabin, when I awoke to flapping overhead. Rather than a bird, it turned out to be four bats. I managed to let two bats out the front door; one bat died, and another found cover in the shadowy wooden recesses of the raised cabin ceiling. Not knowing if the bats were rabid and fearing for the safety of my family, we left the cabin in the middle of the night and made a long drive to the nearest town with a hotel, where we stayed until a bat removal expert from Ohio met me at the cabin the next day. I write about these natural encounters to highlight the so-called status quo experience in Woodford. Certainly, there were some affluent residents in the area, but on the whole, living conditions ranged from small wooden homes to decaying trailers, with a wide range in between.

2. While it is grammatically correct to use the article "the" before ROCOR, I have chosen to omit it for ease of reading.

3. Prior to spending a year in Woodford, I also visited for several weeks in the summer of 2016, and then I returned in January of 2017 to film a short documentary. After I finished my year of fieldwork, I again returned to the community in January of 2019 to spend a festal holiday weekend with lay members of the monastery community. In total, I was with the community for almost thirteen months. Throughout 2020–2021, I conducted additional interviews with former members of the community and other members of ROCOR. Because of the COVID-19 pandemic, these subsequent interviews were conducted digitally.

4. Nelson Goodman, *Ways of Worldmaking* (Indianapolis: Hackett Publishing Group, 1978); Keith Hollinshead, Irena Ateljevic, and Nazia Ali, "Worldmaking Agency–Worldmaking Authority: The Sovereign Constitutive Role of Tourism," *Tourism Geographies* 11, no. 4 (2009): 27–443. Nathalie Karagiannis and Peter Wagner, eds., *Varieties of World-Making: Beyond Globalization* (Liverpool, UK: Liverpool University Press, 2007); Yuriko Saito, *Aesthetics of the Familiar: Everyday Life and World-Making* (London: Oxford University Press, 2017).

5. Jarrett Zigon, *Disappointment: Toward a Critical Hermeneutics of Worldbuilding* (New York: Fordham University Press, 2018).

6. Jarrett Zigon, "A Politics of Worldbuilding," Member Voices, *Fieldsights*, December 5, 2017, https://culanth.org/fieldsights/a-politics-of-worldbuilding. Another excellent theoretical take on worldbuilding is Michael Jackson's notion of lifeworlds, an idea that emphasizes the embodied nature of being and dwelling in worlds. See Michael Jackson, *Lifeworlds: Essays in Existential Anthropology* (Chicago: University of Chicago Press, 2012).

7. Richard B. Drake, *A History of Appalachia* (Lexington: University Press of Kentucky, 2001).

8. For a full breakdown of regional development, see Kelvin M. Pollard, "Population Growth and Distribution in Appalachia: New Realities," Population Reference Bureau and Appalachian Regional Commission, 2005, accessed December 20, 2019, https://www.arc.gov/research/researchreportdetails.asp?REPORT_ID=27.

9. Within the Orthodox Christian tradition, a *skete* is considered to be a small, often isolated, dependency of a larger monastic community, one that potentially still

needs institutional and or financial support for its continuance. St. Basil's monastery was considered a dependency of a much older and more well-established ROCOR monastery for quite a while before it was considered secure enough to stand on its own. By the time I arrived in West Virginia, St. Basil's had its own dependencies in the form of two sketes—one local, and the other in a neighboring state.

10. I have selected not to include a hyperlink to the government website for census statistics, for doing so might divulge too much information about the actual location of Woodford.

11. The monks were quite obvious around town, given their particular religious apparel; however, most lay members of the community wore typical, everyday clothing.

12. Alexei Krindatch, *Atlas of American Orthodox Christian Churches* (Brookline, MA: Holy Cross Orthodox Press, 2011).

13. James Kapaló, in his work on Orthodox converts in contemporary Ireland, notes that there are three different terms used among Irish Orthodox Christians— one of the fastest growing religious groups in that part of Europe because of immigration and conversion—cradle, non-cradle, and convert. In Ireland, converts, often drawn to Orthodoxy because of its seemingly nostalgic pre–Vatican II ethos, combined with a rich and mystical sensorium, sometimes see themselves as creating a pan-Orthodox Irish collective that is both transnational and neo-native. See James A. Kapaló, "Mediating Orthodoxy: Convert Agency and Discursive Autochthonism in Ireland," in *Orthodox Identities in Western Europe: Migration, Settlement, and Innovation*, ed. by Maria Hämmerli and Jean-François Mayer, 229–249 (New York: Routledge, 2014). Berit Synøve Thorbjørnsrud also provides an excellent assessment of Orthodox converts in the European context, showing how new members of the Church are identified and labeled in Norway. See Berit Synøve Thorbjørnsrud, "Who Is a Convert? New Members of the Orthodox Church in Norway," *Temenos* 51, no. 1 (2015): 71–93.

14. I employ the term convert to refer to adults in the community who were catechized and baptized as adults.

15. Clifford Geertz, "Thick Description: Toward an Interpretive Theory of Culture," in *The Interpretation of Cultures: Selected Essays* (New York: Basic Books, 1973), 3–30.

16. I converted to the OCA in 2011. Much in the tradition of Victor and Edith Turner, I found a religious home that I could critically admire. See Edith Turner, *Heart of Lightness: The Life Story of an Anthropologist* (New York: Berghahn Books, 2006). As both a practitioner and a critic, I take my methodological guidance from the writings of American religions scholar Robert Orsi, who provides a model for navigating the uncharted waters of being in but not of the worlds we are studying. Robert A. Orsi, *Between Heaven and Earth: The Religious Worlds People Make and the Scholars Who Study Them* (Princeton, NJ: Princeton University Press, 2004).

17. Nadieszda Kizenko, in her article on gender and Orthodoxy in post-perestroika Russia, notes how despite the entrenched patriarchal systems of power within the Church, women have found places of prominence through lay activities. Historically,

as Kizenko has noted in both written texts and through personal communications, the Russian Church and ROCOR have encouraged lay female and monastic leadership. While this is true to some extent in contemporary U.S. ROCOR cradle communities, American converts often hold traditionalist notions of womanhood that are used to relegate wives and daughters to more quiet modes of production—cooking, cleaning, teaching, and having children—many times silencing the voices of women who want to be theologically or academically engaged with the Church. Nadieszda Kizenko, "Feminized Patriarchy? Orthodoxy and Gender in Post-Soviet Russia," *Signs* 38, no. 3 (2013): 595–621. Throughout my time in the community, I worked with women in various capacities. Cleaning the church, singing in the choir, volunteering at the food pantry, cooking for coffee hour—these were just some of the activities women in the parish took part in regularly. Certainly, these were sites of female solidarity, where the emphasis was on being a godly, productive woman. However, these were not spaces in which women were empowered to transform their circumstances within the Church structure. For the most part, it seemed as if the Orthodox women in Woodford were happy with their roles within the parish and ROCOR more broadly.

18. Agnieszka Pasieka, "Anthropology of the Far-Right: What if We Like the 'Unlikeable' Others?" *Anthropology Today* 35, no.1 (2019): 3–6; Benjamin R. Teitelbaum, "Collaborating with the Radical Right Scholar-Informant Solidarity and the Case for an Immoral Anthropology," *Current Anthropology* 60, no. 3 (June 2019): 414–435.

19. Daniel Bertaux and Martin Kohli, "The Life Story Approach: A Continental View," *Annual Review of Sociology* 10 (1984): 215–237; Faye Ginsburg, "Procreation Stories: Reproduction, Nurturance, and Procreation in Life Narratives of Abortion Activists," *American Ethnologist* 14 (1987): 623–636.

20. Kathleen M. Blee, and Verta Taylor, "The Uses of Semi-Structured Interviews in Social Movement Research," in *Methods in Social Movement Research*, ed. by Bert Klandermans and Suzanne Staggenborg (Minneapolis: University of Minnesota Press, 2002), 92–117.

21. In 2020–2021, I also interviewed a small group of former monks and novices from St. Basil's.

22. In an effort to pay tribute to the Anglo-Saxon roots that so many of the folks in Woodford claimed, I opted primarily to use the names of Irish, Scottish, and English saints as pseudonyms.

23. Facebook and Twitter often connect ROCOR converts across geographies. Much of the data I gathered about the larger discourses and trends in convert ROCOR communities was from my digital ethnographic research of social media sites.

24. For Woodford converts, ROCOR and Russian Orthodoxy were interchangeable. ROCOR and the Russian Orthodox Church (MP) were not interchangeable—they understood the deep social and political differences between the two organizations. However, both institutions, from the perspective of many in

Woodford, are part of the larger sphere of Russian Orthodoxy. Thus, I often use the term Russian Orthodoxy when referring to ROCOR and the ROC, as my interlocutors would. The ROC and the ROC (MP) denote the Russian Orthodox Church in Russia throughout this book.

25. Arlie Russell Hochschild, *Strangers in their Own Land* (New York: New Press, 2016); Robert Wuthnow, *The Left Behind: Decline and Rage in Small-Town America* (Princeton, NJ: Princeton University Press, 2018).

26. Frances FitzGerald, *The Evangelicals: The Struggle to Shape America* (New York: Simon and Schuster, 2017); Robert P. Jones, *The End of White Christian America* (New York: Simon and Schuster, 2017); Thomas S. Kidd, *Who Is an Evangelical? The History of a Movement in Crisis* (New Haven, CT: Yale University Press, 2019).

27. Andrew L. Whitehead and Samuel L. Perry, *Taking America Back for God: Christian Nationalism in the United States* (New York: Oxford University Press, 2020).

28. David Shimer, *Rigged: America, Russia, and One Hundred Years of Covert Electoral Interference* (New York: Knopf Doubleday, 2020).

29. Catherine L. Albanese, ed., *American Spiritualties: A Reader* (Bloomington: Indiana University Press, 2001); Sydney Ahlstrom, *Religious History of the American People* (New Haven, CT: Yale University Press, 1972).

30. Fenella Cannell, ed. *The Anthropology of Christianity* (Durham, NC: Duke University Press, 2006); Webb Keane, *Christian Moderns: Freedom and Fetish in the Mission Encounter* (Berkeley: University of California Press, 2007).

31. Elizabeth Catte, *What You Are Getting Wrong about Appalachia* (Cleveland, OH: Belt Publishing, 2018); Carol Mason, *Reading Appalachia from Left to Right: Conservatives and the 1974 Kanawha County Textbook Controversy* (Ithaca, NY: Cornell University Press, 2011); J. D. Vance, *Hillbilly Elegy: A Memoir of a Family and Culture in Crisis* (New York: HarperCollins, 2018).

32. Stephen L. Fisher, ed., Fighting Back in Appalachia: Traditions of Resistance and Change (Philadelphia: Temple University Press, 1993); Steven Stoll, *Ramp Hollow: The Ordeal of Appalachia* (New York: Hill and Wang, 2017).

33. Wuthnow, *Left Behind*, 2018, 124.

34. Michael Barkun, *A Culture of Conspiracy: Apocalyptic Visions in Contemporary America* (Berkeley: University of California Press, 2013); Susan Harding and Daniel Rosenberg, eds., *Histories of the Future* (Durham, NC: Duke University Press, 2005).

35. The idea of an almost cloistered utopia is also found in other parts of Orthodoxy in the United States. Rod Dreher's best-seller *The Benedict Option* seemed to be a clarion call for many Orthodox converts seeking to flee secular society and build a world of their own. Rod Dreher, *The Benedict Option: A Strategy for Christians in a Post-Christian Nation* (New York: Penguin, 2017).

36. There are numerous scholars in a wide variety of fields in the social sciences and humanities who work in or on midwestern and southern Christianity in the United States. The works I have listed here are incredibly helpful to think with about Christianity in these types of spaces. See James S. Bielo, *Emerging Evangelicals:*

Faith, Modernity, and the Desire for Authenticity (New York: New York University Press, 2011); Darren Dochuk, *From the Bible Belt to the Sunbelt: Plain-Folk Religion, Grassroots Politics, and the Rise of Evangelical Conservatism* (New York: W. W. Norton, 2011); Omri Elisha, *Moral Ambition: Mobilization and Social Outreach in Evangelical Megachurches* (Berkeley: University of California Press, 2011); Kevin M. Lowe, *Baptized with the Soil: Christian Agrarians and the Crusade for Rural America* (New York: Oxford University Press, 2016); Rodney Stark and Roger Finke, *Acts of Faith: Explaining the Human Side of Religion* (Berkeley: University of California Press, 2000); and Robert Wuthnow, *Red State Religion: Faith and Politics in America's Heartland* (Princeton, NJ: Princeton University Press, 2012); *Small-Town America: Finding Community, Shaping the Future* (Princeton, NJ: Princeton University Press, 2013).

37. George E. Demacopoulos and Aristotle Papanikolaou, eds., *Orthodox Constructions of the West* (New York: Fordham University Press, 2013); *Christianity, Democracy, and the Shadow of Constantine* (New York: Fordham University Press, 2017); *Fundamentalism or Tradition: Christianity after Secularism* (New York: Fordham University Press, 2020).

38. For an excellent study of Orthodox materiality, see Timothy Carroll, *Orthodox Christian Material Culture: Of People and Things in the Making of Heaven* (New York: Routledge, 2018).

39. There are quite a few works that are considered classics in the early study of Appalachia. While I note some of them here, most, if not all, are problematic in terms of representation. See Charles K. Bolton, *Scotch-Irish Pioneers in Ulster and America* (Boston: Bacon and Brown, 1910); Harry Caudill, *Night Comes to the Cumberlands: A Biography of a Depressed Area* (Boston: Little, Brown, 1963); Olive Tilford Dargan, *From My Highest Hill: Carolina Mountain Folks* (Knoxville: University of Tennessee Press, 1998 [originally published in 1925]); Allen Hendershott Eaton, *Handicrafts of the Southern Highlands* (New York: Dover, 1973 [orig. 1937]); James Mooney, *Myths of the Cherokee and Sacred Formulas of the Cherokees* (Nashville: C. and R. Elder Booksellers, 1982 [reprint of 1900 and 1891 eds. published by Bureau of American Ethnology]); and Ellen Churchill Semple, "The Anglo-Saxons of the Kentucky Mountains: A Study in Anthropogeography," *Geographical Journal* 17 (June 1901): 588–623.

40. More recently, scholars have begun to examine various aspects of Appalachia that have historically been overlooked. See Dwight B. Billings, Gurney Norman, Katherine Ledford, eds., *Back Talk from Appalachia: Confronting Stereotypes* (Lexington: University Press of Kentucky, 2013); Meredith McCarroll, *Unwhite: Appalachia, Race, and Film* (Atlanta: University of Georgia, 2018); William W. Philliber, Clyde B. McCoy, Harry C. Dillingham, eds., *The Invisible Minority: Urban Appalachians* (Lexington: University Press of Kentucky, 1981); William Schumann and Rebecca Adkins Fletcher, eds., *Appalachia Revisited: New Perspectives on Place, Tradition, and Progress* (Lexington: University Press of Kentucky, 2016); William H. Turner and Edward J. Cabbell, eds., *Blacks in Appalachia* (Lexington: University Press of Kentucky, 1985).

41. For more on the internal colony debate, see Linda Johnson, Donald Askins, and Helen Matthews Lewis, *Colonialism in Modern America: The Appalachian Case* (Boone, NC: Appalachian State University, 2017); Paul J. Nyden, "An Internal Colony: Labor Conflict and Capitalism in Appalachian Coal," *Insurgent Sociologist* 8, no. 4 (January 1979): 33–43; and John Alexander Williams, "Appalachia as Colony and as Periphery: A Review Essay," *Appalachian Journal* 6, no. 2 (1979): 157–161.

42. Anthony Harkins, *Hillbilly: A Cultural History of an American Icon* (New York: Oxford University Press, 2005).

43. Stephen L. Fisher, ed., *Fighting Back in Appalachia: Traditions of Resistance and Change* (Philadelphia: Temple University Press, 1993); Jessica Wilkerson, *To Live Here, You Have to Fight: How Women Led Appalachian Movements for Social Justice* (Urbana: University of Illinois Press, 2018).

44. Catte, *What You Are Getting Wrong about Appalachia*.

45. Deborah Vansau McCauley, *Appalachian Mountain Religion: A History* (Urbana: University of Illinois Press, 1995).

46. McCauley, *Appalachian Mountain Religion*, 55–56.

47. Deborah Vansau McCauley, "Religion," in *High Mountains Rising: Appalachia in Time and Place*, ed. by Richard A. Straw and Blethen H. Tyler (Urbana: University of Illinois Press, 2004), 180.

48. McCauley, "Religion," 182.

49. Ibid.

50. An excellent example of this focus on spectacle can be seen in Peter Adair's 1967 documentary *Holy Ghost People*, chronicling the service of a Pentecostal community in Scrabble Creek, West Virginia, where they practice faith healing, trance, snake handling, speaking in tongues, and singing. Adair uses a mixture of close-ups of the faces of religious believers juxtaposed with shots that follow their physical movements while in trance, creating a kind of visual frenzy, suggesting to the viewer that believers are not in control of themselves and might be a bit wild. Peter Adair, *Holy Ghost People*, Thistle Films (1967), 53 mins.

51. Loyal Jones, "Studying Mountain Religion," *Appalachian Journal* 5, no. 1 (1977): 126.

52. Deborah Wiener's *Coalfield Jews* provides an excellent history of immigration, resettlement, and commerce for Jewish community in Appalachia's most profitable industry. Deborah Wiener, *Coalfield Jews: An Appalachian History* (Urbana: University of Illinois Press, 2006).

53. Helen M. Lewis and Monica Appleby, *Mountain Sisters: From Convent to Community in Appalachia* (Lexington: University Press of Kentucky, 2003).

54. Joseph D. Witt, *Religion and Resistance in Appalachia: Faith and the Fight against Mountaintop Removal Coal Mining* (Lexington: University Press of Kentucky, 2016).

55. Andrew L. Whitehead and Samuel L. Perry, "Is a 'Christian America' a More Patriarchal America? Religion, Politics, and Traditionalist Gender Ideology," *Canadian Review of Sociology* 56, no. 2 (2019): 151–177; Whitehead and Perry, *Taking America Back for God*; Andrew L. Whitehead, Samuel L. Perry, and Joseph

O. Baker, "Make America Christian Again: Christian Nationalism and Voting for Donald Trump in the 2016 Presidential Election," *Sociology of Religion* 79, no. 2 (2018): 147–171.

56. Cas Mudde, *The Far Right in America* (London: Routledge, 2018).

57. Kathleen M. Blee, "Ethnographies of the Far Right," *Journal of Contemporary Ethnography* 36, no. 2 (April 2007): 119–128; and Agnieszka Pasieka, "Taking Far-Right Claims Seriously and Literally: Anthropology and the Study of Right-Wing Radicalism," *Slavic Review* 76, no. S1 (2017): S19–S29.

58. Teitelbaum, "Collaborating with the Radical Right."

59. Susan Harding and Faye Ginsburg also write about the difficulties of dealing with informants who have far different ideological concepts of the world. See Susan Harding, "Representing Fundamentalism: The Problem of the Repugnant Cultural Other," *Social Research* 58, no. 2 (1991): 373–393; Faye Ginsburg, "The Case of Mistaken Identity: Problems in Representing Women on the Right," in *Reflexivity and Voice*, ed. by Rosanne Hertz (Thousand Oaks, CA: Sage, 1997), 283–299.

60. Kalyani Devaki Menon, "Converted Innocents and Their Trickster Heroes: The Politics of Proselytizing in India," in *The Anthropology of Religious Conversion*, ed. by Andrew Buckser and Stephen Glazier (Lanham, MD: Rowman and Littlefield, 2003), 51.

61. Nicholas E. Denysenko, *The Orthodox Church in Ukraine: A Century of Separation* (DeKalb: Northern Illinois University Press, 2018).

62. Carlotta Gall, "Ukrainian Orthodox Christians Formally Break from Russia," *New York Times*, January 6, 2019, accessed March 3, 2019, https://www.nytimes.com /2019/01/06/world/europe/orthodox-church-ukraine-russia.html.

63. Patristic Nectar Films, "Gay Iconoclasm: Holding the Line against the Radical LGBT Agenda," YouTube website, 22:11, accessed November 16, 2018, https://youtu.be/HNXe4P_6dhw; Hatewatch Staff, "World Congress of Families gathering in Tbilisi showcases anti-LGBT rhetoric and conspiracy theories," Southern Poverty Law Center, accessed November 16, 2018, https://www.splcenter .org/hatewatch/2016/06/01/world-congress-families-gathering-tbilisi-showcases-anti -lgbt-rhetoric-and-conspiracy.

64. Holy Trinity Monastery, "Chastity, Purity, Integrity: Orthodox Anthropology and Secular Culture in the Twenty-First Century," Holy Trinity Monastery, accessed January 31, 2019, https://www.jordanville.org/news_190227_1.html. Theological anthropology is a branch of theological inquiry about humanity, the body, and the relationships people have with God. For a thorough yet accessible overview of theological anthropology, see Nonna Verna Harrison, *God's Many-Splendored Image: Theological Anthropology for Christian Formation* (Grand Rapids, MI: Baker Academic, 2010). Orthodox (theological) anthropology is a subspecialty in the broader field of theological anthropology. See John Behr, *Becoming Human: Meditations on Christian Anthropology in Word and Image* (Yonkers, NY: St. Vladimir's Seminary Press, 2013).

65. Ancient Faith Ministries, "Specials: Chastity, Purity, Integrity: Orthodox Anthropology and Secular Culture in the Twenty-First Century," Ancient Faith

Ministries, accessed March 10, 2019, https://www.ancientfaith.com/specials/chastity_purity_integrity.

66. Alexander Agadjanian, "Tradition, Morality, and Community: Elaborating Orthodox identity in Putin's Russia," *Religion, State, and Society,* 45, no. 1 (2017): 39–60; Denis Zhuravlev, "Orthodox Identity as Traditionalism: Construction of Political Meaning in the Current Public Discourse of the Russian Orthodox Church," *Russian Politics and Law,* 55:4–5 (2017): 354–375.

1. Foreign Faith in a Foreign Land: A Discursive History of the Russian Orthodox Church in the United States

1. Father Damascene, interview by author, April 11, 2018.

2. Interview, October 18, 2020. ROCOR's Western Rite was created in 1870 to help converts from Anglican and Catholic backgrounds transition into Russian Orthodox liturgical culture. See Nicholas Denysenko, *Liturgical Reform after Vatican II: The Impact on Eastern Orthodoxy* (Minneapolis, MN: Fortress Press, 2015); Jean-François Mayer, "'We Are Westerners and Must Remain Westerners': Orthodoxy and Western Rites in Western Europe," in *Orthodox Identities in Western Europe: Migration, Settlement, and Innovation* (London: Routledge, 2016), 267–290.

3. For a quick overview of how ROCOR expressed itself in Europe, see Maria Hämmerli and Jean-François Mayer, eds., *Orthodox Identities in Western Europe: Migration, Settlement, and Innovation* (London: Routledge, 2016). Throughout this book, I use "Eastern Orthodoxy" and "Orthodox Christianity" interchangeably. The converts I worked with in Woodford used those terms in their understanding of Orthodoxy as it is broadly construed.

4. Sean Griffin, *The Liturgical Past in Byzantium and Early Rus* (Cambridge: Cambridge University Press, 2019); Christian Raffensperger, *Reimagining Europe: Kievan Rus' in the Medieval World, 988–1146* (Cambridge, MA: Harvard University Press, 2012).

5. Raffensperger, *Reimagining Europe.*

6. Katja Richters, *The Post-Soviet Russian Orthodox Church: Politics, Culture, and Greater Russia* (London: Routledge, 2012), 2.

7. Zoe Knox, *Russian Society and the Orthodox Church: Religion in Russia after Communism* (Richmond: Routledge, 2004), 4–5.

8. Knox, *Russian Society,* 4–5.

9. Knox, 4–5.

10. Valerie A. Kivelson, *Orthodox Russia: Belief and Practice under the Tsars* (Philadelphia: Penn State University Press, 2003), 24; Heather J. Coleman, ed. *Orthodox Christianity in Imperial Russia: A Source Book on Lived Religion* (Bloomington: Indiana University Press, 2014); Vera Shevzov, *Russian Orthodoxy on the Eve of Revolution* (New York: Oxford University Press, 2004).

11. Gregory L. Freeze, "Handmaiden of the State? The Orthodox Church in Imperial Russia Reconsidered," *Journal of Ecclesiastical History* 36 (1985): 82–102;

Jennifer Hedda, *His Kingdom Come: Orthodox Pastorship and Social Activism in Revolutionary Russia* (DeKalb, IL: Northern Illinois University Press, 2007).

12. Knox, *Russian Society*, 2.

13. Daniela Kalkandjieva, *The Russian Orthodox Church, 1917–1948: From Decline to Resurrection* (New York: Routledge, 2015); Edward E. Roslof, *Red Priests: Renovationism, Russian Orthodoxy, and Revolution, 1905–1946* (Bloomington: Indiana University Press, 2002). It is important to note that ways in which my interlocutors understand Russian Orthodox history is only one of many ways intellectual projects in ROCOR and Russian Orthodoxy.

14. Andrii Krawchuk and Thomas Bremer, eds., *Churches in the Ukrainian Crisis* (New York: Springer, 2017).

15. Knox, *Russian Society*, 2.

16. Ivan Mikhaĭlovich Andreev, *Russia's Catacomb Saints: Lives of the New Martyrs*, trans. Father Seraphim Rose (Platina, CA: Saint Herman of Alaska Press, 1982); John and Carol Garrard, *Russian Orthodoxy Resurgent Faith and Power in the New Russia* (Princeton, NJ: Princeton University Press, 2014); Irina Papkova, *The Orthodox Church and Russian Politics* (Washington, DC: Woodrow Wilson Center Press, 2011).

17. Knox, *Russian Society*, 1–3; Jane Ellis, *The Russian Orthodox Church: Triumphalism and Defensiveness* (Basingstoke, UK: Palgrave Macmillan, 1996).

18. John Anderson, "Putin and the Russian Orthodox Church: Asymmetric Symphonia?" *Journal of International Affairs* 611 (2007): 185–201. Marlene Laruelle, "Making Sense of Russia's Illiberalism," *Journal of Democracy* 31, no. 3 (July 2020): 115–129.

19. ROCOR was often called Synod, the Karlovtsy Synod, and the Russian Orthodox Church Abroad in the early part of the twentieth century. For a more detailed examination of the naming complexities, see Alexey Young, *The Russian Orthodox Church Outside of Russia: A History and Chronology* (San Bernardino, CA: St. Willibrord's Press, 1993).

20. John Maximovitch, *The Russian Orthodox Church Abroad: A Short History* (Jordanville, NY: St. Job of Pochaev Press, 1997).

21. The Russian Orthodox Church Outside of Russia, "Ukase No. 362, The Resolutions of His Holiness the Patriarch [Tikhon], of the Sacred Synod and Supreme Ecclesiastical Council of the Russian Orthodox Church, 20/7 November 1920," accessed March 3, 2019, http://www.synod.com/synod/engdocuments/enuk_ukaz362.html. The full text of Ukaz No. 362 can be found here at https://www.synod.com/Istoria/ukaz_362.html (accessed March 2, 2019); The ROC, ROCOR, and many other Orthodox communities follow the Julian calendar (often noted as OS or Old Style); The OCA, along with several other Orthodox jurisdictions, follow the revised Julian calendar (often noted as NS or New Style). The Julian calendar is roughly thirteen days behind the revised Julian calendar. George Demacopoulos points to the idea that the calendar dating system seems to be part of identification logics among conservative or "traditionalist" Orthodox communities. See George

Demacopoulos, "'Traditional Orthodoxy' as a Postcolonial Movement," *Journal of Religion* 97, no. 4 (October 2017): 483–484.

22. Robert Service, *A History of Modern Russia from Nicholas II to Vladimir Putin* (Cambridge, MA: Harvard University Press, 2005).

23. The Orthodox Church in America was known officially as the Russian Orthodox Greek Catholic Church of North America and unofficially as the Metropolia in its early years. See Mark Stokoe and Fr. Leonid Kishkovsky, *Orthodox Christians in North America, 1794–1994* (Syosset, NY: Orthodox Church in America, 1995).

24. *A History of the Russian Orthodox Church Abroad, 1917–1971* (Seattle, WA: St. Nectarios Press, 1972); Maximovitch, *Russian Orthodox Church Abroad.*

25. Aram Sarkisian, "Russian Orthodox Church Outside of Russia," in *Encyclopedia of Christianity in the United States*, vol. 5, ed. George Thomas Kurian and Mark A. Lamport (Lanham, MD: Rowman and Littlefield, 2016), 1996–1998.

26. This is not to say that there was not a range of prerevolutionary Orthodox thought in Russia. However, ROCOR focused on a unique ideological strand of Orthodox intellectual theology prior to the revolution. There were also liberal strands of thought prior to the revolution in Russian Orthodoxy. See Freeze, "Handmaiden of the State?," 82–102; Hedda, *His Kingdom Come*; and Shevzov, *Eve of Revolution.*

27. Stokoe and Kishkovsky, *Orthodox Christians in North America.*

28. Stokoe and Kishkovsky, *Orthodox Christians in North America.*

29. Alexander Bogolepov, *Toward an American Orthodox Church: The Establishment of an Autocephalous Church* (Crestwood, NY: St. Vladimir's Seminary Press, 1968 [2001]).

30. Bogolepov, *Toward an American Orthodox Church.*

31. Ibid.

32. Geraldine Fagan, *Believing in Russia: Religious Policy after Communism* (London: Routledge, 2013).

33. Service, *History of Modern Russia.*

34. Tatyana Veselkina, "Interview with Metropolitan Hilarion," The Russian Orthodox Church Outside of Russia, 2013, accessed May 3, 2019, https://synod.com/synod/engdocuments/enart_mhinterviewancientsaints.html.

35. Ciprian Burlacioiu, "Russian Orthodox Diaspora as a Global Religion after 1918," *Studies in World Christianity* 24, no. 1(2018): 4–24.

36. Rico G. Monge. "'Neither Victim nor Executioner': Essential Insights from Secularization Theory for the Revitalization of the Russian Orthodox Church in the Contemporary World," in "Inward Being and Outward Identity, The Orthodox Churches in the 21st Century," ed. John A. Jillions, special issue, *Religions* 8 (2018): 23.

37. The historical native conversions to Russian Orthodoxy in Alaska have rich textual support and research from a variety of disciplines. Lydia Black, *Russians in Alaska, 1732–1867* (Fairbanks: University of Alaska Fairbanks, 2004); Robert Geraci and Michael Khodarkovsky, eds., *Of Religion and Empire: Missions, Conversion, and*

Tolerance in Tsarist Russia (Ithaca, NY: Cornell University Press, 2018); Viacheslav Vsevolodovich Ivanov, *Native American Traditions: An Attempt at a Multicultural Society, 1794–1912* (Washington, DC: Library of Congress Publication, 1997); Sonja Luehrmann, *Alutiiq Villages under Russian and U.S. Rule* (Fairbanks, AK: University of Alaska, 2008); Ilya Vinkovetsky, *Russian America: An Overseas Colony of a Continental Empire, 1804–1867* (New York: Oxford University Press, 2011); Maria Sháa Tláa Williams, ed., *The Alaska Native Reader: History, Culture, Politics* (Durham, NC: Duke University Press, 2009).

38. Nicholas Chapman, "Virginian Orthodoxy in the Early American Republic," *Orthodox History: The Society for Orthodoxy History in the Americas*, August 26, 2013, accessed March 4, 2018, https://orthodoxhistory.org/2013/08/26/virginian -orthodoxy-in-the-early-american-republic/.

39. "Who Was Philip Ludwell III?," Ludwell.org, accessed September 26, 2021, https://www.ludwell.org/philip-ludwell-iii/.

40. Miguel Palacio, "'Orthodoxy Has a Great Future in Guatemala' Conversation with Abbess Ines, head of the Holy Trinity Monastery in Guatemala," trans. Adrian Fekula, July 16, 2009, accessed January 3, 2017, https://orthochristian .com/31235.html.

41. Tatyana Veselkina, "Interview with Metropolitan Hilarion," The Russian Orthodox Church Outside of Russia, 2013, accessed May 3, 2019, https://synod.com /synod/engdocuments/enart_mhinterviewancientsaints.html.

42. Sarkisian's dissertation broadly examines the idea of American Orthodox Rus' (amerikanskaia pravoslavnaia rus') before and after 1917, focusing on methods of cultural heritage preservation, governmental surveillance, and how the Church struggled with assimilation and missionization. Along the way, Sarkisian highlights the Russian Orthodox Church's English Department as a gateway for male converts to find their way into the Church. In many respects, the figures and institutions in Sarkisian's study helped pave the way for contemporary converts to ROCOR. See Aram Sarkisian, "The Cross between Hammer and Sickle: Russian Orthodox Christians in the United States, 1908–1928," PhD diss., Northwestern University, 2019.

43. Hagiographies of Maximovitch are often found in conjunction with an *akathist* (hymn) to the saint or as a preface to his own theological writings. There are a few hagiographies about the saint written by Russian Orthodox believers. See Anonymous, *A Brief Life of Our Father Among the Saints, Archbishop John, Wonder-Worker of Shanghai and San Francisco* (Jordanville, NY: St. Job of Pochaev Press, 1997); John Dunlop, *Exodus: St. John Maximovitch Leads His Flock Out of Shanghai* (Yonkers, NY: St. Vladimir's Seminary Press, 2017); and Peter Perekrestov, *Man of God: St. John of Shanghai and San Francisco* (New York: Nikodemos Orthodox Publications, 1994).

44. Anonymous, *Brief Life of Our Father*, 6–21.

45. Anonymous, 17.

46. Anonymous, 19.

47. Marcus Plested, "Between Rigorism and Relativism: The Givenness of Tradition," *Public Orthodoxy*, May 25, 2017, accessed March 13, 2019, https://public orthodoxy.org/2017/05/25/between-rigorism-and-relativism/.

48. Yekaterina Sinelschikova, "Why Do Some Americans Join the Russian Orthodox Church?" *Russian Beyond*, September 4, 2018, accessed May 3, 2019, https://www.rbth.com/lifestyle/329076–americans-join-russian-church.

49. Sinelschikova, "Why Do Some Americans Join the Russian Orthodox Church?"

50. Ibid.

51. Father Hubert, interview by author, May 16, 2018.

52. Father Hubert, interview by author, May 16, 2018.

53. John P. Burgess, *Holy Rus': The Rebirth of Orthodoxy in the New Russia* (New Haven, CT: Yale University Press, 2017); Burgess writes that post-Soviet Orthodox Christians' veneration of Tsar Nicholas II is part of their "call for a Russian government that will support the Church and Orthodox moral values. They hope for the restoration of Holy Rus'" (151). Yet as scholars of religion in Russia have noted, "post-Soviet Orthodoxy itself is not the same as the prerevolutionary Russian Orthodox Church" (Filatov and Stiopina 54). Sergei Filatov and Aleksandra Stiopina, "Russian Lutheranism: Between Protestantism, Catholicism, and Russian Orthodoxy," in *Religion and Politics in Russia: A Reader*, ed. Marjorie Mandelstam Balzer (London: Routledge, 2010), 54–75.

54. Mary Douglas, *Purity and Danger: An Analysis of Concepts of Pollution and Taboo* (London: Routledge, 2002), 63.

2. Church of God: Traditionalism, Authenticity, and Conversion to Russian Orthodoxy in Appalachia

1. Father Romanos, interview by author, August 12, 2018.

2. Anthropological work on selective conversion (not forced) to Christianity does exist, although it is limited. Among others, see John Barker, "Secondary Conversion and the Anthropology of Christianity in Melanesia." *Archives De Sciences Sociales Des Religions* 57, no. 157 (2012): 67–87; Andrew Buckser and Stephen D. Glazier, eds., *The Anthropology of Religious Conversion* (Lanham, MD: Rowman and Littlefield, 2003); Fenella Cannell, ed., *The Anthropology of Christianity* (Durham, NC: Duke University Press, 2006); Giuseppe Giordan, ed., *Conversion in the Age of Pluralism*, volume 16 (Leiden: Brill, 2009); Henri Gooren, *Religious Conversion and Disaffiliation: Tracing Patterns of Change in Faith Practices* (New York: Palgrave Macmillan, 2010); Robert W. Hefner, *Conversion to Christianity: Historical and Anthropological Perspectives on a Great Transformation* (Berkeley: University of California Press, 1993); Martijn Oosterbaan, *Transmitting the Spirit: Religious Conversion, Media, and Urban Violence in Brazil* (University Park: Penn State University Press, 2017); Mathijs Pelkmans, ed., *Conversion after Socialism: Disruptions, Modernisms, and Technologies of Faith in the Former Soviet Union*

(New York: Berghahn Books), 2009; Lewis R. Rambo, *Understanding Religious Conversion* (New Haven, CT: Yale University Press, 1993); Lewis R. Rambo and Charles E. Farhadian, eds., *The Oxford Handbook of Religious Conversion* (Oxford: Oxford University Press).

3. Lisbeth Haas, *Saints and Citizens: Indigenous Histories of Colonial Missions and Mexican California* (Berkeley: University of California Press, 2014); Webb Keane, *Christian Moderns: Freedom and Fetish in the Mission Encounter* (Berkeley: University of California Press, 2007); Joel Robbins, *Becoming Sinners: Christianity and Moral Torment in a Papua New Guinea Society* (Berkeley: University of California Press, 2004); Nathaniel Roberts, *To Be Cared For: The Power of Conversion and Foreignness of Belonging in an Indian Slum* (Berkeley: University of California Press, 2016).

4. Diane Austin-Broos, "The Anthropology of Conversion: An Introduction," in *The Anthropology of Religious Conversion, ed.* Andrew Buckser and Stephen D. Glazier (Lanham, MD: Rowman and Littlefield, 2003), 2.

5. Wade Clark Roof, *A Generation of Seekers: The Spiritual Journeys of the Baby Boom Generation* (New York: HarperCollins, 1993); *Spiritual Marketplace: Baby Boomers and the Remaking of American Religion* (Princeton, NJ: Princeton University Press, 2001[reprint]). Stark's early work on religious commitment is some of the first of its kind to ask *why* people select certain religious options over and against others. In many respects his work paved the way for contemporary understandings of the spiritual marketplace. See Rodney Stark and Charles Y. Glock, *American Piety: The Nature of Religious Commitment* (Berkeley: University of California Press, 1968). In recent years, more literature on the spiritual marketplace that elaborates on Wade Clark Roof's earlier contributions has developed; yet it is still beholden to an understanding of selective conversion as simply part and parcel of mass options available. Nonetheless, this type of research provides a helpful lens through which to examine the relationship between travel, tourism, and spirituality more broadly in order to think through the issues of privilege that accompany selective shifts in religious adherence. See Nancy Tatom Ammerman, *Sacred Stories, Spiritual Tribes: Finding Religion in Everyday Life* (New York: Oxford University Press, 2014); Alex Norman, *Spiritual Tourism: Travel and Religious Practice in Western Society* (London: Continuum, 2011); Jan Stievermann, Philip Goff, and Detlef Junke, eds., *Religion and the Marketplace in the United States* (New York: Oxford University Press, 2015). Much of this literature is also indebted to the work of sociologist Robert Wuthnow, whose research has helped shape the way scholars of American religion understand practice and belief, particularly among rural, conservative populations. See *After Heaven: Spirituality in America Since the 1950s* (Berkeley: University of California Press, 1998); *Experimentation in American Religion: The New Mysticisms and Their Implications for the Churches* (Berkeley: University of California Press, 1978).

6. Amy Slagle's sociological work on Orthodox conversion in both the Delta region of Mississippi and the Pennsylvania coal fields employs theories of the spiritual marketplace, suggesting that by focusing on the availability of choices we can better understand conversion within the shifting social economies of the

American religious landscape. See Amy Slagle, *The Eastern Church in the Spiritual Marketplace: American Conversions to Orthodox Christianity* (DeKalb, IL: Northern Illinois University Press), 2011. Slagle's monograph is a revision of her dissertation, a text that provides far more theoretical analysis of her ethnographic encounters with converts. Slagle sees the conversion process as a search between self-reflexive choices that continued, even after the converts had settled into the Orthodox faith, to analyze the relationship between "self and the other" (25). Where converts in Slagle's sites focused on choice, believers in Woodford stressed correctness and authenticity as key drivers in their spiritual quests to find true Christianity. See Amy Slagle, "'Nostalgia without Memory': A Case Study of American Converts to Eastern Orthodoxy in Pittsburgh, Pennsylvania," (PhD diss., University of Pittsburgh, 2008).

7. See Thomas Bremer, *Formed from This Soil: An Introduction to the Diverse History of Religion in America* (Malden, MA: Wiley-Blackwell, 2015); Carla Doggett, *Dr. Andrew Turnbull and the New Smyrna Colony of Florida* (Eustis, FL: Founders Publishing, 1994); Gwenn A. Miller, *Kodiak Creole: Communities of Empire in Early Russian America* (Ithaca, NY: Cornell University, 2010); Mark Stokoe and Leonid Kishkovsky, *Orthodox Christians in North America, 1794–1994* (Syosset, NY: Orthodox Christian Publications Center, 1995).

8. Nicholas Chapman, "The Righteous Shall Be an Everlasting Remembrance: Further Reflections on Colonel Philip Ludwell III," Orthodox History: The Society for Orthodox History in the Americas, accessed January 2, 2019, https://orthodox history.org/2013/03/22/the-righteous-shall-be-in-everlasting-remembrance-further -reflections-on-colonel-philip-ludwell-iii/.

9. Chapman, "The Righteous Shall Be an Everlasting Remembrance."

10. Associates of Colonel Philip Ludwell III, "Structure 'S': The First Orthodox Chapel in America?" Associates of Colonel Philip Ludwell III, accessed December 30, 2018, https://www.ludwell.org/project/greenspring-structure-s.

11. Lincoln Mullen, *The Chance of Salvation: A History of Conversion in America* (Cambridge, MA: Harvard University Press, 2017).

12. Sergei Kan, *Memory Eternal: Tlingit Culture and Russian Orthodox Christianity through Two Centuries* (Seattle: University of Washington Press, 1999).

13. Oliver Herbel, *Turning to Tradition: Converts and the Making of an American Orthodox Church* (New York: Oxford University Press, 2013).

14. Phillip Charles Lucas, "Enfants Terribles: The Challenge of Sectarian Converts to Ethnic Orthodox Churches in the United States," *Nova Religio: The Journal of Alternative and Emergent Religions* 7, no. 2 (November 2003): 5–23.

15. Slagle, "Nostalgia without Memory"; Slagle, *Eastern Church*. Daniel Winchester, "Converting to Continuity: Temporality and Self in Eastern Orthodox Conversion Narratives," *Journal for the Scientific Study of Religion* 54 (2015): 439–460.

16. My understanding of the techniques of conversion is indebted to Pierre Hadot's psycho-philosophical concept of the term that allows for both rhetorical and process forms of conversion historically. In this case, I am more interested in techniques of

conversion that allow for inclusion into a particular community. Hadot is helpful in thinking through conversion, for he sees it as both a process of changing one's orientation in the world and a rebirth. See Pierre Hadot, "Conversion," *Encyclopaedia Universalis* 4 (1968): 979–981.

17. Arnold Van Gennep, *The Rites of Passage*, trans. Monika B. Vizedom and Gabrielle L. Caffee (Chicago: University of Chicago Press, 1960 [1906]) and Victor Turner, *The Ritual Process: Structure and Anti-Structure* (New York: Routledge, 2017 [1969]).

18. Hugh Wybrew, *The Orthodox Liturgy: The Development of the Eucharistic Liturgy in the Byzantine Rite* (Crestwood, NY: St. Vladimir's Seminary Press, 2003).

19. Alexander Schmemann, *Of Water and the Spirit: A Liturgical Study of Baptism* (Crestwood, NY: St. Vladimir's Seminary Press, 1974), 23. For a helpful guide to the service, see Isabel Hapgood, *Service Book of the Holy Orthodox-Catholic Apostolic (Greco-Russian) Church* (Boston: Houghton Mifflin, 1906), 272–273.

20. Interview by author, April 24, 2018.

21. George Marsden, "Fundamentalism as an American Phenomenon, A Comparison with English Evangelicalism," in *Fundamentalism and Evangelicalism*, ed. Martin E. Marty (Berlin: De Gruyter, 1993), 37.

22. Sara Moslener, *Virgin Nation: Sexual Purity and American Adolescence* (Oxford: Oxford University Press, 2015); Katherine Stewart, *The Power Worshippers: Inside the Dangerous Rise of Religious Nationalism* (London: Bloomsbury, 2020).

23. Irene Taviss Thomson, *Culture Wars and Enduring American Dilemmas* (Ann Arbor: University of Michigan Press, 2010).

24. Debbie Ging, "Alphas, Betas, and Incels: Theorizing the Masculinities of the Manosphere," *Men and Masculinities* 22, no. 4 (October 2019): 638–657; Emma Green, "A Christian Insurrection," *Atlantic*, January 8, 2021, under "Politics," accessed January 9, 2021, https://www.theatlantic.com/politics/archive/2021/01/evangelicals -catholics-jericho-march-capitol/617591/.

25. Haralambos Ventis, "Fundamentalism as 'Orthodoxism,'" Public Orthodoxy, accessed September 4, 2018, https://publicorthodoxy.org/2018/07/03/fundamentalism -as-orthodoxism/; Vaseilios Thermos, "Fundamentalism: Theology in the Service of Psychosis," Public Orthodoxy, accessed May 30, 2018, https://publicorthodoxy .org/2018/05/30/fundamentalism-and-psychosis/.

26. Some scholars have suggested that ROCOR in the United States collaborated with the Nazis during World War II. See Karen Dawisha and Bruce Parrott, *Russia and the New States of Eurasia: The Politics of Upheaval* (New York: Cambridge University Press, 1994); Michael Kellogg, *The Russian Roots of Nazism: White Émigrés and the Making of National Socialism 1917–1945* (New York: Cambridge, 2005).

27. Nathaniel Davis, *A Long Walk to Church: A Contemporary History of Russian Orthodoxy* (New York: Routledge, 2003).

28. Trine Stauning Willert and Lina Molokotos-Liederman, eds., *Innovation in the Christian Orthodox Tradition?: The Question of Change in Greek Orthodox Thought and Practice* (Burlington, VT: Ashgate, 2012).

29. Willert and Liederman, *Innovation in the Christian Orthodox Tradition?*

30 Aristotle Papanikolaou, "I am a Traditionalist, Therefore I am," Public Orthodoxy, accessed March 1, 2019, https://publicorthodoxy.org/2019/02/19/i-am-a-traditionalist-therefore-i-am/.

31. Alexander Agadjanian, "Breakthrough to Modernity, Apologia for Traditionalism: the Russian Orthodox View of Society and Culture in Comparative Perspective," *Religion, State, and Society* 31, no. 4 (2003): 327–346.

32. Aristotle Papanikolaou, "I am a Traditionalist, Therefore I am," Public Orthodoxy, accessed March 1, 2019, https://publicorthodoxy.org/2019/02/19/i-am-a-traditionalist-therefore-i-am/. In the course of the article, Papanikolaou goes on to say that the rhetoric of traditionalists and nontraditionists takes away from the diversity of Orthodoxy's living tradition, with both parties using the term traditional in a political way to demonize specific communities within the Church.

33. The Russian Orthodox Church Department for External Church Relations, "The Basis of the Social Concept," The Russian Orthodox Church, accessed February 3, 2019, https://mospat.ru/en/documents/social-concepts/.

34. Marlene Laruelle, *Is Russia Fascist? Unraveling Propaganda East and West* (Ithaca, NY: Cornell University Press, 2021).

35. Laruelle, *Is Russia Fascist?*, 108.

36. Laruelle, 108.

37. Laruelle, 120.

38. Kristina Stoeckl and Kseniya Medvedeva, "Double Bind at the UN: Western Actors, Russia, and the Traditionalist Agenda," *Global Constitutionalism* 7, no. 3 (2018): 383–421.

39. Benjamin R. Teitelbaum, *War for Eternity: Inside Bannon's Far-Right Circle of Global Power Brokers* (New York: HarperCollins, 2020), 159.

40. Teitelbaum, *War for Eternity*, 159.

41. Teitelbaum, 159.

42. Crucial to note here is distinction between canonical and noncanonical traditionalist Orthodox communities. Institutions such as The Center for Traditionalist Orthodox Studies in Etna, California, is not considered to be a legitimate entity because it is not under the jurisdictional authority of one of the sitting Patriarchs within Eastern Orthodoxy.

43. Oliver Herbel, *Turning to Tradition: Converts and the Making of an American Orthodox Church* (London: Oxford Press, 2013), 5–6.

44. Ernest Gellner, *Nations and Nationalism* (Ithaca, NY: Cornell University Press, 1983), 1–3; 33–35.

45. Pål Kolstø and Helge Blakkisrud, eds., *The New Russian Nationalism: Imperialism, Ethnicity and Authoritarianism 2000–2015* (Edinburgh, UK: University of Edinburgh Press, 2016).

46. Father Tryphon, interview by author, May 9, 2018.

47. John Garrard and Carol Garrard, *Russian Orthodoxy Resurgent: Faith and Power in the New Russia* (Princeton, NJ: Princeton University Press, 2008); Andrew

Greeley, "A Religious Revival in Russia?" *Journal for the Scientific Study of Religion* 33, no. 3 (September 1994): 253–277; Juliet Johnson, Marietta Stephaniants, and Benjamin Forest, eds., *Religion and Identity in Modern Russia: The Revival of Orthodoxy and Islam* (New York: Routledge, 2017).

48. My understanding of affective logics rests in literature from both media studies and politics, in which the term is used in different ways, but ultimately nods to mediation and relationality. See Emma Hutchinson, *Affective Communities in World Politics: Collective Emotions after Trauma* (Cambridge: Cambridge University Press, 2016); Jan Slaby and Christian von Scheve, eds., *Affective Societies: Key Concepts* (London: Routledge, 2019).

49. Simon Coleman and John Elsner, "Performing Pilgrimage: Walsingham and the Ritual Construction of Irony," in *Ritual, Performance, and Media,* ed. Felicia Hughes-Freeland (London: Routledge, 1998), 46.

50. John Burgess, *Holy Rus': The Rebirth of Orthodoxy in the New Russia* (New Haven, CT: Yale University Press, 2017); John Fennel, A *History of the Russian Church to 1448* (New York: Routledge, 2013).

51. Fyodor Dostoevsky, *The Idiot* (New York: Macmillan, 1913).

52. Interview by author, December 30, 2017.

53. Interview by author, December 30, 2017.

54. Father Tryphon, interview by author, May 9, 2018. Aldous Huxley, *The Perennial Philosophy* (New York: HarperCollins, 1944).

55. Father Tryphon, interview by author, May 9, 2018.

56. Ann Taves, *Revelatory Events: Three Case Studies of the Emergence of New Spiritual Paths* (Princeton, NJ: Princeton University Press, 2016).

57. With the case of the Woodford community, a traditional afterlife is based squarely in Russian Orthodox mystical philosophy concerning toll houses. See St. Anthony's Greek Orthodox Monastery, *The Departure of the Soul According to the Teaching of the Orthodox Church* (Florence, AZ: St. Anthony's Greek Monastery, 2017).

58. Father Tryphon, interview by author, May 9, 2018.

59. Monk Damascene Christensen, *Not of This World: The Lie and Teaching of Fr. Seraphim Rose, Pathfinder to the Heart of Ancient Christianity* (Forestville, CA: Fr. Seraphim Rose Foundation, 1993).

60. Christensen, *Not of This World.*

61. Christensen, *Not of This World,* 11.

62. Christensen, 17.

63. Christensen, 22.

64. Christensen, 36–37.

65. Christensen, 61.

66. For an overview of Guénon and other traditionalist thinkers, including Aleksandr Dugin, see Mark J. Sedgwick, *Against the Modern World: Traditionalism and the Secret Intellectual History of the Twentieth Century* (New York: Oxford University Press, 2004).

67. Christensen, *Not of this World,* 190–191.

68. Christensen, 202.

69. Christensen, 186–187.

70. Christensen, 266.

71. One vital thing to note here is that Rose never received an academic theological education from an Orthodox institution. This is not uncommon among ROCOR convert laity in the United States, who often are seemingly rushed through the process of ordination (for the priesthood or the diaconate) with little to no theological training in an environment of higher education. This is not to say that there are no centers of ROCOR education in the United States. Indeed, Holy Trinity Seminary in Jordanville, NY, is arguably one of the epicenters of émigré ROCOR education.

72. Christensen, *Not of this World*, 127.

73. Fr. Seraphim Rose, *God's Revelation of the Human Heart* (Platina, CA: St. Herman of Alaska Brotherhood, 1987); *Soul After Death* (Platina, CA: St. Herman of Alaska Brotherhood, 1980).

74. Cathy Scott, *Seraphim Rose: The True Story and Private Letters* (Salisbury, MA: Regina Orthodox Press, 2000).

75. Scott, *Seraphim Rose*, 72.

76. Emil Edenborg, "Homophobia as Geopolitics: 'Traditional Values' and the Negotiation of Russia's Place in the World," in *Gendering Nationalism: Intersections of Nation, Gender and Sexuality*, ed. Jon Mulholland, Nicola Montagna, and Erin Sanders-McDonagh (London: Palgrave Macmillan, 2018), 67–87.

77. Sophie Bjork-James, *The Divine Institution: White Evangelicalism's Politics of the Family* (Newark, NJ: Rutgers University Press, 2021).

78. Scott, *Seraphim Rose*, 230.

79. Fr. Seraphim Rose, *Lectures of Fr. Seraphim Rose, Volume One (Living the Orthodox Worldview)* (St. Herman of Alaska Brotherhood, CD, 2015 [2007]).

80. Fr. Theodosius, interview by author, July 5, 2018.

81. Interview, July 5, 2018.

82. Interview, July 5, 2018.

83. Interview, July 5, 2018.

84. Interview, July 5, 2018.

85. Interview, July 5, 2018.

86. Interview, July 5, 2018.

87. Interview, July 5, 2018.

88. Interview, July 5, 2018.

89. Interview, July 5, 2018.

90. Interview, July 5, 2018.

91. Interview, July 5, 2018.

92. Christensen, *Not of This World*, 473. Monk Damascene Christensen is not the same figure as Fr. Damascene who lived at St. Basil's monastery. One trouble we have in the Orthodox world is clergy with the same name. It's not uncommon to be in a room where everyone turns when a popular name such as John or Luke is called out.

93. Christensen, xi.

94. Kristin Kobes Du Mez, *Jesus and John Wayne: How White Evangelicals Corrupted a Faith and Fractured a Nation* (New York: Liveright, 2020).

95. Rod Dreher, *The Benedict Option: A Strategy for Christians in a Post Christian Nation* (New York: Peguin, 2017), 10.

96. Rod Dreher, "Religion of Head and Heart," The American Conservative, December 20, 2018, accessed January 3, 2019, https://www.theamericanconservative .com/dreher/religion-head-heart-orthodoxy-catholicism/.

97 Rod Dreher, "Thinking and the Bid Divide," TheAmericanConservative.com, January 28, 2015, accessed January 3, 2019, https://www.theamericanconservative.com /dreher/thinking-and-the-big-divide/.

98. Interview by author, December 31, 2017.

99. Not muscular Christianity in the sense of competitive sports and religiosity; rather, I am thinking of this term in conjunction with Marie Dallam's work on cowboy Christians, who veer away from "feminized" spirituality in favor of a religious experience that is difficult and seemingly manly. Marie W. Dallam, *Cowboy Christians* (Oxford: Oxford University Press, 2018). For a broader understanding of how muscular Christianity is linked tightly to sports, nationalism, and patriotism, see Clifford Putney, *Muscular Christianity: Manhood and Sports in Protestant America, 1880–1920* (Cambridge, MA: Harvard University Press, 2003).

100. Kristen Kobes Du Mez, *Jesus and John Wayne: How White Evangelicals Corrupted a Faith and Fractured a Nation* (New York: Liveright, 2020). As I have mentioned previously, patriarchally inclined traditionalism is one of many different ideologies in ROCOR and Orthodox Christianity more broadly. However, with the influx of former evangelicals and other fundamentalists Christians it seems, from my fieldwork and digital ethnography, that ideologies such as those are gaining more traction.

101. Fr. John Peck and Fr. Anthony Perkins, "Good Guys Wear Black: Discerning your Vocation in the Orthodox Church," accessed September 3, 2019, https://good guyswearblack.org.

102. Fr. Andrew Lemeshonok, "Q&A with a Priest: What Does It Mean to Be a Priest's Wife?" Good Guys Wear Black: Discerning your Vocation in the Orthodox Church, entry posted December 3, 2018, accessed September 3, 2019, https://good guyswearblack.org/2018/12/03/qa-with-a-priest-what-does-it-mean-to-be-a-priests-wife/.

103. Lemeshonok, "Q&A with a Priest."

104. Lemeshonok, "Q&A with a Priest."

3. America the Beautiful: Of Guns, God, and Vodka

1. Godfrey Hodgson, *The Myth of American Exceptionalism* (New Haven, CT: Yale University Press, 2009).

2. Matthew McManus, *The Rise of Post-Modern Conservatism: Neoliberalism, Post-Modern Culture, and Reactionary Politics* (Cham, Switzerland: Palgrave Macmillan, 2019).

3. Scholars have noted that memes are often among the preferred forms of social communication and ideological dissemination of ideas for those affiliated with the alt-right. Viveca S. Greene, "'Deplorable' Satire: Alt-Right Memes, White Genocide Tweets, and Redpilling Normies," *Studies in American Humor* 5, no. 1 (2019): 31–69; George Hawley, *Making Sense of the Alt-Right* (New York: Columbia University Press, 2017); Annie Kelly, "The Alt-Right: Reactionary Rehabilitation for White Masculinity: US Alt-Right Extremism Is a Logical Consequence of Mainstream Neo-Conservatism," *Soundings: A Journal of Politics and Culture* 68 (2017): 68–78.

4. Interview by author, April 24, 2018.

5. Members of ROCOR communities have often pointed out to me that if a married man is interested in Orthodoxy, his spouse will typically fall in line and convert as well, although this process can often take years.

6. In Woodford, there was a noted outlier to this conservative convert model. Nikon was a longtime convert, but often the brunt of jokes by his friends in the parish because he was outspoken in his anti-firearm ideologies. He had the additional distinction of having married a "career woman" who was from a different "modern" Orthodox community.

7. Klaus Larres and Ruth Wittlinger, eds. *Understanding Global Politics: Actors and Themes in International Affairs* (London: Routledge, 2019).

8. Henry Kissinger, *Diplomacy* (New York: Simon and Schuster, 1995), 142.

9. Robert A. Saunders, *Popular Geopolitics and Nation Branding in the Post-Soviet Realm* (London: Routledge, 2016); Marlene Laruelle, *Russian Eurasianism: An Ideology of Empire* (Baltimore, MD: Johns Hopkins University Press, 2012).

10. Peter J. S. Duncan, *Russian Messianism: Third Rome, Revolution, Communism, and After* (London: Routledge, 2002).

11. Hilde Eliassen Restad, *American Exceptionalism: An Idea That Made a Nation and Remade the World* (London: Routledge, 2014).

12. Ian Tyrell, *Reforming the World: The Creation of America's Moral Empire* (Princeton, NJ: Princeton University Press, 2010).

13. Dennis R. Hoover, ed., *Religion and American Exceptionalism* (London: Routledge, 2013).

14. Lisa McGirr, *Suburban Warriors: The Origins of the New American Right* (Princeton, NJ: Princeton University Press, 2015).

15. Kristin Kobes Du Mez, *Jesus and John Wayne: How White Evangelicals Corrupted a Faith and Fractured a Nation* (New York: Liveright, 2020). Sarah Posner, *Unholy: Why White Evangelicals Worship at the Altar of Donald Trump* (New York: Random House, 2020).

16. Donald T. Critchlow, *The Conservative Ascendancy: How the GOP Right Made Political History* (Cambridge, MA: Harvard University Press, 2007).

17. Kevin M. Kruse, *One Nation Under God: How Corporate America Invented Christian America* (New York: Basic Books, 2015).

18. Mary C. Brennan, *Turning Right in the Sixties: The Conservative Capture of the GOP* (Chapel Hill: University of North Carolina Press, 2005); Donald T. Critchlow,

Phyllis Schlafly and Grassroots Conservatism: A Woman's Crusade (Princeton, NJ: Princeton University Press, 2018).

19. David T. Courtwright, *No Right Turn: Conservative Politics in a Liberal America* (Cambridge, MA: Harvard University Press, 2010), 122–23.

20. Daniel Hummel, "Revivalist Nationalism since World War II: From 'Wake up, America!' to 'Make America Great Again,'" *Religions* 7 (2006): 123–124.

21. Fritz Detwiler, *Standing on the Premises of God: The Christian Right's Fight to Redefine America's Public Schools* (New York: New York University Press, 1999); Steven Patrick Miller, *The Age of Evangelicalism: America's Born-Again Years* (New York: Oxford University Press, 2014).

22. Matthew Avery Sutton, *American Apocalypse: A History of Modern Evangelicalism* (Cambridge, MA: Harvard University Press, 2014).

23. Philip Jenkins, *The Cold War at Home: The Red Scare in Pennsylvania, 1945–1960* (Chapel Hill: University of North Carolina, 2011).

24. Jonathan Michaels, *McCarthyism: The Realities, Delusions, and Politics behind the 1950s Red Scare* (New York: Routledge, 2017).

25. Michaels, *McCarthyism*; Jonathan P. Herzog, *The Spiritual-Industrial Complex: America's Religious Battle against Communism in the Early Cold War* (New York: Oxford University Press, 2011).

26. Mary C. Brennan, *Wives, Mothers, and the Red Menace: Conservative Women and the Crusade against Communism* (Boulder: University of Colorado Press, 2011).

27. Richard Moss, *Nixon's Back Channel to Moscow: Confidential Diplomacy and Détente* (Lexington: University Press of Kentucky, 2017).

28. Thomas Kiffmeyer, *Reformers to Radicals: The Appalachian Volunteers and the War on Poverty* (Lexington: University Press of Kentucky, 2009); Huey Perry, *They'll Cut off Your Project: A Mingo County Chronicle* (Morgantown: West Virginia University Press, 2011).

29. Mark Francis, "Media Event: Russian Surprised by Turn of Events in Mingo County," *Raleigh Register*, December 19, 1977; Gregory Jaynes, "Stranded Mining Town Awaits Bridge," *New York Times*, December 16, 1978.

30. Richard Grimes, "The Mouse Is Roaring: Mingo Mayor Will Ask Russians to Build a Bridge," *Charleston Daily Mail*, August 4, 1977.

31. Grimes, "The Mouse Is Roaring."

32. Ibid.

33. Ibid.

34. Article, "West Virginian Dedicates Bridge He Once Asked Russians to Build: Worldwide Publicity 'Story Was Embarrassing,'" *New York Times*, July 5, 1980. Iona Andronov decided to stay in the United States on a tour of the nation. By 1985 he was back in Appalachia, in eastern Kentucky, where he was attacked by "two well-dressed men," while he was interviewing coal workers striking on the picket line. According to an article in the *Los Angeles Times*, Andronov claimed the men shouted, "You bloody Russian," as they attacked him. Article, "Soviet Reporter Says He Was Attacked on U.S. Picket Line," *Los Angeles Times*, September 26, 1985.

35. Article, "West Virginian Dedicates Bridge."

36. Article, "West Virginian Dedicates Bridge."

37. Article, "West Virginian Dedicates Bridge." Organized socialist parties in West Virginia were quite present in the first part of the twentieth century, but by the 1920s internal factors and external political forces eventually brought about their demise. Much pressure to deconstruct organized socialism in the state came from political leaders, who, by 1919 saw the activities as un-American. See Frederick A. Barkey, *Working Class Radicals: The Socialist Party in West Virginia, 1898–1920* (Morgantown: West Virginia University Press, 2012); John C. Hennen, *The Americanization of West Virginia: Creating a Modern Industrial State, 1916–1925* (Lexington: University Press of Kentucky, 2015).

Grassroots forms of socialism were and still are present in West Virginia, with a growing number of millennials taking up the cause through social media endeavors and in local politics. Within Appalachian Instagram circles, the user @cornbreadcommunism, who has upward of 10,000 followers, has been prolific in creating and disseminating meme content about the socialist and communist efforts in the region. Often jointly noted with the very popular account @queerappalachia, who has upward of 260,000 followers, @cornbreadcommunism and other similar accounts use hashtags such as #cornbreadcommunism, #nohateinmyholler, and #ruralresistance to help spread awareness of the leftist, liberal rural contingent that is so often overlooked in U.S. media coverage of politics in these areas. Regional public historian Elizabeth Catte argues that the one-dimensional portrait of Appalachia only seeks to reinforce the stereotypes of poor, rural whites. See Elizabeth Catte, eds., *Left Elsewhere: Finding the Future in Radical Rural America* (Boston: Boston Review Forum/MIT Press, 2019).

38. Jason W. Stevens, *God-Fearing and Fear: A Spiritual History of America's Cold War* (Cambridge, MA: Harvard University Press, 2010), viii.

39. Stevens, *God-Fearing and Fear*, x.

40. Stevens, 3–4.

41. John Fea, *Believe Me: The Evangelical Road to Donald Trump* (Grand Rapids, MI: Wm. B. Eerdmans, 2018); Frances Fitzgerald, *The Evangelicals: The Struggle to Shape America* (New York: Simon and Schuster, 2017).

42. Cas Mudde and Cristóbal Rovira Kaltwasser, eds., *Populism in Europe and the Americas: Threat or Corrective for Democracy?* (New York: Oxford University Press, 2012).

43. Jonathan P. Herzog, *The Spiritual-Industrial Complex: America's Religious Battle against Communism in the Early Cold War* (New York: Oxford University Press, 2011); Mark Juergensmeyer, *The New Cold War? Religious Nationalism Confronts the Secular State* (Berkeley: University of California Press, 1994).

44. Scholars of Russian politics have noted that this view stems much from the rhetoric Vladimir Putin and Patriarch Kirill have used when addressing Russian public audiences. Mikhail Suslov and Dmitry Uzlaner, eds., *Contemporary Russian Conservatism: Problems, Paradoxes, and Perspectives* (Leiden, Netherlands: Brill, 2019).

45. Bethany Moreton, *Slouching Toward Moscow: American Evangelicals and the Romance of Russia* (Cambridge, MA: Harvard University Press, forthcoming).

46. Anthony M. Petro, *After the Wrath of God: AIDS, Sexuality, and American Religion* (New York: Oxford University Press, 2015); Heather R. White, *Reforming Sodom: Protestants and the Rise of Gay Rights* (Chapel Hill: University of North Carolina Press, 2015).

47. Fr. Josiah Trenham, "Gay Iconoclasm: Holding the Line against the Radical LGBT Agenda," World Congress of Families X, May 15, 2016, accessed May 3, 2018, https://youtu.be/HNXe4P_6dhw.

48. Christine Pappas, Jeanette Mendez, and Rebekah Herrick, "The Negative Effects of Populism on Gay and Lesbian Rights," *Social Science Quarterly* 90, no.1 (March 2009): 150–163.

49. Jennifer Suchland "The LGBT Specter in Russia: Refusing Queerness, Claiming 'Whiteness,'" *Gender, Place, and Culture* 25, no. 7 (2018): 1073–1088.

50. Pippa Norris and Ronald Inglehart, *Cultural Backlash: Trump, Brexit, and Authoritarian Populism* (Cambridge: Cambridge University Press, 2019), 7–8.

51. Ruth Wodak, *The Politics of Fear: What Right-Wing Populist Discourses Mean* (London: Sage, 2015).

52. Interview by author, November 1, 2017. The idea that Trump is "one of us" highlights the clever way in which his media team positioned him as a candidate. For a man who is seemingly a wealthy reactionary with no concept of labor, he did have somewhat of an appeal for working class conservatives. Aurelien Mondon and Aaron Winter, "Whiteness, Populism and the Racialisation of the Working Class in the United Kingdom and the United States," *Identities* 26, no. 5 (2019): 510–528; Paul Pierson, "American Hybrid: Donald Trump and the strange merger of populism and plutocracy," *The British Journal of Sociology* 68, S1 (2017): S105–119.

53. Mondon and Winter, "Whiteness."

54. Cas Mudde, *The Far Right Today* (Cambridge: Polity Press, 2019).

55. Andrew L. Whitehead and Samuel L. Perry, "Is a 'Christian America' a More Patriarchal America? Religion, Politics, and Traditionalist Gender Ideology," *Canadian Review of Sociology* (2019): 153.

56. Deborah Vansau McCauley, *Appalachian Mountain Religion: A History* (Urbana: University of Illinois Press, 1995).

57. Catherine Albanese, *America, Religions, and Religion* (Toronto: Wadsworth, 1981), 230.

58. Karl B. Raitz, Richard Ulack, and Thomas R. Leinbach, *Appalachia: A Regional Geography: Land, People, and Development* (New York: Routledge, 2018 [1984]).

59. Richard B. Drake, *A History of Appalachia* (Lexington: University Press of Kentucky, 2004).

60. John Anderson, *Conservative Christian Politics in Russia and the United States: Dreaming of Christian Nations* (New York: Routledge, 2014); Seth Dowland, *Family Values and the Rise of the Christian Right* (Philadelphia: University of Pennsylvania Press, 2015).

61. Sophie Bjork-James, *The Divine Institution: White Evangelicalism's Politics of the Family* (New Brunswick, NJ: Rutgers University Press, 2021), 68.

62. Doris Buss and Didi Herman, *Globalizing Family Values: The Christian Right in International Politics* (Minneapolis: University of Minnesota Press, 2003 [1998]).

63. Damien McGuinness, "Thousands Protest in Georgia Over Gay Rights Rally," BBC, May 17, 2013, accessed May 2, 2018, https://www.bbc.com/news/world -europe-22571216; Orthodox Christianity, "Family Purity Day Is Not against Anyone, but for Georgia—Patriarch Ilia," *Orthodox Christianity*, accessed May 8, 2019, http://orthochristian.com/121266.html.

64. Patristic Nectar Films, "Gay Iconoclasm: Holding the Line against the Radical LGBT Agenda," YouTube website, 22:11, accessed November 16, 2018, https://youtu.be/HNXe4P_6dhw; Hatewatch Staff, "World Congress of Families Gathering in Tbilisi Showcases Anti-LGBT Rhetoric and Conspiracy Theories," Southern Poverty Law Center, accessed November 16, 2018, https://www.splcenter .org/hatewatch/2016/06/01/world-congress-families-gathering-tbilisi-showcases-anti -lgbt-rhetoric-and-conspiracy.

65. Katherine Stewart, "What Was Maria Butina Doing at the National Prayer Breakfast?," *New York Times*, July 18, 2018, https://www.nytimes.com/2018/07/18/ opinion/maria-butina-putin-infiltration.html.

66. Stewart, "What Was Maria Butina Doing?"

67. Tom Porter, "The Christian Right Is Looking to Putin's Russia to Save Christianity from the Godless West," *Newsweek*, July 15, 2018, https://www.newsweek .com/how-evangelicals-are-looking-putins-russia-save-christianity-godless-west-1115164.

68. Dmitry Uzlaner and Kristina Stoeckl, "The Legacy of Pitirim Sorokin in the Transnational Alliances of Moral Conservatives," *Journal of Classical Sociology* 1, no. 2 (2017).

69. Sanna Turoma and Kaarina Aitamurto, "Renegotiating Patriotic and Religious Identities in the Post-Soviet and Post-Secular Russia," *Transcultural Studies* 12 (2016): 1–14.

70. Kristina Stoeckl, *The Russian Orthodox Church and Human Rights* (London: Routledge, 2014).

71. Sam Haselby, *The Origins of American Religious Nationalism* (New York: Oxford University Press, 2016).

72. Andrew L. Whitehead and Samuel L. Perry, *Taking America Back for God: Christian Nationalism in the United States* (New York: Oxford University Press, 2020).

73. Whitehead and Perry, "Is a 'Christian America' a More Patriarchal America?," 152–177.

74. John Anderson, *Conservative Christian Politics in Russia and the United States: Dreaming of Christian Nations* (London: Routledge, 2014).

75. Jordan B. Peterson, "Tradition and Things That Don't Fit with Jonathan Pageau, November 29, 2016, accessed December 4, 2017, https://www.youtube.com /watch?time_continue=95&v=eob5mnuKQvs.

76. Jeffrey W. Robbins, "What's the Matter with Populism?" *Soundings: An Interdisciplinary Journal* 102, no. 2–3 (2019): 261–273.

4. Port of the Tsar: Material Monarchism and the End of Days

1. In her work on the rise of new forms of nationalism in Russia, Marlene Laruelle suggests that there has been a resurgent interest in the imperial flag among particular Russian nationalist movements tied to, among other things, a deep devotion to the Romanovs (164–201). With groups ranging from "Slavic Strength (*Slavianskaia sila*)" to the "Russian Orthodox Army," the flag seems to represent everything from a "revival of political Orthodoxy" with notions stemming from a resuscitated Black Hundreds group to white power imperialism that has global ties to white supremacy networks (164–203). Marlene Laruelle, *Russian Nationalism: Imaginaries, Doctrines, and Political Battlefields* (London: Routledge, 2019).

2. Wendy Slater, *The Many Deaths of Tsar Nicholas II: Relics, Remains, and the Romanovs* (London: Routledge, 2007), 110.

3. See Tom Balmforth, "Russian Orthodox Nationalists Hope for Tsar's Return," *Reuters*, August 9, 2018, accessed November 20, 2018, https://www.reuters.com /article/us-russia-nationalists/russian-orthodox-nationalists-hope-for-tsars-return -idUSKBN1KU1C7?feedType=RSS&feedName=topNews&utm_source=twitter& utm_medium=Social.

4. Nikolay Andreyev, "Filofey and His Epistle to Ivan Vasil'yevich," *The Slavonic and East European Review* 38, no. 90 (December 1959): 1–31. Andreyev is drawing on the work of V. N. Malinin, *Starets Eleazarova Monastyrya Filofey i yego poslaniya. Istoriko-literaturnoye issledovaniye* (Kiev, 1901), using his rendering of Filofey's letter found in appendix vii, (3).

For an excellent assessment of Third Rome in its varying manifestations, see Jardar Østbø, *The New Third Rome: Readings of a Russian Nationalist Myth* (Stuttgart: ibidem-Verlag, 2016). It is also important to point out that not all scholars agree with the importance of the Third Rome theory. See Daniel B. Rowland, "Moscow—The Third Rome or the New Israel?" *Russian Review* 55, no. 4 (October 1996): 591–614.

5. Vincent W. Lloyd, *The Problem with Grace: Reconfiguring Political Theology* (Stanford, CA: Stanford University Press, 2011), 9.

6. Cyril Hovorun, *Political Orthodoxies: The Unorthodoxies of the Church Coerced* (Minneapolis, MN: Fortress Press, 2018), 9.

7. Dieter Grimm, *Sovereignty: The Origin and Future of a Political and Legal Concept*, trans. Belinda Cooper (New York: Columbia University Press, 2015 [2009]).

8. David Graeber and Marshall Sahlins, *On Kings* (Chicago: University of Chicago Press, 2017), 2.

9. Graeber and Sahlins, *On Kings*, 4.

10. Marshall Sahlins, "The Original Political Society," in *On Kings*, David Graeber and Marshall Sahlins (Chicago: University of Chicago Press, 2017), 39–40.

11. Stephen Freeman, *Everywhere Present: Christianity in a One-Storey Universe* (Chesterton, IN: Conciliar Press, 2010).

12. Sahlins, "The Original Political Society," 39–40.

13. For an academic yet accessible primer on the history of political theology, see Elizabeth Phillips, *Political Theology: A Guide for the Perplexed* (London: Bloomsbury, 2012).

14. Orthodox scholar Paul Valliere suggests that these Orthodox theological philosophers were part of the patristic renewal in many respects. See Paul Valliere, *Modern Russian Theology: Bukharev, Soloviev, Bulgakov: Orthodox Theology in a New Key* (Grand Rapids, MI: Wm. B. Eerdmans, 2000). Dugin would be an outlier to this group for Valliere.

15. Within the Greek Orthodox tradition there are several conservative strands of belief that have formed around elders. Members of the Woodford community seem to have a deep affinity for the writings of Elder Ephrem, who was considered a grace-filled *starets* for traditional believers. Originally a monastic on Mount Athos, he resided in Arizona, where he had a large following among ROCOR and Old-Calendarists (Greek and Russian), until his death in December 2019. Virtually no academic works exist about Elder Ephrem or his new following in the United States. For a brief reference to the elder, see Christopher D. L. Johnson, *The Globalization of Hesychasm and the Jesus Prayer: Contesting Contemplation* (London: Continuum, 2010).

16. Irina Paert, *Spiritual Elders: Charisma and Tradition in Russian Orthodoxy* (DeKalb: Northern Illinois University Press, 2010).

17. In his article on traditionalism and Eastern Orthodoxy in the post-colonial period, Orthodox theologian George Demacopoulos explores the historical complexities that have brought about pushback against "Western and/or modern contamination of Orthodox teaching and practice" (476). Demacopoulos suggests that identity of traditionalist Orthodox Christianity as distinct "morally, ideologically, and (sometimes) sacramentally from the broader Orthodox community is bound up in quests for social relevance that were quite possibly shaped by the historic "cultural captivity" it experienced during the Ottoman empire (479–80). Furthermore, he goes on to show that traditionalist, which we could easily replace with fundamentalist, Orthodoxy in the post-colonial period is not a new phenomenon; rather it is a new incarnation of historic efforts to somehow thwart modernization efforts (483). George Demacopoulos, "'Traditional Orthodoxy' as a Postcolonial Movement," *Journal of Religion* 97, no. 4 (October 2017): 475–499.

18. Abbot Spyridon, interview by author, March 13, 2018.

19. Restorationism movements range from early incarnations of Mormonism to recent trends of new monasticism and house churches. See Paul Keith Conkin, *American Originals: Homemade Varieties of Christianity* (Chapel Hill: University of North Carolina Press, 1997); Wes Markofski, *New Monasticism and the Transformation of American Evagelicalism* (New York: Oxford University Press, 2015).

20. John Maximovitch, "The Question of Uniformity in the Church Services Discussed at the Council of Hierarchs of the Russian Orthodox Church Abroad (1951)," trans. Akim Provatakis, *Orthodox Life* 41, no. 4 (1991): 42–45.

21. Vincent W. Lloyd, *The Problem with Grace: Reconfiguring Political Theology* (Stanford, CA: Stanford University Press, 2011), 3.

22. Carlota McAllister and Valentina Napolitano, "The Powers of Powerlessness," *Political Theology Network*, accessed January 28, 2019, https://politicaltheology.com /the-powers-of-powerlessness/.

23. Aristotle Papanikolaou, "Byzantium, Orthodoxy, and Democracy," *Journal of the American Academy of Religion* 71, no. 1 (2003): 75–98.

24. Justinian's Sixth Novella lays out a detailed understanding of the importance of a God-ordained emperor and the concept that would later develop properly into symphonia. For a high-quality English-language translation, see Peter Sarris, ed., *The Novels of Justinian: A Complete Annotated English Translation*, trans. David D. J. Miller (Cambridge: Cambridge University Press, 2018).

25. Sarris, *Novels of Justinian*.

26. Aristotle Papanikolaou, *The Mystical as Political: Democracy and Non-Radical Orthodoxy* (Notre Dame, IN: University of Notre Dame, 2012).

27. Oliver O'Donovan and Joan Lockwood O'Donovan, eds. *From Irenaeus to Grotius: A Sourcebook in Christian Political Thought* (Grand Rapids, MI: Wm. B. Eerdmans, 1999), 60.

28. Zoe Knox, *Russian Society and the Orthodox Church: Religion in Russia after Communism* (London: Routledge, 2004), 106.

29. Papanikolaou, *Mystical as Political*, 19.

30. Knox, *Russian Society and the Orthodox Church*, 107.

31. Wendy Slater, "Relics, Remains, and Revisionism: Narratives of Nicholas II in Contemporary Russia," *Rethinking History: The Journal of Theory and Practice* 9, no. 1 (2005): 53–70.

32. John Maximovitch, "Tsar-Martyr Nicholas II," *Orthodox Word* 4, no. 21 (July–August 1968): 137.

33. Maximovitch, "Tsar-Martyr Nicholas II."

34. The cultic interest in the Romanovs is often centered on the macabre events that transpired around their deaths, which has led to everything from wild speculation to conspiracy theories that have been become fodder for the media, to their glorification (canonization) two times. Public scholarship and investigative reporting about the life, death, and controversial remains of the royal family abound.

35. Interview by author, December 31, 2017.

36. Wil van den Berken, "The Canonisation of Nicholas II in Iconographical Perspective," in *Orthodox Christianity and Contemporary Europe*, ed. J. Sutton and W. van den Bercken (Leuven: Peeters, 2003), 185–211.

37. Scholars are beginning to take notice of the both the influence and issues Orthodox Christians face in the digital age. See Mikhail Suslov, ed., *Digital Orthodoxy in the Post-Soviet World: The Russian Orthodox Church and the Web 2.0* (Stuttgart: *ibidem*-Verlag, 2016).

38. His Holiness Patriarch Kirill, [26:19] interview, *60 Minut, Rossiya Odna*, January 7, 2019, https://www.youtube.com/watch?v=kV6SuZ7t9gs&feature=youtu.be.

39. Jesse Dominick, "In Memory of the Royal Martyrs, Through Personal Testimony," *Pravoslavie*, accessed December 30, 2018, http://www.pravoslavie.ru /80716.html#_ftn7.

40. Dominick, "In Memory of the Royal Martyrs."

41. Dominick, "In Memory of the Royal Martyrs."

42. Radio Free Europe, "Russian Patriarch Says Gay Marriage 'Sign of Apocalypse," July 21, 2013, https://www.rferl.org/a/patriarch-russia-gay-apocalypse -kirill/25052758.html.

43. RIA Novosti, "Patriarkh Kirill predupredil o priblizhenii kontsa sveta," November 21, 2017, https://ria.ru/20171120/1509166583.html.

44. The saintly status of the Romanovs is not without controversy between ROCOR and the ROC. ROCOR sees the Romanovs as martyrs at the hands of Bolsheviks and labeled them as such in 1981. However, the ROC canonized the family as passion-bearers in 2000, right before the reunification with ROCOR, moving away from the trope of godless assassination in order to avoid confronting their own cooperation with the Bolshevism (Knox and Mitrofanova 2014). See Zoe Knox and Anastasia Mitrofanova, "The Russian Orthodox Church," in *Eastern Christianity and Politics in the Twenty-First Century*, ed. Lucian N. Leustean (New York: Routledge, 2014), 38–66.

45. 2 Thessalonians 2:7 (New Revised Standard Version). Since most converts quote varying versions of this verse, I chose to cite the version generally accepted by both the American Academy of Religion and the Society for Biblical Literature.

46. Father Tryphon, interview by author, May 9, 2018.

47. Interview, May 9, 2018.

48. Robert A. Orsi, *History and Presence* (Cambridge, MA: Harvard University Press, 2018).

49. Betsy Perabo, *Russian Orthodoxy and the Russo-Japanese War* (New York: Bloomsbury, 2017). The icon never reached its intended location during the Russo-Japanese war. However, in 2004, in honor of the Port Arthur's defense, the icon sailed around Asia on a blessing tour that brought the icon to sites throughout China and Japan where Russian sailors had perished during the battles a hundred years before. See Edyta M. Bojanowska, *A World of Empires: The Russian Voyage of the Frigate Pallada* (Cambridge, MA: Harvard University Press, 2018).

50. Vera Shevzov, *Russian Orthodoxy on the Eve of Revolution* (New York: Oxford University Press, 2003).

51. Abbot Spyridon, interview by author, March 13, 2018.

52. Interview, March 13, 2018.

53. Interview, March 13, 2018.

54. Interview, March 13, 2018.

55. The icon's official name is the Port Arthur Triumph of the Theotokos, but is generally referred to as the Port Arthur, Port Arthur Mother of God, or the Port Arthur Theotokos colloquially.

56. Fr. Theodosius created the rubrics and hymnody for the divine services, which include Vigil, Matins, and Liturgy, all of which would be serviced for the feast day within a twenty-four-hour cycle.

57. Anonymous, Service for "The Commemoration of the Triumph of Our Lady of Port Arthur Icon," Unpublished, 2014.

58. Anonymous, "Commemoration."

59. Anonymous, "Commemoration."

60. Anonymous, "Commemoration."

61. Anonymous, "Commemoration."

62. Anonymous, "Commemoration."

63. This turn of phrase is from Hebrews 12:1 (NASB): "Therefore, since we have so great a cloud of witnesses surrounding us, let us also lay aside every encumbrance and the sin which so easily entangles us, and let us run with endurance the race that is set before us." It is often used in reference to the saints watching the lives of believers on earth and aiding them in the journey to heaven.

64. Anonymous, "Commemoration."

65. Interview, March 13, 2018.

66. Anonymous, "Commemoration."

5. Palace of Putin: Political Ideologies in Orthodox Appalachia

1. Interview by author, December 31, 2017.

2. Interview, December 31, 2017.

3. In recent years, far-right conservatism has not only been on the rise in rural areas of the United States, but also throughout Europe, with these seemingly disparate areas of the world connected by the digital forces of globalization that allow for rapid networking and dissemination of ideas. See Chris Atton, *An Alternative Internet: Radical Media, Politics, and Creativity* (Edinburgh, UK: Edinburgh University Press, 2014); Hans-Georg Betz, *Radical Right-Wing Populism in Western Europe* (New York: Palgrave Macmillan, 1994); Manuela Caiani and Linda Parenti, *European and American Extreme Right Groups and the Internet* (London: Routledge Press, 2016); Jean-Yves Camus and Nicolas Lebourg, *Far-Right Politics in Europe*, trans. Jane Marie Todd (Cambridge, MA: Harvard University Press, 2017); Katherine J. Cramer, *The Politics of Resentment: Rural Consciousness in Wisconsin and the Rise of Scott Walker* (Chicago: University of Chicago Press, 2016); Paul Hainsworth, ed., *The Extreme Right in Europe and the USA* (London: Bloomsbury, 1992); Arlie Russell Hochschild, *Strangers in Their Own Land: Anger and Mourning on the American Right* (New York: New Press, 2016); Jeffrey Kaplan and Leonard Weinberg, *The Emergence of a Euro-American Radical Right* (New Brunswick, NJ: Rutgers University Press, 1998); Cas Mudde, *The Far Right in America* (London: Routledge, 2018).

4. George Hawley, *Making Sense of the Alt-Right* (New York: Columbia University Press, 2017); Cyril Hovorun, *Political Orthodoxies: The Unorthodoxies of the Church Coerced* (Minneapolis, MN: Fortress Press, 2018). It is crucial to remember that the

Russian Orthodox Church Outside of Russia (ROCOR) has a distinct history from the Russian Orthodox Church (ROC) and the Moscow Patriarchate (MP), even though they are now reconciled and are in full communion with each other.

5. By new Russia, I am referring to the contemporary period seen as Russia after the Soviet Union, but particularly since the late 1990s, during which Vladimir Putin began holding various forms of public governmental authority. Perhaps another term, one that is often used in public scholarship regarding this time frame, would be "Putin's Russia." A wide variety of periodicals and paperbacks on the mass market use that term, although it is generally used pejoratively in analyzing the increasing authoritarian framework of contemporary Russia. See Peter Baker and Susan Glasser, *Kremlin Rising: Vladimir Putin's Russia and the End of Revolution* (New York: Simon and Schuster, 2005); Steven Lee Myers, *The New Tsar: The Rise and Reign of Vladimir Putin* (New York: Simon and Schuster, 2015); and Anna Politkovskaya, *Putin's Russia: Life in a Failing Democracy* (New York: Metropolitan Books, 2007). Some scholars of Vladimir Putin and Russian politics also make use of the term "Putin's Russia," often focusing on resistance groups in what seems to be an increasingly oppressive political moment in Russia's history. See Elena A. Chebankova, *Civil Society in Putin's Russia* (New York: Routledge, 2013); Mischa Gabowitsch, *Protest in Putin's Russia* (Malden, MA: Polity Press, 2017); and Julie Hemment, *Youth Politics in Putin's Russia: Producing Patriots and Entrepreneurs* (Bloomington: Indiana University Press, 2015) among others. While there are a wide variety of published monographs that deal with the political figure of Vladimir Putin, this sphere of influence, his resisters, and contemporary Russia in relationship to the rest of the world, there is very little written about Putin's appeal outside of Russia and what that might mean given the conservative turn in many countries and nations around the globe.

6. In a recent monograph, sociologist of American religion Robert Wuthnow discusses how moral outrage among inhabitants of rural communities can be felt in the ballot booth. Wuthnow suggests that rage is expressed in these communities because of varying factors, one of those being the "corrosive effects" of modernity (116). Wuthnow draws on statistics and stories to explain how Protestants and Catholics worry about "the moral decline of the nation at large" (119). For the rural believers in Wuthnow's study, the specifics of their outrage often mirror that of those in the Appalachian Orthodox community—abortion, homosexuality, and the growing diversity of the United States are key factors for these voters, causing them to lash out through their ballots. As Wuthnow notes in his epilogue, moral order is part of the constructive cultural of reality of these communities (161). Robert Wuthnow, *The Left Behind: Decline and Rage in Rural America* (Princeton, NJ: Princeton University Press, 2018).

7. David S. Foglesong, *The American Mission and the "Evil Empire"* (Cambridge: Cambridge University Press, 2007); Ernest, Gellner, *Postmodernism, Reason, and Religion* (London: Routledge, 1992); George M. Marsden, *Fundamentalism and American Culture* (New York: Oxford University Press, 1980); Martin E. Marty and R. Scott Appleby, eds., *Fundamentalisms and the State:*

Remaking Polities, Economies, and Militance (Chicago: University of Chicago Press, 1996).

8. Christopher Lamb and M. Darrol Bryant, eds. *Religious Conversion: Contemporary Practices and Controversies* (London: Bloomsbury, 1999). When I refer to political theology or use the term "theo-political," I am not only referencing the sociohistorical relationship between church and government in a variety of Orthodox contexts; I am also acknowledging Orthodox understandings of the relationship between divinity and humanity. See Aristotle Papanikolaou, *The Mystical as Political: Democracy and Non-Radical Orthodoxy* (Notre Dame, IN: Notre Dame University Press, 2012); Kristina Stoeckl, Ingeborg Gabriel, and Aristotle Papanikolaou, eds., *Political Theologies in Orthodox Christianity: Common Challenges—Divergent Positions* (London: Bloomsbury, 2017).

9. My use of disaffected is in no way an attempt to reinforce stereotypes of rural sociality in this region. Rather, it stems from conversations, interviews, and experiences with local interlocutors during my time in Appalachia. Many citizens in Woodford felt neglected by the U.S. government, which in turn caused them to feel disaffected. The sense of alienation among non-Orthodox Christians in the region often stemmed from economic decline and a sense that those outside of Appalachia do not care about the area or its inhabitants, whereas Orthodox converts, by contrast, often felt discontent with the way society is evolving socially. For them, the fact that outsiders do not care about the region was beneficial. One convert mentioned that West Virginia is often seen as fifty years behind times in terms of infrastructure and social mores; he believed living in the state where modernity had not yet creeped in was beneficial to salvation.

One of the main goals of Putin's *Russkii mir* was the preservation and expansion of the Russian language. However, that was only part of his agenda, for he desired to spread Russian culture as well. This aspect of his project is vital, for it is a point of commonality between him and many Russian Orthodox Christians around the globe who sought, during the 2010s, to spread Russian Orthodox moral values to the far corners of the earth.

10. Fenella Cannell, ed., *The Anthropology of Christianity* (Durham, NC: Duke University Press, 2006); Webb Keane, *Christian Moderns: Freedom and Fetish in the Mission Encounter* (Berkeley: University of California Press, 2007).

11. There was one Russian-born man who lived nearby the monastery and would attend sporadically. He would often work at the monastery as well.

12. Derek Hastings, *Nationalism in Modern Europe: Politics, Identity, and Belonging Since the French Revolution* (London: Bloomsbury, 2018); Lloyd Kramer, *Nationalism in Europe and America: Politics, Cultures, and Identities Since 1775* (Durham: University of North Carolina Press, 2011).

13. Frances FitzGerald, *The Evangelicals: The Struggle to Shape America* (New York: Simon and Schuster, 2017); Susan Harding, *The Book of Jerry Falwell: Fundamentalist Language and Politics* (Princeton, NJ: Princeton University Press, 2000); Daniel K. Williams, *God's Own Party: The Making of the Christian Right* (Oxford: Oxford University Press, 2010).

14. Jonathan Wiseman, *Semitism: Being Jewish in America in the Age of Trump* (New York: St. Martin's Press, 2018).

15. In a 2018 lecture at Columbia University's Society of Fellows, historian of American Religions Bethany Moreton argued that traditional Catholicism and Russian Orthodoxy are both part and parcel of the white nationalism movement that helped push Trump into the White House. While many of the ROCOR converts in Woodford voted for Trump, they primarily did so as way to block Hillary Clinton from winning the election and because Trump seemed to have positive political and economic relations with Russia generally. Bethany Moreton, "Our Lady of the Alt-Right: Catholic Traditionalism, Russian Orthodoxy, and the Theology of White Nationalism," accessed November 14, 2018, http://societyoffellows.columbia. edu/events/our-lady-of-the-alt-right-catholic-traditionalism-russian-orthodoxy-the -theology-of-nationalism/.

Perhaps one of the most famous white nationalist converts to Orthodox Christianity is Matthew Heimbach, who was a member of the Antiochian Archdiocese of North America until he was excommunicated in late 2014. While Heimbach was seemingly enamored with Russia, he never sought membership in ROCOR. For more information on white nationalism in American Orthodox circles, see Katherine Kelaidis, "How Orthodox Christianity Became the Spiritual Home of White Nationalism," Religious Dispatches, entry posted November 30, 2016, accessed September 12, 2018, http://religiondispatches.org/how-orthodox-christianity-became-the-spiritual-home-of-white-nationalism/; Katherine Kelaidis, "White Supremacy and Orthodox Christianity: A Dangerous Connection Rears Its Head in Charlottesville," Religious Dispatches, entry posted August 18, 2017, accessed September 12, 2018, http://religion dispatches.org/white-supremacy-and-orthodox-christianity-a-dangerous-connection -rears-its-head-in-charlottesville/; Inga Leonova, "Deafening Silence," Public Orthodoxy, entry posted August 16, 2017, accessed August 1, 2018, https://publicorthodoxy .org/2017/08/16/deafening-silence/.

16. Father Basil, interview by author, August 12, 2018.

17. While many of these ideologies are featured quite prominently in current media portrayals of conservatives, paleoconservatism is quite often ignored. This might be because the idea has fallen out of fashion politically. Popular in the 1980s, paleoconservatism was a reactionary response to neoconservatism, which was a moderate leaning group. Fearing a shift to the left, the paleoconservative movement was born. It pushed for a return to older forms of conservatism opposing state-sponsored programs for racial equality and any type of U.S. foreign intervention (29–33). George Hawley, *Making Sense of the Alt-Right* (New York: Columbia University Press, 2017).

18. Hovorun, in his work on Orthodox political theology, notes that anti-Semitism has long been part of the Russian Orthodox tradition. Cyril Hovorun, *Political Orthodoxies: The Unorthodoxies of a Church Coerced* (Minneapolis, MN: Fortress Press, 2018).

19. Hawley, *Making Sense of the Alt-Right*, 4.

20. Aleksandr Dugin, *Filosofiia politiki* (Moscow: Arktogeia, 2004). Ilya Yablokov draws our attention to how conservative Russian thinkers such as Aleksandr Dugin and Nataliia Narochnitskaia are proponents of the same types of conspiratorial, anti-globalist, moral-culture-wars rhetoric that converts in Woodford used to describe Russia's role in the salvation of the world from secularism and Western influences. See Ilya Yablokov, *Fortress Russia: Conspiracy Theories in the Post-Soviet World* (Cambridge: Polity Press, 2018).

21. Daniela Kalkandjieva, *The Russian Orthodox Church, 1917–1948: From Decline to Resurrection* (New York: Routledge, 2015); Fr. Alexey Young, *The Russian Orthodox Church Outside Russia: A History and Chronology* (San Bernardino, CA: St. Willibrord's Press, 1993).

22. Daniel P. Payne, "Spiritual Security, the Russian Orthodox Church, and the Russian Foreign Ministry: Collaboration or Cooptation?," *Journal of Church and State* 52, no. 4 (2010): 712–727.

23. Geoffrey Hosking, Russia and the Russians: A History (Cambridge, MA: Harvard University Press, 2011); Dmitri Sidorov, "Post-Imperial Third Romes: Resurrections of a Russian Orthodox Geopolitical Metaphor," *Geopolitics* 11, no. 2 (2006): 317–347.

24. For a theological analysis of Moscow as the Third Rome from a nationalistic ROCOR perspective, see Matthew Raphael Johnson, *The Third Rome, Holy Russia, Tsarism, and Orthodoxy* (Washington, DC: Foundation for Economic Liberty, 2004).

25. J. M. Lotman and B.A. Uspenskij, "Echoes of the Notion of 'Moscow as the Third Rome' in Peter the Great's Ideology," trans. N.F.C. Owen, in Ann Shukman, ed., *The Semiotics of Russian Culture* (Ann Arbor: University of Michigan, 1984).

26. For a take on the way the language of Third Rome has been expressed in Soviet political history, see Katerina Clark, *Moscow, the Fourth Rome: Stalinism, Cosmopolitanism, and the Evolution of Soviet Culture, 1931–1941* (Cambridge, MA: Harvard University Press, 2011).

27. Sidorov, "Post-Imperial Third Romes," 322.

28. Marshall Poe, "Moscow, the Third Rome: The Origins and Transformations of a 'Pivotal Moment,'" *Jahrbücher für Geschichte Osteuropas, Neue Folge* 49, no. 3 (2001): 412–429.

29. Justyna Doroszczyk, "Moscow—Third Rome as Source of Anti-Western Russian Geopolitics," *Historia i Polityka* 24, no. 3 (2018): 47. It is crucial to note, of course, that this ideology is not universal in Russia.

30. Father Tryphon, interview by author, May 9, 2018.

31. Protestant theologian John Burgess, who conducted ethnographic research in Russia 2011–2012, offers up the idea that the veneration of Tsar Nicholas II and other Royal Martyrs might be a democratizing force in Russia, noting that representations of the ROC need not always be that of an institution opposed to democracy. See John P. Burgess, "Retrieving the Martyrs in Order to Rethink the Political Order: The Russian Orthodox Case," *Journal of the Society of Christian Ethics* 34, no. 2 (2014): 177–201.

32. Elena Chebankova, "Russian Fundamental Conservatism: In Search of Modernity," *Post-Soviet Affairs* 29, no. 2 (2013): 300–304. http://doi.org/10.1080/10605 86x.2013.786579. In recent years, Putin has seemingly shifted the tasks of the *Russkii mir* project onto the members of the World Congress of Compatriots Living Abroad. This group comprises Russians who are ethnically, spiritually, and socially linked to the traditional values and ideas of the Russian homeland.

33. John Garrad and Carol Garrad, *Russian Orthodoxy Resurgent: Faith and Power in the New Russia* (Princeton, NJ: Princeton University Press, 2008).

34. Marlene Laruelle, "Ideological Complementarity or Competition? The Kremlin, the Church, and the Monarchist Idea in Today's Russia," *Slavic Review* 79, 2 (Summer 2020): 345.

35. Mikhail Suslov, "The Genealogy of the Idea of Monarchy in the Post-Soviet Political Discourse of the Russian Orthodox Church," *State, Religion, and Church* 3, no. 1 (2016): 27–62; "'Holy Rus': The Geopolitical Imagination in the Contemporary Russian Orthodox Church," *Russian Politics and Law* 52, no. 3 (May–June 2014): 67–86.

36. Nun Nectaria McLees, *A Gathered Radiance: The Life of Alexandra Romanov, Russia's Last Empress* (Chico, CA: Valaam Society of America, 1992), 126.

37. Elizabeth Castelli, *Martyrdom and Memory: Early Christian Culture Making* (New York: Columbia University Press, 2004), 7–9.

38. Zoe Knox, "The Symphonic Ideal: The Moscow Patriarchate's Post-Soviet Leadership," *Europe-Asia Studies* 55, no. 4 (2003): 575. For further reading on the idea of *symphonia* in its applicability in various forms of secular governance, see Aristotle Papanikolaou, "Byzantium, Orthodoxy, and Democracy," *Journal of the American Academy of Religion* 71, no. 1 (2003): 75–98; Aristotle Papanikolaou and George E. Demacopoulos, "Outrunning Constantine's Shadow," in *Christianity, Democracy, and the Shadow of Constantine*, ed. Aristotle Papanikolaou and George E. Demacopoulos (New York: Fordham University Press, 2017), 1–8; Catherine Wanner, "Southern Challenges to Eastern Christianity: Pressures to Reform the Church-State Model," *Journal of Church and State* 52, no. 4 (2010): 644–661.

39. Scholar of Russian Orthodoxy Kathy Rousselet, in her work on the moral meanings behind contemporary devotions to the Royal Martyrs in Russia, suggests that believers do not attach monarchic ideology to the veneration of Tsar Nicholas II or desire to return to prerevolutionary Russian Orthodoxy. Rather, as her work highlights, the cult of royal saints is a way for devotees to make sense of their world through a nostalgic lens that is infused with distinctive notions of morality linked to tradition. See Kathy Rousselet, "Constructing Moralities around the Tsarist Family," in *Multiple Moralities and Religions in Post-Soviet Russia*, ed. Jarrett Zigon, 146–167 (New York: Berghahn Books, 2011).

40. See Andras Fekete, "Vladimir the Savior: The New Symbol of Russia to Open at Kremlin's Gates," *Moscow Times*, November 3, 2016. https://themoscow times.com/articles/vladimir-the-savior-the-new-symbol-of-russia-to-open-at-the -kremlins-gates-56012; Neil MacFarquhar, "Another Huge Statue in Russia? Not

Rare but Hugely Divisive," *New York Times*, May 28, 2015, https://www.nytimes.com /2015/05/29/world/europe/another-huge-statue-in-russia-not-rare-but-hugely-divisive .html?module=inline; "A New Vladimir Overlooking Moscow," *New York Times*, November 4, 2016, https://www.nytimes.com/2016/11/05/world/europe/vladimir -statue-moscow-kremlin.html.

41. The event streamed on the Russian government–run news agency, RT, which is the outlet of choice for most of my interlocutors.

42. His All-Holiness Patriarch Kirill, "Putin attends ceremony for anniversary of Rus' conversion to Christianity (Streamed Live)," RT YouTube Channel, aired July 28, 2018, https://www.youtube.com/watch?v=jvpmYH9pF6E.

43. Interview, May 9, 2018.

44. Nun Nectaria McLees, *A Gathered Radiance: The Life of Alexandra Romanov, Russia's Last Empress* (Chico, CA: Valaam Society of America, 1992), 13.

45. Facebook, Russian Imperial Union-Order East Coast About Page, Russian Imperial Union-Order East Coast, https://www.facebook.com/pg/riuoeast/about/ ?ref=page_internal, accessed June 1, 2018.

46. Facebook, Russian Imperial Union-Order East Coast About Page, Russian Imperial Union-Order East Coast, https://www.facebook.com/pg/riuoeast/about /?ref=page_internal, accessed June 1, 2018.

47. Metropolitan Hilarion (Alfeyev) of Volokolamsk, The Theology of Freedom. Christianity and Secular Power: From the Edict of Milan to the Present, lecture, Pontifical Theology Faculty of Southern Italy, October 17, 2014, https://mospat.ru /en/2014/10/18/news109757/.

48. Alexander Dugin, *The Fourth Political Theory*, English Edition (United Kingdom: Arktos Media, 2012), 86.

49. Dugin, *Fourth Political Theory*, 15–31.

50. Aleksandr Dugin, [56:51], interviewed by Lauren Southern Brittany Pettibone, *Lauren Southern YouTube Channel*, June 19, 2018, https://youtu.be/sl2--OHvxK4.

51. Aleksandr Dugin, [56:51], interviewed by Lauren Southern Brittany Pettibone, *Lauren Southern YouTube Channel*, June 19, 2018, https://youtu.be/sl2--OHvxK4.

52. Daniel Payne, "Spiritual Security, the Russian Orthodox Church, and the Russian Foreign Ministry: Collaboration or Cooptation?," *Journal of Church and State* 52, no. 4 (2010): 712.

53. Interview by author, July 30, 2018

54. Interview, July 30, 2018.

55. Interview by author, June 12, 2018.

56. Wuthnow, *The Left Behind*.

57. Abbott Spyridon, interview by author, July 18, 2018.

58. In 2020–2021, I also interviewed several former converts who had been a part of the Woodford community but left before my arrival in 2017. While each person had individual reasons for leaving the parish or the monastery, most highlighted the fervent focus on Putin and Russian intervention as a motivating factor in their decision to leave both the community and ROCOR.

59. Interview by author, August 3, 2018.

60. Interview, August 3, 2018.

61. Interview, August 3, 2018.

62. Mark Lilla, *The Shipwrecked Mind: On Political Reaction* (New York: New York Review of Books, 2016), xii.

63. Feminists, homosexuals, and transgender are the three words that peppered many conversations Orthodox converts had with me. Believers are acutely sensitive to gender and sexuality as forms of boundary making and transgressing in this community.

64. Anonymous, "Truth, Compassion and the Transgender Movement," *Remembering Sion* https://www.rememberingsion.com/2018/06/25/truth-compassion-transgender-movement/

65. Pierre Bourdieu, *Outline of a Theory of Practice*, trans. Richard Nice (Cambridge: Cambridge University Press, 2015 [1977]).

66. Anonymous, "About Page," *The Sobornost* http://thesobornost.org/about/, accessed August 2, 2018. Typically, Sobornost is spelled *sobornost'*, but that is not the case with this blog title.

67. Anonymous, "Orthodoxy and Community: Introduction to the Orthodox World View," *The Sobornost*, accessed August 2, 2018, http://thesobornost.org/2017/06/orthodoxy-and-community-intro-orthodox-worldview/.

68. Igumen Phillip Ryabykh, "The Orthodox Church and Society. Part I: Historic Roots of Church-State Relations," *Pravoslavie*, accessed August 1, 2018, http://pravoslavie.ru/49277.html.

69. Ryabykh, "Orthodox Church and Society."

70. Ibid.

71. Bourdieu, *Theory of Practice*, 165.

72. Ryabykh, "Orthodox Church and Society."

73. Ibid.

74. Father Artemy Vladimirov, "A Russian Priest: My Work with English-Speaking Converts Part II," *Road to Emmaus Journal* 4 (2001): 8, http://www.roadtoemmaus.net/back_issue_articles/RTE_04/My_Work_with_English_Speaking_Converts_Part_II.pdf.'

75. Vladimirov, "A Russian Priest."

76. Bourdieu, *Theory of Practice*, 90.

77. Tom Boylston, in his work with an Ethiopian Orthodox Church on the Zege peninsula, notes the detailed levels of gendered interaction, restriction, and prohibition, all of which have some overlap with ROCOR forms of ritual purity and access. See Tom Boylston, *The Stranger at the Feast: Prohibition and Mediation in an Ethiopian Orthodox Christian Community* (Berkeley: University of California Press, 2018).

78. Cynthia Lynn Lyerly, "In Service, Silence, and Strength: Women in Southern Churches," in *Religion and Public Life in the South: In the Evangelical Mode*, ed. Charles Reagan Wilson and Mark Silk (New York: AltaMira Press, 2005), 101–124.

79. Bourdieu, *Theory of Practice*, 165–171.

80. For a highly readable introduction to theological anthropology, see Nonna Verna Harrison, *God's Many-Splendored Image: Theological Anthropology for Christian Formation* (Grand Rapids, MI: Baker Academic, 2010).

81. In many respects, focus on hierarchal leadership, on kingship, and on strict rules of social conduct is quite unnatural in terms of the region and the so-called spirit of West Virginia. Locals pride themselves on being independent, self-reliant, and free-born mountain folk. The state motto, "Montani Semper Liberi," which was adopted in 1872–1873 translates into English as "Mountaineers Are Always Free." See Robert M. Bastress, *The West Virginia State Constitution: A Reference Guide* (Westport, CT: Greenwood Publishing Group, 1995), 42.

82. Fr. Seraphim Rose, Living the Orthodox World View (A talk delivered by Hieromonk Seraphim [Rose] at the St. Herman Pilgrimage, August 1982, St. Herman of Alaska Monastery, Platina, California). Seraphim Rose, *Lectures of Fr. Seraphim Rose, Volume One: Living the Orthodox Worldview.* Compact Disc (Platina, CA: St. Herman of Alaska Brotherhood, 2015 [2007]).

83. Interview by author, July 4, 2018.

84. Frederick Cooper, *Colonialism in Question: Theory, Knowledge, History* (Berkeley: University of California Press, 2005).

6. A People Set Apart: Intra-Community Politics and Regionalism

1. Scholars often note that intentional religious communities, especially new religious movements and fundamentalist sects, can be highly insular as a way to create and protect their ideological boundaries (Harding 2000; Marty 1992). In many respects, as I discussed in the previous chapter, the Orthodox converts in Woodford fall into this category of religious sociality. These types of Orthodox communities are often hard to pin down theoretically (and even methodologically) for analysis, because they are not Christian fundamentalists in the traditional American religious history framework. Nor can they be considered as a New Religious Movement (NRM). This is not to say that the Woodford converts do not possess many of the same attributes that fundamentalist communities have; indeed, they do. Yet to simply label them fundamentalists negates the global history and complexities of Orthodox Christianity that have brought about the rise of Russian Orthodox converts *with* fundamentalist ideologies. Whether or not the fundamentalist ideologies espoused are good or bad à la Žižek (2009), I assert that ROCOR converts are fundamentalist Christians, but they are also traditionalists. Indeed, traditionalist and or traditional were often descriptors that converts used to describe themselves in relationship to both other Orthodox communities and society more broadly. Some scholars of Orthodoxy refer to these types of communities as "neotraditionalists," although I view them as traditionalists. See Paul Ladouceur, "Neo-Traditionalist Ecclesiology in Orthodoxy," *Scottish Journal of Theology* 72 (2019): 398–413; Slavoj Žižek, *The Parallax View* (Cambridge, MA: The MIT Press, 2009).

In framing my understanding of this intentional, insular community, I turned to colleagues at the New York Working Group on Jewish Orthodoxies, which is a joint project between Fordham University and the American Academy of Jewish Research, with affiliations with New York University and other universities around the world. As a member of the group, and the only person working on Christianity, I often discussed method and theory in the study of orthodox communities as they are broadly constructed. Many times, the theoretical frameworks used to analyze Hasidic communities were far more beneficial in thinking about U.S. Orthodox converts than those often used in the study of right-wing American Christians, even Catholics. In particular, conversations with Samuel Heilman and Ayala Fader have helped flesh out new models for thinking about tradition, fundamentalism, and community.

2. Bruce Lincoln, *Holy Terrors: Thinking about Religion after September 11* (Chicago: University of Chicago Press, 2002), 7.

3. The idea of being a good Christian is often caught up in philosophical and psychological understandings of what constitutes ethical or virtuous practices. These notions tend to be, in the neoliberal period, an offshoot of questions about natural law and common good, but in this case the idea of good person *and* Christian has far more to do with external practices of social well-being than theological belief. See Omri Elisha, *Moral Ambition: Mobilization and Social Outreach in Evangelical Megachurches* (Berkeley: University of California Press, 2011).

4. I was able to talk with many pastors in the area and gather some of their ideas about the Orthodox community, but very few were willing to sit down for a more formal conversation.

5. The notion of lifelong pilgrimage is often found in Orthodox spiritual literature. The much revised and anonymous *Pilgrim's Tale* from the revered Optina monastery has provided a Slavic Orthodox example of transitory spirituality for generations of Orthodox Christians, although some scholars called the final transformations of the text took place in Greece on Mount Athos. See Aleksei Pentkovsky, ed., *The Pilgrim's Tale*, trans. T. Allan Smith (Minneapolis, MN: Paulist Press, 1999). Crucial to the book's short story format are ideas of elderism, ascetic struggle (*podvig*), and lifelong pilgrimage.

Within anthropology, pilgrimage is often analyzed for its embodied, kinetic, class, and mobile features. Ritual aspects of the liminal practice are important, of course, but much of the material shies away from theological ideas or analyzing the psychosocial dimensions of spirituality. The Orthodox concept of being a lifelong pilgrim is not easy to understand under the umbrella of pilgrimage unless the spiritual aspects are first addressed.

6. Leslie Baynes, *The Heavenly Book Motif in Judeo-Christian Apocalypses, 200 B.C.E.–200 C.E.* (Leiden, Netherlands: Brill, 2012), 197. Anthropologist Girish Daswani, in his ethnography of Ghanaian Pentecostals in the United Kingdom, suggests that the idea of being "citizens of heaven" was crucial in the way his interlocutors not only understood the world spiritually, but also politically, for it "superseded their citizenship any nation-state" (2015, 182). Girish Daswani, *Looking*

Back, Moving Forward: Transformation and Ethical Practice in the Ghanaian Church of Pentecost (Toronto: University of Toronto Press, 2015).

7. This lecture was delivered in 1981 in San Francisco at an Orthodox youth conference. Eventually the lecture was published. Hieromonk Seraphim Rose, "The Future of Russia and the End of the World," *The Orthodox Word*, vol. 17, no. 5–6 (1981): 205–217.

8. Daswani, *Looking Back, Moving Forward*.

9. Anonymous, Service for "The Commemoration of the Triumph of Our Lady of Port Arthur Icon," Unpublished, 2014.

10. Lincoln, *Holy Terrors*, 6.

11. Typically, alongside icons of Christ and the Theotokos, most churches have images of their patron saints and saints who are seemingly popular, such as St. Nicholas of Myra, St. George the Wonderworker, St. Seraphim of Sarov, and St. Herman of Alaska, to name a few.

12. In the fall of 2019, I received news from Fr. Cyril that Coleman had finally agreed to sell the church building and land to the parish. By winter of the same year, the sale had gone through and the parish began working on their next phase of expansion.

13. While none of the local Orthodox converts attended the monastery full-time as their primary place of worship, many locals who attended the parish regularly visited the monastery and frequented the services. Fr. Cyril encouraged his parishioners to attend weekend liturgies at St. Basil's whenever it was feasible.

14. Johann von Gardner, *Russian Church Singing: Orthodox Worship and Hymnography, Vol. 1* (Yonkers, NY: St. Vladimir's Seminary Press, 1980).

15. Vyacheslav Karpov, Elena Lisovskaya, and David Barry, "Ethnodoxy: How Popular Ideologies Fuse Religious and Ethnic Identities," in *Journal for the Scientific Study of Religion* 51, no. 4 (2012): 638–655.

16. Connor Bailey, Leif Jensen, and Elizabeth Ransom, eds., *Rural America in a Globalizing World: Problems and Prospects for the 2010s* (Morgantown: West Virginia University Press, 2014).

17. Removing the *antimins* from an altar is a serious material accusation against either a priest or the parish community, for it indicates that the hierarchical blessing for conducting the divine services and consecrating the Eucharist have been removed from the parish.

18. As I noted in the beginning of this book, my informants have pseudonyms. However, in the case of Father Alexey (Ambrose) Young, I have chosen to use his given name. Father Alexey, in a similar fashion to Father Seraphim Rose, was an influential figure in the history of the Russian Orthodox Church Outside of Russia in the United States, with published works and spiritual kinship networks that have been kept alive in Orthodox digital social spaces.

19. Alexey Young, ed., *Letter from Father Seraphim: The Twelve-Year Correspondence between Hieromonk Seraphim (Rose) and Father Alexey Young* (Richfield Springs, NY: Nikodemos Orthodox Publishing Society, 2001). The correspondence

between the two men and Rose's letters to other friends and followers were published after the monk's death by Young. While the book is out of print, copies are still available for purchase, although typically at exorbitant prices, pushing many Orthodox bloggers to type out the letters in blog post form on their websites, as a way to disseminate the teachings of Rose.

20. Moravians began missionizing what is now considered Appalachia during the eighteenth century in Schaghticoke territory. While the Moravians encouraged indigenous conversions, their form of Christian colonization was not as violent as some other forms present in North America during this time and following. This seems to be the case because Moravians encouraged Schaghticoke people to keep their own traditions and incorporate them into their Christians identities. See Lynne P. Sullivan and Susan C. Prezzano, eds., *Archaeology of the Appalachian Highlands* (Knoxville: University of Tennessee Press, 2001).

21. Loyal Jones, *Appalachian Values* (Ashland, KY: Jesse Stuart Foundation, 1994 [1973]).

22. An excellent example of this sensationalized media exposure of the region is the photography work of Robert Coles. See Robert Coles, *Still Hungry in America* (New York: Penguin, 1972), which was instrumental in procuring government aid for Appalachians. A filmic critique of this type of photography is found in the excellent documentary *Stranger with a Camera* that was produced by Appalshop. Elizabeth Barret, *Stranger with a Camera*, DVD (Whitesburg, KY: Appalshop, 2000).

23. Thomas Kiffmeyer, *Reformers to Radicals: The Appalachian Volunteers and the War on Poverty* (Lexington: University Press of Kentucky, 2009).

24. Huey Perry, *They'll Cut off Your Project: A Mingo County Chronicle* (Morgantown: West Virginia University Press, 2011).

25. Helen Matthews Lewis, Linda Johnson, Donald Askins, eds., *Colonialism in Modern America: The Appalachian Case* (Boone, North Carolina: Appalachian State University, 2017 [1978]).

26. Deborah Vansau McCauley, *Appalachian Mountain Religion: A History* (Urbana: University of Illinois Press, 1995).

27. Elena Namli, "Orthodox Theology, Politics, and Power," in *Political Theologies in Orthodox Christianity: Common Challenges-Divergent Positions*, ed. Kristina Stoeckl, Ingeborg Gabriel, and Aristotle Papanikolaou, 265–282 (London: Bloomsbury, 2017), 268.

28. Heather D. Curtis, *Holy Humanitarians: American Evangelicals and Global Aid* (Cambridge, MA: Harvard, 2018).

29. Christopher Veniamin, *The Orthodox Understanding of Salvation: Theosis in Scripture and Tradition* (Dalton, PA: Mount Thabor Publishing, 2013).

30. Examples of this are seen in popular press nonfiction accounts of the opioid crisis that seek to investigate the reasons behind heavy drug use in the region, but instead reinforce stereotypes of Appalachia communities. See Beth Macy, *Dope Sick: Dealers, Doctors, and the Drug Company that Addicted America* (Boston: Little, Brown, 2019).

31. John Denver, *Country Roads, Take Me Home*, RCA, 1971.

32. John Raby, "Almost Heaven: West Virginia starts new tourism campaign," *Associated Press*, April 11, 2018, accessed May 10, 2018, https://apnews.com/034ade58 0c7b4265bd54d181dd8e4f41/
Almost-heaven:-West-Virginia-starts-new-tourism-campaign.

33. Helen Matthews Lewis, Linda Johnson, Donald Askins, eds., *Colonialism in Modern America: The Appalachian Case* (Boone, NC: Appalachian State University, 2017 [1978]); Chad Montrie, *To Save the Land and People: A History of Opposition to Surface Coal Mining in Appalachia* (Durham: University of North Carolina Press, 2003). Steven Stoll, *Ramp Hollow: The Ordeal of Appalachia* (New York: Hill and Wang, 2017).

34. Nancy Isenberg, *White Trash: The 400-Year Untold History of Class in America* (New York: Penguin, 2017 [Reprint]).

35. Elizabeth Catte, *What You Are Getting Wrong About Appalachia* (Cleveland, OH: Belt Publishing, 2018).

36. Katherine Ledford, Gurney Norman, and Dwight B. Billings, eds., *Back Talk from Appalachia: Confronting Stereotypes* (Lexington: University Press of Kentucky, 2013).

37. Woodford is located in what is typically referred to as Central or Southern Appalachia by scholars of the region.

38. Frank Wilson, interview by author, July 9, 2018.

39. Andrew L. Whitehead and Samuel L. Perry, "Is a 'Christian America' a More Patriarchal America? Religion, Politics, and Traditionalist Gender Ideology," *Canadian Review of Sociology* 56, no. 2 (May 2019): 153.

40. Bill J. Leonard, ed., *Christianity in Appalachia: Profiles in Regional Pluralism* (Knoxville: University of Tennessee Press, 1999); Helen M. Lewis and Monica Appleby, *Mountain Sisters: From Convert to Community in Appalachia* (Lexington: University Press of Kentucky, 2003).

41. Eugene Rose, "Orthodoxy and Modern Thought: The Self-Liquidation of Christianity," *The Orthodox Word* 2, no. 3 (9) (July–August 1966): 101.

42. Rose, "Orthodoxy and Modern Thought."

43. Anonymous, "The Character and Path of the Orthodox Mission," *The Orthodox Word* 1, no. 6 (November–December 1965): 209. This article is anonymous, which means that is most likely written by the journal editors—Rose and Podmoshensky.

44. Andrew Louth, *Modern Orthodox Thinkers: From the Philokalia to the Present* (Dower's Grove, IL: InterVarsity Press, 2015), 80.

45. Alexander Agadjanian, "Breakthrough to Modernity, Apologia for Traditionalism: The Russian Orthodox View of Society and Culture in Comparative Perspective," *Religion, State, and Society* 31, no. 4 (2003): 334.

46. Victor Turner, *The Ritual Process: Structure and Anti-Structure* (New York: Routledge, 2017 [1969]); Arnold Van Gennep, *The Rites of Passage* (New York: Routledge, 2004 [1960]).

47. Fr. Seraphim Rose to Alexey Young, June 5/18, 1972. Published in Alexey Young, ed., *Letter from Father Seraphim: The Twelve-Year Correspondence Between*

Hieromonk Seraphim (Rose) and Father Alexey Young (Richfield Springs, NY: Nikodemos Orthodox Publishing Society, 2001), 50–1.

48. Fr. Seraphim Rose to Alexey Young, June 5/18, 1972.

49. Fr. Seraphim Rose to Alexey Young, June 5/18, 1972.

50. Fr. Seraphim Rose to Alexey Young, June 5/18, 1972.

51. Fr. Seraphim Rose to Alexey Young, June 5/18, 1972.

52. Georges Florovsky, "Antinomies of Christian History: Empire and Desert," in *The Collected Works of Georges Florovsky*, vol. 2, ed. Richard S. Haugh (Belmont, MA: Norland Publishing Company, 1974), 68; Eugen J. Pentiuc, *The Old Testament in Eastern Orthodox Tradition* (Oxford: Oxford University Press, 2014), 293.

7. The "Holler Feast": Spiritual Geographies and Temporalities

1. Interview by author, August 22, 2018. Marian hagiography is quite developed in most of the Orthodox World; this is especially true in ROCOR, which has a multitude of "lesser" feast days devoted to regional or iconic feasts of the Theotokos, such as the celebration of the Kursk Root icon. For more on Orthodox Mariology and feast days, see Archbishop John Maximovitch, *The Orthodox Veneration of the Mother of God* (Platina, CA: St. Herman Press, 1987); Hugh Wybrew, *Orthodox Feasts of Jesus Christ and the Virgin Mary* (Yonkers, NY: St. Vladimir's Seminary Press, 2000.

2. Wybrew, *Orthodox*.

3. James Davison Hunter, *Culture Wars: The Struggle to Define America* (New York: HarperCollins, 1991), 43.

4. Hunter, *Culture Wars*, 24–25.

5. I use the word "modern" rather tentatively given its weighty complexity. Certainly, many would argue that the 2010s were already deeply entrenched in the postmodern period, and that might well be the case. Perhaps in a similar fashion to Bruno Latour, I understand the modern to have two different practical formations (1993, 10). First, I see modern as part of a social rhetoric deployed by far-right Christians as a way of curating their "traditional" identity in the world. Second, I see modern as part of the larger understanding of modernity as it relates to secularism. Latour might argue that the idea of modern serves to linguistically and ontologically create instability and ambiguity, and in the case of converts to the Russian Orthodox Church Outside of Russia, this might be true. The notion of modern for many in the community was drenched in fear of the other, of what might happen, of what could be. Modernity clouded their temporalities and clarified their cosmologies, creating boundaries, delineating what was right and what was wrong. Bruno Latour, *We Have Never Been Modern*, trans. Catherine Porter (Cambridge, MA: Harvard University Press, 1993).

6. Kristina Stoeckl suggests that the contemporary positioning of Russia as a moral compass for the world is part of the geopolitics of soft power that Putin is using to expand the boundaries of his illiberal regime. In doing so, he turns to the ROC and Patriarch Kirill to explain why and how his ideas are part of a religious

242

NOTES TO PAGES 163-164

legacy of morality that is lacking in other parts of the world. See Kristina Stoeckl, "Postsecular Conflicts and the Global Struggle for Traditional Values," *State, Religion, and Church* 2/3 (2016): S102–116; "The Russian Orthodox Church's Conservative Crusade," *Current History* 116/792 (2017): 271.

7. Nicholas Denysenko, *Theology and Form: Contemporary Orthodox Architecture in America* (Notre Dame, IN: University of Notre Dame Press, 2017); Richard Kieckhefer, *Theology in Stone: Church Architecture from Byzantium to Berkeley* (New York: Oxford University Press, 2005).

8. Margaret Paxson's ethnohistorical examination of Russian Orthodox icon corners provides excellent examples of how these corners were used by laity in everyday life, focusing on their social and political dimensions. See Paxson, *Solovyovo: The Story of Memory in a Russian Village* (Indianapolis: Indiana University Press, 2005).

9. Frederica Mathewes-Green, *Facing East: A Pilgrim's Journey into Mysteries of Orthodoxy* (New York: HarperCollins, 1997). Mathewes-Green's autobiographical conversion story was incredibly popular in the Orthodox market, going through several reprints. She followed up with a book that focused on guiding believers through the Divine Liturgy as a way to make sense of contemporary life, still focusing on the East, modernity, and ancient belief as key selling points. Frederica Mathewes-Green, *At the Corner of East and Now: A Modern Life in Ancient Christian Orthodoxy* (New York: Putnam, 1999).

In her work on media conceptions of the Middle East, American Studies scholar Melani McAlister highlights how the East (as an Orientalist construct) is often viewed through the lens of holiness. Drawing on the work of Anne McClintock, McAlister shows how the notion of a holy (Middle) East is tied to imperialistic notions of space and time that seek to perpetuate American and European ideas of Western modernity in juxtaposition to Eastern primitive exoticism (14–15). While American conceptions of Russia are different, in part because of the Cold War, the same type of impulse toward essentialist notions of the other are very much a part of conversion rhetoric about the Orthodox East, especially Russia. In this case, however, modernity was not a sign of progress but of decline. Melani McAlister, *Epic Encounters: Culture, Media, and U.S. Interests in the Middle East Since 1945* (Berkeley: University of California Press, 2005).

10. One of the early attempts to engage with the rhetoric of turning to the East for true spirituality was taken up by Harvey Cox, who highlighted how Orientalism was at the heart of shift in religious practices by white Americans. Harvey Cox, *Turning East: The Promise and Peril of New Orientalism* (New York: Simon and Schuster, 1997). An earlier and bit more problematic study was conducted by Robert S. Ellwood, Jr., who focused on religious traditions beyond Judeo-Christianity. Rife with essentializing assumptions about spiritual traditions and why Americans would be drawn to them, Ellwood's sociological study exemplifies how social scientists studying U.S. religions often reinforce Orientalism, even if it is not intended. See Robert S. Ellwood, Jr., *Alternative Altars: Unconventional and Eastern Spirituality in America* (Chicago: University of Chicago Press, 1979).

11. Courtney Bender, *The New Metaphysicals: Spirituality and the American Religious Imagination* (Chicago: University of Chicago Press, 2010). Wade Clark Roof, *Spiritual Marketplace: Baby Boomers and the Remaking of American Religion* (Princeton, NJ: Princeton University Press, 1999).

12. Victor Roudometof, *Globalization and Orthodox Christianity: The Transformations of a Religious Tradition* (New York: Routledge, 2014), 1.

13. Gil Anidjar, "Secularism," *Critical Inquiry* 33, no. 1 (Autumn 2006): 56.

14. Edward Said, *Orientalism* (New York: Random House, 1978).

15. Anidjar, "Secularism."

16. For a thorough yet brief history of the Orientalist approaches to Orthodoxy, see Christopher D. L. Johnson, "He Has Made the Dry Bones Live": Orientalism's Attempted Resuscitation of Eastern Christianity," *Journal of American Academy of Religion* 82, no. 3 (September 2014): 811–840.

17. Sabrina P. Ramet, "The Way We Were—and Should Be Again? European Orthodox Churches and the 'Idyllic Past,'" in *Religion in an Expanding Europe*, ed. T. Byrnes and P. Katzenstein (Cambridge: Cambridge University Press 2006), 148.

18. Aristotle Papanikolaou and George E. Demacopoulos, eds., *Fundamentalism or Tradition: Christianity after Secularism* (New York: Fordham University Press, 2020).

19. Oliver Herbel, *Turning to Tradition: Converts and the Making of an American Orthodox Church* (New York: Oxford University Press, 2014), 2–6.

20. The focus on equating conversion to ROCOR with Restorationism was also present to some extent in the queries I have received from scholars about why the Woodford community did not chose to be part of the Latter-Day Saints, which is a Restorationist movement. Quite simply, Woodford converts were not interested in breaking traditions to create new ones that were more authentic. They found in ROCOR valid sacraments and links to the apostolic tradition that did not need to be restored from their vantage point. Theologically, the idea of *sola scriptura* was something converts eschewed as a Protestant ideology. Converts were far more willing to consider Catholicism than Protestant Restorationist groups, such as the Church of Christ, independent Christian Churches, and Pentecostal movements, which many of them had fled in their efforts to find true, hierarchal Christianity. For detailed histories of the Restorationist movements in the United States, see William R. Baker, ed., *Evangelicalism and the Stone Campbell Movement* (Downers Grove, IL: InterVarsity Press, 2002); Edith L. Blumhofer, *Restoring the Faith: The Assemblies of God, Pentecostalism, and American Culture* (Urbana: University of Illinois Press, 1993).

21. Interrogating the project of colonialism, conversion, and modernity amidst globalization is one that scholars have worked on mostly outside of the United States. See Peter van der Veer, ed., *Conversions to Modernities: The Globalization of Christianity* (New York: Routledge, 1996).

22. Herbel, *Turning to Tradition*, 10.

23. Alexander Agadjanian, "Breakthrough to Modernity, Apologia for Traditionalism: The Russian Orthodox View of Society and Culture in Comparative Perspective," *Religion, State, and Society* 31, no. 4 (2003): 327–346.

24. Agadjanian, "Breakthrough to Modernity." Andreas E. Buss, *The Russian-Orthodox Tradition and Modernity* (Leiden, Netherlands: Brill, 2003).

25. Trine Stauning Willert and Lina Molokotos-Liederman, eds., *Innovation in the Orthodox Christian Tradition? The Question of Change in Greek Orthodox Thought and Practice* (New York: Routledge, 2012).

26. R. Scott Appleby, "Fundamentalists, Rigorists, and Traditionalists: An Unorthodox Trinity," in *Fundamentalism and Tradition: Christianity after Secularism*, ed. Aristotle Papanikolaou and George E. Demacopoulos (New York: Fordham University Press, 2020), 152–164.

27. Appleby, "An Unorthodox Trinity," 168–169.

28. Ibid., 170.

29. Ibid.

30. Ibid., 170.

31. Ibid.

32. Ibid.

33. I use Fr. Artmey's given name rather than a pseudonym because of his public profile and celebrity status in Russian Orthodoxy globally.

34. Scott M. Kenworthy, *The Heart of Russia: Trinity-Sergius, Monasticism, and Society after 1825* (New York: Oxford University Press, 2010).

35. Martin Phillips, "Rural Gentrification and the Process of Class Colonization," *Journal of Rural Studies* 9, no. 2 (1993): 123–140.

36. Rod Dreher, *The Benedict Option: A Strategy for Christians in a Post-Christian Nation* (New York: Penguin, 2017).

37. Many of the group members self-identified as converts to ROCOR.

38. Facebook, "Introduction," Moving to Russia (public group).

39. Facebook, "Introduction," Moving to Russia (public group).

40. Facebook, Moving to Russia (public group), November 27, 2019.

41. Facebook, Moving to Russia (public group), March 21, 2017.

42. Mikhail Suslov, "'Holy Rus': The Geopolitical Imagination in the Contemporary Russian Orthodox Church," *Russian Politics and Law* 52, no. 3 (May–June 2014): 67–86.

43. Suslov, "Holy Rus'," 70.

44. Webb Keane, *Christian Moderns: Freedom and Fetish in the Mission Encounter* (Berkeley: University of California Press, 2006), 42.

45. David Curry, "About," *Russian Faith*, accessed December 2, 2019, https://russian-faith.com/pages/about.

46. Curry, "About," *Russian Faith*.

47. As an aside, the son-in-law of a St. Basil's parishioner visited while I was in Woodford; he bore a striking resemblance to David Curry. My face must have given away my shock, since the mother-in-law leaned over to proclaim, "He looks just like David Curry, doesn't he?" I agreed and she continued, "If only!" Expats, within ROCOR convert circles, are often viewed as the wholesale devotees to the faith, those who are willing to give up everything for the faith and move abroad for the moral sake of their children.

48. An interview with Fr. Joseph and a sociologist from the University of Yaroslav, was originally published in Russian on *Today News* and then translated into English and reposted on *Russian Faith*. Artemy Schmidt, "Vse dorogi vedut v Tretiy Rim," *Today.tj*, March 13, 2018, accessed September 19, 2019, http://today.tj/religiya/12088 -vse-dorogi-vedut-v-tretiy-rim.html; Father Joseph Gleason and Artemy Schmidt, "US Orthodox Priest, Wife, and 8 Children Move to Russia (Rostov-the-Great) — Interview," *Russian Faith: Christian Renaissance*, March 16, 2018, accessed September 19, 2019, https://russian-faith.com/family-values/. us-orthodox-priest-wife-and-8-children-move-russia-rostov-great-interview-n1336.

49. Alex Jones and Charles Bausman, "Alex Jones: Extended Interview with *Russia Insider's* Charles Bausman," *Russian Insider*, November 1, 2019, https://russia -insider.com/en/alex-jones-extended-interview-russia-insiders-charles-bausman -studio/ri27820.

50. Ibid. (2:16).

51. Ibid. (10:39).

52. Herbel, *Turning to Tradition*; Amy Slagle, *The Eastern Church in the Spiritual Marketplace: American Conversions to Orthodox Christianity* (DeKalb: Northern Illinois University Press, 2011).

53. Svetlana Boym, *The Future of Nostalgia* (New York: Basic Books, 2002).

54. John Erikson, *Orthodox Christians in America* (New York: Oxford University Press, 1999); Mark Stokoe and Leonid Kishkovsky, *Orthodox Christians in North America, 1794–1994* (Syosset, NY: Orthodox Church in America, 1995).

55. Theodore Saloutos, "The Greek Orthodox Church in the United States and Assimilation," *The International Migration Review* 7, no. 4 (Winter 1973): 395–407.

56. For a detailed study of the Evangelical Orthodox Church, Campus Crusade, and other early Orthodox convert communities, see Phillip Charles Lucas, *The Odyssey of a New Religion: The Holy Order of MANS from New Age to Orthodoxy* (Bloomington: Indiana University Press, 1995). Aaron Sokoll's doctoral work also explores the social politics of the EOC, particularly their shift into the Antiochian Archdiocese and the various issues of identity that they grappled with. See Aaron J. Sokoll, "'We're Not Ethnic': Ethnicity, Pluralism, and Identity in Orthodox Christian America." (PhD diss. University of California at Santa Barbara, 2018), https://escholarship.org/uc/item/9f61p9hw.

57. The deeply entrenched homophobia that I have found among converts to the Orthodox Church, their push back against liberalism and its effects, and their fears of religious practices and beliefs being squelched by governmental powers are not isolated within Orthodox communities. Sabrina P. Ramet has noted that European Orthodox churches have been resolute in their conservative stance, guided by the past in order to create the future (Ramet 2009). While I agree with Ramet with regards to the conservative focus of Orthodox broadly, I find her assessment of Orthodoxy as being preoccupied with the past because it did not participate in the Renaissance or the Enlightenment to be essentializing and Orientalist. Ramet assumes the intellectual histories of European Orthodoxy are at the least inferior and at the worst primitive, because of the Slavic influence. It also negates the intellectual flows of

information that have historically been present throughout Eurasia, such as the relationship between Voltaire and Catherine the Great. Additionally, Ramet's biased assumptions do a disservice to the liberal philosophical, intellectual traditions of Orthodoxy in Europe. One only has to think of the Paris school to see the development of more progressive, even liberal, Orthodox theologies and philosophies. For an intellectual history of the Paris school, see Andrew Louth, *Modern Orthodox Thinkers: From the Philokalia to the Present* (Dowers Grove, IL: InterVarsity Press, 2015).

58. Andrew L. Whitehead and Samuel L. Perry, *Taking America Back for God: Christian Nationalism in the United States* (New York: Oxford University Press, 2020). Katherine Stewart, *The Power Worshippers: Inside the Dangerous Rise of Religious Nationalism* (New York: Bloomsbury, 2020). Unlike the powerfully aligned and entrenched evangelicals, Orthodox Christians, who possess many of the same social fears, do not have deep financial and social connections to American political structures.

59. Aristotle Papanikolaou, *The Mystical as Political: Democracy and Non-Radical Orthodoxy* (Notre Dame, IN: University of Notre Dame Press, 2012).

60. Interview by author, April 11, 2018.

61. Interview, April 11, 2018.

62. Agadjanian, "Breakthrough to Modernity," 327–346.

63. Pippa Norris and Ronald Ingelhart, *Cultural Backlash: Trump, Brexit, and Authoritarian Populism* (Cambridge: Cambridge University Press, 2019); Kurt Weyland and Raul L. Madrid, eds., *When Democracy Trumps Populism: European and Latin American Lessons for the United States* (Cambridge: Cambridge University Press, 2019).

64. Norris and Ingelhart, *Cultural Backlash*; Weyland and Madrid, *When Democracy Trumps Populism*.

65. Father Tryphon, interview by author, May 9, 2018.

66. Andrew L. Whitehead and Samuel L. Perry, *Taking America Back for God: Christian Nationalism in the United States* (New York: Oxford University Press, 2020).

Conclusion: In Soviet America, Russia Converts You!

1. Monk Damascene Christensen, *Not of This World: The Life and Teaching of Fr. Seraphim Rose, Pathfinder to the Heart of Ancient Christianity* (Forestville, CA: Fr. Seraphim Rose Foundation, 1993), xiii.

2. Christensen, *Not of This World*, xi.

3. Interview by author, May 30, 2018.

4. Elizabeth Catte, ed., *Left Elsewhere: Finding the Future in Radical Rural America* (Boston: Boston Review Forum/MIT Press, 2019).

5. Elizabeth Catte, ed., "What We Talk about When We Talk about the Working Class," in *Left Elsewhere: Finding the Future in Radical Rural America* (Boston: Boston Review Forum/MIT Press, 2019), 64.

6. Since the 2016 election cycle, scholarship in post-truth studies—particularly work engaged with media forms—have accelerated. Especially in light of the potential cyber interference from Russia and the work of Russian bots to shape the trajectory of American politics, writers have been grappling with the mediated relationships between news, reality, and the real. This work not only focuses on facts, but also on curation of content, thinking through the challenges media pose to democracy globally.

7. Catte, *Left Elsewhere*, 4.

8. Catte, "What We Talk About," 64.

9. *New State Co. Ice v. Liebmann*, 285 U.S. 262, 52 S.Ct. 371, 76 L.Ed. 747 (1932).

Epilogue

1. Interview by author, October 19, 2020.

2. Interview, October 19, 2020.

3. Interview, October 19, 2020. The birther movement or conspiracy asserted that President Barak Obama was a foreign-born illegal alien and Muslim who wanted to institute Sharia law in the United States. See Jonathan Kay, *Among the Truthers: A Journey Through America's Growing Conspiracist Underground* (New York: HarperCollins, 2011).

4. Interview, October 19, 2020.

5. Interview, October 19, 2020.

6. Michael Sisco, "Platform," Michael Sisco for Congress, accessed June 1, 2021, https://sisco2022.com/platform.

7. Interview, October 19, 2020.

8. Interview by author, April 8, 2021.

9. Cynthia Miller-Idriss, *Hate in the Homeland: The New Global Far Right* (Princeton, NJ: Princeton University Press, 2020).

10. For a history of the America First movement, see Sarah Churchwell, *Behold, America: The Entangled History of "America First" and "The American Dream"* (New York: Basic Books, 2018).

11. Svetlana Boym, *The Future of Nostalgia* (New York: Basic Books, 2001), xvi.

12. Boym, *Future of Nostalgia*, xv.

13. Emily Brown, "Death to the World: The Last True Rebellion," *TheOutline.com*, December 21, 2016, under "Culture," accessed August 20, 2019, https://theoutline.com/post/715/death-to-the-world.

14. Alexey Young, ed., *Letters from Father Seraphim: The Twelve-Year Correspondence Between Hieromonk Seraphim (Rose) and Father Alexey Young* (Richfield Springs, NY: Nikodemos Orthodox Publishing Society, 2001), 51–52.

15. Young, *Letters from Father Seraphim*, 267.

16. Alexander Schmemann, *Liturgy and Tradition*, ed. Thomas Finch (Crestwood, NY: St. Vladimir's Seminary Press, 1990), 10.

17. Boym, *Future of Nostalgia*, 354.

18. Monk Damascene Christensen, *Not of This World: The Life and Teaching of Fr. Seraphim Rose, Pathfinder to the Heart of Ancient Christianity* (Forestville, CA: Fr. Seraphim Rose Foundation, 1993), 999.

19. Rod Dreher, *The Benedict Option: A Strategy for Christians in a Post-Christian Nation* (New York: Penguin, 2017). For an overview of just a small handful of the many communitarian groups that have sprung forth in American religion(s), see Donald E. Pitzer, *America's Communal Utopias* (Chapel Hill: University of North Carolina Press, 1997).

20. Elizabeth Shakman Hurd and Winnifred Fallers Sullivan, eds., *At Home and Abroad: The Politics of American Religion* (New York: Columbia University Press, 2021).

21. Hurd and Sullivan, *At Home and Abroad.* Winnifred Fallers Sullivan and Elizabeth Shakman Hurd, eds., *Theologies of American Exceptionalism* (Bloomington: Indiana University Press, 2021).

22. Marshall Sahlins, *Historical Metaphors and Mythical Realities: Structure in the Early History of the Sandwich Islands Kingdom* (Ann Arbor: University of Michigan, 1981 [2009]), vii.

23. Jarrett Zigon, *Disappointment: Toward a Critical Hermeneutic of World-building* (New York: Fordham University Press, 2018), 158.

24. Mia Bloom and Sophie Moskalenko, *Pastels and Pedophiles: Inside the Mind of QAnon* (Stanford, CA: Stanford University Press, 2021); Magda Teter, *Blood Libel: On the Trail of an Anti-Semitic Myth* (Cambridge, MA: Harvard University Press, 2020).

25. Beth Allison Barr, *The Making of Biblical Womanhood: How the Subjugation of Women Became Gospel Truth* (Grand Rapids, MI: Brazos Press).

Bibliography

Adair, Peter. *Holy Ghost People*. Directed by Peter Adair. DVD and Streaming (public domain). Thistle Films. 1967.

Agadjanian, Alexander. "Breakthrough to Modernity, Apologia for Traditionalism: The Russian Orthodox View of Society and Culture in Comparative Perspective." *Religion, State, and Society* 31, no. 4 (2003): 327–346.

———. "Tradition, Morality and Community: Elaborating Orthodox Identity in Putin's Russia." *Religion, State, and Society* 45, no. 1 (2017): 39–60.

Ahlstrom, Sydney. *Religious History of the American People*. New Haven, CT: Yale University Press, 1972.

Albanese, Catherine. *America, Religions, and Religion*. Toronto: Wadsworth, 1981.

Albanese, Catherine L., ed. *American Spiritualties: A Reader*. Bloomington: Indiana University Press, 2001.

Alfeyev, Hilarion (Metropolitan of Volokolamsk). "The Theology of Freedom. Christianity and Secular Power: From the Edict of Milan to the Present." Lecture. Pontifical Theology Faculty of Southern Italy. October 17, 2014. https://mospat.ru/en/2014/10/18/news109757/.

Ammerman, Nancy Tatom. *Sacred Stories, Spiritual Tribes: Finding Religion in Everyday Life*. New York: Oxford University Press, 2014.

Ancient Faith Ministries. "Specials: Chastity, Purity, Integrity: Orthodox Anthropology and Secular Culture in the Twenty-First Century." Ancient Faith Ministries. Accessed March 10, 2019. https://www.ancientfaith.com/specials/chastity_purity_integrity.

Anderson, John. *Conservative Christian Politics in Russia and the United States: Dreaming of Christian Nations*. London: Routledge, 2014.

———. "Putin and the Russian Orthodox Church: Asymmetric Symphonia?" *Journal of International Affairs* 611 (2007): 185–201.

Andreev, Ivan Mikhaĭlovich. *Russia's Catacomb Saints: Lives of the New Martyrs*. Translated by Father Seraphim Rose. Platina, CA: Saint Herman of Alaska Press, 1982.

Andreyev, Nikolay. "Filofey and His Epistle to Ivan Vasil'yevich." *The Slavonic and East European Review* 38, no. 90 (December 1959): 1–31.

Anidjar, Gil. "Secularism," *Critical Inquiry* 33, no. 1 (Autumn 2006): 52–77.

Anonymous. "About Page." Accessed August 2, 2018. *The Sobornost*. http://theso bornost.org/about/.

Anonymous. *A Brief Life of Our Father Among the Saints, Archbishop John, Wonder-Worker of Shanghai and San Francisco*. Jordanville, NY: St. Job of Pochaev Press, 1997.

Anonymous. "The Character and Path of the Orthodox Mission." *The Orthodox Word* 1, no. 6 (November–December 1965): 207–209.

Anonymous. *A History of the Russian Orthodox Church Abroad, 1917–1971*. Seattle, WA: St. Nectarios Press, 1972.

Anonymous. "Orthodoxy and Community: Introduction to the Orthodox World View," *The Sobornost*. Accessed August 2, 2018. http://thesobornost.org/2017/06 /orthodoxy-and-community-intro-orthodox-worldview/.

Anonymous. *Service for "The Commemoration of the Triumph of Our Lady of Port Arthur Icon."* Unpublished, 2014.

Anonymous. "Truth, Compassion, and the Transgender Movement." *Remembering Sion*. Accessed September 13, 2019. https://www.rememberingsion.com/2018/06/25 /truth-compassion-transgender-movement/.

Appleby, R. Scott. "Fundamentalists, Rigorists, and Traditionalists: An Unorthodox Trinity." In *Fundamentalism and Tradition: Christianity after Secularism*. Edited by Aristotle Papanikolaou and George E. Demacopoulos. New York: Fordham University Press, 2020.

Associates of Colonel Philip Ludwell III. "Structure 'S': The First Orthodox Chapel in America?" *Associates of Colonel Philip Ludwell III*. Accessed December 30, 2018. https://www.ludwell.org/project/greenspring-structure-s.

Atton, Chris. *An Alternative Internet: Radical Media, Politics, and Creativity*. Edinburgh, UK: Edinburgh University Press, 2014.

Austin-Broos, Diane. "The Anthropology of Conversion: An Introduction." In *The Anthropology of Religious Conversion*. Edited by Andrew Buckser and Stephen D. Glazier. 1–14. Lanham, MD: Rowman and Littlefield, 2003.

Bailey, Connor, Leif Jensen, and Elizabeth Ransom, eds. *Rural America in a Globalizing World: Problems and Prospects for the 2010s*. Morgantown: West Virginia University Press, 2014.

Baker, Peter, and Susan Glasser. *Kremlin Rising: Vladimir Putin's Russia and the End of Revolution*. New York: Simon and Schuster, 2005.

Baker, William R., ed. *Evangelicalism and the Stone Campbell Movement*. Downers Grove, IL: InterVarsity Press, 2002.

Barker, John. "Secondary Conversion and the Anthropology of Christianity in Melanesia." *Archives De Sciences Sociales Des Religions* 57, no. 157 (2012): 67–87.

Barkey, Frederick A. *Working Class Radicals: The Socialist Party in West Virginia, 1898–1920.* Morgantown: West Virginia University Press, 2012.

Barkun, Michael. *A Culture of Conspiracy: Apocalyptic Visions in Contemporary America.* Berkeley: University of California Press, 2013.

Barr, Beth Allison. *The Making of Biblical Womanhood: How the Subjugation of Women Became Gospel Truth.* Grand Rapids, MI: Brazos Press.

Barret, Elizabeth. *Stranger with a Camera.* DVD. Whitesburg, KY: Appalshop, 2000.

Bastress, Robert M. *The West Virginia State Constitution: A Reference Guide.* Westport, CT: Greenwood Publishing Group, 1995.

Baynes, Leslie. *The Heavenly Book Motif in Judeo-Christian Apocalypses, 200 B.C.E.–200 C.E.* Leiden, Netherlands: Brill, 2012.

Behr, John. *Becoming Human: Meditations on Christian Anthropology in Word and Image.* Yonkers, NY: St. Vladimir's Seminary Press, 2013.

Bell, Catherine. *Ritual: Perspectives and Dimensions.* New York: Oxford University Press, 1997.

Bender, Courtney. *The New Metaphysicals: Spirituality and the American Religious Imagination.* Chicago: University of Chicago Press, 2010.

Benz, Ernst. *The Eastern Orthodox Church: Its Thought and Life.* London: Routledge, 2017[1975].

Bertaux, Daniel, and Martin Kohli. "The Life Story Approach: A Continental View." *Annual Review of Sociology* 10 (1984): 215–237.

Betz, Hans-Georg. *Radical Right-Wing Populism in Western Europe.* New York: Palgrave Macmillan, 1994.

Bielo, James S. *Emerging Evangelicals: Faith, Modernity, and the Desire for Authenticity.* New York: New York University Press, 2011.

Billings, Dwight B., Gurney Norman, and Katherine Ledford, eds. *Back Talk from Appalachia: Confronting Stereotypes.* Lexington: University Press of Kentucky, 2013.

Bjork-James, Sophie. *The Divine Institution: White Evangelicalism's Politics of the Family.* New Brunswick, NJ: Rutgers University Press, 2021.

Black, Lydia. *Russians in Alaska, 1732–1867.* Fairbanks: University of Alaska Fairbanks, 2004.

Blee, Kathleen M. "Ethnographies of the Far Right." *Journal of Contemporary Ethnography* 36, no. 2 (April 2007): 119–128.

Blee, Kathleen M., and Verta Taylor. "The Uses of Semi-Structured Interviews in Social Movement Research." In *Methods in Social Movement Research.* Edited by Bert Klandermans and Suzanne Staggenborg. Minneapolis: University of Minnesota Press, 2002.

Bloom, Mia, and Sophie Moskalenko. *Pastels and Pedophiles: Inside the Mind of QAnon.* Stanford, CA: Stanford University Press, 2021.

Blumhofer, Edith L. *Restoring the Faith: The Assemblies of God, Pentecostalism, and American Culture*. Urbana: University of Illinois Press, 1993.

Bogolepov, Alexander. *Toward an American Orthodox Church: The Establishment of an Autocephalous Church*. Crestwood, NY: St. Vladimir's Seminary Press, 1968 [2001].

Bojanowska, Eydta M. *A World of Empires: The Russian Voyage of the Frigate Pallada*. Cambridge, MA: Harvard University Press, 2018.

Bolton, Charles Knowles. *Scotch-Irish Pioneers in Ulster and America*. Boston: Bacon and Brown, 1910.

Bourdieu, Pierre. *Outline of a Theory of Practice*. Translated by Richard Nice. Cambridge: Cambridge University Press, 2015 [1977].

Boylston, Tom. *The Stranger at the Feast: Prohibition and Mediation in an Ethiopian Orthodox Christian Community*. Berkeley: University of California Press, 2018.

Boym, Svetlana. *The Future of Nostalgia*. New York: Basic Books, 2001.

Bremer, Thomas. *Formed from This Soil: An Introduction to the Diverse History of Religion in America*. Malden, MA: Wiley-Blackwell, 2015.

Brennan, Mary C. *Turning Right in the Sixties: The Conservative Capture of the GOP*. Chapel Hill: University of North Carolina Press, 2005.

———. *Wives, Mothers, and the Red Menace: Conservative Women and the Crusade against Communism*. Boulder: University of Colorado Press, 2011.

Brown, Emily. "Death to the World: The Last True Rebellion." *TheOutline.com*. December 21, 2016, under "Culture." Accessed August 20, 2019). https://theout line.com/post/715/death-to-the-world.

Buckser, Andrew, and Stephen D. Glazier, eds. *The Anthropology of Religious Conversion*. Lanham, MD: Rowman and Littlefield, 2003.

Burgess, John P. *Holy Rus': The Rebirth of Orthodoxy in the New Russia*. New Haven, CT: Yale University Press, 2017.

———. "Retrieving the Martyrs in Order to Rethink the Political Order: The Russian Orthodox Case." *Journal of the Society of Christian Ethics* 34, no. 2 (2014): 177–201.

Burlacioiu, Ciprian. "Russian Orthodox Diaspora as a Global Religion after 1918." *Studies in World Christianity* 24, no. 1(2018): 4–24.

Buss, Andreas E. *The Russian-Orthodox Tradition and Modernity*. Leiden, Netherlands: Brill, 2003.

Buss, Doris, and Didi Herman. *Globalizing Family Values: The Christian Right in International Politics*. Minneapolis: University of Minnesota Press, 2003 [1998].

Caiani, Manuela, and Linda Parenti. *European and American Extreme Right Groups and the Internet*. London: Routledge Press, 2016.

Camus, Jean-Yves, and Nicolas Lebourg. *Far-Right Politics in Europe*. Translated by Jane Marie Todd. Cambridge, MA: Harvard University Press, 2017.

Cannell, Fenella, ed. *The Anthropology of Christianity*. Durham, NC: Duke University Press, 2006.

Carroll, Timothy. *Orthodox Christian Material Culture: Of People and Things in the Making of Heaven*. New York: Routledge Press, 2018.

Castelli, Elizabeth A. *Martyrdom and Memory: Early Christian Culture Making.* New York: Columbia University Press, 2004.

Catte, Elizabeth ed. *Left Elsewhere: Finding the Future in Radical Rural America.* Boston: Boston Review Forum/MIT Press, 2019.

Catte, Elizabeth. *What You Are Getting Wrong about Appalachia.* Cleveland, OH: Belt Publishing, 2018.

Caudill, Harry. *Night Comes to the Cumberlands: A Biography of a Depressed Area.* Boston: Little, Brown, 1963.

Chapman, Nicholas. The Righteous Shall Be an Everlasting Remembrance: Further Reflections on Colonel Philip Ludwell III." *Orthodox History: The Society for Orthodox History in the Americas.* Accessed January 2, 2019. https:// orthodoxhistory.org/2013/03/22/the-righteous-shall-be-in-everlasting-remembrance -further-reflections-on-colonel-philip-ludwell-iii/.

———. "Virginian Orthodoxy in the Early American Republic." *Orthodox History: The Society for Orthodox Christian History in the Americas.* August 26, 2013. Accessed March 4, 2018. https://orthodoxhistory.org/2013/08/26/ virginian-orthodoxy-in-the-early-american-republic/.

Chebankova, Elena. *Civil Society in Putin's Russia.* New York: Routledge, 2013.

———. "Russian Fundamental Conservatism: In Search of Modernity." *Post-Soviet Affairs* 29, no. 2 (2013): 300–304.

Christensen, Monk Damascene. *Not of This World: The Life and Teaching of Fr. Seraphim Rose, Pathfinder to the Heart of Ancient Christianity.* Forestville, CA: Fr. Seraphim Rose Foundation, 1993.

Churchwell, Sarah. *Behold, America: The Entangled History of "America First" and "The American Dream."* New York: Basic Books, 2018.

Clark, Katerina. *Moscow, the Fourth Rome: Stalinism, Cosmopolitanism, and the Evolution of Soviet Culture, 1931–1941.* Cambridge, MA: Harvard University Press, 2011.

Coleman, Heather J., ed. *Orthodox Christianity in Imperial Russia: A Source Book on Lived Religion.* Bloomington: Indiana University Press, 2004.

Coleman, Simon, and John Elsner. "Performing Pilgrimage: Walsingham and the Ritual Construction of Irony." In *Ritual, Performance, and Media.* Edited by Felicia Hughes-Freeland. 46–66. London: Routledge, 1998.

Coles, Robert. *Still Hungry in America.* New York: Penguin, 1972.

Conkin, Paul Keith. *American Originals: Homemade Varieties of Christianity.* Chapel Hill: University of North Carolina Press, 1997.

Cooper, Frederick. *Colonialism in Question: Theory, Knowledge, History.* Berkeley: University of California Press, 2005.

Courtwright, David T. *No Right Turn: Conservative Politics in a Liberal America.* Cambridge, MA: Harvard University Press, 2010.

Cox, Harvey. *Turning East: The Promise and Peril of New Orientalism.* New York: Simon and Schuster, 1997.

Cramer, Katherine J. *The Politics of Resentment: Rural Consciousness in Wisconsin and the Rise of Scott Walker.* Chicago: University of Chicago Press, 2016.

Critchlow, Donald T. *The Conservative Ascendancy: How the GOP Right Made Political History*. Cambridge, MA: Harvard University Press, 2007.

———. *Phyllis Schlafly and Grassroots Conservatism: A Woman's Crusade*. Princeton, NJ: Princeton University Press, 2018.

Curry, David. "About." *Russian Faith*. Accessed December 2, 2019. https://russian-faith.com/pages/about.

Curtis, Heather D. *Holy Humanitarians: American Evangelicals and Global Aid*. Cambridge, MA: Harvard University Press, 2018.

Dallam, Marie W. *Cowboy Christians*. New York: Oxford University Press, 2018.

Dargan, Olive Tilford. *From My Highest Hill: Carolina Mountain Folks*. Knoxville: University of Tennessee Press, 1998 [originally published in 1925].

Daswani, Girish. *Looking Back, Moving Forward: Transformation and Ethical Practice in the Ghanaian Church of Pentecost*. Toronto: University of Toronto Press, 2015.

Davis, Nathaniel. *A Long Walk to Church: A Contemporary History of Russian Orthodoxy*. New York: Routledge, 2003.

Dawisha, Karen, and Bruce Parrott. *Russia and the New States of Eurasia: The Politics of Upheaval*. New York: Cambridge University Press, 1994.

Demacopoulos, George E., and Aristotle Papanikolaou, eds. *Christianity, Democracy, and the Shadow of Constantine*. New York: Fordham University Press, 2017.

———. *Orthodox Constructions of the West*. New York: Fordham University Press, 2013.

Demacopoulos, George E. "'Traditional Orthodoxy' as a Postcolonial Movement," *Journal of Religion* 97, no. 4 (October 2017): 475–499.

Denver, John. *Country Roads, Take Me Home*. RCA. 1971.

Denysenko, Nicholas E. *Liturgical Reform after Vatican II: The Impact on Eastern Orthodoxy*. Minneapolis, MN: Fortress Press, 2015.

———. *The Orthodox Church in Ukraine: A Century of Separation*. DeKalb: Northern Illinois University Press, 2018.

———. *Theology and Form: Contemporary Orthodox Architecture in America*. Notre Dame, IN: University of Notre Dame Press, 2017.

Detwiler, Fritz. *Standing on the Premises of God: The Christian Right's Fight to Redefine America's Public Schools*. New York: New York University Press, 1999.

Dochuk, Darren. *From the Bible Belt to the Sunbelt: Plain-Folk Religion, Grassroots Politics, and the Rise of Evangelical Conservatism*. New York: W. W. Norton, 2011.

Doggett, Carla. *Dr. Andrew Turnbull and the New Smyrna Colony of Florida*. Eustis, FL: Founders Publishing, 1994.

Dominick, Jesse. "In Memory of the Royal Martyrs, Through Personal Testimony." *Pravoslavie*. Accessed December 30, 2018. http://www.pravoslavie.ru/80716.html #_ftn7.

Doroszczyk, Justyna. "Moscow—Third Rome as a Source of Anti-Western Russian Geopolitics." *Historia i Polityka* 24, no. 3 (2018): 47–59.

Dostoevsky, Fyodor. *The Idiot*. New York: Macmillan, 1913.

Douglas, Mary. *Purity and Danger: An Analysis of Concepts of Pollution and Taboo*. London: Routledge, 2002.

Dowland, Seth. *Family Values and the Rise of the Christian Right*. Philadelphia: University of Pennsylvania Press, 2015.

Drake, Richard B. *A History of Appalachia*. Lexington: University Press of Kentucky, 2001.

Dreher, Rod. *The Benedict Option: A Strategy for Christians in a Post-Christian Nation*. New York: Penguin, 2017.

———. "Religion of Head and Heart." *The American Conservative*. December 20, 2018. Accessed January 3, 2019. https://www.theamericanconservative.com/dreher/religion-head-heart-orthodoxy-catholicism/.

———. "Thinking, and the Big Divide." *The American Conservative*. January 28, 2015. Accessed January 3, 2019. https://www.theamericanconservative.com/dreher/thinking-and-the-big-divide/.

Dugin, Aleksandr. *Filosofiia politiki*. Moscow: Arktogeia, 2004.

———. *The Fourth Political Theory*. English Edition. United Kingdom: Arktos Media, 2012.

Du Mez, Kristin Kobes. *Jesus and John Wayne: How White Evangelicals Corrupted a Faith and Fractured a Nation*. New York: Liveright, 2020.

Duncan, Peter J. S. *Russian Messianism: Third Rome, Revolution, Communism and After*. London: Routledge, 2002.

Dunlop, John. *Exodus: St. John Maximovitch Leads His Flock Out of Shanghai*. Yonkers, NY: St. Vladimir Seminary Press, 2017.

Eaton, Allen Hendershott. *Handicrafts of the Southern Highlands*. New York: Dover, 1973 [1937].

Edenborg, Emil. "Homophobia as Geopolitics: 'Traditional Values' and the Negotiation of Russia's Place in the World." In *Gendering Nationalism: Intersections of Nation, Gender, and Sexuality*. Edited by Jon Mulholland, Nicola Montagna, and Erin Sanders-McDonagh. 67–87. London: Palgrave Macmillan, 2018.

Elisha, Omri. *Moral Ambition: Mobilization and Social Outreach in Evangelical Megachurches*. Berkeley: University of California Press, 2011.

Ellis, Jane. *The Russian Orthodox Church: Triumphalism and Defensiveness*. Basingstoke, UK: Palgrave Macmillan, 1996.

Ellwood, Jr. Robert S. *Alternative Altars: Unconventional and Eastern Spirituality in America*. Chicago: University of Chicago Press, 1979.

Erikson, John. *Orthodox Christians in America*. New York: Oxford University Press, 1999.

Fagan, Geraldine. *Believing in Russia: Religious Policy after Communism*. London: Routledge, 2013.

Fea, John. *Believe Me: The Evangelical Road to Donald Trump*. Grand Rapids, MI: Wm. B. Eerdmans, 2018.

Fennell, John. *A History of the Russian Church to 1448*. New York: Routledge, 2013.

Filatov, Sergei, and Aleksandra Stiopina, "Russian Lutheranism: Between Protestant-ism, Catholicism, and Russian Orthodoxy." In *Religion and Politics in Russia: A Reader.* Edited by Marjorie Mandelstam Balzer. London: Routledge, 2010.

Fisher, Stephen L. ed. *Fighting Back in Appalachia: Traditions of Resistance and Change.* Philadelphia: Temple University Press, 1993.

Fitzgerald, Frances. *The Evangelicals: The Struggle to Shape America.* New York: Simon and Schuster, 2017.

Florovsky, Georges. "Antinomies of Christian History: Empire and Desert." In *The Collected Works of Georges Florovsky, vol. 2.* Edited by Richard S. Haugh. Belmont, MA: Norland Publishing, 1974.

Foglesong, David S. *The American Mission and the "Evil Empire."* Cambridge: Cambridge University Press, 2007.

Freeman, Stephen. *Everywhere Present: Christianity in a One-Storey Universe.* Chesterton, IN: Conciliar Press, 2010.

Freeze, Gregory L. "Handmaiden of the State? The Orthodox Church in Imperial Russia Reconsidered." *Journal of Ecclesiastical History* 36 (1985): 82–102.

Gabowitsch, Mischa. *Protest in Putin's Russia.* Malden, MA: Polity Press, 2017.

Garrard, John, and Carol Garrard. *Russian Orthodoxy Resurgent: Faith and Power in the New Russia.* Princeton, NJ: Princeton University Press, 2014.

Geertz, Clifford. "Thick Description: Toward an Interpretive Theory of Culture." In *The Interpretation of Cultures: Selected Essays.* New York: Basic Books, 1973.

Gellner, Ernest. *Nations and Nationalism.* Ithaca, NY: Cornell University Press, 1983.

———. *Postmodernism, Reason, and Religion.* London: Routledge, 1992.

Geraci, Robert, and Michael Khodarkovsky, eds. *Of Religion and Empire: Missions, Conversion, and Tolerance in Tsarist Russia.* Ithaca, NY: Cornell University Press, 2018.

Ging, Debbie. "Alphas, Betas, and Incels: Theorizing the Masculinities of the Manosphere." *Men and Masculinities* 22, no. 4 (October 2019): 638–657.

Ginsburg, Faye. "The Case of Mistaken Identity: Problems in Representing Women on the Right." In *Reflexivity and Voice.* Edited by Rosanne Hertz. Thousand Oaks, CA: Sage, 1997.

———. "Procreation Stories: Reproduction, Nurturance, and Procreation in Life Narratives of Abortion Activists." *American Ethnologist* 14 (1987): 623–636.

Giordan, Giuseppe ed. *Conversion in the Age of Pluralism, vol. 16.* Leiden, Nether-lands: Brill, 2009.

Goodman, Nelson. *Ways of Worldmaking.* Indianapolis: Hackett Publishing Group, 1978.

Gooren, Henri. *Religious Conversion and Disaffiliation: Tracing Patterns of Change in Faith Practices.* New York: Palgrave Macmillan, 2010.

Gorski, Philip S. *American Babylon: Christianity and Democracy Before and After Trump.* London: Routledge, 2020.

Graeber, David, and Marshall Sahlins. *On Kings.* Chicago: University of Chicago Press, 2017.

Greeley, Andrew. "A Religious Revival in Russia?" *Journal for the Scientific Study of Religion* 33, no. 3 (September 1994): 253–277.

Green, Emma. "A Christian Insurrection." *Atlantic*, January 8, 2021. Under "Politics." Accessed January 9, 2021. https://www.theatlantic.com/politics/archive/2021/01 /evangelicals-catholics-jericho-march-capitol/617591/.

Greene, Viveca S. "'Deplorable' Satire: Alt-Right Memes, White Genocide Tweets, and Redpilling Normies." *Studies in American Humor* 5, no. 1 (2019): 31–69.

Griffin, Sean. *The Liturgical Past in Byzantium and Early Rus*, Cambridge: Cambridge University Press, 2019.

Grimm, Dieter. *Sovereignty: The Origin and Future of a Political and Legal Concept*. Translated by Belinda Cooper. New York: Columbia University Press, 2015 [2009].

Haas, Lisbeth. *Saints and Citizens: Indigenous Histories of Colonial Missions and Mexican California*. Berkeley: University of California Press, 2014.

Hadot, Pierre. "Conversion." *Encyclopaedia Universalis* 4 (1968): 979–981.

Hainsworth, Paul, ed. *The Extreme Right in Europe and the USA*. London: Bloomsbury, 1992.

Hatewatch Staff. "World Congress of Families Gathering in Tbilisi Showcases Anti-LGBT Rhetoric and Conspiracy Theories." Southern Poverty Law Center. Accessed November 16, 2018. https://www.splcenter.org/hatewatch/2016/06/01 /world-congress-families-gathering-tbilisi-showcases-anti-lgbt-rhetoric-and -conspiracy.

Hämmerli, Maria, and Jean-François Mayer, eds. *Orthodox Identities in Western Europe: Migration, Settlement, and Innovation*. London: Routledge, 2016.

Hapgood, Isabel. *Service Book of the Holy Orthodox-Catholic Apostolic (Greco-Russian) Church*. Boston: Houghton Mifflin, 1906.

Harding, Susan. *The Book of Jerry Falwell: Fundamentalist Language and Politics*. Princeton, NJ: Princeton University Press, 2000.

———. "Representing Fundamentalism: The Problem of the Repugnant Cultural Other." *Social Research* 58, no. 2 (1991): 373–393.

Harding, Susan, and Daniel Rosenberg, eds. *Histories of the Future*. Durham, NC: Duke University Press, 2005.

Harkins, Anthony. *Hillbilly: A Cultural History of an American Icon*. New York: Oxford University Press, 2005.

Harrison, Nonna Verna. *God's Many-Splendored Image: Theological Anthropology for Christian Formation*. Grand Rapids, MI: Baker Academic, 2010.

Haselby, Sam. *The Origins of American Religious Nationalism*. New York: Oxford University Press, 2016.

Hastings, Derek. *Nationalism in Modern Europe: Politics, Identity, and Belonging Since the French Revolution*. London: Bloomsbury, 2018.

Hawley, George. *Making Sense of the Alt-Right*. New York: Columbia University Press, 2017.

Hedda, Jennifer. *His Kingdom Come: Orthodox Pastorship and Social Activism in Revolutionary Russia*. DeKalb: Northern Illinois University Press, 2007.

Hefner, Robert W. *Conversion to Christianity: Historical and Anthropological Perspectives on a Great Transformation.* Berkeley: University of California Press, 1993.

Hemment, Julie. *Youth Politics in Putin's Russia: Producing Patriots and Entrepreneurs.* Bloomington: Indiana University Press, 2015.

Hennen, John C. *The Americanization of West Virginia: Creating a Modern Industrial State, 1916–1925.* Lexington: University Press of Kentucky, 2015.

Herbel, Oliver. *Turning to Tradition: Converts and the Making of an American Orthodox Church.* London: Oxford University Press, 2013.

Herzog, Jonathan P. *The Spiritual-Industrial Complex: America's Religious Battle against Communism in the Early Cold War.* New York: Oxford University Press, 2011.

Hochschild, Arlie Russell. *Strangers in their Own Land.* New York: New Press, 2016.

Hodgson, Godfrey. *The Myth of American Exceptionalism.* New Haven, CT: Yale University Press, 2009.

Hollinshead, Keith, Irena Ateljevic, and Nazia Ali. "Worldmaking Agency– Worldmaking Authority: The Sovereign Constitutive Role of Tourism." *Tourism Geographies* 11, no. 4 (2009): 27–443.

Holy Trinity Monastery. "Chastity, Purity, Integrity: Orthodox Anthropology and Secular Culture in the Twenty-First Century." Holy Trinity Monastery. Accessed January 31, 2019. https://www.jordanville.org/news_190227_1.html.

Hoover, Dennis R. ed. *Religion and American Exceptionalism.* London: Routledge, 2013.

Hosking, Geoffrey. *Russia and the Russians: A History.* Cambridge, MA: Harvard University Press, 2011.

Hovorun, Cyril. *Political Orthodoxies: The Unorthodoxies of the Church Coerced.* Minneapolis, MN: Fortress Press, 2018.

Hummel, Daniel. "Revivalist Nationalism since World War II: From "Wake Up, America!" to "Make America Great Again."" *Religions* 7 (2006): 123–124.

Hunter, James Davison. *Culture Wars: The Struggle to Define America.* New York: HarperCollins, 1991.

Hurd, Elizabeth Shakman, and Winnifred Fallers Sullivan, eds. *At Home and Abroad: The Politics of American Religion.* New York: Columbia University Press, 2021.

Hutchinson, Emma. *Affective Communities in World Politics: Collective Emotions after Trauma.* Cambridge: Cambridge University Press, 2016.

Huxley, Aldous. *The Perennial Philosophy.* New York: HarperCollins, 1944.

Isenberg, Nancy. *White Trash: The 400-Year Untold History of Class in America.* New York: Penguin, 2017 [Reprint].

Ivanov, Viacheslav Vsevolodovich. *Native American Traditions: An Attempt at a Multicultural Society, 1794–1912.* Washington, DC: Library of Congress Publication, 1997.

Jackson, Michael. *Lifeworlds: Essays in Existential Anthropology.* Chicago: University of Chicago Press, 2012.

Jenkins, Philip. *The Cold War at Home: The Red Scare in Pennsylvania, 1945–1960*. Chapel Hill: University of North Carolina Press, 2011.

Johnson, Christopher D. L. *The Globalization of Hesychasm and the Jesus Prayer: Contesting Contemplation*. London: Continuum, 2010.

———. "He Has Made the Dry Bones Live": Orientalism's Attempted Resuscitation of Eastern Christianity." *Journal of American Academy of Religion* 82, no. 3 (September 2014): 811–840.

Johnson, Juliet, Marietta Stephaniants, and Benjamin Forest, eds. *Religion and Identity in Modern Russia: The Revival of Orthodoxy and Islam*. New York: Routledge, 2017.

Johnson, Linda, Donald Askins, and Helen Matthews Lewis, eds. *Colonialism in Modern America: The Appalachian Case*. Boone, NC: Appalachian State University, 2017.

Johnson, Matthew Raphael. *The Third Rome, Holy Russia, Tsarism, and Orthodoxy*. Washington, DC: Foundation for Economic Liberty, 2004.

Jones, Loyal. *Appalachian Values*. Ashland, KY: Jesse Stuart Foundation, 1994 [1973].

———. "Studying Mountain Religion." *Appalachian Journal* 5, no. 1 (1977): 125–130.

Jones, Robert P. *The End of White America*. New York: Simon and Schuster, 2017.

Juergensmeyer, Mark. *The New Cold War? Religious Nationalism Confronts the Secular State*. Berkeley: University of California Press, 1994.

Kalkandjieva, Daniela. *The Russian Orthodox Church, 1917–1948: From Decline to Resurrection*. New York: Routledge, 2015.

Kan, Sergei. *Memory Eternal: Tlingit Culture and Russian Orthodox Christianity through Two Centuries*. Seattle: University of Washington Press, 1999.

Kapaló, James A. "Mediating Orthodoxy: Convert Agency and Discursive Autochthonism in Ireland." In *Orthodox Identities in Western Europe: Migration, Settlement, and Innovation*. Edited by Maria Hämmerli and Jean-François Mayer. 229–249. New York: Routledge, 2014.

Kaplan, Jeffrey, and Leonard Weinberg. *The Emergence of a Euro-American Radical Right*. New Brunswick, NJ: Rutgers University Press, 1998.

Karagiannis, Nathalie, and Peter Wagner, eds. *Varieties of World-Making: Beyond Globalization*. Liverpool, UK: Liverpool University Press, 2007.

Karpov, Vyacheslav, Elena Lisovskaya, and David Barry. "Ethnodoxy: How Popular Ideologies Fuse Religious and Ethnic Identities." In *Journal for the Scientific Study of Religion* 51, no. 4 (2012):638–655.

Kay, Jonathan. *Among the Truthers: A Journey Through America's Growing Conspiracist Underground*. New York: HarperCollins, 2011.

Keane, Webb. *Christian Moderns: Freedom and Fetish in the Mission Encounter*. Berkeley: University of California Press, 2007.

Kelaidis, Katherine. "How Orthodox Christianity Became the Spiritual Home of White Nationalism." *Religious Dispatches*. November 30, 2016. Accessed September 12, 2018. http://religiondispatches.org/how-orthodox-christianity-became-the -spiritual-home-of-white-nationalism/.

———. "White Supremacy and Orthodox Christianity: A Dangerous Connection Rears Its Head in Charlottesville." *Religious Dispatches*. August 18, 2017. Accessed September 12, 2018. http://religiondispatches.org/white-supremacy-and-orthodox -christianity-a-dangerous-connection-rears-its-head-in-charlottesville/.

Kellogg, Michael. *The Russian Roots of Nazism: White Émigrés and the Making of National Socialism 1917–1945*. New York: Cambridge University Press, 2005.

Kelly, Annie. "The Alt-Right: Reactionary Rehabilitation for White Masculinity: US Alt-Right Extremism Is a Logical Consequence of Mainstream Neo-Conservatism." *Soundings: A Journal of Politics and Culture* 68 (2017): 68–78.

Kenworthy, Scott M. *The Heart of Russia: Trinity-Sergius, Monasticism, and Society after 1825*. New York: Oxford University Press, 2010.

Kidd, Thomas S. *Who Is an Evangelical? The History of a Movement in Crisis*. New Haven, CT: Yale University Press, 2019.

Kieckhefer, Richard. *Theology in Stone: Church Architecture from Byzantium to Berkeley*. New York: Oxford University Press, 2005.

Kiffmeyer, Thomas. *Reformers to Radicals: The Appalachian Volunteers and the War on Poverty*. Lexington: University Press of Kentucky, 2009.

Kissinger, Henry. *Diplomacy*. New York: Simon and Schuster, 1995.

Kivelson, Valerie A. *Orthodox Russia: Belief and Practice under the Tsars*. Philadelphia: Penn State University Press, 2003.

Kizenko, Nadieszda. "Feminized Patriarchy? Orthodoxy and Gender in Post-Soviet Russia." *Signs* 38, no. 3 (2013): 595–621.

Knox, Zoe. *Russian Society and the Orthodox Church: Religion in Russia after Communism*. London: Routledge, 2004.

———. "The Symphonic Ideal: The Moscow Patriarchate's Post-Soviet Leadership." *Europe-Asia Studies* 55, no. 4 (2003): 575–596.

Knox, Zoe, and Anastasia Mitrofanova. "The Russian Orthodox Church." In *Eastern Christianity and Politics in the Twenty-First Century*. Edited by Lucian N. Leustean. 38–66. New York: Routledge, 2014.

Kolstø, Pål, and Helge Blakkisrud, eds. *The New Russian Nationalism: Imperialism, Ethnicity and Authoritarianism 2000–2015*. Edinburgh, UK: University of Edinburgh Press, 2016.

Kramer, Lloyd. *Nationalism in Europe and America: Politics, Cultures, and Identities Since 1775*. Durham: University of North Carolina Press, 2011.

Krawchuk, Andrii, and Thomas Bremer, eds. *Churches in the Ukrainian Crisis*. New York: Springer, 2017.

Krindatch, Alexei. *Atlas of American Orthodox Christian Churches*. Brookline, MA: Holy Cross Orthodox Press, 2011.

Kruse, Kevin M. *One Nation Under God: How Corporate America Invented Christian America*. New York: Basic Books, 2015.

Ladouceur, Paul. "Neo-traditionalist ecclesiology in Orthodoxy." *Scottish Journal of Theology* 72 (2019): 398–413.

Lamb, Christopher, and M. Darrol Bryant, eds. *Religious Conversion: Contemporary Practices and Controversies*. London: Bloomsbury, 1999.

Larres, Klaus, and Ruth Wittlinger, eds. *Understanding Global Politics: Actors and Themes in International Affairs*. London: Routledge, 2019.

Laruelle, Marlene. "Ideological Complementarity or Competition? The Kremlin, the Church, and the Monarchist Idea in Today's Russia." *Slavic Review* 79, no. 2 (Summer 2020): 345–364.

———. *Is Russia Fascist? Unraveling Propaganda East and West*. Ithaca, NY: Cornell University Press, 2021).

———. "Making Sense of Russia's Illiberalism." *Journal of Democracy* 31, no. 3 (July 2020): 115–129.

———. *Russian Eurasianism: An Ideology of Empire*. Baltimore, MD: Johns Hopkins University Press, 2012.

———. *Russian Nationalism: Imaginaries, Doctrines, and Political Battlefields*. London: Routledge, 2019.

Latour, Bruno. *We Have Never Been Modern*. Translated by Catherine Porter. Cambridge, MA: Harvard University Press, 1993.

Ledford, Katherine, Gurney Norman, and Dwight B. Billings, eds. *Back Talk from Appalachia: Confronting Stereotypes*. Lexington: University Press of Kentucky, 2013.

Lemeshonok, Andrew Fr. "Q&A with a Priest: What Does It Mean to Be a Priest's Wife?" Good Guys Wear Black: Discerning Your Vocation in the Orthodox Church. December 3, 2018. Accessed September 3, 2019. https://goodguyswear black.org/2018/12/03/qa-with-a-priest-what-does-it-mean-to-be-a-priests-wife/.

Leonard, Bill J. ed. *Christianity in Appalachia: Profiles in Regional Pluralism*. Knoxville: University of Tennessee Press, 1999.

Leonova, Inga. "Deafening Silence." *Public Orthodoxy*. Orthodox Christian Studies Center, Fordham University. Accessed August 1, 2018. https://publicorthodoxy .org/2017/08/16/deafening-silence/.

Lewis, Helen Matthews, Linda Johnson, Donald Askins, eds. *Colonialism in Modern America: The Appalachian Case*. Boone, NC: Appalachian State University, 2017 [1978].

Lewis, Helen M., and Monica Appleby. *Mountain Sisters: From Convent to Community in Appalachia*. Lexington: University Press of Kentucky, 2003.

Lilla, Mark. *The Shipwrecked Mind: On Political Reaction*. New York: New York Review of Books, 2016.

Lincoln, Bruce. *Holy Terrors: Thinking about Religion after September 11*. Chicago: University of Chicago Press, 2002.

Lloyd, Vincent W. *The Problem with Grace: Reconfiguring Political Theology*. Stanford, CA: Stanford University Press, 2011.

Lotman, J. M., and B.A. Uspenskij. "Echoes of the Notion of 'Moscow as the Third Rome' in Peter the Great's Ideology." Translated by N.F.C. Owen. In *The Semiotics of Russian Culture*. Edited by Ann Shukman. Ann Arbor: University of Michigan Press, 1984.

Louth, Andrew. *Modern Orthodox Thinkers: From the Philokalia to the Present*. Dowers Grove, IL: InterVarsity Press, 2015.

Lowe, Kevin M. *Baptized with the Soil: Christian Agrarians and the Crusade for Rural America*. New York: Oxford University Press, 2016.

Lucas, Phillip Charles. "Enfants Terribles: The Challenge of Sectarian Converts to Ethnic Orthodox Churches in the United States." *Nova Religio: The Journal of Alternative and Emergent Religions* 7, no. 2 (November 2003): 5–23.

———. *The Odyssey of a New Religion: The Holy Order of MANS from New Age to Orthodoxy*. Bloomington: Indiana University Press, 1995.

Luehrmann, Sonja. *Alutiiq Villages under Russian and U.S. Rule*. Fairbanks, AK: University of Alaska, 2008.

Lyerly, Cynthia Lynn. "In Service, Silence, and Strength: Women in Southern Churches." In *Religion and Public Life in the South: In the Evangelical Mode*. Edited by Charles Reagan Wilson and Mark Silk. New York: AltaMira Press, 2005.

Macy, Beth. *Dope Sick: Dealers, Doctors, and the Drug Company that Addicted America*. Boston: Little, Brown, 2019.

Markofski, Wes. *New Monasticism and the Transformation of American Evangelicalism*. New York: Oxford University Press, 2015.

Marsden, George. *Fundamentalism and American Culture*. New York: Oxford University Press, 1980.

———. "Fundamentalism as an American Phenomenon, A Comparison with English Evangelicalism." In *Fundamentalism and Evangelicalism*. Edited by Martin E. Marty. Berlin: De Gruyter, 1993.

Marty, Martin E., and R. Scott Appleby, eds. *Fundamentalisms and the State: Remaking Polities, Economies, and Militance*. Chicago: University of Chicago Press, 1996.

Mason, Carol. *Reading Appalachia from Left to Right: Conservatives and the 1974 Kanawha County Textbook Controversy*. Ithaca, NY: Cornell University Press, 2011.

Mathewes-Green, Frederica. *At the Corner of East and Now: A Modern Life in Ancient Christian Orthodoxy*. New York: Putnam, 1999.

———. *Facing East: A Pilgrim's Journey into the Mysteries of Orthodoxy*. New York: HarperCollins, 1997.

Maximovitch, John. *The Orthodox Veneration of the Mother of God*. Platina, CA: St. Herman Press, 1987.

———. "Tsar-Martyr Nicholas II." Orthodox Word 4, no. 21 (July–August 1968): 137.

———. "The Question of Uniformity in the Church Services Discussed at the Council of Hierarchs of the Russian Orthodox Church Abroad (1951)." Translated by Akim Provatakis. *Orthodox Life* 41, no. 4 (1991): 42–45.

———. *The Russian Orthodox Church Abroad: A Short History*. Jordanville, NY: St. Job of Pochaev Press, 1997.

Mayer, Jean-François. "'We are Westerners and Must Remain Westerners': Orthodoxy and Western Rites in Western Europe." 267–290. *Orthodox Identities in Western Europe: Migration, Settlement, and Innovation*. Edited by Maria Hämmerli and Jean-François Mayer. London: Routledge, 2016.

McAlister, Melani. *Epic Encounters: Culture, Media, and U.S. Interests in the Middle East Since 1945*. Berkeley: University of California Press, 2005.

McAllister, Carlota, and Valentina Napolitano. "The Powers of Powerlessness." *Political Theology Network.* Accessed January 28, 2019. https://politicaltheology.com/the-powers-of-powerlessness/.

McCarroll, Meredith. *Unwhite: Appalachia, Race, and Film.* Atlanta: University of Georgia, 2018.

McCauley, Deborah Vansau. *Appalachian Mountain Religion: A History.* Urbana: University of Illinois Press, 1995.

———. "Religion." In *High Mountains Rising: Appalachia in Time and Place.* Edited by Richard A. Straw and H. Tyler Blethen. 179–96. Urbana: University of Illinois Press, 2004.

McGirr, Lisa. *Suburban Warriors: The Origins of the New American Right.* Princeton, NJ: Princeton University Press, 2015.

McLees, Nun Nectaria. *A Gathered Radiance: The Life of Alexandra Romanov, Russia's Last Empress.* Chico, CA: Valaam Society of America, 1992.

McManus, Matthew. *The Rise of Post-Modern Conservatism: Neoliberalism, Post-Modern Culture, and Reactionary Politics.* Cham, Switzerland: Palgrave Macmillan, 2019.

Menon, Kalyani Devaki. "Converted Innocents and Their Trickster Heroes: The Politics of Proselytizing in India." In *The Anthropology of Religious Conversion.* Edited by Andrew Buckser and Stephen Glazier. Lanham, MD: Rowman and Littlefield, 2003.

Michaels, Jonathan. *McCarthyism: The Realities, Delusions, and Politics behind the 1950s Red Scare.* New York: Routledge, 2017.

Miller, Gwenn A. *Kodiak Creole: Communities of Empire in Early Russian America.* Ithaca, NY: Cornell University Press, 2010.

Miller, Steven Patrick. *The Age of Evangelicalism: America's Born-Again Years.* New York: Oxford University Press, 2014.

Miller-Idriss, Cynthia. *Hate in the Homeland: The New Global Far Right.* Princeton, NJ: Princeton University Press, 2020.

Mondon, Aurelien, and Aaron Winter. "Whiteness, Populism and the Racialisation of the Working Class in the United Kingdom and the United States." *Identities* 26, no. 5 (2019): 510–528.

Monge Rico G. "'Neither Victim nor Executioner': Essential Insights from Secularization Theory for the Revitalization of the Russian Orthodox Church in the Contemporary World." In *Inward Being and Outward Identity: The Orthodox Churches in the Twenty-First Century.* Edited by John A. Jillions. Special Issue. *Religions* 8 (2018): 170.

Montrie, Chad. *To Save the Land and People: A History of Opposition to Surface Coal Mining in Appalachia.* Durham: University of North Carolina Press, 2003.

Mooney, James. *Myths of the Cherokee and Sacred Formulas of the Cherokees.* Nashville: C. and R. Elder Booksellers, 1982 [reprint of 1900 and 1891 eds. published by Bureau of American Ethnology].

Moreton, Bethany. *Slouching Toward Moscow: American Evangelicals and the Romance of Russia.* Cambridge, MA: Harvard University Press, forthcoming.

Moslener, Sara. *Virgin Nation: Sexual Purity and American Adolescence.* New York: Oxford University Press, 2015.

Moss, Richard. *Nixon's Back Channel to Moscow: Confidential Diplomacy and Détente.* Lexington: University Press of Kentucky, 2017.

Mudde, Cas. *The Far Right in America.* London: Routledge, 2018.

———. *The Far Right Today.* Cambridge: Polity Press, 2019.

Mudde, Cas, and Cristóbal Rovira Kaltwasser, eds. *Populism in Europe and the Americas: Threat or Corrective for Democracy?* New York: Oxford University Press, 2012.

Mullen, Lincoln. *The Chance of Salvation: A History Conversion in America.* Cambridge, MA: Harvard University Press, 2017.

Myers, Steven Lee. *The New Tsar: The Rise and Reign of Vladimir Putin.* New York: Simon and Schuster, 2015.

Namli, Elena. "Orthodox Theology, Politics, and Power." In *Political Theologies in Orthodox Christianity: Common Challenges-Divergent Positions.* Edited by Kristina Stoeckl, Ingeborg Gabriel, and Aristotle Papanikolaou. 265–282. London: Bloomsbury, 2017.

Norman, Alex. *Spiritual Tourism: Travel and Religious Practice in Western Society.* London: Continuum, 2011.

Norris, Pippa, and Ronald Ingelhart. *Cultural Backlash: Trump, Brexit, and Authoritarian Populism.* Cambridge: Cambridge University Press, 2019.

Nyden, Paul J. "An Internal Colony: Labor Conflict and Capitalism in Appalachian Coal." *Insurgent Sociologist* 8, no. 4 (January 1979): 33–43.

O'Donovan, Oliver, and Joan Lockwood O'Donovan, eds. *From Irenaeus to Grotius: A Sourcebook in Christian Political Thought.* Grand Rapids, MI: Wm. B. Eerdmans, 1999.

Oosterbaan, Martijn. *Transmitting the Spirit: Religious Conversion, Media, and Urban Violence in Brazil.* University Park: Penn State University Press, 2017.

Orsi, Robert A. *Between Heaven and Earth: The Religious Worlds People Make and the Scholars Who Study Them.* Princeton, NJ: Princeton University Press, 2004.

———. *History and Presence.* Cambridge, MA: Harvard University Press, 2018.

Østbø, Jardar. *The New Third Rome: Readings of a Russian Nationalist Myth.* Stuttgart: ibidem-Verlag, 2016.

Paert, Irina. *Spiritual Elders: Charisma and Tradition in Russian Orthodoxy.* DeKalb: Northern Illinois University Press, 2010.

Palacio, Miguel. "'Orthodoxy Has a Great Future in Guatemala' Conversation with Abbess Ines, Head of the Holy Trinity Monastery in Guatemala." Translated by Adrian Fekula. *Orthodox Christianity.* July 16, 2009, Accessed January 3, 2017. https://orthochristian.com/31235.html.

Papanikolaou, Aristotle. "Byzantium, Orthodoxy, and Democracy." *Journal of the American Academy of Religion* 71, no. 1 (2003): 75–98.

———. "I am a Traditionalist, Therefore I am." *Public Orthodoxy.* Orthodox Christian Studies Center, Fordham University. Accessed March 1, 2019. https://publicorthodoxy.org/2019/02/19/i-am-a-traditionalist-therefore-i-am/.

———. *The Mystical as Political: Democracy and Non-Radical Orthodoxy.* Notre Dame, IN: University of Notre Dame Press, 2012.

Papanikolaou, Aristotle, and George E. Demacopoulos, eds. *Fundamentalism or Tradition: Christianity after Secularism.* New York: Fordham University Press, 2020.

Papkova, Irina. *The Orthodox Church and Russian Politics.* Washington, DC: Woodrow Wilson Center Press, 2011.

Pappas, Christine, Jeanette Mendez, and Rebekah Herrick. "The Negative Effects of Populism on Gay and Lesbian Rights." *Social Science Quarterly* 90, no.1 (March 2009): 150–163.

Pasieka, Agnieszka. "Anthropology of the Far-Right: What if We Like the 'Unlikeable' Others?" *Anthropology Today* 35, no.1 (2019): 3–6.

———. "Taking Far-Right Claims Seriously and Literally: Anthropology and the Study of Right-Wing Radicalism." *Slavic Review* 76, no. S1 (2017): S19–S29.

Patristic Nectar Films. "Gay Iconoclasm: Holding the Line against the Radical LGBT Agenda." YouTube. Accessed November 16, 2018. https://youtu.be/HNXe 4P_6dhw.

Paxson, Margaret. *Solovyovo: The Story of Memory in a Russian Village.* Indianapolis: Indiana University Press, 2005.

Payne, Daniel P. "Spiritual Security, the Russian Orthodox Church, and the Russian Foreign Ministry: Collaboration or Cooptation?" *Journal of Church and State* 52, no. 4 (2010): 712–727.

Peck, Fr. John, and Fr. Anthony Perkins. "Good Guys Wear Black: Discerning Your Vocation in the Orthodox Church." Accessed September 3, 2019. https://good guyswearblack.org.

Pelkmans, Mathjis, ed. *Conversion after Socialism: Disruptions, Modernisms, and Technologies of Faith in the Former Soviet Union.* New York: Berghahn Books, 2009.

Pentiuc, Eugen J. *The Old Testament in Eastern Orthodox Tradition.* New York: Oxford University Press, 2014.

Pentkovsky, Aleksei ed. *The Pilgrim's Tale.* Translated by T. Allan Smith. Minneapolis, MN: Paulist Press, 1999.

Perabo, Betsy. *Russian Orthodoxy and the Russo-Japanese War.* New York: Bloomsbury, 2017.

Perekrestov, Peter. *Man of God: St. John of Shanghai and San Francisco.* New York: Nikodemos Orthodox Publications, 1994.

Perry, Huey. *They'll Cut off Your Project: A Mingo County Chronicle.* Morgantown: West Virginia University Press, 2011.

Peterson, Jordan B. "Tradition and Things That Don't Fit with Jonathan Pageau." YouTube. November 29, 2016. Accessed December 4, 2017. https://www.youtube .com/watch?time_continue=95&v=eob5mnuKQvs.

Petro, Anthony M. *After the Wrath of God: AIDS, Sexuality, and American Religion.* New York: Oxford University Press, 2015.

Philliber, William W., Clyde B. McCoy, Harry C. Dillingham, eds. *The Invisible Minority: Urban Appalachians.* Lexington: University Press of Kentucky, 1981.

Phillips, Elizabeth. *Political Theology: A Guide for the Perplexed*. London: Bloomsbury, 2012.

Phillips, Martin. "Rural Gentrification and Process of Class Colonization." *Journal
of Rural Studies* 9, no. 2 (1993): 123–140.

Pierson, Paul. "American Hybrid: Donald Trump and the Strange Merger of
Populism and Plutocracy." *The British Journal of Sociology* 68, S1 (2017): S105–119.

Pitzer, Donald E. *America's Communal Utopias*. Chapel Hill: University of North
Carolina Press, 1997.

Plested, Marcus. "Between Rigorism and Relativism: The Givenness of Tradition."
Public Orthodoxy. Orthodox Christian Studies Center, Fordham University.
Accessed March 13, 2019. https://publicorthodoxy.org/2017/05/25/
between-rigorism-and-relativism/.

Poe, Marshall. "Moscow, the Third Rome: The Origins and Transformations of a
'Pivotal Moment.'" *Jahrbücher für Geschichte Osteuropas, Neue Folge* 49, no. 3
(2001): 412–429.

Politkovskaya, Anna. *Putin's Russia: Life in a Failing Democracy*. New York:
Metropolitan Books, 2007.

Pollard, Kelvin M. "Population Growth and Distribution in Appalachia: New Realities." Population Reference Bureau and Appalachian Regional Commission.
2005. Accessed December 20, 2019. https://www.arc.gov/research/researchreport
details.asp?REPORT_ID=27.

Posner, Sarah. *Unholy: Why White Evangelicals Worship at the Altar of Donald
Trump*. New York: Random House, 2020.

Putney, Clifford. *Muscular Christianity: Manhood and Sports in Protestant America,
1880–1920*. Cambridge, MA: Harvard University Press, 2003.

Raffensperger, Christian. *Reimagining Europe: Kievan Rus' in the Medieval World,
988–1146*. Cambridge, MA: Harvard University Press, 2012.

Raitz, Karl B., Richard Ulack, and Thomas R. Leinbach, *Appalachia: A Regional
Geography: Land, People, and Development*. New York: Routledge, 2018 [1984].

Rambo, Lewis R. *Understanding Religious Conversion*. New Haven, CT: Yale
University Press, 1993.

Rambo, Lewis R., and Charles E. Farhadian, eds. *The Oxford Handbook of Religious
Conversion*. New York: Oxford University Press, 2014.

Ramet, Sabrina P. "The Way We Were—and Should Be Again? European Orthodox
Churches and the 'Idyllic Past.'" In *Religion in an Expanding Europe*. Edited by
T. Byrnes and P. Katzenstein. Cambridge: Cambridge University Press 2006.

Restad, Hilde Eliassen. *American Exceptionalism: An Idea That Made a Nation and
Remade the World*. London: Routledge, 2014.

Riccardi-Swartz, Sarah. "American Conversions to Russian Orthodoxy Amid the
Global Culture Wars." Berkeley Forum. https://berkleycenter.georgetown
.edu/responses/american-conversions-to-russian-orthodoxy-amid-the-global
-culture-wars.

————. "Fieldwork and Fallout with the Far Right." American Ethnologist website. June 18, 2020. https://americanethnologist.org/features/reflections/fieldwork-and -fallout-with-the-far-right.

————. "The Hybridity of Rural Fascism." Hotspots, American Anthropologist. April 15, 2021. https://culanth.org/fieldsights/the-hybridity-of-rural-fascism.

————. "Putin's American Comrades and Our Post-Truth Moment." Sightings. University of Chicago Divinity School. December 10, 2020. https://divinity .uchicago.edu/sightings/articles/putins-american-comrades-and-our-post-truth -moment.

————. "Seeking a Sovereign for the End of Democracy: Monarchism and the Far Right." Canopy Forum, August 10, 2021. https://canopyforum.org/2021/08/10 ./seeking-a-sovereign-for-the-end-of-democracy-monarchism-and-the-far-right/.

Richters, Katja. The Post-Soviet Russian Orthodox Church: Politics, Culture, and Greater Russia. London: Routledge, 2012.

Robbins, Jeffrey W. "What's the Matter with Populism?" Soundings: An Interdisciplinary Journal 102, no. 2–3 (2019): 261–273.

Robbins, Joel. Becoming Sinners: Christianity and Moral Torment in a Papua New Guinea Society. Berkeley: University of California Press, 2004.

Roberts, Nathaniel. To Be Cared For: The Power of Conversion and Foreignness of Belonging in an Indian Slum. Berkeley: University of California Press, 2016.

Roof, Wade Clark. A Generation of Seekers: The Spiritual Journeys of the Baby Boom Generation. New York: HarperCollins, 1993.

————. Spiritual Marketplace: Baby Boomers and the Remaking of American Religion. Princeton, NJ: Princeton University Press, 2001 [reprint].

Rose, Eugene (Seraphim). "Orthodoxy and Modern Thought: The Self-Liquidation of Christianity." The Orthodox Word 2, no. 3 (9) (July–August 1966): 100–101.

Rose, Fr. Seraphim. "The Future of Russia and the End of the World." The Orthodox Word, vol. 17, no. 5–6 (1981): 205–217.

————. God's Revelation of the Human Heart. Platina, CA: St. Herman of Alaska Brotherhood, 1987.

————. Lectures of Fr. Seraphim Rose, vol. 1 (Living the Orthodox Worldview). St. Herman of Alaska Brotherhood. CD. 2015 [2007].

————. Soul After Death. Platina, CA: St. Herman of Alaska Brotherhood, 1980.

Roslof, Edward E. Red Priests: Renovationism, Russian Orthodoxy, and Revolution, 1905–1946. Bloomington: Indiana University Press, 2002.

Roudometof, Victor. Globalization and Orthodox Christianity: The Transformations of a Religious Tradition. New York: Routledge, 2014.

Rousselet, Kathy. "Constructing Moralities around the Tsarist Family." In Multiple Moralities and Religions in Post-Soviet Russia. Edited by Jarrett Zigon. New York: Berghahn Books, 2011).

Rowland, Daniel B. "Moscow-The Third Rome or the New Israel?" Russian Review 55, no. 4 (October 1996): 591–614.

The Russian Orthodox Church Department for External Church Relations. "The Basis of the Social Concept," The Russian Orthodox Church. Accessed February 3, 2019. https://mospat.ru/en/documents/social-concepts/.

The Russian Orthodox Church Outside of Russia. "Ukase No. 362, The Resolutions of His Holiness the Patriarch [Tikhon], of the Sacred Synod and Supreme Ecclesiastical Council of the Russian Orthodox Church, 20/7 November 1920." The Russian Orthodox Church Outside of Russia. Accessed March 3, 2019. http://www.synod.com/synod/engdocuments/enuk_ukaz362.html.

Ryabykh, Igumen Phillip. "The Orthodox Church and Society, Part I: Historic Roots of Church-State Relations." Pravoslavie. Accessed August 1, 2018. http://pravoslavie.ru/49277.html.

Sahlins, Marshall. Historical Metaphors and Mythical Realities: Structure in the Early History of the Sandwich Islands Kingdom. Ann Arbor: University of Michigan Press, 1981 [2009].

————. "The Original Political Society." In On Kings, by David Graeber and Marshall Sahlins. Chicago: University of Chicago Press, 2017.

Said, Edward. Orientalism. New York: Random House, 1978.

Saint Anthony's Greek Orthodox Monastery. The Departure of the Soul According to the Teaching of the Orthodox Church. Florence, AZ: St. Anthony's Greek Monastery, 2017.

Saito, Yuriko. Aesthetics of the Familiar: Everyday Life and World-Making. London: Oxford University Press, 2017.

Saloutos, Theodore. "The Greek Orthodox Church in the United States and Assimilation." The International Migration Review 7, no. 4 (Winter 1973): 395–407.

Sarkisian, Aram. "The Cross between Hammer and Sickle: Russian Orthodox Christians in the United States, 1908–1928." PhD diss., Northwestern University, 2019.

————. "Russian Orthodox Church Outside of Russia." In Encyclopedia of Christianity in the United States, vol. 5. Edited by George Thomas Kurian and Mark A. Lamport. 1996–1998. London: Rowman and Littlefield, 2016.

Sarris, Peter, ed. The Novels of Justinian: A Complete Annotated English Translation. Translated by David D.J. Miller. Cambridge: Cambridge University Press, 2018.

Saunders, Robert A. Popular Geopolitics and Nation Branding in the Post-Soviet Realm. London: Routledge, 2016.

Schmemann, Alexander. Liturgy and Tradition. Edited by Thomas Finch. Crestwood, NY: St. Vladimir's Seminary Press, 1990.

————. Of Water and the Spirit: A Liturgical Study of Baptism. Crestwood, NY: St. Vladimir's Seminary Press, 1974.

Schumann, William, and Rebecca Adkins Fletcher, eds. Appalachia Revisited: New Perspectives on Place, Tradition, and Progress. Lexington: University Press of Kentucky, 2016.

Scott, Cathy. Seraphim Rose: The True Story and Private Letters. Salisbury, MA: Regina Orthodox Press, 2000.

Sedgwick, Mark J. *Against the Modern World: Traditionalism and the Secret Intellectual History of the Twentieth Century.* New York: Oxford University Press, 2004.

Semple, Elaine. "The Anglo-Saxons of the Kentucky Mountains: A Study in Anthropogeography." *Geographical Journal* 17 (June 1901): 588–623.

Service, Robert. *A History of Modern Russia from Nicholas II to Vladimir Putin.* Cambridge, MA: Harvard University Press, 2005.

Shevzov, Vera. *Russian Orthodoxy on the Eve of Revolution.* New York: Oxford University Press, 2007.

Shimer, David. *Rigged: America, Russia, and One Hundred Years of Covert Electoral Interference.* New York: Knopf Doubleday, 2020.

Sidorov, Dmitri. "Post-Imperial Third Romes: Resurrections of a Russian Orthodox Geopolitical Metaphor." *Geopolitics* 11, no. 2 (2006): 317–347.

Sinelschikova, Yekaterina. "Why Do Some Americans Join the Russian Orthodox Church?" *Russia Beyond.* September 4, 2018. Accessed May 3, 2019. https://www.rbth.com/lifestyle/329076-americans-join-russian-church.

Slaby, Jan, and Christian von Scheve, eds. *Affective Societies: Key Concepts.* London: Routledge, 2019.

Slagle, Amy. *The Eastern Church in the Spiritual Marketplace: American Conversions to Orthodox Christianity.* DeKalb: Northern Illinois University Press, 2011.

———. "'Nostalgia without Memory': A Case Study of American Converts to Eastern Orthodoxy in Pittsburgh, Pennsylvania." PhD diss., University of Pittsburgh, 2008.

Slater, Wendy. *The Many Deaths of Tsar Nicholas II: Relics, Remains, and the Romanovs.* London: Routledge, 2007.

Sokoll, Aaron J. "'We're Not Ethnic': Ethnicity, Pluralism, and Identity in Orthodox Christian America." PhD diss. University of California at Santa Barbara, 2018. https://escholarship.org/uc/item/9f61p9hw.

Stark, Rodney, and Roger Finke. *Acts of Faith: Explaining the Human Side of Religion.* Berkeley: University of California Press, 2000.

Stark, Rodney, and Charles Y. Glock. *American Piety: The Nature of Religious Commitment.* Berkeley: University of California Press, 1968.

Stevens, Jason W. *God-Fearing and Fear: A Spiritual History of America's Cold War.* Cambridge, MA: Harvard University Press, 2010.

Stewart, Katherine. *The Power Worshippers: Inside the Dangerous Rise of Religious Nationalism.* New York: Bloomsbury, 2020.

Stievermann, Jan, Philip Goff, and Detlef Junke, eds. *Religion and the Marketplace in the United States.* New York: Oxford University Press, 2015.

Stoeckl, Kristina. "Postsecular Conflicts and the Global Struggle for Traditional Values." *State, Religion, and Church* 2/3 (2016): S102–116.

———. *The Russian Orthodox Church and Human Rights.* London: Routledge, 2014.

———. "The Russian Orthodox Church's Conservative Crusade." *Current History* 116/792 (2017): 271–276.

Stoeckl, Kristina, Ingeborg Gabriel, and Aristotle Papanikolaou, eds. *Political Theologies in Orthodox Christianity: Common Challenges—Divergent Positions.* London: Bloomsbury, 2017.

Stoeckl, Kristina, and Kseniya Medvedeva. "Double Bind at the UN: Western Actors, Russia, and the Traditionalist Agenda." *Global Constitutionalism* 7, no. 3 (2018): 383–421.

Stokoe, Mark, and Fr. Leonid Kishkovsky. *Orthodox Christians in North America, 1794–1994.* Syosset, NY: Orthodox Church in America, 1995.

Stoll, Steven. *Ramp Hollow: The Ordeal of Appalachia.* New York: Hill and Wang, 2017.

Suchland, Jennifer. "The LGBT Specter in Russia: Refusing Queerness, Claiming 'Whiteness.'" *Gender, Place, and Culture* 25, no. 7 (2018): 1073–1088.

Sullivan, Lynne P., and Susan C. Prezzano, eds. *Archaeology of the Appalachian Highlands.* Knoxville: University of Tennessee Press, 2001.

Sullivan, Winnifred Fallers, and Elizabeth Shakman Hurd, eds. *Theologies of American Exceptionalism.* Bloomington: Indiana University Press, 2021.

Suslov, Mikhail. "The Genealogy of the Idea of Monarchy in the Post-Soviet Political Discourse of the Russian Orthodox Church." *State, Religion, and Church* 3, no. 1 (2016): 27–62.

———. "Holy Rus'": The Geopolitical Imagination in the Contemporary Russian Orthodox Church." *Russian Politics and Law* 52, no. 3 (May–June 2014): 67–86.

Suslov, Mikhail, ed. *Digital Orthodoxy in the Post-Soviet World: The Russian Orthodox Church and the Web 2.0.* Stuttgart: ibidem-Verlag, 2016.

Suslov, Mikhail, and Dmitry Uzlaner, eds. *Contemporary Russian Conservatism: Problems, Paradoxes, and Perspectives.* Leiden, Netherlands: Brill, 2019.

Sutton, Matthew Avery. *American Apocalypse: A History of Modern Evangelicalism.* Cambridge, MA: Harvard University Press, 2014.

Taves, Ann. *Revelatory Events: Three Case Studies of the Emergence of New Spiritual Paths.* Princeton, NJ: Princeton University Press, 2016.

Teitelbaum, Benjamin Raphael. "Collaborating with the Radical Right: Scholar-Informant Solidarity and the Case for an Immoral Anthropology." *Current Anthropology* 60, no. 3 (June 2019): 414–435.

———. *War for Eternity: Inside Bannon's Far-Right Circle of Global Power Brokers.* New York: HarperCollins, 2020.

Teter, Magda. *Blood Libel: On the Trail of an Anti-Semitic Myth.* Cambridge, MA: Harvard University Press, 2020.

Thermos, Vaseilios. "Fundamentalism: Theology in the Service of Psychosis." *Public Orthodoxy.* Orthodox Christian Studies Center, Fordham University. Accessed May 30, 2018. https://publicorthodoxy.org/2018/05/30/fundamentalism-and-psychosis/.

Thomson, Irene Taviss. *Culture Wars and Enduring American Dilemmas.* Ann Arbor: University of Michigan Press, 2010.

Thorbjørnsrud, Berit Synøve. "Who Is a convert? New Members of the Orthodox Church in Norway." *Temenos* 51, no. 1 (2015): 71–93.

Trenham, Josiah Fr. "Gay Iconoclasm: Holding the Line against the Radical LGBT Agenda." World Congress of Families X. May 15, 2016. Accessed May 3, 2018. https://youtu.be/HNXe4P_6dhw.

Turner, Edith. *Heart of Lightness: The Life Story of an Anthropologist.* New York: Berghahn Books, 2006.

Turner, Victor. *The Ritual Process: Structure and Anti-Structure.* New York: Routledge, 2017 [1969].

Turner, William H., and Edward J. Cabbell, eds. *Blacks in Appalachia.* Lexington: University Press of Kentucky, 1985.

Turoma, Sanna, and Kaarina Aitamurto. "Renegotiating Patriotic and Religious Identities in the Post-Soviet and Post-Secular Russia," *Transcultural Studies* 12 (2016) 1–14.

Tyrell, Ian. *Reforming the World: The Creation of America's Moral Empire.* Princeton, NJ: Princeton University Press, 2010.

Uzlanėr, Dmitry, and Kristina Stoeckl. "The Legacy of Pitirim Sorokin in the Transnational Alliances of Moral Conservatives." *Journal of Classical Sociology* 1, no. 2 (2017): 133–153.

Valliere, Paul. *Modern Russian Theology: Bukharev, Soloviev, Bulgakov: Orthodox Theology in a New Key.* Grand Rapids, MI: Wm. B. Eerdmans, 2000.

van den Berken, Wil. "The Canonisation of Nicholas II in Iconographical Perspective." In *Orthodox Christianity and Contemporary Europe.* Edited by J. Sutton and W. van den Berken. Leuven: Peeters, 2003.

van der Veer, Peter, ed. *Conversions to Modernities: The Globalization of Christianity.* New York: Routledge, 1996.

Van Gennep, Arnold. *The Rites of Passage.* Translated by Monika B. Vizedom and Gabrielle L. Caffee. Chicago: University of Chicago Press, 1960 [1906].

Vance, J. D. *Hillbilly Elegy: A Memoir of a Family and Culture in Crisis.* New York: HarperCollins, 2018.

Veniamin, Christopher. *The Orthodox Understanding of Salvation: Theosis in Scripture and Tradition.* Dalton, PA: Mount Thabor Publishing, 2013.

Ventis, Haralambos. "Fundamentalism as 'Orthodoxism.'" *Public Orthodoxy.* Orthodox Christians Studies Center, Fordham University. Accessed September 4, 2018. https://publicorthodoxy.org/2018/07/03/fundamentalism-as-orthodoxism/.

Veselkina, Tatyana. "Interview with Metropolitan Hilarion." The Russian Orthodox Church Outside of Russia, 2013. Accessed May 3, 2019. https://synod.com/synod/engdocuments/enart_mhinterviewancientsaints.html.

Vinkovetsky, Ilya. *Russian America: An Overseas Colony of a Continental Empire, 1804–1867.* New York: Oxford University Press, 2011.

Vladimirov, Father Artemy. "A Russian Priest: My Work with English-speaking Converts Part II." *Road to Emmaus Journal* 4 (2001): 1–28. http://www.roadto

emmaus.net/back_issue_articles/RTE_04/My_Work_with_English_Speaking
_Converts_Part_II.pdf.

von Gardner, Johann. *Russian Church Singing: Orthodox Worship and Hymnography, vol. 1*. Yonkers, NY: St. Vladimir's Seminary Press, 1980.

Wanner, Catherine. "Southern Challenges to Eastern Christianity: Pressures to Reform the Church-State Model." *Journal of Church and State* 52, no. 4 (2010): 644–661.

Weyland, Kurt, and Raul L. Madrid, eds. *When Democracy Trumps Populism: European and Latin American Lessons for the United States*. Cambridge: Cambridge University Press, 2019.

Whitehead, Andrew L., and Samuel L. Perry. "Is a 'Christian America' a More Patriarchal America? Religion, Politics, and Traditionalist Gender Ideology." *Canadian Review of Sociology* (2019): 152–177.

———. *Taking America Back for God: Christian Nationalism in the United States*. New York: Oxford University Press, 2020.

Whitehead, Andrew L., Samuel L. Perry, and Joseph O. Baker. "Make America Christian Again: Christian Nationalism and Voting for Donald Trump in the 2016 Presidential Election." *Sociology of Religion* 79, no. 2 (2018): 147–171.

Wiener, Deborah. *Coalfield Jews: An Appalachian History*. Urbana: University of Illinois Press, 2006.

Wilkerson, Jessica. *To Live Here, You Have to Fight: How Women Led Appalachian Movements for Social Justice*. Urbana: University of Illinois Press, 2018.

Willert, Trine Stauning, and Lina Molokotos-Liederman, eds. *Innovation in the Christian Orthodox Tradition?: The Question of Change in Greek Orthodox Thought and Practice*. Burlington, VT: Ashgate, 2012.

Williams, Daniel K. *God's Own Party: The Making of the Christian Right*. New York: Oxford University Press, 2010.

Williams, John Alexander. "Appalachia as Colony and as Periphery: A Review Essay." *Appalachian Journal* 6, no. 2 (1979): 157–161.

Williams, Maria Sháa Tláa, ed. *The Alaska Native Reader: History, Culture, Politics*. Durham, NC: Duke University Press, 2009.

Winchester, Daniel. "Converting to Continuity: Temporality and Self in Eastern Orthodox Conversion Narratives." *Journal for the Scientific Study of Religion* 54 (2015): 439–460.

Wiseman, Jonathan. *Semitism: Being Jewish in America in the Age of Trump*. New York: St. Martin's Press, 2018.

Witt, Joseph D. *Religion and Resistance in Appalachia: Faith and the Fight against Mountaintop Removal Coal Mining*. Lexington: University Press of Kentucky, 2016.

Wodak, Ruth. *The Politics of Fear: What Right-Wing Populist Discourses Mean*. London: Sage, 2015.

Wuthnow, Robert. *After Heaven: Spirituality in America Since the 1950s*. Berkeley: University of California Press, 1998.

————. *Experimentation in American Religion: The New Mysticisms and Their Implications for the Churches.* Berkeley: University of California Press, 1978.

————. *The Left Behind: Decline and Rage in Small-Town America.* Princeton, NJ: Princeton University Press, 2018.

————. *Red State Religion: Faith and Politics in America's Heartland.* Princeton, NJ: Princeton University Press, 2012.

————. *Small-Town America: Finding Community, Shaping the Future.* Princeton, NJ: Princeton University Press, 2013.

Wybrew, Hugh. *Orthodox Feasts of Jesus Christ and the Virgin Mary.* Yonkers, NY: St. Vladimir's Seminary Press, 2000.

————. *The Orthodox Liturgy: The Development of the Eucharistic Liturgy in the Byzantine Rite.* Crestwood, NY: St. Vladimir's Seminary Press, 2003.

Yablokov, Ilya. *Fortress Russia: Conspiracy Theories in the Post-Soviet World.* Cambridge: Polity Press, 2018.

Young, Alexey, ed. *Letters from Father Seraphim: The Twelve-Year Correspondence Between Hieromonk Seraphim (Rose) and Father Alexey Young.* Richfield Springs, NY: Nikodemos Orthodox Publishing Society, 2001.

————. *The Russian Orthodox Church Outside of Russia: A History and Chronology.* San Bernardino, CA: St. Willibrord's Press, 1993.

Zhuravlev, Denis. "Orthodox Identity as Traditionalism: Construction of Political Meaning in the Current Public Discourse of the Russian Orthodox Church." *Russian Politics and Law* 55, no. 4–5 (2017): 354–375.

Zigon, Jarrett. *Disappointment: Toward a Critical Hermeneutic of Worldbuilding.* New York: Fordham University Press, 2018.

————. "A Politics of Worldbuilding." Member Voices. *Fieldsights*, December 5, 2017. https://culanth.org/fieldsights/a-politics-of-worldbuilding.

Žižek, Slavoj. *The Parallax View.* Cambridge, MA: MIT Press, 2009.

Index

2016 presidential election, 8, 65, 71–72, 76, 81, 109–111, 122–124, 168–169, 176

abortion, 66, 71–72, 81, 96, 125, 129
aesthetics, Russian, 36
affective logics, 50–51, 61–63
akathist (hymn), 103, 192
Alaska, 40, 104
alterity, 72, 111, 136, 158–159; as rhetoric, 164–166
alt-right, xiii, 15, 17, 20, 65–66, 108, 110–112, 120–121, 123, 127, 133, 172–173, 187–188
America First, xiii, 187–189, 192
American dream, 50, 68–69, 176
American exceptionalism, 65–68, 109
American Family Association, 48
Americanization, 35–36; in Orthodox Christianity, 174
analoys (icon stands), 141
Ancient Faith Ministries, 22
anthropology: methods, 7–12; theological, 131; theories of conversion, 38
anti-intellectualism, 72, 78
anti-Semitism, 111–112, 188, 193
Antichrist: and the apocalypse, 160; and the Internet, 96–97; Obama as, 186; relationship to democracy, 81; Rose and modernity, 55–56, 104, 179, 191–192
Antimins (consecrated fabric with relics), 147
Antiochian Archdiocese, 24, 35, 41; and converts, 133–134, 174
Apocalypse, 96–98, 108, 112, 117, 122, 125, 160, 163, 173, 179, 189–190, 192; moral, 113, 121, 167; secular, 134

aposticha (hymn), 139
Appalachia, 4–6, 9, 12–13, 73–74, 83, 96, 107, 110–111, 113–114, 121, 133–134, 181–184, 188–189; addiction, 154–155, 158; alterity, 15–16, 135; border making, 129; Christian colonization of, 138; coal and identity, 151–152; colonization of, 21, 151–152; connections to socialism, 70; converts' transformation of, 185; diversity in, 145, 156, 182; economic decline, 123; economic stimulation, 122; fetishization of poverty, 151; as a focus of study, 14–16; as an image of Holy Rus', 162; isolation, 123; missionization of, 137–138, 151–155; mountain religion, 16; mountain sociality, 123, 156; narratives of incapability and backwardness, 15–16, 17; neocolonialism, 182; as not converts' homeland, 139; political ideologies, 108–112; poor whites in need of a savior, 151; Port Arthur service, 103–104; poverty, 123; relationship between spirituality and ecology, 16; religion, 16; Russian-born residents, 125; Russian Orthodox Church Outside of Russia missionization in, 151, 153–154; Russian Orthodoxy in, 21; socioeconomic transformation of, 169; spiritual geographies, 162, 171, 183; stereotypes, 13–16; West Virginia, 155
aşkesis (self-discipline), 138
assimilation: as innovation, 134, 174; of the Orthodoxy in the United States, 24–25, 190–191
atheism, 26
attire, 136

SARAH RICCARDI-SWARTZ is a Postdoctoral Fellow in the Recovering Truth: Religion, Journalism, and Democracy in a Post-Truth Era project in the Center for the Study of Religion and Conflict at Arizona State University.

Orthodox Christianity and Contemporary Thought
Aristotle Papanikolaou and Ashley M. Purpura, series editors